Families, Disability, and Empowerment

Families, Disability, and Empowerment

Active Coping Skills and Strategies for Family Interventions

edited by

George H.S. Singer, Ph.D.
Director

and

Laurie E. Powers, Ph.D.
Co-Director

Hood Center for Family Support
Dartmouth Medical School
Lebanon, New Hampshire

·P A U L·H·
BROOKES
PUBLISHING CO

Baltimore·London·Toronto·Sydney

Paul H. Brookes Publishing Co.
P.O. Box 10624
Baltimore, Maryland 21285-0624

Typeset by The Composing Room of Michigan, Inc., Grand
Rapids, Michigan.
Manufactured in the United States of America by
The Rose Printing Company, Tallahassee, Florida.

Library of Congress Cataloging-in-Publication Data
Families, disability, and empowerment : active coping skills
    and strategies for family interventions / edited by George
    H.S. Singer and Laurie E. Powers.
        p.   cm.
    Includes bibliographical references and index.
    ISBN 1-55766-126-X
    1. Handicapped—United States—Family relationships.   2.
Social work with the handicapped—United States.   I. Singer,
George H. S. II. Powers, Laurie E.
HV1153.F348   1993
362.4′043′0973—dc20   93-16956
CIP

British Library Cataloging-in-Publication data are available
from the British Library.

Contents

v

Contributors

Richard W. Albin, Ph.D.
University of Oregon
Specialized Training Program
Eugene, Oregon 97403-1235

Valerie Bateman
6420 Angela Drive
Mobile, Alabama 36695

W. Carl Cooley, M.D.
Dartmouth-Hitchcock Medical
  Center
Dartmouth Center for Genetics
  and Child Development
1 Medical Center Drive
Lebanon, New Hampshire
  03756-0001

Carl J. Dunst, Ph.D.
Senior Research Scientist
Early Childhood Intervention
  Program
Allegheny-Singer Research
  Institute
320 East North Avenue
Pittsburgh, Pennsylvania 15212

Betsy Gibbs, Ph.D.
Positive Developments Consulting
RFD 1, Box 210
Newport, New Hampshire 03773

Nancy J. Gordon, M.A.
Research Assistant
Center for Family Studies
Western Carolina Center
300 Enola Road
Morganton, North Carolina
  28655-4608

Nancy E. Hawkins, Ph.D.
996 Ferry Lane
Eugene, Oregon 97401

Jack Hegreness, Ph.D.
Oregon Health Sciences Center
3181 SW Sam Jackson Park Road
Portland, Oregon 97207

Larry K. Irvin, Ph.D.
Oregon Research Institute
149 West 12th Street
Eugene, Oregon 97401

Blair Irvine, Ph.D.
Oregon Research Institute
149 West 12th Street
Eugene, Oregon 97401

Russell Jackson, Ph.D.
Oregon Health Sciences Center
3181 SW Sam Jackson Park Road
Portland, Oregon 97207

Donna Lea Johnson
512 Peppermint Drive
Sand Springs, Oklahoma 74063

Esther Lerner, M.S.
Computer Applications Unit
Schiefelbusch Institute for Life
  Span Studies
University of Kansas
Lawrence, Kansas 66045

**Jacqui Lichtenstein, Ph.D.,
  M.S.W.**
Oregon Research Institute
149 West 12th Street
Eugene, Oregon 97401

Joseph M. Lucyshyn, M.S.
University of Oregon
Specialized Training Program
Eugene, Oregon 97403-1235

Janet Marquis, Ph.D.
Computer Applications Unit
Schiefelbusch Institute for Life
  Span Studies
University of Kansas
Lawrence, Kansas 66045

John B. Moeschler, M.D.
Dartmouth-Hitchcock Medical
  Center
Dartmouth Center for Genetics
  and Child Development
1 Medical Center Drive
Lebanon, New Hampshire
  03756-0001

Nan D. Nelson
5902 Harwick Road
Bethesda, Maryland 20816

Charles D. Nixon, Ph.D.
Oregon Research Institute
149 West 12th Street
Eugene, Oregon 97401

Laurie E. Powers, Ph.D.
Co-Director
Hood Center for Family Support
Assistant Professor
Department of Pediatrics
Dartmouth Medical School
Lebanon, New Hampshire
  03756-0001

Lloyd W. Robertson, Ph.D.
1160 Cannon Valley Drive #65
Northfield, Minnesota 55057

Betsy Santelli, M.Ed.
Beach Center on Families and
  Disability
Schiefelbusch Institute for Life
  Span Studies
University of Kansas
Lawrence, Kansas 66045

Marilyn S. Shank, Ph.D.
Assistant Professor
University of South Alabama
Department of Special Education
ILB 215
Mobile, Alabama 36688

George H.S. Singer, Ph.D.
Director
Hood Center for Family Support
Associate Professor
Department of Pediatrics
Dartmouth Medical School
Lebanon, New Hampshire
  03756-0001

A. Lauren Starnes, B.A.
Research Assistant
Center for Family Studies
Western Carolina Center
300 Enola Road
Morganton, North Carolina
  28655-4608

Bonnie Todis, Ph.D.
Center on Human Development
University of Oregon
Eugene, Oregon 97403

Carol M. Trivette, Ph.D.
Director
Center for Family Studies
Family, Infant and Preschool
  Program
Western Carolina Center
300 Enola Road
Morganton, North Carolina
  28655-4608

Ann P. Turnbull, Ed.D.
Beach Center on Families and
  Disability
Schiefelbusch Institute for Life
  Span Studies
University of Kansas
Lawrence, Kansas 66045

Barbara Walker, Ph.D.
Oregon Research Institute
149 West 12th Street
Eugene, Oregon 97401

Paul Yovanoff, Ph.D.
Alder Group Data Management
  Consultants
1346 Alder Street
Eugene, Oregon 97401

Foreword

During the 1980s and early 1990s, as families' views about "helpful help" have been articulated and heard, there has been a notable shift in philosophy and thought regarding support for families of persons with disabilities. The perspectives of the public, of professionals, and of families themselves have matured from a view of families as long-suffering and needy to a more hopeful and realistic assessment of their strengths and needs. Along with this shift in attitude, the nature of formal and informal family support efforts has also changed. This evolution has been characterized by a movement from a more professionally controlled "provision of service" approach to a strengths-based collaboration that acknowledges the expertise and contributions of both parents and professionals.

Predictably, this shift in attitudes and ideas has been accompanied by a growing amount of published material describing family support concepts, practice, and research. But nowhere, until now, have so many of the vital elements of a comprehensive approach to family support been gathered in one place. These elements include a clearly articulated philosophy, a well-developed conceptual framework, logically organized practical information, and much needed research and systematic evaluation of family support efforts. Through the blending of these ingredients, *Families, Disability, and Empowerment: Active Coping Skills and Strategies for Family Interventions* truly represents a "next generation" of information about family support in the disability field.

The importance of a clearly articulated philosophy and conceptual framework is heightened by the recent popularity and use of terms such as *family-centered, family-based,* and *family support.* Unfortunately, much that is called *family-centered* is in reality only a shift in emphasis from the individual as the unit of analysis to the entire family as the target for change, and is not necessarily reflective of a commitment to family-driven systems or to partnership. *Family-based* service has come to be a shorthand term for a particular set of services provided to families, usually in their own homes, when there is risk of out-of-home placement for a child or adolescent. And the term *family support* also has taken on a variety of meanings. These range from a very specific reference to family support groups, usually for parents, to family support as a comprehensive, individualized response to the dynamic needs of all family members, including both formal and informal services.

The philosophy of family support presented by Singer and Powers in the first chapter is explicitly threaded throughout the entire work. A deep respect for families, an unwavering belief in family strengths and the importance of self-determination, and a commitment to moving parent–professional collaboration "beyond rhetoric" comprises the framework within which the other chapters have been developed. But the volume is balanced; it recognizes that a commitment to building on strengths does not deny the pain and need for assistance that many families experience during some periods of their development.

Achieving and preserving wellness and resilience in families are goals around which the conceptual framework is crafted. This framework and a dedication to helping families find and develop their power are woven together and echoed throughout the remainder of the book to an extent that is rare in edited volumes.

The practical information presented in this book is notable in that each of the chapters written to provide guidance for practice reflects the overall philosophy of the book, provides a coherent framework for action, and presents a set of specific (in some cases, step-by-step) strategies. Chapter 6 by Cooley and Moeschler, which discusses supporting families through the primary health care relationship, is but one good example of this combination. The authors make a strong case for the importance of operating within a collaborative relationship with families, provide some general guidelines, and then take the reader carefully through various phases of the physician–family relationship. At each step they point out opportunities for providing support, always balancing their family-centered approach with reminders about the rights of individuals with disabilities, and acknowledging tough issues and choices faced by families and health care professionals alike.

A very important contribution of this book is the considerable attention given to the evaluation of specific family support strategies. The research efforts that are presented keep the overall philosophy and conceptual framework in view, and as a group, add to the body of evidence about how family support strategies may be designed and delivered, as well as responding to the question, "What good do they do?" Some of the chapters also provide an instructive lesson about how "family-changing" interventions can fit within an empowerment perspective. Nixon's chapter on the treatment of self-blame and guilt in parents of children with disabilities is a good example of this amalgam. The evaluation and research discussions in this chapter as well as others greatly enrich the book because they provide a last necessary step linking philosophy, thought, and action.

Families, Disability, and Empowerment makes a very important contribution to the literature in the disability field and far beyond. It will be a valuable resource to families, professionals, and policy makers as they work to shift the focus from "whether family support" to a concern about how family support can be designed in ways that are family-centered—built on strengths, responsive to the changing needs of individual families, respectful, collaborative, and effective.

Barbara J. Friesen, Ph.D.
Director, Research and Training Center on
Family Support and Children's Mental Health
Portland State University
Portland, Oregon

Acknowledgments

We are endeavoring to create a body of empirically validated work on ways to strengthen families of persons with disabilities. This program of research necessarily is a long-term project that involves teamwork and cooperation with many colleagues. The authors of these chapters have been more than contributors to a volume. As colleagues at the Oregon Research Institute and at Dartmouth Medical School they have been truly collegial and have worked to create something that transcends our individual ambitions and endeavors. Above all we have learned from the families who have been our guides, companions, and challengers. To the extent that we have succeeded in lending a helping hand to them, it has been a mutual process whereby they have taught and given at least as much as they have received.

Our thanks are due to the publishing staff at Brookes Publishing Co., who have been helpful and patient in producing this volume, and to Cindi LaPointe, who has kept us organized.

Special thanks goes to Joanne Singer, who has been a colleague, advisor, and supporter in the long and often challenging work that this volume represents.

Families, Disability, and Empowerment

1

Contributing to Resilience in Families

An Overview

George H. S. Singer and Laurie E. Powers

Innovative interventions to help families of persons with disabilities offer great promise as a way to promote well-being, strengthen families, and alleviate suffering. These innovations embrace a variety of emerging practices, including parent-to-parent self-help groups, governmental support programs, and an array of cognitive-behavioral counseling interventions. All of these interventions share a common shift in values and emphases in public policy and social science. This chapter describes this shift and presents an overview of emerging values.

The purpose of this chapter is: 1) to provide an overview of the history and tenets of the family support movement, 2) to explore the nature of personal and family resilience as related to emerging principles of family support, 3) to articulate the essential role of reliable alliance in family support, and 4) to highlight the contributions of self-help and professional models to family support.

The work on this chapter was funded in part by grant no. H023T80013-90 from the U.S. Department of Education to the Hood Center for Caregiving Families at the Dartmouth-Hitchcock Medical Center. The views stated herein are not necessarily those of the funder.

FAMILY SUPPORT MOVEMENT

The family support movement consists of many grass-roots efforts to strengthen and empower families in their traditional caregiving roles (Kagan, Powell, Weisbourd, & Zigler, 1987). During the 1980s, the family support movement has gained momentum and shaped social policy in several states as well as influenced efforts at national reform. In particular, family support has emerged as a major policy initiative in the field of developmental disabilities (Knoll, Covert, Orsuch, O'Connor, & Blaney, 1990). Parents have impressed upon policymakers the fact that families serve as the primary source of support to a majority of persons with developmental disabilities.

Concurrent with the emergence of the family support movement, families have been undergoing rapid demographic and economic changes that strain traditional caregiving roles (Singer & Irvin, 1990). Advocates for persons with disabilities have urged that social policy should reflect the importance of the family, and that disincentives to home living for persons with disabilities should be abolished. As a result, several states have initiated new family support programs aimed at enhancing the capacity of families to take care of their own members. These initiatives attempt to put families in control of efforts to support their caregiving capacity.

The new family support initiatives represent a substantial break with traditional social policy regarding families in the United States. Historically, many forms of family support have been created as part of an emergency "safety net" that is designed to serve families once they have already been damaged. This tradition has been most pronounced in the field of child welfare where the state intervenes once families have become highly dysfunctional. This approach of providing a minimal "safety net" once families have failed has been called "residualism" by Moroney (1986). Although other more preventative approaches to families are as old as the Settlement House movement in the United States, efforts to focus on the promotion of well-being and prevention of problems in targeted populations are, for the most part, recent developments. Table 1 shows several characteristics of the residualist model and contrasts it with features of the new family support movement.

The Larger Movement

Family support initiatives in the area of disability are part of a much larger national and international family support movement. This movement has primarily arisen from a variety of grass-roots efforts to strengthen the traditional role of families at a time when

Table 1. Models of family support approaches

Residualist model	New family models
Controlled by professionals	Family driven
Views families as dysfunctional	Assumes all families have strengths and can learn
Intervenes after families are in crisis	Aims to prevent dysfunction, promote well-being, and ameliorate crises
Devotes resources to out-of-home placements	Devotes resources to family
Focuses on person with disability as client	Views whole family as client
Emphasizes formal programs	Activates informal as well as formal support systems
Invests in remote institutions	Builds local community capacity
Emphasizes pathology	Emphasizes adaptation, skill learning, and viewing families as experts and allies
Emphasizes safeguards against fraud and abuse	Stresses flexibility and rapid response to need
Serves poor families	Serves across all socioeconomic levels

such trends as high divorce rates, economic stagnation, employment of young mothers, geographic mobility, and immigration have made the endeavor of raising a family increasingly challenging. In response to many of these trends, most of the nations of western Europe have developed policies and services aimed at supporting families (Moroney, 1986).

In the United States this movement has emerged incrementally, with initiatives launched on several fronts. One strand of the movement has grown out of various efforts at early intervention for young children. As practitioners have gained experience since the 1970s, they have realized that the family and community context that surrounds a young child is often the proper focus for assistance (Dunst, Trivette, & Deal, 1988). At the other end of the life cycle, advocates for elderly citizens have demanded alternatives to nursing homes and means to permit elderly persons to live in their own homes or with family members (Monk, 1983). Furthermore, a revolution in medical care and technology has created an entirely new phenomenon; long-term technologically dependent life sustenance in home settings (Lehr, 1990). Such diverse groups as hospice organizations, AIDS advocates, families of persons with traumatic brain injury, and parents of infants who are dependent on ventilators at home have called for increased assistance and support to families. In the field of child welfare, reformers have initiated efforts to preserve high-risk families and to create sustained support for foster or adoptive families when they are necessary (Wells & Biegel, 1991).

Tenets of Traditional Family Support

One way to clarify the nature of emerging models of family support is to contrast them with traditional models of caring for families that emphasize residualism, professional dominance, and pathology. Moroney (1986) eloquently described the way in which traditional family welfare practices have been based upon a set of ideas that he called *residualism*. According to this approach, society assists only a small residual number of families who are unable to perform their traditional functions. As such, society plays a role in providing a safety net for families under dire circumstances; programs are often dominated by eligibility requirements and enforcement bureaucracies aimed at assuring that only those deemed worthy receive help. In the worst case, assistance is provided in a paternalistic and punitive fashion. The residualist tradition has dominated family welfare practices in much of the United States.

Until recently, residualist thinking influenced the rationale for assisting families of persons with developmental disabilities. The few programs that were available to families had rigid eligibility requirements that limited them to assisting families at risk of breaking apart, thereby preventing out-of-home placements. This thinking also shaped the way policy makers evaluated early family support programs. A prime indicator of success was out-of-home placement rates. The first generation of evaluations revealed that small family support efforts failed to significantly reduce placements (Slater, Bates, & Eicher, 1986). The fact that there might be other valued outcomes of family support was not considered.

A second tenet in traditional family support has been oriented toward *professional control* and *the fitting of the families to the programs*. It is assumed that special expertise is required to assist troubled families and that it is usually better to give help after problems have reached a crisis stage. There is an implicit assumption that, because they are troubled, family members should turn over decision making to professionals and program administrators. Additionally, programs are designed to address professionally perceived, generic needs of families with little attention directed to personalizing support.

A third principle of traditional models of family support holds that *families are necessarily pathological* because of the burdens imposed by raising a child with a disability. This orientation stresses family problems and often uses language derived from medicine in which *pathology, treatment, cure,* and *prescription* are common terms. It is assumed that parents require training, need assistance to learn how to raise their children, and are invariably distressed. Turnbull, Blue-Banning, Behr, and Kerns (1986) identified some of the assumptions that have been promoted in the professional literature, including blanket generalizations about the negative impact of living with a person with developmental disabilities. In this negative tradition, the assumption has been that all such families are, to state the case in the extreme, cursed with a terrible misfortune from which they never recover. Under the shadow of this broad condemnation, specific negative concepts have included the idea that families are permanently fixed in early stages of familial development, marriages are unavoidably damaged, and parents are likely to suffer psychopathologically. Recent reviews of the literature on families suggest that, in fact, the picture is far more complicated than the negative thesis. It is now clear that most families view their child with a disability as a positive contributor to the family's quality of life (Summers, Behr, & Turnbull, 1989). The evidence about marriage is equivocal with at least a few studies showing that some marital relationships are strengthened in these families (Benson & Gross, 1989).

New Principles of Support

The ideology of the new family support movement represents a considerable divergence from this negative tradition. Foremost, it emphasizes that all families have strengths. When problems are identified by a family, practitioners recognize that people have the capacity to change and grow when the proper facilitating conditions exist. It also assumes that family members with disabilities are positive contributors to their families and their communities. Practitioners try to identify resources and match them to family needs *as the family perceives them* rather than trying to fit families into rigid programs. Thus, there is an emphasis on "doing what it takes" and on flexibility. In addition, the relationship between practitioners and family members is an equal partnership in which the ultimate power of decision making resides with the family. A successful partnership in this model results in family members becoming more efficacious at attaining their goals and more resilient in the face of future stressors.

Dunst and his colleagues (Dunst, Trivette, Starnes, Hamby, & Gordon, 1993) have extracted from the literature on family support a set of defining principles that clarify the philosophy and practices that characterize these diverse efforts. They identified six basic principles of the family support movement:

Enhance a sense of community   Family support programs aim to integrate families into the mainstream of the community. They do so by emphasizing the common needs of all people rather than individual differences. They work to improve the capacity of the family to link up with the broader community for a range of social support provisions.

Mobilize resources and support   Family support programs work to address the broad-based needs of families in addition to specific child-focused concerns. The services are available to the whole family as opposed to individual members. They make resources available in flexible, individualized, and responsive ways. Furthermore, they build upon or strengthen existing social networks.

Encourage shared responsibility and collaboration   Professionals treat families as partners. They assume that all families have strengths and that when problems are identified in a family, people can learn to solve these problems given the opportunity to acquire skills and resources. Professionals assume a broad range of roles and functions in order to meet the individualized needs of families. The programs promote reciprocity so that families have a chance to offer time and energy as well as to consume. Professionals behave in ways that encourage trust, honesty, respect, and open communication.

Strengthen and protect the integrity of the family unit   Family support programs aim to encourage stable and healthy relationships among all family members. They value and protect the cultural beliefs of all families. They try to minimize intrusion upon the family by respecting family boundaries and privacy. These programs also try to prevent abuse and neglect in families. In the exceptional cases when a child must be removed from a family, the programs aim for reunification.

Operate according to enabling and empowering principles that enhance and promote competence of the family and individual family members   These principles create opportunities for family members to acquire knowledge, skills, and capacities so that they may become more capable and competent. They build on family strengths. The programs and face-to-face interactions are configured in a way that maximizes family control and encourages informed decisionmaking.

Follow proactive human services approaches   The programs are resource-based rather than service-based. That is, they aim to identify family needs and mobilize the needed social and material resources to meet them as opposed to trying to fit families into a program. They adopt a holistic orientation toward the family as a unit and as a member of a wider community as opposed to child-focused models. These programs are consumer-driven and consumer-governed. The services emphasize promotion of well-being and enhancement of life quality as opposed to prevention and treatment. And finally, they are community-based rather than located in centralized sites apart from the community.

Theoretical Approaches to Resilience

So far this chapter has described the new family support movement and contrasted it with some traditional models of family assistance. In this section, approaches to resilience are discussed, as presented in the social sciences and helping professions and as they relate to new models of family support. These ideas come from schools of thought as diverse as community psychology, applied behavior analysis, cognitive-behavioral psychology, studies of resilient persons, family-centered early intervention, and research on family adaptation to stress.

The idea has gradually entered the social sciences and the helping disciplines that human wellness and resilience are the proper parameters for a framework for understanding how people may assist one another. This perspective assumes that most of the time, people adapt to significant challenges in their lives in ways that provide them with renewed strength and energy. The central focus is on identifying ways that people successfully transform stressors into challenges and emerge from difficulties while having been strengthened from the process. Similarly, the central focus of efforts to assist people under stress involves identifying ways to provide assistance in such a fashion as to minimize suffering and maximize future adaptability. In this framework, helpgiving is effective if it strengthens a person's ability to cope with new stressors; that is, it makes a person more resilient. There are three essential constituents of resilience: flexible meaningfulness, balanced coping, and flexible interdependence.

Meaningfulness: Creatively Managing Uncertainty

Humans are meaningmakers and meanings are established and transmitted by social communities. People exist in a world that is suffused with language and its underlying concepts. When difficult life events occur, sometimes preestablished ways of understanding the world are challenged. For example, one line of research in social psychology has established that most people believe in the "just world hypothesis," the notion that fate deals people the hand that they deserve. This persistent faith that life is essentially orderly and in some sense fair can be challenged by an unwanted, uncontrolled event such as a sudden loss. For some people the birth of a child with a disability is such an event. Some parents are thrown into a state of turmoil and disorientation and attempt to find a reason why their child has emerged as a different person than they had dreamed. Thus, efforts to cope with the birth of a child with a disability often involve striving both to understand what it means to have a child with a disability and to find a reason why it has happened.

The process of acquiring new meanings is, in part, a social one. Meanings are conveyed by social communities; different groups attach different meanings to the same phenomena. Also, for a person to acquire a new way of understanding the meaning of an event, he or she often must enter into a trusting relationship with people who convey these new meanings. Helping approaches that are congruent with family support principles create relationships with parents and siblings of children with disabilities in ways that allow them to be open to more positive meanings about disability than those commonly conveyed by the mainstream culture. Connections between parents of children with disabilities play a vital role in this process. People are most likely to be influenced by someone with whom they can identify and develop a sense of trust, someone whose experiences have been similar enough to make their orientation plausible. As is discussed in greater detail later, the quality of the helping relationship is a key ingredient in allowing people to process new meanings.

Aaron Antonovsky is one researcher who has demonstrated a link between a sense of meaning and life adjustment (Antonovsky, 1987). His central construct is called a *sense of coherence*, which consists of the beliefs that life is sufficiently orderly to be understandable, that actions are likely to lead to results, and that others can be trusted as resources. Antonovsky also points out that there is such a thing as a rigid sense of coherence—a set of inflexible beliefs that do not allow ready adaptation to change even though they provide a cognitive map that works in some environments. Thus, adaptation is facilitated by the adoption of flexible meanings that promote tolerance of ambiguity and uncertainty. One role of a helpgiver is to assist people in formulating a sense of meaning about their situation. Another is to assist them in tolerating a lack of clarity or meaning while continuing to cope and search.

Flexible Coping: Achievement of Goals, Hope, and Acceptance

New meanings are conveyed as much through the attitudes that people adopt while carrying out daily tasks as they are through more abstract belief statements. Consequently, the role of parent-to-parent or sibling-to-sibling contact is not simply to convey a credo regarding disability as a challenge rather than as a tragedy but, more importantly, to illustrate the ways that this understanding translates into day-to-day coping. Meanings are embedded in practical coping activities, everyday arrangements, and mundane strategies for daily living. Coping with day-to-day demands through a process of goal-setting, striving, and attainment or modification of goals can lead to a sense of efficacy and a related sense of hope. Recent studies have identified two aspects of hope, *goal* and *agency* (Snyder et al., 1991). A goal is a representation of a desirable outcome. Agency is the belief that it is possible to act in ways that will lead to attainment of a goal. Thus, self-efficacy and hope are interrelated, with both nurtured through effective helping interventions.

The ability to envision a goal, determine a plan of action, and act to achieve it is a major contributor to a sense of self-efficacy. The role of the helper is to assist a parent, sibling, or person with a disability to clarify goals and to develop strategies to achieve them. The helper may sometimes ask questions or probe to stimulate examination of his or her goals, provide information about ways to achieve them, or serve as a coach and skill trainer to teach means of acting toward a goal. In addition, the helper may link the family member to other people who can model ways of reaching goals. Coaching and skill-building may focus on encouraging the development of active, overt skills such as making assertive requests or carrying out an exercise regimen, or covert processes such as promoting basic attitudinal shifts that facilitate coping with challenges.

The most effective goal-striving is accomplished within a context of personal acceptance of challenge. Acceptance is a set of meta-affective and metacognitive responses. As such, it is a multidimensional construct that represents a stance that a person takes toward a broad range of individual situations and stressors. An accepting stance can be characterized as an attitude toward life difficulties that embraces hope and willingness to proceed while at the same time acknowledging pain or suffering. In regard to a family member with a disability, acceptance includes the appreciation of the contributions that the person with disabilities makes to the family as well as the benefits that accrue as a result of facing the challenges and quandaries posed by disability. At the same time, it does not gloss over the difficulties and sorrows that also arise.

The helper assists people in three main ways: helping them to identify and accept their feelings, communicating that they are valued and respected, and linking them to others who have come to terms with similar challenges. Many of the skills that are traditionally taught to counselors are essential to the process of promoting acceptance (Ivey, 1988). It is in their methods of training people to be active listeners, express positive regard, empathize, and take the other's perspective that the counseling professions can make some of their greatest contributions to the family support movement.

Flexible Interdependence

Historically, a primary value in the United States has been self-reliant individualism (Bellah, Madsen, Sullivan, Swidler, & Tipton, 1985). The predominant culture places great emphasis on the ability of individuals to act independently and autonomously. In keeping with this value, psychologists have studied empowerment and individualization from many different perspectives. For example, one line of research has studied the construct of locus of control (Johnson & Sarason, 1978). A considerable body of evidence has found that persons who generally believe that they can influence their own fate, make their own major life choices, and determine their future are also more likely to have positive self-esteem and are less likely to be depressed. In addition, they are able to adapt to chronic conditions more effectively than people who view their lives as out of their control. Schools of individual psychology as well as community psychology have adopted empowerment as an organizing framework for their disciplines. They have studied the ways in which various approaches to assisting individuals and groups can enhance their sense of autonomy and efficacy. At the level of individual assistance, practices such as assertiveness training and assisting people to set and achieve their own goals help to promote empowerment and autonomy.

However, personal empowerment appears to be maximized through social support and collective action. Many cultures have a more collectivist orientation in which individuals achieve success through identification and membership with a group. These cultures place an emphasis on interdependence with others achieved through cooperation and teamwork. In the western world, activities such as community organizing, formation of self-help groups, and political advocacy enhance the sense of personal and group efficacy among persons who have formerly been disenfranchised or devalued. People who believe that they are supported by others are likely to experience fewer major life stressors and more likely to adapt to severe stress without ill effects (Sarason, Levine, & Pierce, 1990). Consequently, efforts to support individual resilience also must take into account a person's social network and the availability of several different kinds of social assistance that friends, neighbors, and kin commonly provide to one another.

Professionals and self-help organizations have developed methods for assisting people to garner social support. Social skills training protocols have been developed for helping isolated and shy people to connect with others and to act assertively (Rakos, 1990). Self-help organizations have promoted the building of parent networks through one-to-one parent matching and by sponsoring group support activities. Additional methodologies have been identified to assist people to map their social worlds and develop circles of support (Gottlieb, 1988).

PROMOTING FAMILY RESILIENCE

The concept of resilience applies to families as well as individuals. As a unit, families can experience periods of intense stress, learn from the experience, and emerge stronger. Most families encounter difficult circumstances that force family members to change the ways they interact, assign tasks, and think of their circumstances. As with individuals, circumstances such as unemployment, natural disaster, separation due to war, or a death in the family can fracture and fragment families or strengthen them.

One way to look at family resilience is to consider the characteristics of successful families. The study of successful adaptation to disability is in its infancy. However, scholars have mined some preliminary visions from the existing literature. Patterson (1991) reviewed the literature on families of children with chronic illness. She reported that successful families with a child with a chronic health challenge coped well by doing many of the things that any successful family must accomplish. Patterson (1991) described the following characteristics of resilient families of children with chronic illness.

Maintenance of Family Boundaries   Families who successfully maintain an external boundary manage to retain a sense of control over their households despite the need for intrusive involvements with a variety of professionals. Families who interact with outside organizations with assertiveness and have a clear perception of their needs in relation to the organization are more likely to maintain a sense of identity and integrity as a unit.

Developing Communicative Competence   Patterson (1991) points out that families with a child with a disability or chronic illness have to make more frequent decisions and often must deal with novel situations in which no clear normative basis for action is available. As such, families who are organized and can resolve conflicts appear to do better when faced with long-term caregiving demands. A major obstacle to communication in some caregiving families is the expression of affect. Family members may believe that they must suppress feelings of grief, sorrow, or anger over disability in the family. Parents may feel that they must protect children from negative feelings. Partners may believe that they must spare each other the burden of their feelings. However, there is some evidence suggesting that families in which members openly express feelings to one another are likely to be more successful in caring for children with chronic illness (Patterson, 1991).

Attributing Positive Meanings to the Situation   As with individual resilience, family resilience consists partly of finding positive meanings in challenging situations. Just as individuals develop cognitive maps of their circumstances, families also generate their own conceptual paradigms—ways that the family as a group assigns attributions to events. Attributional agreement among family members will usually promote cohesion and adaptation, so long as the shared meanings facilitate functional responses.

Maintaining Family Flexibility   Resilient families appear to be able to transfer roles and tasks within the family when needed. Risk-taking and a willingness to try new things may also mark these well-coping families. Several of the coping skills in this volume, notably problem solving, can contribute to flexibility in the family.

Maintaining a Commitment to the Family Unit   Families who maintain a sense of teamwork and cooperation are more likely to be resilient. Efforts to support siblings and utilize joint family meetings to resolve problems and to plan can contribute to family cohesion. Similarly, in two-parent families, cohesion is strengthened when the parental dyad can carry out its executive function through open communication and problem solving.

Engaging in Active Coping Efforts   Resilient families are active problem solvers and efficient users of coping skills. They rarely approach challenges with a sense of passive resignation. Mutual goal-setting, internal strategies for negotiation, and a focus on seeking out and using resources are hallmarks of active family coping.

Maintaining Social Integration Families who remain embedded in positive social networks appear to cope better with adversity than do isolated families. Disability in the family can pose a threat to social integration if the community is not accepting of disability, if families are made to feel stigmatized, or if caregiving demands do not allow time for normal friendships and participation in activities. Resilient families work at maintaining social links despite these challenges.

Developing Collaborative Relationships with Professionals Families of people with disabilities or chronic health problems have many more interactions with professionals than do typical families. Family stress research suggests that all too often these interactions are a source of distress. In order to change this situation, parents and professionals have asserted the importance of collaborative and mutually respectful relationships (Patterson, 1991). Thus, through numerous individual and family efforts, resilience is developed and bolstered. It is clear that support from others directed toward facilitating family resilience is an essential contributor to adaptation. The provision of family support, whether in the form of information, encouragement, or practical assistance, appears to have as its foundation the establishment of a reliable alliance between the family and helper. The following section discusses the nature of such an alliance.

THE ROLE OF A RELIABLE ALLY

Weiss (1974) studied loneliness and social support in older persons. One of his findings was that emotional support is best provided by a person who is perceived to be a reliable ally. A *reliable alliance* exists when a person feels that there is someone to call on in a time of emotional distress. Parents describe a reliable ally with phrases such as, "I know I can count on her," or, "He is there when I need him." There is a sense of stability and dependability in the relationship. Perceptions of reliability usually require repeated interactions to establish a mutual history. Thus, one aspect of reliable alliance is *instrumental and practical* in the sense that concrete facts of availability and repeated support over time help to establish a sense of enduring trustworthiness.

The second aspect of reliable alliance is *affective*. Parents use phrases such as "kind," "understanding," "knows where I'm coming from," and "believes in me." This dimension of a reliable alliance consists of the perception that *intersubjectivity* has been attained. Intersubjectivity is the perception that persons' subjective experiences overlap. Parents describe the attainment of intersubjectivity with a phrase such as, "She really understands what I've been through." Commonality of experience often sets the stage for intersubjectivity. For example, two survivors of a natural disaster are likely to assume that each understands the other's use of the phrase "a hell of a storm." In the same way, a parent who has felt nervous before an individualized education program (IEP) meeting is likely to subjectively understand the experience of another parent who reports missing sleep over an upcoming meeting.

Commonality of experience is not the sole constituent of intersubjectivity. There also must be a mutual attribution of positive intent in the relationship. Such is the case in most self-help organizations in which the reason why people come together is publicly stated and often repeated. It serves as a kind of framework that defines the relationship. For example, parents who join the Alliance for the Mentally Ill understand that the purpose of the organization is to provide support and to counter commonplace prejudice against families of persons with mental illness (Orford, 1987). Thus, the affective component of a reliable alliance is aided by perceived commonality of experience and mutual attributions of positive intent. Self-help groups provide a potent environment for generating intersubjectivity because they bring together people who have had similar experiences and who have the stated intent of acting benevolently toward one another.

Just as there must be an overlap of subjective meanings in a reliable alliance, there also must be some overlap of the dominant affect that both parties express. Thoits (1986) reports that emotional support is most effective if offered by someone who has had similar experiences and whose affect falls within a narrow range of compatibility. This band of compatibility refers to the match between the emotional state of the ally and the person seeking help. An ally cannot be so positive as to seem to be an unrealistic or unsympathetic listener. Neither can the ally's affect be so negative in tone that he or she appears to be worse off than the person who seeks help. Ideally, the ally can express sympathy and empathy so that the person being helped knows that his or her pain has been understood while, at the same time, the ally demonstrates that he or she has been able to move beyond the distress to less suffering. In this fashion the reliable ally can model cognitive adaptation.

Along with affective overlap, reliable alliance is most likely to arise when people communicate in a style of discourse that is similar to the way they normally talk about their daily lives. Communication in technical contexts such as the doctor's office or a public school follows a structure and uses language that is highly rational, formal, and technical. For example, Mischler (1984) studied the way physicians and patients speak to one another during a medical interview. He found that physicians ignore much of what patients say, ask a series of closed-ended questions, rarely speak about affect or meaning, and usually use technical language. By contrast, he found that patients usually tell stories that set a context for their symptoms, describe the meaning attributed to the illness, and often express feelings about it. Mischler called the one form of discourse "the voice of medicine" and the other "the voice of the life world." Reliable alliances are facilitated when people speak to one another in similar styles and shared terminology normally used to think and talk about everyday experience.

SELF-HELP AND PROFESSIONAL CONTRIBUTIONS TO FAMILY SUPPORT

The preceding discussion of resilience and the nature of reliable alliance provides a framework for the identification of the essential elements of both well-coping and facilitative support. Within this context, it is appropriate to consider next the specific contributions to the promotion of these elements by the two primary mechanisms for the provision of formal support to families of persons with disabilities: self-help organizations and professional services.

Self-Help Organizations

Levine and Perkins (1987) studied a variety of self-help organizations and identified six common ways by which these groups support their members. Their findings suggest that self-help organizations: 1) promote a psychological sense of community; 2) provide an ideology that serves as a philosophical antidote to the typical devaluing by the larger community; 3) provide an opportunity for confession, catharsis, and mutual criticism; 4) provide role models; 5) teach effective coping strategies for day-to-day problems; and 6) provide a network of social relationships.

Santelli and Turnbull (chap. 2, this volume) found that *parent-to-parent groups* offer two major forms of social support: emotional support and informational support. Members of parent-to-parent groups share the experience of day-to-day coping with disability in the family. They share lived reality and, consequently, are able to speak with a kind of authenticity and authority that is not available from others. Also, their knowledge is embedded in naturalistic, "real-life" conditions that they can describe in everyday language. They do not have to resort to the highly technical language of professional discourse. They can tell stories and make jokes. They do not have to refer to a lexicon of arcane terms or to a language structure that exclusively emphasizes rational understandings at the expense of affective information.

The fact that helping parents know the day-to-day details of life with a child with special needs also means that they have a tremendous amount of practical knowledge available to each other. The theory of the social construction of reality addresses the fact that knowledge is not evenly distributed. Berger and Luckmann (1989) write, ". . . knowledge of everyday life is structured in terms of relevances" (p. 45). Relevant knowledge is most available from others who have similar concerns. For example, parents of children without disabilities are less likely to know such practical facts as: 1) how to find a trusted baby-sitter for a child with special medical needs, 2) what to do when strangers stare at a child and ask rude questions, 3) which doctor in the local community knows about disability, or 4) how and where to go on a vacation with a young child with a disability. All of this information is likely to be available to a more experienced parent of a child with a disability because it derives from their lived, 24-hour-a-day experience. Not only is relevant knowledge concentrated in the possession of persons with shared life circumstances, but also their information is more likely to be more persuasive and believable.

The parent-to-parent movement has also exerted a vital influence upon new models of family support. Parents of persons with disabilities have actively organized national advocacy groups since the end of World War II (Scheerenberger, 1983). In addition to acting as agents for social change, parents have functioned as effective helpers to others in parent-to-parent networks, mentorship programs, and parent information centers. Increasingly, professional helpers are learning to rely upon the expertise of activist parents. Parent helpers have achieved a unique authority based upon their competence and first-hand knowledge of the challenges that families face and the benefits that can be gained from effectively facing challenges. Legislative mandates and public policy initiatives have also begun to reflect the key role that parents can play as colleagues in the design and management of services available to families. For example, in New Hampshire, following much grass-roots organizing by parents, family support legislation was recently passed that places family councils at the helm of governance for family support programs. The notion that support should empower families is taken quite literally to mean that the chief consumers of services are the leaders of policy and advisory governance structures.

Contributions of the Professions

The principles of the new family support movement and theories of individual and family resilience suggest a set of practices that will be useful in providing family support. There are a number of professional approaches that have a tradition of training practitioners to work with people who request assistance and doing this work in a way that enhances individual and family resilience. These approaches are found within social work, counseling, psychology, clinical psychology, special education, marriage and family counseling, and early childhood intervention. It is possible to identify schools of thought within each of these professions that are consistent with family support principles and the enhancement of individual and family resilience.

These diverse approaches share some important practices. They all involve repeated face-to-face encounters between people who ask for assistance and people who want to be helpful. Interactions are based on a professional commitment to understand and communicate respect for the family's personal perceptions of the world. Most importantly, helping relations involve collaborative efforts between families and professionals in which families are key intervention decisionmakers and primary evaluators of intervention efficacy.

The major contributions of professional approaches to family support are summarized in Table 2. The first such contribution is a normative approach to adaptation and helping. In the normative approach, a helper makes available skills and resources for other equally important reasons: to promote well-being, to enrich and enhance the quality of life, and to prevent suffering. The normative

Table 2.   Contributions of professional approaches to family support

1. A normative frame of reference directed toward promotion and enhancement of well-being
2. A methodology of identifying and training relationship skills
3. Well-developed ethics for supportive relationships
4. A methodology for psychoeducational skill training
5. Knowledge of strategies to enhance formal and informal social support
6. Commitment to collaboration with self-help organizations

approach emphasizes proactive helping practices in which enrichment and prevention prior to the onset of problems are emphasized. The normative frame of reference leads professionals to emphasize ways in which individuals and families share common challenges and strengths.

Normative Approach to Adaptation and Helping

There are several examples of the application of the normative approach within the professions. For example, in the field of social work, Slater and Wikler (1984) have proposed a *normalization model* for assisting families of children with disabilities. They suggest that the role of the social worker is to assist families to attain a normative life-style as an integrated part of the community. Within psychology, researchers have used skill training to try to enrich family life and to prevent interpersonal problems. For example, Markham and colleagues (Markham, Floyd, Stanley, & Storaasli, 1988) taught communication and problem-solving skills to young couples early in their relationship and showed that 5 years later these couples had higher levels of marital satisfaction and lower levels of divorce than a randomly assigned comparison group. Additionally, Guerney and his colleagues (Guerney, Guerney, & Cooney, 1985) have developed family enrichment courses that have been widely used by church and community groups to help couples to promote positive relationships. Research on enrichment interventions has found positive effects in improving couples' relationships as well as parent–child relationships. Other psychologists have developed and disseminated support group methods for single parents and for stepparents (Dinkmeyer, McKay, & McKay, 1987).

Within the helping professions, researchers and clinicians have also worked on designing ways to assist people in developing positive meanings around challenging life circumstances. These diverse approaches include logotherapy, meditation training, and cognitive-behavioral therapy. In all of these approaches, helpers assist people whose belief systems have been challenged to develop methods of integrating difficult life experiences into their normal ways of coping. In the field of developmental disabilities and families, Behr and her colleagues have presented a theory of cognitive coping (Summers, Behr, & Turnbull, 1989) and other researchers have shown that cognitive behavioral interventions can improve well-being in parents of children with disabilities (Singer, 1993; Singer, Irvin, & Hawkins, 1988; see also Singer et al., chap. 3, this volume, and Nixon, chap. 7, this volume). These cognitive and behavioral approaches to helping again assume a normative framework. That is, they are premised on the idea that stress and adaptation are normal parts of life experience.

IDENTIFICATION AND TRAINING OF RELATIONSHIP SKILLS

Another contribution that the professions can make to the family support movement is that they have devoted a great deal of thought, time, and effort to *identifying and teaching key relationship skills* essential to the promotion of reliable alliance. In order to prepare counselors-in-training, it has been necessary to examine the skills that make up an effective helping interaction. Also, in order to assist people in improving a variety of social relationships, researchers in these professions have studied the behaviors that contribute to effective relationships and have developed methods for teaching them. Both the identification of relationship skills and the development of relationship-building training methods are useful to the family support movement.

Ivey (1988) has developed a task analysis of helping interactions and has then used it to create a teaching system. These skills and methods have become commonplace in the curricula for helping professions and are often called *active listening skills*. Ivey pioneered the use of brief video examples and role-plays to train counselors. These microteaching methods have been widely used to improve communication skills among teachers, social workers, and parents of children with disabilities (Walker, 1989).

Active listening is but one set of the useful interpersonal skills that professionals have studied and taught. Others that have been identified and effectively taught include *problem solving, communication, assertiveness,* and *negotiation.* In each case, researchers have studied the behavior of people who communicate well, developed a curriculum, and taught these skills to people who wanted to learn them. These methods and materials should be very useful to family support providers and to parents who are helping other parents because they are based on the assumptions that people can learn new skills and apply them in order to resolve problems.

ETHICAL PRACTICES

All of the helping professions have had extensive experience with the ethical issues that arise in the course of a helping relationship. Most have developed guidelines for practice that are aimed at protecting the privacy and autonomy of people who make their private lives open to a helper. Family support activities may also necessarily involve some of the more private and vulnerable aspects of personal interaction. It is essential that family support workers enter this territory with a thorough knowledge of ethical practices. One of the most important is the practice of gathering valid consent from family members before beginning any kind of intervention or assistance. Guidelines for gathering valid consent have been well developed in the medical, ethical, and psychological literature (e.g., Culvert & Gert, 1982). Informed consent is much more than a simple legal procedure. It represents a general principle for working with families. The principle is that a helper makes extensive efforts to safeguard the privacy and autonomy of the family and to ensure that family members are willing participants in the helping interaction. At each stage of an intervention with a family, people who intend to be helpful should clearly state their purposes and goals, make sure that family members understand these aims, and confirm that they want to participate. The process of gathering informed consent should go on as a continuous part of the supportive relationship.

A METHODOLOGY FOR TEACHING PSYCHOEDUCATIONAL SKILLS

Some approaches within the helping professions have emphasized the importance of "giving skills away" to people. This approach contrasts with an expert model in which it is assumed that the professional has difficult-to-attain knowledge that can only be held by a few individuals. While the expert model is unavoidable in many areas of knowledge, it does not make sense as a way of helping families where the goal is to support and enhance the ability of a family to carry out its many roles. This is not to say that family support providers should not be thoroughly trained. However, their training should emphasize how to give away their expertise as well as how to interact with family members. As other contributions to this volume are steeped in methods of teaching psychoeducational skills, examples of these approaches will not be detailed here. However, it is important to note that such approaches share many common elements including the use of video examples, role-plays, homework, coaching, modeling, prompting, programmed instruction, and mutual support.

ENHANCING FORMAL AND INFORMAL SOCIAL SUPPORT

The professions have also addressed the need to assist people in building and maintaining supportive social networks. For example, community psychologists have developed methods of convening the social networks around families and eliciting help from people in communities (Gottlieb, 1988). These methods have recently become popular in creating circles of support for persons with disabilities and their families. Two sets of helping practices that complement network interventions are social skills training methods developed by behavioral psychologists and family interaction methods developed by family therapists (L'Abate, 1984).

Researchers and practitioners in psychology and social work have also learned a great deal about how to activate formal supports for troubled families (Kaplan, 1986). They recognize that multiple systems, including schools, neighborhood organizations, churches, insurance companies, and a host of government agencies, affect families. Activating these supports, negotiating collaboration between the different groups, and advocating for families are all parts of the social–ecological approach to assisting families (e.g., Dunst et al., 1988). Those helping professions that recognize the importance of networking and nesting families in supportive communities have developed skills and expertise in these endeavors. This body of information also can be of use to the family support movement.

COLLABORATION WITH SELF-HELP GROUPS

Practitioners and researchers in several of the helping disciplines have recognized the importance of the self-help movement. For example, community psychologists (Levine & Perkins, 1987) have argued that there will never be sufficient numbers of professionals to assist all those who experience major life crises or who suffer from a range of common psychosocial problems. Consequently, they have stressed the importance of self-help organizations in which people offer aid to one another. Many professionals also recognize that self-help groups provide elements of support that cannot be given in any other way and are, in many cases, superior to professional assistance (Thoits, 1986). Likewise, they realize that self-help organizations can be powerful allies in assisting families. Some self-help organizations have also developed collaborative relationships with professional helpers and self-help facilitators such that they have well-developed, mutually supportive roles (e.g., Compassionate Friends, an organization for bereaved parents). This body of experience is also relevant to the family support movement.

CONCLUSION

A new view of families and children with disabilities breaks the mold of residualist thinking. Families are now increasingly being considered partners and allies with professionals. Professionals have much to learn and gain from this alliance. In the same way, there are important schools of thought within the helping professions that have some extremely valuable methods and programs that can benefit families. A true alliance of families, professionals, and family support services promises to build resilience in families and to contribute to positive adaptation to disability. There is much to be gained in this endeavor.

The field of family support for persons with disabilities and their relatives has gained considerable momentum since the mid-1980s with the passage of new federal policy initiatives and funding of research and training centers devoted to family issues. The notion that families are central to the well-being of persons with disabilities has gained widespread acceptance. At the same time, practical guidance as to how to assist families in their many roles is still sketchy and a data base for guiding family support work is only in a nascent state. This volume emphasizes the value of various cognitive-behavioral interventions and self-help programs in assisting families to promote well-being, prevent distress, and alleviate difficulties associated with stress. Several of the authors have published data validating the efficacy of these procedures. Contributing to a necessary body of knowledge about how to form effective partnerships with caregiving families is the focus of this book.

Family support is based upon the notion that families can and do adapt positively to challenges posed by disability. In this chapter, recent ideas regarding resilience and adaptation in families are discussed. An important value base for the family support movement is respect for the immense contribution that families make to the well-being of persons with disabilities. Increasingly, parents and their professional allies have come to appreciate that some of the best resources for families come from other families.

In Chapter 2, Santelli and Turnbull describe the recent growth of the family-to-family self-help movement. In Chapter 3, Singer and his colleagues provide an example of a multi-element family support model that combines cognitive-behavioral interventions, community support, and parent-to-parent helping. Dunst and his colleagues describe the values that underlie family centered intervention and give examples of how values translate into helpgiving behavior in Chapter 4.

Several chapters in this book focus on specific kinds of assistance for issues that commonly arise in supporting families. In Chapter 5, Powers describes her work on grieving and adaptation. In Chapter 6, Cooley and Moeschler discuss some of the ways that physicians can provide support for family adjustment. Nixon discusses a cognitive group intervention in Chapter 7 to help parents who are dealing with guilt and self-blame. In Chapter 8, Todis and her colleagues describe a new approach to parent training that focuses on promotion of positive self-esteem in children with disabilities. In Chapter 9, Shank and Turnbull present a cognitive-behavioral intervention to assist single parents, a large and growing part of the population. In Chapter 10, Lichtenstein discusses some of the ways that she has applied behavioral marital therapy to assist couples who have a child with disabilities. In Chapter 11, Walker and Singer describe a framework for understanding the development of alliances over time between parents and professionals with an emphasis on the parent–teacher relationship. They also review an intervention developed by Walker for promoting improved communication. Hawkins and her colleagues describe the use of short-term behavioral therapy in Chapter 12 to assist families with specific problems that can be addressed within the family system. Gibbs focuses on siblings and ways of supporting them in Chapter 13. In the final chapter, Lucyshyn and Albin discuss an approach to providing in-home behavioral support to families.

REFERENCES

Antonovsky, A. (1987). *Unraveling the mystery of health: How people manage stress and stay well*. San Francisco: Jossey-Bass.

Bellah, R.M., Madsen, R. Sullivan, W.M., Swidler, A., & Tipton, S.M. (1985). *Habits of the heart: Individualism and commitment in American life*. New York: Harper & Row.

Benson, B.A., & Gross, A.M. (1989). The effects of a congenitally handicapped children upon the marital dyad: A review of the literature. *Clinical Psychology Review, 9*, 747–758.

Berger, P.L., & Luckmann, T. (1989). *The social construction of reality: A treatise in the sociology of knowledge*. New York: Doubleday.

Birenbaum, A., Guyot, D., & Cohen, H.J. (1990). *Health care financing for severe developmental disabilities*. Washington, DC: American Association on Mental Retardation Publications.

Culvert, C.M., & Gert, B. (1982). *Philosophy in medicine: Conceptual and ethical issues in medicine and psychiatry*. New York: Oxford University Press.

Dinkmeyer, D., McKay, G.D., & McKay, J.L. (1987). *New beginnings: Skills for single parents and stepfamily parents*. Champaign, IL: Research Press.

Dunst, C., Trivette, C., & Deal, A. (1988). *Enabling and empowering families: Principles and guidelines for practice*. Cambridge, MA: Brookline Books.

Dunst, C.J., Trivette, C.M., Starnes, A.L., Hamby, D.W., & Gordon, N.J. (1993). *Building and evaluating family support initiatives: A national study of programs for persons with developmental disabilities*. Baltimore: Paul H. Brookes Publishing Co.

Gottlieb, B.H. (1988). *Marshalling social support: Formats, processes and effects*. Newbury Park, CA: Sage Publications.

Guerney, B.C., Guerney, L., & Cooney, T. (1985). Marital and family problem prevention and enrichment programs. In L. L'Abate (Ed.), *The handbook of family psychology and therapy* (pp. 1179–1217). Homewood, IL: Dorsey Press.

Ivey, A.E. (1988). *Intentional interviewing and counseling: Facilitating client development*. Pacific Grove, CA: Brooks/Cole Publishing Co.

Johnson, J., & Sarason, I. (1978). Life stress, depression, and anxiety: Internal–external control as a moderator variable. *Journal of Psychosomatic Research, 22*, 205–208.

Kagan, S.L., Powell, D.R., Weissbourd, B., & Zigler, E.F. (Eds.). (1987). *America's family support programs: Perspectives and prospects*. New Haven, CT: Yale University Press.

Kaplan, L. (1986). *Working with multiproblem families*. New York: Lexington Books.

Knoll, J., Covert, S., Orsuch, R., O'Connor, S., & Blaney, B. (1990). *Family support services in the United States: An end of decade status report*. Cambridge, MA: Human Services Research Institute.

L'Abate, L. (Ed.). (1985). *The handbook of family psychology and therapy*. Homewood, IL: Dorsey Press

Lehr, D.H. (1990). Preparation of personnel to work with students with complex health care needs. In A.P. Kaiser & C.M. McWhorter (Eds.), *Preparing personnel to work with persons with severe disabilities* (pp. 135–152). Baltimore: Paul H. Brookes Publishing Co.

Levine, M., & Perkins, D.V. (1987). *Principles of community psychology*. Oxford: Oxford University Press.

Markham, H.J., Floyd, F.J., Stanley, S.M., & Storaasli, R.D. (1988). Prevention of marital distress: A longitudinal investigation. *Journal of Consulting and Clinical Psychology, 56*(2), 210–217.

Mischler, E.G. (1984). *The discourse of medicine: Dialectics of medical interviews*. Norwood, NJ: Ablex Publishing Co.

Monk, A. (1983). Family supports in old age. In R. Perlman (Ed.), *Family home care: Critical issues for services and policies* (pp. 101–111). New York: Hawthorne Press.

Moroney, R.M. (1986). *Shared responsibility: Families and social policy*. New York: Aldine.

Orford, J. (Ed.). (1987). *Treating the disorder, treating the family*. Baltimore: Johns Hopkins University Press.

Patterson, J. (1991). Family resilience to the challenge of a child's disability. *Pediatric Annals, 20*(9), 491–500.

Rakos, R.F. (1990). *Assertive behavior*. New York: Routledge, Chapman & Hall.

Sarason, B.R., Levine, I.G., & Pierce, G.R. (Eds.). (1990). *Social support: An interactional view*. New York: John Wiley & Sons.

Scheerenberger, R.C. (1983). *A history of mental retardation*. Baltimore: Paul H. Brookes Publishing Co.

Singer, G.H.S. (1993). When it's not so easy to change your mind: Some reflections on cognitive interventions for parents of children with disabilities. In A.P. Turnbull, J.M. Patterson, S.K. Behr, D.L. Murphy, J.G. Marquis, & M.J. Blue-Banning (Eds.), *Cognitive coping, families, and disability* (pp. 207–220). Baltimore: Paul H. Brookes Publishing Co.

Singer, G.H., & Irvin, L.K. (1990). Family support: Emerging practices, issues and questions. In L.H. Meyer, C.A. Peck, & L. Brown (Eds.), *Critical issues in the lives of people with severe disabilities* (pp. 271–312). Baltimore: Paul H. Brookes Publishing Co.

Singer, G.H.S., Irvin, L.K., & Hawkins, N. (1988). Stress management training for parents of severely handicapped children. *Mental Retardation, 26,* 269–277.

Slater, M.A., Bates, M., & Eicher, L. (1986). Survey: Statewide family support programs. *Applied Research in Mental Retardation, 7,* 241–257.

Slater, M.A., & Wikler, L. (1984). Normalized family resources for families with a developmentally disabled child. *Social Work, 31,* 385–390.

Snyder, R., Harris, C., Anderson, J.R., Holleran, S.A., Irving, L.M., Sigmon, S.T., Yoshinobu, L., Gibb, J., Langelle, C., & Harney, P. (1991). The will and the ways: Development and validation of an individual differences measure of hope. *Journal of Personality and Social Psychology, 60*(4), 570–585.

Summers, J.A., Behr, S.K., & Turnbull, A.P. (1989). Positive adaptation and coping strengths of families who have children with disabilities. In G.H.S. Singer & L.K. Irvin (Eds.), *Support for caregiving families: Enabling positive adaptation to disability* (pp. 27–40). Baltimore: Paul H. Brookes Publishing Co.

Thoits, P.A. (1986). Social support as coping assistance. *Journal of Consulting and Clinical Psychology, 54,* 416–423.

Turnbull, A.P., Blue-Banning, M., Behr, S., & Kerns, G. (1986). Family research and intervention: A value and ethical examination. In P.R. Dokecki & R.M. Zaner (Eds.), *Ethics of dealing with persons with severe handicaps: Toward a research agenda* (pp. 119–140). Baltimore: Paul H. Brookes Publishing Co.

Walker, B. (1989). Strategies for improving parent–professional cooperation. In G.H.S. Singer & L.K. Irvin (Eds.), *Support for caregiving families: Enabling positive adaptation to disability* (pp. 103–119). Baltimore: Paul H. Brookes Publishing Co.

Weiss, R.S. (1974). The provisions of social relationships. In Z. Rubin (Ed.), *Doing unto others.* Englewood Cliffs, NJ: Prentice Hall.

Wells, K., & Biegel, D.E. (1991). *Family preservation services: Research and review.* Newbury Park, CA: Sage Publications.

2

Parent to Parent Programs

A Unique Form of Mutual Support for Families of Persons with Disabilities

Betsy Santelli, Ann P. Turnbull, Esther Lerner, and Janet Marquis

Parent to Parent programs offer an individualized and personalized form of support to families who have a member with a disability. Both emotional and informational support are provided by a trained "veteran" parent who is carefully and systematically matched with a newly referred parent on the basis of similar disability and family experiences. This one-to-one match is the foundation of the Parent to Parent approach.

Parent to Parent programs first appeared in the United States in the early 1970s. The first program of record was started in 1971 in Omaha, Nebraska, by four parents of children with disabilities who petitioned the Greater Omaha Arc[1] for assistance in establishing

We gratefully acknowledge the assistance of Lynn Blanchard and Carey Maynard-Moody for their contributions, both to their Parent to Parent programs and to this chapter.

Many of the quotes in this chapter were shared with the Beach Center on Families and Disability by parents participating in the Parent to Parent National Survey Project. These parents were happy to share their thoughts but preferred to do so anonymously.

[1]This is a local chapter of The Arc, formerly Association for Retarded Citizens of the United States.

Pilot Parents. The program grew quickly, and within 3 years the support of the Nebraska State Developmental Disabilities Council enabled a full-time parent coordinator to oversee this rapid growth.

Convinced that the emotional and informational support that one experienced parent could give to another parent was uniquely valuable and could only be provided "parent to parent," the co-founders of Pilot Parents soon sought additional funding to expand the program into neighboring states. The model has since spread throughout the United States, and currently there are an estimated 350 Parent to Parent programs nationwide serving over 20,000 parents (Santelli, 1992; Santelli, Turnbull, Marquis, & Lerner, in press). Parent to Parent is also prevalent in other countries, particularly in Canada, Australia, New Zealand, the United Kingdom, and Denmark (Boukydis, 1987; Hornby, 1988; Hornby, Murray, & Jones, 1987; Iscoe & Bordelon, 1985).

This chapter: 1) provides a rationale for Parent to Parent programs, 2) describes and summarizes the results of the national survey of Parent to Parent programs conducted by the Beach Center on Families and Disability at The University of Kansas, 3) presents two Parent to Parent program development stories that exemplify successful strategies for implementing and expanding a Parent to Parent program, 4) overviews new developments in Parent to Parent, and 5) describes several national resources for parents and professionals who have an interest in Parent to Parent.

RATIONALE FOR PARENT TO PARENT PROGRAMS

Special Challenges Faced by Families

Families who have a member with a disability must not only cope with the typical demands of family life, but also deal with a host of disability-related issues that accompany their transition from the culture of nondisability to the culture of disability. They must learn about the disability itself and what it means for the individual as well as for the whole family; they must learn the languages of the medical, legal, financial, and special education worlds; they must find their way in a service system that may or may not provide appropriate support opportunities; and they often must face the loss of their more familiar social supports as relatives and friends distance themselves out of fear and/or misunderstanding. Additionally, as new members of a minority group in our society, they must meet all of these challenges while struggling to understand and adjust to their own new identities and roles.

Several studies document the challenges faced by families of a person with a disability. For families who learn that their child has a disability at birth, the experience is often emotionally overwhelming, shattering many of their hopes and expectations for the future (Pearson & Sternberg, 1986). The family's long-term goals and security are suddenly no longer in clear focus, and replacement goals and avenues to family security are not yet defined. Parents may feel guilty, angry (with each other and with the many professionals who are now in and out of their family lives), depressed, numb, lonely, and/or confused (Seligman & Darling, 1989). Intensifying many of these feelings are the day-to-day logistics of caring for a young child with special needs. These logistics include repeated visits to hospitals and medical clinics and the resulting medical bills, often demanding and time-consuming caregiving (and sometimes life-sustaining) home responsibilities, little opportunity for respite, managing the concerns and acceptance (or rejection) of family and friends, and juggling the needs of the parent(s) and other siblings—significant challenges to say the least (Gallagher, Beckman, & Cross, 1983; Schell, 1981).

These challenges will be present throughout the child's lifetime, and will be augmented by additional child and family needs as the family moves into and through the service system. Transitions between service settings require adjustments on the part of all family members as new visions and goals are established and new issues and challenges appear. Questions about educational programming, medical interventions, inclusion in the social mainstream, employment, and independent living appear and reappear as the child grows up. Families struggle with these questions and with the uncertainties associated with not knowing what is around the corner. For many families, there are no appropriate opportunities around the corner except those they themselves will develop. As one parent of a 14-month-old boy with cerebral palsy related:

> For us, the scariest part of being a family for Mark is that there are so many unknowns—for him and for us. Will he be able to make himself understood by using a communication board? Will he have friends who accept him as he is? Will a quality educational program be available for him in our community? How much will our insurance pay for his upcoming surgery? Who can we talk to when we are "down?" Will Mark ever be able to live and work on his own? Who will look after him when we can no longer do so?

Where once-strong family networks existed that often helped families to meet the challenges of family life (with or without disability), the societal trends of increased mobility and decreased interdependence mean that today members of the extended family often live in communities far away (Kazak & Marvin, 1984); roles played by neighborhoods and churches in the lives of families are also constricted (Madara, 1983). As a result, many families are left to face these challenges alone.

When families of persons with disabilities are asked who would be best able to support them emotionally, they often mention as their first choice other parents who share their experiences (Boukydis, 1984). Sharing family stories with someone who has a similar story to share apparently is an important source of support. Such relationships may develop naturally and spontaneously within existing social networks among families who do not have a member with a disability. For families of a person with a disability, social networks tend to be smaller; finding a family with similar experiences and needs is often difficult (Dunst, Trivette, & Cross, 1985).

Social Support as a Buffer to Challenge

Social support has been defined as "the attachments among individuals or between individuals and groups that serve to improve adaptive competence in dealing with short-term crises and life transitions as well as long-term challenges, stresses, and privations" (Caplan & Killilea, 1976, p. 41). Social support operates on several different levels, from the very intimate social support that is provided by a spouse or other close family member or friend, to the more casual support that may be received from neighborhood, community, and/or professional connections. The type of support provided through social support networks varies and includes information, material assistance, and emotional empathy and understanding (Henderson, Byrne, & Duncan-Jones, 1981).

The idea that social support may be beneficial to family members has been corroborated in family research. Crnic, Greenberg, Ragozin, Robinson, and Basham (1983) found that when mothers of young children received social support from a variety of sources— neighbors, friends, members of the extended family—they reported greater parenting satisfaction and more positive parent–child interactions. Pilon and Smith (1985) observed that parents became better health care managers for their young children (as measured by the child's weight gain, hospital usage, use of the educational system, and self-ratings) when they participated in weekly parent support groups. Thus, parental social support systems can be a coping support under the various stressful conditions that accompany the parenting experience.

Because families of persons who have disabilities have smaller social support networks and tend to obtain their support from many of the same members of their small, interconnected, family-dominated networks (Kazak & Marvin, 1984), their opportunities for benefiting from the support of a highly developed friendship network are reduced. Yet, because of the additional challenges that accompany a disability in the family, their need for support may be increased. Parent to Parent programs have evolved in the last 20 years in response to the unique needs of these families.

Parent to Parent programs involve matching an experienced "veteran" parent of a family member with a disability in a one-to-one relationship with a new or referred parent who is just beginning the experience of parenting a child with a disability. Many parents who are experiencing the adjustment to the diagnosis or the challenges of transition can be helped in a unique way by other veteran parents who have already had these same life experiences. Because veteran parents have "been there" and have experienced the presence of a family member with a disability, they are in a unique position to establish a meaningful bond with referred parents and to provide them with emotional support and information through this one-to-one match. These shared experiences often become the foundation for relationships that develop into lifelong friendships, thus alleviating the isolation often reported by families of people with disabilities. As one mother relates:

> When my third daughter was born with Down syndrome, isolation was what I felt . . . [Despite being] surrounded by supportive people at the time of (her) birth and diagnosis—the medical people who dealt with us were very sensitive; my husband and close family were incredibly helpful; our friends were trying desperately to understand what had happened—through the first few weeks I felt isolated. . . . almost as if I were insulated from the very people who were trying to reach me the hardest. I felt desperately that no one, absolutely no one, knew what I was going through. (Mariska, 1984, p. 6)

Another mother tells of a different set of circumstances with similar results:

> Family and friends fell by the wayside in a fantastic pattern of despair. . . . like a chain of dominoes. Many of these friends were professionals that I had the utmost confidence in. Pillars of strength and guidance drifted away like straws in the wind. . . . I knew then that from that day forward my whole life must change if [my son] were to survive. His vulnerability frightened me. I knew what I must do. I could no longer go it alone. I needed other mothers, other fathers to relate to. (Pizzo, 1983, p. 25)

These mothers were looking for social support to help them cope, to help them deal with their feelings of isolation, to help them learn their way in their new world. Parent to Parent programs offer such social support, but in a way that is different from the ways used by more general parent support groups. While parent support groups usually have regularly scheduled meetings for parents to come together around common issues, Parent to Parent programs use peer support to provide emotional and informational support to parents through a carefully constructed one-to-one match. Matches between a trained veteran parent and a newly referred parent are made based upon similar disability and family issues, and each matched relationship evolves according to the needs and preferences of the referred parent. The support, therefore, is more informal, flexible, spontaneous, and individualized than the support that is generated within a group setting.

THE PARENT TO PARENT NATIONAL SURVEY

Parent to Parent programs have been providing emotional and informational support to families of persons with disabilities for 20 years. However, because most Parent to Parent programs are relatively small grass-roots efforts fueled by the energies and dedication of a few veteran parents, there has been little systematic study or description of the programs themselves. Other than a small international study conducted in 1985 that included seven Pilot Parent programs in the United States and six in Canada (Iscoe & Bordelon, 1985), and a few articles describing individual Parent to Parent programs in the United States (Bassin & Kreeb, 1978; Boukydis, 1987; Brookman, 1988; Menolascino & Coleman, 1980; Mott, Deal, & Skidmore, 1986; Scott & Doyle, 1984), the literature contains little on Parent to Parent programs.

The Parent to Parent National Survey Project at the Beach Center on Families and Disability at The University of Kansas, in response to this lack of information, is conducting a national survey of Parent to Parent programs. Its aim is to identify Parent to Parent programs throughout the United States, to gather and analyze descriptive information from Parent to Parent program administrators and from Parent to Parent program participants through a mail survey, and to use the information to develop resources for families and professionals who have an interest in Parent to Parent.

Phases of the National Survey of Parent to Parent Programs

There are three phases to the survey effort. During Phase 1, a questionnaire was developed that contained 62 questions relating to: 1) program demographics; 2) participating family demographics; 3) administrative characteristics of the program, including annual budget and expenses, sources of funds, staffing patterns, and in-kind supports from a sponsoring agency; and 4) program components, supports and services (including the supports provided to referred parents and the strategies for providing these supports), the supports for veteran parents, activities for persons with disabilities and for other family members, training opportunities provided to other professionals, and materials available from the program.

In the fall of 1989, 634 programs that identified themselves as doing Parent to Parent matching received the survey. Over the next 15 months, 55% of these programs returned their surveys to the Beach Center on Families and Disability. Some of these 346 programs that returned surveys were not actually Parent to Parent programs, leaving 267 programs that were doing systematic one-to-one matching between a trained veteran parent and a newly referred parent.

Of the 45% of the programs that did not return surveys, 10% did not respond because they were not providing one-to-one matching, 14% cited lack of staff time or capability to respond, and the reasons for the remaining 21% were unknown. Based on conversations with the non-respondents about their reasons for not participating in the survey, the authors believe that the 267 Parent to Parent programs that returned surveys represent about 75% of the currently existing Parent to Parent programs across the country.

For Phase 2 of the project, two separate survey booklets were developed—one for veteran parents and one for referred parents. Each of the parent surveys contained questions relating to: 1) family demographics, 2) the supports and services offered to and received by referred parents and how they ranked these various supports in importance, and 3) other program activities provided above and beyond the matched experience. The survey for veteran parents included additional questions relating to the supports and services available specifically for them.

In the fall of 1990, each participating Parent to Parent program was asked to assist in reaching veteran and referred parents who were active in their program. Approximately 3,000 referred parents and 1,600 veteran parents received invitations to join the survey effort. Over the next several months, 704 referred parents and 629 veteran parents requested a survey booklet; 239 referred parents and 327 veteran parents actually returned their completed survey protocols to the Beach Center. The data collected in Phases 1 and 2 of the project provide a national picture of how several hundred

Parent to Parent programs are operating today. This data can form guidelines for newly developing programs.

Phase 3 of the project is devoted to the development of products and resources for parents and professionals interested in participating in the Parent to Parent experience and/or starting a Parent to Parent program in their community. A list of these products and resources appears at the end of this chapter.

Parent to Parent Program Highlights

Parent to Parent programs responded to our national survey from every state except Alaska, Mississippi, and Wyoming, with fairly even distribution among the 10 federally defined regions of the country. The greatest percentage of programs operate in communities of over 100,000 people.

The oldest Parent to Parent programs that responded have been supporting families for close to 20 years. Most programs responding to our survey, however, were less than 6 years old, with many in their first year of operation. Parent to Parent programs range in size from very small programs that may have only two veteran parents serving four to six referred parents, to very large programs with groups of several hundred veteran parents matched with several hundred referred parents. The greatest percentage of programs serve 13–25 referred parents.

About half (52%) of the responding Parent to Parent programs have a formal relationship with a sponsoring agency and receive a significant percentage of their funds from their sponsor. The remaining programs are autonomous and receive most of their funding support through fundraising efforts and grant-writing. Approximately 50% of nonsponsored programs listed fundraising as a source of their annual income, and 66% of nonsponsored programs mentioned private donations as a source of funds. The greatest percentage of programs have annual budgets of less than $5,000; only about half of the programs have a paid coordinator, who in most cases works part-time.

The vast majority of Parent to Parent programs are cross-disability in focus and meet the needs of families dealing with a variety of disabilities—physical, intellectual, and emotional—as well as health care needs. The few single disability programs that responded devote their energies to Down syndrome or match parents nationally based on a rare disorder. While most Parent to Parent programs are providing services to families with younger children (birth to 6 years), more matches are being made for families who have adolescents and/or young adults with disabilities as the programs and their veteran parents age.

As is true for most other parent support efforts, the majority of the families participating in Parent to Parent programs are Caucasian, two-parent, middle-income households. When asked if parent participation reflected the cultural diversity of the home community, however, 61% of the programs indicated that this was true for their program. Parent to Parent programs struggle to reach families who are traditionally underrepresented in the service system, and several programs have developed very successful outreach strategies, particularly with Hispanic and Native American families. Perhaps the Parent to Parent experience eventually will be widely available to all families across disability and across the life span.

At the very heart of Parent to Parent programs is the one-to-one match; all of the programs responding to the national survey reported that the matched opportunity is the foundation of their program. While 89% of the programs reported using the one-to-one match between two parents most often, other forms of matching are also occurring (e.g., couple to couple, family to family, sibling to sibling, grandparent to grandparent, and individual with the disability to individual with the disability).

Another hallmark of Parent to Parent programs is the training component for veteran parents. In 76% of the responding Parent to Parent programs, formal training is provided to veteran parents before they are placed in a match. Many programs also offer veteran parents ongoing training opportunities and informal support from the program coordinator once they are matched with newly referred parents. In over 90% of Parent to Parent programs, the content of veteran parent training includes: 1) communication and listening skills, 2) the adjustment process that families experience as they cope with disability-related issues, 3) information about disabilities and community resources, and 4) the referral process and continued support from the Parent to Parent program. Among all Parent to Parent programs nationally, 78% provide at least 1–3 hours of training to veteran parents.

Because the quality of the support that will be offered by the veteran parent is so dependent on the relationship between the referred parent and the veteran parent, great care is taken when making a match. Approximately 96% of programs nationally match parents on similarity of the disability, and 91% match parents based on similarity of family problems/issues. Programs also reported using an average of six different factors (age of child, age of parents, family structure, family socioeconomic status, primary language spoken at home, location of residence) when making a match.

Once a newly referred parent has agreed to be matched, most Parent to Parent programs encourage the veteran parent to contact the referred parent within 24 hours. Nationally, 58% of Parent to Parent programs strive to have this first contact between the veteran and the referred parent occur within 24 hours of the referral. A quick response may help to alleviate any anxiety the referred parent may have about becoming involved in the program. Once a match is underway, the evolution of the matched experience is fully determined by the needs and preferences of the referred parent. Fifteen percent of referred parents reported that their matches lasted less than 1 month; 22% participated in matches lasting from 1 to 6 months; 14% had active matches from 6 to 12 months; and 50% of referred parents had been in matches for more than 1 year.

Although a variety of supports and services are provided through the one-to-one match, the vast majority of Parent to Parent programs (more than 90% of the responding programs) reported offering each of the following: someone to listen and understand, information about the disability, information about community resources, assistance with referrals, and problem-solving support. These key support opportunities, delivered through a carefully implemented one-to-one match between a trained veteran parent and a newly referred parent, are the very essence of Parent to Parent. While some programs reported other program activities beyond the one-to-one match, the delivery of these support opportunities is the common denominator among all of the Parent to Parent programs that responded to the survey.

Additional information about specific survey findings from the national survey of Parent to Parent programs is found in Santelli (1992) and Santelli et al. (in press).

STRATEGIES FOR PROGRAM DEVELOPMENT

Because Parent to Parent programs deliver emotional and informational support through the volunteer efforts of trained veteran parents, starting a Parent to Parent program requires little more than a small group of dedicated volunteer parents. Florene Poyadue, the executive director of Parents Helping Parents in San Jose, California, and a national Parent to Parent leader, describes her highly successful 15-year old-program as having been started very simply by two "mono-maniacs with a mission." An important beginning step is finding and channeling the energies of a core group of parents—the "mono-maniacs" who are committed to the importance of one-to-one Parent to Parent support and who will lead the program development effort.

Can a professional who is not a parent of a child or young adult with a disability successfully launch a Parent to Parent program? The answer is a resounding "yes," but this is uncommon. Of the program administrators responding to the national survey, 78% were themselves parents of children/young adults with disabilities. Moreover, anecdotal data from the surveys are consistent in suggesting the importance of a parent-driven program. Just as the relationship between a veteran parent and a referred parent is solidified by the credibility of the shared common experiences of the two parents, so too does the strength of a Parent to Parent program appear to be bolstered by the credibility of the shared common experiences of the parents coordinating the program and the parents participating in the program.

A professional who is not a parent of a child or young adult with a disability, however, can and often does play an important role in a developing Parent to Parent program. Florene Poyadue describes the ideal role for a professional who is supporting a newly developing Parent to Parent program as the "guide at the side." A professional with established visibility and credibility may serve as an important link to the service system and to potential referral sources and funding prospects. The professional's academic training may very well include knowledge and information that will facilitate the program's establishment and growth. A professional sharing these experiences with parents as a part of the program development team, while recognizing the importance of parent-determined directions, can be an extremely valuable team member.

Once the program development team is identified, the real effort of planning and launching the program begins. Described below is the evolution of two program development activities under quite different circumstances, but with surprisingly similar outcomes. Each of these program stories comes in part from the Beach Center's actual contacts with developing Parent to Parent programs, and from the data from the national survey of Parent to Parent programs. Parents and professionals who work to develop their own Parent to Parent program may often encounter some of these same issues. The national survey data and the suggested strategies and resources described in the two program stories will likely be useful in aiding their efforts.

A New Parent to Parent Program in North Carolina

A small group of parents in rural North Carolina became friends after joining a community-based parent support group for families of children who have disabilities. After attending several group meetings, they decided that they would like to start a Parent to Parent program to offer parents the opportunity to be matched one-to-one with another parent sharing their experiences. These four parents were the required "mono-maniacs with a mission" and became the program development team.

Because these parents lived in North Carolina, they knew about the Family Support Network—the North Carolina statewide Parent to Parent program located in Chapel Hill. Since 1985, the Family Support Network has provided training and technical assistance to newly developing Parent to Parent programs in North Carolina, and today there are 25 local Parent to Parent chapters that are connected with the Family Support Network. Excited to have such a resource in their state, the parents contacted the Family Support Network.

With the guidance and consulting support of the Family Support Network staff (including on-site visits and follow-up telephone contacts), the program development team made some important initial decisions that determined the philosophy and direction of the program. The team members elected not to pursue sponsorship from an existing service provider agency such as The Arc, a hospital, or a school district. While recognizing that there were some advantages to sponsorship, they nonetheless wished for their program to have full autonomy and to be able to develop in the directions indicated by the parents. They met to write their program's mission statement and goals, and they enjoyed the freedom that a nonsponsored status allowed them in determining their own agenda. Next, using a sample provided by the Family Support Network, they developed their program brochure—one that was similar in format to brochures used by other Parent to Parent programs in North Carolina.

The Family Support Network staff provided additional support to the program development team by matching their newly developing program with an established Parent to Parent program in a nearby community. The program coordinator of this "veteran" Parent to Parent program was able to share information and strategies with the "referred" Parent to Parent program development team in much the same way that a veteran parent shares with a newly referred parent.

Because it did not have a sponsor, the Parent to Parent program housed itself in the family room of one of the parent's homes. With the assistance of the Family Support Network, the parents applied for a small grant from a local community group for $500 in seed money to cover their start-up costs. With these funds, they purchased a separate telephone line for the program and an answering machine to take incoming calls 24 hours a day. While they felt that the answering machine was a bit impersonal, they believed that all calls needed to be answered and that a machine was better than no answer at all. The seed money also paid for the printing costs for the program brochure. They printed their local Parent to Parent telephone number and the number for the Family Support Network on the brochure, just to be sure that parents connected with someone in Parent to Parent.

Using the sample training manuals from the Family Support Network, the parents next worked to develop their training component for new veteran parents. Following the lead of 76% of the programs responding to the national survey, the program development team believed in the importance of training veteran parents before they are matched. They also believed that their program's credibility would be strengthened in the eyes of potential referral sources by advertising the fact that each veteran parent is carefully trained. The manuals from the Family Support Network were comprehensive and served as a basis for their own training sessions. With the help of the Family Support Network's manuals, the parents developed their own 6-hour training component, to be divided into two 3-hour evening sessions. Content areas of the training included: listening and communication skills; understanding the adjustment process; information about disabilities; community resources and the referral process; and the philosophy of Parent to Parent.

At the same time the training sessions for veteran parents were being designed, recruitment efforts for veteran parents were underway. The parents started with their own social networks of friends. They also approached service providers in the community who were involved in helping to meet the needs of families of people with disabilities. Such personal face-to-face meetings, as a way to promote a Parent to Parent program and to seek the assistance of service providers in reaching parents, are used by 89% of the programs that responded to the survey.

During each meeting with an agency representative, the parents shared their own family stories and their commitment to the value of the one-to-one match. They described the features of their Parent to Parent program (sometimes they used the videotape on Parent to Parent support that was developed by the Family Support Network), and copies of their program brochure and a letter explaining the veteran parent opportunity were available to be mailed or sent home with the children. In this way, confidentiality for the families participating within the agency was protected and the cooperating agency needed to expend only minimum staff time to distribute the information.

Once a core group of veteran parents was trained, the program development team moved to promote and advertise the program within the community, particularly with potential referral sources. Because the single largest source of referrals to Parent to Parent programs nationally is the medical profession (88% of the responding programs indicated that they received referrals from this group of professionals), they initially concentrated their efforts on the medical community.

Several different methods were used to promote the program— person-to-person contacts, presentations to agency staffs, distribution of the program brochures, and announcements in various agency newsletters. Camera-ready print ads and a 30-second public service announcement for TV and radio from the Family Support Network made these important public awareness efforts easier; the seed money helped with printing and mailing costs. With each contact, the parents educated the community about the program and also began to develop positive working relationships that might eventually result in some financial support for the activities of the program. Without a sponsoring agency, long-term financial security for the program was an important issue. By the end of the program's first year, they had been successful in obtaining a small grant from the United Way to cover their basic operating costs. Their annual budget was $2,000.

Their first referral came from a nurse at one of the local hospitals. A woman had just given birth to a daughter who had Down syndrome. The nurse had talked with her about the Parent to Parent program and had given her and her husband the program's brochure. When the nurse asked them if they would like to be contacted by the Parent to Parent program, the family agreed and gave the nurse permission to share their telephone number with the Parent to Parent program. Only with the permission of the referred parent(s) are families contacted by the program.

The referral came in at 8:30 P.M., and the nurse and the Parent to Parent representative talked about the family and the disability-related issues—just enough to share information that would be useful in determining the best match. Fortunately, one of the new veteran parents was a mother who had a toddler with Down syndrome. After talking with the nurse, the Parent to Parent representative called the new veteran parent to see if she would like to be matched. The veteran parent was delighted to have a referral, and the next morning, she called the referred parent at the hospital and asked if she could come by to visit later in the day. Their match began just as most matches do nationwide, with the initial contact between the veteran parent and the referred parent being by telephone, and subsequent contacts being both in person and by telephone.

The referred parent from North Carolina describes her experiences with the Parent to Parent program:

> Our support parent has been terrific from the very first moment she walked into the hospital room. My husband and I were so numb with shock that we didn't know which way to turn, and we needed someone to give us some direction. She cried with us—real tears that only another parent can generate—and then helped us to see our way through some major decisions. When our daughter was diagnosed with a major heart defect that would require open-heart surgery, she gave blood for her surgery. She took us out to eat while our daughter was in intensive care, and later she even came to her first birthday party. She has become one of our dearest, closest friends.

The North Carolina veteran parent relates:

> When my son was born, there was no local Parent to Parent program, and I felt very alone and scared. There was simply no one who could possibly understand what I was feeling. For that first year until I finally connected with another parent in our new Parent to Parent program, I kept all of my feelings tightly inside. Meeting another parent whose child also had Down syndrome helped me to reconnect with life. So when I first walked into that hospital room to meet my referred parent, so many memories filled my heart—both painful ones and joyful ones. I so wanted to help her stay connected with life.

> I am very proud of our program and the parents who make it go, because we are all volunteers. I feel improved because we have each taken our negative experience regarding the births of our children and made something good come out of it by contributing to Parent to Parent.

Another early match for the program was made involving a veteran couple—a husband and wife who had trained together to be veteran parents after their daughter was born 10 weeks prematurely. Their experiences in the neonatal intensive care unit (NICU) had been so frightening and confusing that they vowed to do whatever they could to help other families whose birth experiences were similarly complicated.

The referred couple was experiencing an unexpected plunge into the world of the NICU—with all of its tiny, vulnerable, and often medically fragile infants being kept alive by life support machines that dwarfed the size of the babies even more. Although the doctors explained the procedures and the necessary treatments to the young couple, the explanations were often unclear because the labels and descriptors, so commonplace for the medical staff, were all new for them. They wanted desperately to hold their baby, stroke his cheek, and speak the soft and comforting words that are such an important part of the parent–child bonding experience—yet they were afraid that their loving gestures might disrupt the life support interventions that were keeping their son alive. They were scared and felt very isolated and alone in their rocky introduction to the parenting experience.

Fortunately, an empathetic NICU nurse informed them of Parent to Parent support. Because the hospital had been informed about the new group of trained veteran parents and knew about the availability of a couple who had had experience themselves in the NICU, the nurse was able to offer the matching services of the Parent to Parent program.

The veteran parents came right away to the hospital to visit the family. They brought pictures of their own daughter when she had been in the same NICU 2 years earlier along with pictures of the joyful toddler she had become. They visited the NICU together with the referred couple and began to explain some of the machinery and terminology that are a part of the NICU. Perhaps most importantly, they urged the couple to ask to hold their son, reassuring them that this important contact was usually not life-threatening, and was indeed often quite the opposite. The new mother recounts:

> I was so afraid that our son wouldn't make it through those first few days, and that I would never have a chance to hold him close to my heart. I didn't see how I possibly could with all of the tubes and machines all around. The nurses on the unit were always so busy keeping these babies alive that I didn't dare ask if I could simply hold my son. And yet my arms ached. To have [the veteran parent] practically insist that I make my own needs known to the NICU staff was exactly the gentle push that I needed. And holding him was exactly what we all three needed to see us through those first few days.

Over the next 3 months, there were many contacts between the two couples—in the NICU, at each others' homes, and over the telephone. On the day that the referred parents brought their son home from the hospital, the veteran couple provided the transportation and planned a small homecoming celebration for the family. The veteran couple's first-hand experience with an apnea monitor made the first few nights at home much easier for the referred parents, and there were many telephone calls made back and forth.

The couples have continued to say in close touch, and to share the ongoing concerns that parents of babies born prematurely often have even when the NICU experience is behind them. The two fathers have discovered a mutual interest in bowling and have joined a league together, finding this father-to-father time to be yet another type of mutual support. The referred father shared the following:

> I was terrified when my son was born so early, especially since my wife had just seen the doctor that afternoon. The rush to the emergency room was the longest journey of my life. And then to see this tiny, tiny human being fighting for his life with every breath—I felt so helpless, so afraid. And yet as husband and father, I wanted to be strong— strong for my wife and strong for my new son. Where and how to begin?

> When the veteran couple came to see us in the hospital, just their presence made all the difference in the world to me. Being able to talk (and cry) with another father who knew what I was going through gave me the strength I so desperately wanted to have for us all.

At the end of the first year in operation, the Parent to Parent program in North Carolina had a core group of 12 trained veteran parents, including the father described above. Eleven referrals were made to the program, and 10 of the veteran parents were involved in a match, with one veteran carrying two matched relationships. The other two veteran parents were involved in fundraising and the publication of the program newsletter while awaiting their first matched opportunity. Documentation of these matches was sent to the Family Support Network for inclusion on their statewide database.

Public awareness efforts were actively underway to continue to build the program's credibility in the community. The first issue of the program newsletter was printed, and a second round of veteran parent training was soon to occur. Four of the 11 parents who were referred into the program during the year will soon be trained to serve as veteran parents.

Because the program development team has a special interest in educating professionals about the parent perspective and about the importance of "family-friendly" ways of working and talking with families, they have plans to develop some training materials for service providers. They are also planning to begin a speakers' bureau of parents who are willing to make presentations about the program. The Family Support Network often receives requests for parent nominations to various task forces, commissions, and advisory boards, and the speakers' bureau will provide a pool of parents for these opportunities as well. Support opportunities for siblings are also in the planning stages.

The United Way has continued to fund the basic operational costs of the program at the same level and the founding parents are exploring grant-writing opportunities with the staff of the Family Support Network. After attending a statewide workshop on Parent to Parent given by the Family Support Network for program coordinators, energies and motivation are high to expand the program.

This Parent to Parent program in North Carolina is a small but growing parent-driven program that is functioning actively and successfully without a sponsor. As is true for about half of the North Carolina Parent to Parent programs, there is no paid coordinator. Their annual budget is small and fundraising is a continuing issue for program implementation and expansion. The development of this program was facilitated by the presence of a statewide Parent to Parent network in North Carolina. The careful and systematic one-to-one match between a trained veteran parent and a newly referred parent based on similar disability and family issues is the foundation of the program's services. Additional program activities are being planned in response to the preferences and needs of the participating parents.

A New Parent to Parent Program in Kansas

After receiving some information on Parent to Parent from the Beach Center on Families and Disability, a social worker in a special education cooperative providing services to several small independent public school districts in eastern Kansas decided to initiate a Parent to Parent program. Several parents were interested in working with her, and thus a parent–professional program development team (i.e., the "mono-maniacs with a mission") was formed.

Because in Kansas there is not yet a fully developed statewide Parent to Parent program, the program development team contacted the Beach Center for technical assistance. Information from the national survey was useful to the members of the program development team in describing the characteristics of other Parent to Parent programs nationally, and in providing guidelines for the development of their own program. Sample training manuals, program brochures, and newsletters, combined with the survey information from several hundred other Parent to Parent programs, formed the basis for their own program development. Thus, in much the same way that Parent to Parent programs facilitate information sharing between experienced parents and newly referred parents, so too can the Beach Center on Families and Disability facilitate information sharing between "veteran" Parent to Parent programs and newly developing Parent to Parent programs.

The program development team members in Kansas presented the idea for their Parent to Parent program to the special education parent advisory council, school administrators, and members of the school board. The response was favorable, and the decision was made to proceed under the sponsorship of the special education cooperative. While the program development team recognized that sponsorship might mean some loss of autonomy in determining the direction of the program, they appreciated the advantages that sponsorship offered to them: in-kind supports, such as the use of meeting rooms, a telephone line, the copy machine, and other office supplies and equipment; increased visibility and credibility for the program; easier access to school district professionals for assistance with referrals and training; and use of an already existing not-for-profit status for fundraising and grant-writing.

Just as was true for the North Carolina Parent to Parent effort, one of the first tasks undertaken by the program development team in Kansas was the development of the mission statement, goals and objectives for the program, and the program brochure. The special education cooperative printed the brochures and disseminated them to each of the local school districts. An article announcing the establishment of the program appeared in each of the local school district newsletters.

Under the sponsorship of the special education cooperative, the Parent to Parent program was located in the office of the social worker. Because the social worker was also a parent of a child with special needs and was permitted by the special education cooperative to develop and implement the Parent to Parent program as a part of her paid position, she assumed the role of the program coordinator. Incoming referrals were made through her office—no need for an answering machine, but calls could only be received during the school day.

The veteran training component of their Parent to Parent program, which was designed from sample training materials that the Beach Center provided, was based on an informal needs assessment of the parents who were interested in being trained as veterans. A 6-hour training session, to be presented in a full-day Saturday session, was developed covering the content areas of sharing family stories, listening and communication skills, understanding the adjustment process, the referral and matching process, and the philosophy of Parent to Parent.

Unlike the North Carolina communitywide effort to recruit veteran parents, the efforts of the Kansas Parent to Parent program were directed at only the school districts belonging to the special education cooperative. In many ways, the recruitment of veteran parents had already been accomplished during earlier awareness presentations about the program to parents and school district personnel and through several school district newsletter articles on the Parent to Parent opportunity. The group of parents who emerged to work with the social worker on developing the program was virtually the same group that wished to be trained as veteran parents. All had children attending the special education cooperative programs—except for a grandmother who joined the program on behalf of both her grandson, who had severe multiple disabilities, and her daughter, the mother of the child with disabilities.

Public awareness efforts increased once the core group of veteran parents had been trained. Because the program was sponsored by the school district special education cooperative, initial efforts were directed "in-house" to families with children in the special education programs. Access to the staff and families within the special education cooperative was facilitated because of the program's sponsored status. Awareness of the program's existence was spread through presentations made at teacher in-service meetings and to the district psychologists, brochures distributed to the school counselors and at preschool screenings, articles in the various school newsletters, and announcements sent home with children. Communitywide efforts were directed primarily toward the medical centers.

The first referral to the program came from a special education teacher on behalf of a family new to the district. The new arrival in her classroom was a 7-year-old boy with cerebral palsy, whose family had previously lived in rural western Kansas. He used a wheelchair and a communication board to assist in his daily activities. His mother was a single parent and had never before had an opportunity to meet and talk with other parents who were encountering issues similar to her own. When the special education teacher explained the Parent to Parent program to her at the initial staffing, she was delighted to learn of the opportunity to connect with other parents. Parent to Parent participation became one of the goals on her son's individualized education program (IEP).

After reading the program brochure and the article about the Parent to Parent program in the school newsletter, the mother decided to contact the program coordinator on her own behalf. She shared her family story, including the feelings of isolation and loneliness that often accompany the experience of parenting a child with special needs in a very rural area. A part of her story included her concern for her younger daughter who did not have a disability but was struggling with having an older brother who did. She specifically requested to be matched with a single parent of a child with cerebral palsy and, if possible, a younger child without disabilities.

After going back to the roster of trained veteran parents, the program coordinator called the new mother back to talk a bit more about the match opportunities. Because the Parent to Parent program was new and had only a small number of trained veteran parents, a match with another parent who was single and had two children, the older of whom had cerebral palsy, was not possible. However, the program coordinator explained that she could "double match" for her if she would be interested in having two veteran parents. The young mother was thrilled.

Within the next 2 days, the program coordinator contacted two veteran parents. The first veteran, while married, had a son who was 9 years old and had cerebral palsy. The second veteran was a single mom herself who had an 8-year-old son with attention deficit disorder and a 6-year-old daughter without a disability. Both of these veteran parents were excited to be able to share their respective and unique experiences. Each was given the new mother's telephone number and they agreed to work together in timing their contacts with her. As the matches evolved, the new mother found that her two veterans were very different resources to her, and she very much appreciated having such tailor-made support. She shared the following:

> I feel so lucky to have two caring veteran parents, especially when I know that too many parents have not even one. But for me, my needs as a single mom are just as unique as my needs as a parent of a child with cerebral palsy. When I'm feeling overwhelmed because I am parenting alone, I call my veteran parent who knows from firsthand experience about the isolation and exhaustion that sometimes come with being a single parent. When my son's cerebral palsy needs become too much for me to bear, well, then my other veteran parent knows just what I am talking about, and her similar experiences help to see us through.

One of the veteran parents from Kansas relates:

> To have two of us matched with [her] is Parent to Parent at its best! We each have something special to give, and yet we all three share the common experiences of disability.

A very different but no less important match also occurred during the early months of the program. The parents of a 6-year-old girl in kindergarten were very concerned about a recommendation they had just received from their pediatrician that their daughter's hyperactivity should be treated with Ritalin (methylphenidate). While they recognized that their daughter's short attention span sometimes interfered with her own progress, not to mention the progress of the other children in the classroom, they were uncomfortable with the idea of using drugs to control her hyperactivity. They asked the doctor if he knew of any other parents who had been faced with this same choice. He told them about the Parent to Parent program and gave them the number of the coordinator. The parents were delighted with the opportunity to talk with someone who had dealt with these same issues and the mother contacted the program the next morning.

A match was quickly made with a veteran parent whose son had taken Ritalin for the better part of his second- and third-grade years in school. The two mothers arranged to meet for coffee the next afternoon to share experiences and do some brainstorming about options. While the veteran parent's experiences with her son taking Ritalin had been largely positive, she was careful not to make a recommendation to the referred parent. Instead she listened carefully to the referred parent's concerns, frustrations, and fears and then simply shared her own family's experiences with her son taking Ritalin. Together they talked about different choices that might be made and what the possible outcomes might be for each option. The veteran parent had a couple of articles about Ritalin that she loaned to the referred parent. They agreed to meet again in 1 week.

At their next meeting, the referred parent shared with the veteran parent her tentative decision, after reading and thinking on her own, to follow the doctor's recommendation that her daughter be treated with Ritalin. Knowing firsthand the fears that accompany such a decision, the veteran parent then helped the referred parent to map out her own plan for monitoring her daughter's reaction to the Ritalin and her progress and to develop her own alternatives in case the Ritalin did not have the desired effect. Once the decision had been made, the referred parent needed no further support from the veteran parent, and the match was concluded. As the referred parent notes:

> I found the support from the veteran parent to be extremely useful to me during a time when I needed to make a difficult decision. Because she had also had to make this same decision, her perspective was much more helpful than that of others who had not. She shared many of her own family experiences with Ritalin, and in fact I even had a chance to talk with her son about how the Ritalin had been for him. Their collective wisdom was just what I needed to make my own decision with confidence.

At the end of their first year, the Parent to Parent program in Kansas had nine trained veteran parents. Each of these veteran parents had a child or grandchild who received special services through the special education cooperative. Six referred parents, who also had a child attending classes through the special education cooperative, were receiving informational and emotional support through their matches (and in one case, a double match) with a veteran parent. A grandparent-to-grandparent match was also arranged. While the program development team has made some awareness presentations about the program in the wider community, the program is still functioning solely "in-house" within the school districts that make up the special education cooperative.

Keeping the program visible in the community and to families is an ongoing task that requires much in the way of personal time and attention, but the effort is vital to the overall success of the program. For the Kansas Parent to Parent program, public awareness efforts continue to be a priority activity. Program brochures and response postcards for parents to use to contact the program are being distributed to doctors' offices in the community, and articles about the program continue to appear in the school district newsletters. While the program began with a focus on school district families, the program development team hopes that the program will expand to become community-based.

A second round of training is planned, and the program development team hopes to expand the number of hours of training offered to 12. They are planning to train a new group of veteran parents and to offer additional training for the original group of veteran parents. Both groups will attend the entire 12 hours of training, giving the new veteran parents an opportunity to benefit from the experiences of the original group of veteran parents. Perhaps matches will be arranged between the new veteran parents and the experienced veteran parents.

The program still has no official budget, but rather continues to be supported by the special education cooperative as the sponsoring agency. As the program grows, the program development team will consider the possibility of applying for state funding to support its continued expansion of the program.

The Kansas Parent to Parent program is an example of a small but growing effort that is driven by the energies of a parent–professional team and is functioning actively in a state that does not yet have a statewide Parent to Parent network. The program provides its supports and services under the sponsorship of a special education cooperative of several public school districts. The coordinator of the program is a paid employee of the special education cooperative and performs Parent to Parent functions as a part of her paid position. Many other in-kind financial supports are provided by the sponsoring agency, but the program development team is aware that the special education cooperative can only absorb a limited portion of the financial costs necessary for the program's activities. Soliciting funds from other sources will be required to support the program's growth.

The careful and systematic one-to-one match between a trained veteran parent and a newly referred parent based upon similar disability and family issues is the foundation of the program's services. Additional program activities are being planned according to the preferences and needs of the participating parents and school district personnel.

NEW DEVELOPMENTS IN PARENT TO PARENT

Newly developing Parent to Parent programs can benefit from the diverse program options and experiences of existing programs. While still in the minority, there are many mature, comprehensive Parent to Parent programs that are providing an array of supports and services above and beyond the one-to-one match in very creative ways. Some of these programs are expanding into areas such as: 1) collaboration with other community agencies and universities to bring the Parent to Parent experience to more families and to train professionals in family-centered care, 2) the use of computers, 3) wrestling with the ethical ramifications of matching parents prenatally, and 4) meeting the needs of families who are often underrepresented in the service system (e.g., families challenged by their social, educational, and economic situations; families for whom English is a second language; teenage parents). The Beach Center will compile these best practices in a manual that will be ready for dissemination to families and professionals in July 1993.

Parent-Directed Family Resource Centers

In addition to the development of many new and individual best practices in supporting families of persons with disabilities, approximately 15–20 of the Parent to Parent programs responding to the national survey are beginning to take on new identities—that of parent-directed family resource centers. As family resource centers, these Parent to Parent programs are expanding their services to meet all of the needs that families may have—financial, legal, transportation, respite, medical, and educational needs—as well as providing informational and emotional support. Hoping to be a "one-stop shop" for families, these programs are engaged in either the direct provision of some of these services, or more often, in the referral of resources for families. As such, they help families to make their way through the maze of services and to connect with the services that they need. The important features of these family resource centers include the following:

1. A family need only to come to one agency to get connected to all of the supports and services that a community offers.
2. Comprehensive family support is delivered in the informal, sensitive, respectful Parent to Parent way with the careful, systematic one-to-one match at the very heart of the service.
3. The centers emphasize parent-directed management, with professionals serving as the "guides at the side."

Parent to Parent and Personnel Preparation

In response to federal legislation for early intervention, specifically Part H of the Individuals with Disabilities Education Act (PL 99-457 as amended by PL 102-119), and its emphasis on family-centered care, colleges and universities are developing personnel preparation programs to train early intervention specialists. Faculty members, recognizing the power of the family experience as a teaching device, are beginning to connect with local and state Parent to Parent programs. In some universities, parents from Parent to Parent programs are actually employed by the university as "community faculty members." These parents participate in planning and teaching roles in university classes and welcome and involve students in their family lives and homes as a part of the students' practicum experiences. These opportunities provide early intervention students with firsthand and real-life family experiences that, according to students and families, are very effective in sensitizing the students to the day-to-day challenges and frustrations, as well as the special joys, that accompany life with a family member who has a disability. Similar collaborative efforts with Parent to Parent programs are also beginning to appear in medical schools across the country.

NATIONAL RESOURCES FOR PARENT TO PARENT

The number of Parent to Parent programs in the United States has grown from a very small number of newly developing programs in the early 1970s to 350 active programs in 1992. This exciting growth has meant that the one-to-one Parent to Parent matched experience is now more widely available to families of persons with disabilities.

Several different national efforts have facilitated the evolution of Parent to Parent into a national resource for families. Each of these national opportunities for support has a similar mission—to enhance the quality of life for children with disabilities and their families—but the focus of specific activities is slightly different for each. Parents and professionals who are interested in Parent to Parent, by utilizing the resources of each one of these organizations, can avail themselves of a broad range of technical assistance and support.

The Beach Center on Families and Disability

The Beach Center on Families and Disability at The University of Kansas is a federally funded research and training center. Eight different research projects on family issues related to disability, including the Parent to Parent National Survey Project, are being conducted at the Beach Center. Using the information generated from these research projects, the Beach Center is developing resources and training materials for families and professionals. The products from the Parent to Parent National Survey Project that will be available in July 1993 are listed in the Suggested Readings section at the end of this chapter. Information about the availability of these resources, and the many other products developed at the Beach Center, can be obtained by contacting:

> Beach Center on Families and Disability
> The University of Kansas
> 3111 Haworth Hall
> Lawrence, KS 66045
> (913) 864-7600

National Center on Parent-Directed Family Resource Centers

Another national resource in Parent to Parent program development is the National Center on Parent-Directed Family Resource Centers in San Jose, California. As a part of the Parents Helping Parents program, the federally funded National Center on Parent-Directed Family Resource Centers, directed by Florene Poyadue, provides training and technical assistance to those interested in starting a Parent to Parent program. Telephone consultation and printed materials are available at minimal cost to those interested in developing their own programs. More intensive technical assistance, including on-site visits from the center staff, can also be arranged, and a network of regional technical assistance centers is being developed. The National Center on Parent-Directed Family Resource Centers is an invaluable resource for parents and professionals interested in learning more about family resource centers. Information about technical assistance opportunities provided by the National Center on Parent-Directed Family Resource Centers can be obtained by contacting:

> Florene Poyadue, Executive Director
> National Center on Parent-Directed Family Resource Centers
> Parents Helping Parents
> 535 Race Street, Suite 140
> San Jose, CA 95126
> (408) 288-5010

National Parent Network on Disabilities

The National Parent Network on Disabilities (NPND) was founded originally in 1988 as the National Network of Parent Centers, a coalition of federally funded Parent Training Centers. In 1990, under the leadership of Patty McGill Smith, who was the first paid Parent to Parent coordinator of the original Greater Omaha Arc Pilot Parents Program in Nebraska, the name of the organization was changed and the membership was expanded. Today the National Parent Network on Disabilities is a national coalition of parent support programs, disability organizations, research and training centers, the federally funded Parent Training and Information Centers, state developmental disability councils, and individual professionals, parents, and persons with disabilities.

As a coalition of more than 135 member organizations and individuals, the NPND provides support to Parent to Parent programs nationally by working collaboratively to create a national climate that is more conducive to the development of comprehensive support opportunities for families with persons who have a disability by:

- serving as a national presence and voice representing the needs of individuals with disabilities and their families to the federal government
- informing parents and professionals about current planning and policymaking at the national level
- providing assistance to local and state parent organizations for maximizing their effectiveness in their own communities

Through awareness and advocacy efforts, the NPND works to bring about changes in legislation and to reform policies at the national level. NPND may be contacted at:

National Parent Network on Disabilities
Patty McGill Smith, Executive Director
1600 Prince Street, Suite 115
Alexandria, VA 22314
(703) 684-6763

Parent Training and Information Centers

There are 61 federally funded Parent Training and Information Centers that provide information about disability and educational issues, parent education, and advocacy training to parents in their home states. Each of these Parent Training and Information Centers views parents as full partners with professionals in the educational process and emphasizes the support and assistance that parents can and do offer to each other. Specifically, Parent Training and Information Centers help parents to:

- better understand the nature and needs of the disability of their child.
- receive follow-up support for the educational programs of their child with a disability.
- communicate more effectively with special and regular educators, administrators, related service personnel, and other relevant professionals.
- participate in educational decision-making processes, including the development of the child's individualized education program (IEP).
- obtain information about the programs, services, and resources available to their child with a disability and the degree to which those programs, services, and resources are appropriate (Federation for Children with Special Needs, 1991).

Further information about local Parent Training and Information Centers can be obtained by contacting:

Technical Assistance for Parent Programs (TAPP)
Martha Ziegler, Project Director
Federation for Children with Special Needs
95 Berkeley Street, Suite 104
Boston, MA 02116
(617) 482–2915

Statewide Parent to Parent Programs

Fourteen states have a statewide Parent to Parent program that supports the local efforts of newly developing Parent to Parent programs, and the nature and level of support that statewide Parent to Parent programs provide to local efforts varies by state. In some states, the statewide program actually provides many of the services that are important for the success of the local program and may even have funding support for local efforts. In other states, the statewide program is simply a resource, leaving the actual program development and implementation up to individual programs.

For parents who are not sure whether their state has a statewide Parent to Parent program, a good place to start is with their state's Parent Training and Information Center. In some states, the statewide Parent to Parent program is also the Parent Training and Information Center; in others, both a statewide Parent to Parent program and a Parent Training and Information Center exist; and some states have just a Parent Training and Information Center.

While there is no one national Parent to Parent network that provides an easy way for all Parent to Parent programs (and the participating parents) to be connected, each of these state and national resources facilitates parent connections and information sharing to those who have a special interest in Parent to Parent.

SUMMARY

The growth of Parent to Parent since the early 1970s has been both dramatic and exciting. In 1971, fewer than 50 parents received emotional and informational support from one Parent to Parent program—the Greater Omaha Arc Pilot Parents Program. Today, well over 20,000 parents are involved, either as referred parents or veteran parents, in more than 350 Parent to Parent programs. Fourteen states have Parent to Parent networks, and there are several national organizations that are available as resources to those interested in Parent to Parent. A national Parent to Parent conference occurs every 2 years, drawing together national leaders in Parent to Parent and family support, professionals, policymakers, and entire families. The growth of Parent to Parent has had a significant impact on the emergence of family support as an important national issue in its own right.

Despite all of these exciting developments, the heart and soul of Parent to Parent remains unchanged and continues to be the solid foundation of Parent to Parent efforts nationwide. This common theme—providing emotional and informational support to families of persons with disabilities by carefully and systematically matching a trained veteran parent and a newly referred parent in a one-to-one relationship—is the very essence of Parent to Parent. The pure simplicity of Parent to Parent—one parent helping another parent—is its greatest hallmark.

REFERENCES

Bassin, J., & Kreeb, D.D. (1978). *Reaching out to parents of newly diagnosed retarded children: A guide to developing a parent-to-parent intervention program.* St. Louis: St. Louis Association for Retarded Children.

Boukydis, C.F. (1984, October). *The importance of parenting networks.* Paper presented at Parent Care Conference, Salt Lake City, UT.

Boukydis, C.F. (1987, October). *An overview of parent support groups.* Paper presented at the Fourth Parent Care Conference, Philadelphia.

Brookman, B.A. (1988). Parent to Parent: A model for parent support and information. *Topics in Early Childhood Special Education, 8*(2), 88–93.

Caplan, G., & Killilea, M. (1976). *Support systems and mutual help.* New York: Grune & Stratton.

Crnic, K.A., Greenberg, M.T., Ragozin, A.S., Robinson, N.M., & Basham, R. (1983). Effects of stress and social support on mothers and premature and full-term infants. *Child Development, 54,* 209–217.

Dunst, C., Trivette, C., & Cross, A. (1985). Roles and support networks of mothers of handicapped children. In R. Fewell & P. Vadasy (Eds.), *Families of handicapped children: Needs and supports across the life-span.* Austin, TX: PRO-ED.

Federation for Children with Special Needs. (1991). *Directory of parent training and information projects.* (OSERS publication through Cooperative Agreement G0087C3042). Prepared by Technical Assistance for Parent Programs (TAPP). Project funded by the U.S. Department of Education, Minneapolis, MN.

Gallagher, J., Beckman, P., & Cross, A.H. (1983). Families of handicapped children: Sources of stress and its amelioration. *Exceptional Children, 50*(1), 10–17.

Henderson, S., Byrne, D.G., & Duncan-Jones, P. (1981). *Neurosis in the social environment.* New York: Academic Press.

Hornby, G. (1988). Launching Parent-to-Parent schemes. *British Journal of Special Education, 15*(2), 77–78.

Hornby, G., Murray, R., & Jones, R. (1987). Establishing a Parent-to-Parent service. *Child Care Health & Development, 13,* 277–288.

Iscoe, L., & Bordelon, K. (1985). Pilot Parents: Peer support for parents of handicapped children. *Children's Health Care, 14*(2), 103–109.

Kazak, A.E., & Marvin, R.S. (1984). Differences, difficulties, and adaptations: Stress and social networks in families with a handicapped child. *Family Relations, 33,* 67–77.

Madaran, E.J. (1983). Self-help and how we teach tomorrow. *What's New in Home Economics, 17*(4), 3–4.

Mariska, J. (1984). Finding and founding support groups. In S. Duffy, K. McGlynn, J. Mariska, & J. Murphy (Eds.), *Acceptance is only the first battle: How some parents of young handicapped children have coped with common problems* (pp. 6–10). Missoula: Montana University Affiliated Program, University of Montana.

Menolascino, F.J., & Coleman, R. (1980). The Pilot Parent Program: Helping handicapped children through their parents. *Child Psychiatry and Human Development, 11*(1), 41–48.

Mott, D.W., Deal, A.G., & Skidmore, D. (1986). *Project HOPE: A parent-to-parent support program.* Morganton, NC: Family, Infant and Preschool Program (FIPP), Western Carolina Center.

Pearson, J.E., & Sternberg, A. (1986). A mutual-project for families of handicapped children. *Journal of Counseling & Development, 65,* 213–215.

Pilon, B.H., & Smith, K.A. (1985). A parent group for the Hispanic parents of children with severe cerebral palsy. *Children's Health Care, 14*(2), 96–102.

Pizzo, P. (1983). *Parent to Parent.* Boston: Beacon Press.

Santelli, B. (1992, April). *Parent to Parent National Survey Project.* Paper presented at the National Parent to Parent Conference, Phoenix.

Santelli, B., Marquis, J., Lerner, E., & Turnbull, A. (1992). *Parent to Parent: A special resource for parents and for educators.* Unpublished manuscript, Beach Center on Families and Disability, University of Kansas.

Santelli, B., Turnbull, A., Marquis, J., & Lerner, E. (in press). Parent to Parent programs: Ongoing support for parents of young adults with special needs. *Journal of Vocational Rehabilitation.*

Schell, G.C. (1981). The young handicapped child: A family perspective. *Topics in Early Childhood Special Education, 1*(3), 21–27.

Scott, S., & Doyle, P. (1984). Parent to Parent support. *The Exceptional Parent, 14*(1), 15–22.

Seligman, M., & Darling, R. (1989). *Ordinary families, special children: A systems approach to childhood disability.* New York: Guilford Press.

SUGGESTED READINGS

The following resources are available from the Beach Center on Families and Disability:

The National Directory of Parent to Parent Programs
Provides a single-page descriptive listing of each Parent to Parent program with information about the program's demographics, services, materials developed, and types of disabilities represented. This resource is useful for families and service providers who may be looking for Parent to Parent support, and for other Parent to Parent programs that may be looking for networking opportunities.

Bibliography of Parent to Parent Literature and Resources
Contains a descriptive listing of the resources in the literature on Parent to Parent, as well as Parent to Parent materials that have been developed by Parent to Parent programs nationwide.

Parent to Parent National Survey Results—A Summary
Summarizes the major findings of the national survey, with a discussion of the implications of the findings for families, practitioners, administrators, and policymakers.

Best Practices in Parent to Parent
Describes state-of-the-art practices in Parent to Parent program development and implementation.

The World of Parents of Children with Disabilities

Lloyd W. Robertson

It all started with Katie's jitters. She emerged from the womb, a slender baby and incredibly long to this new father's eyes, and she was "jittery," as the doctor and nurses said. They suctioned her, dried her, wrapped her in a towel, took her to be weighed, and brought her back, and said she was jittery—like a baby who had been badly chilled. The doctor said it could be various things, and various possible solutions would be tried, especially making sure the levels of sugar and certain minerals in the blood were correct. The baby was born at 10:30 A.M. in the morning; by 4 P.M. in the afternoon, the doctor was telling me the baby would travel from our local hospital to Minneapolis Children's (MCMC) by ambulance. At one point she said it might be something "neurological," so I heard that word in connection with Katie before she was a day old.

A DIFFERENT WORLD

Friday was Day 3, and late in the afternoon, Dr. B. found us (Katie was now in the Transitional Nursery) and told us the results of the MRI. This is another scene we will never forget. The doctor began to tell me the results as we stood outside the nursery, right where he had found me. I asked him to wait and tell Laura at the same time, so we went to the Family Lounge where Laura was waiting, still resting from her ordeal. Magnetic Resonance Imaging is a new technology that allows images to be taken from different angles and perspectives, allowing for a complete and precise picture of the structure of the brain. We still have a copy of some of the pictures Dr. B. discussed with us that day. Katie, it turned out, was almost completely missing her cerebellum, and this fact explained her jitteriness and hypertonicity. The

implications were still extremely unclear. She could have severe disabilities, not only in motor coordination, but in intelligence as well. On
the other hand, some good outcomes were also possible. The doctor
told us that some patients had been able to walk and, indeed, had been
"handicapped" very little. We clung to the hope he was giving us, but
we also started getting used to the phrase "brain damage." We both
knew our lives had changed, and we had entered a different world—
the world of parents of children with disabilities.

ROUGH NIGHTS

We want to try to recall some of the special experiences, good and bad,
which we could only have had in this different world into which we
have been plunged. Many episodes concern our own case, but we have
learned a great deal from other parents as well. The first kind of
experience I would put under the heading "learning just how miser-
able life can be." All parents have stories about rough nights; as one
nurse told us, everything is scarier at night—it seems worse even if it is
not. Parents of "special" children have stories that seem to come from
way off in the Twilight Zone. We know a mother who has had her baby
sent off by helicopter with pneumonia—not once or twice, but five or
six times. She and her husband have also given CPR in the night—
sometimes more than once in the same night.

By comparison, our stories are mostly of the "losing sleep" variety, but we will never forget the night before the long hospital stay. We
had gone to the [Twin] Cities to see various doctors, mostly to prepare
for the insertion of the stomach tube.

We also had other problems to discuss. Laura had been sure from
the beginning that Katie snorted too much, as though she were strain-
ing to breathe. The cardiologist, whom we had waited two weeks to
see, confirmed immediately that the heart murmur was caused by a
problem in the airway. We stayed the night in a special residence
attached to the hospital, so as to see Dr. B. the next day and discuss all
the problems we had seen and heard about. As soon as Dr. B. saw
Katie, he decided she should be admitted to the hospital.

The night before, however, after seeing the cardiologist and other
doctors, we were on our own with her, knowing she was very sick, not
knowing whether to call a doctor, and if so, which. We paced, we sang
(we sang a lot in those days; it was always "Bicycle Built for Two" with
gavage feedings), we tried to comfort her, and she would not sleep.
She snorted and wheezed, she squirmed and choked (she was still
regurgitating). We had to give her two or three gavage feedings; she
did not yet have the "built-in" tube which would make life so much

easier. By the end of the hospital stay which was about to begin, we would be able to give her a sedative to ease her agitation; on that night we had nothing, and it was easily the worst night of either of our lives.

A NEW LOW

The second worst was probably when we brought Katie and all her equipment home for the first time, after a month in the hospital. We had not planned well and left the trip till too late in the day. We simply could not figure out all the equipment: a humidifier to supply humidity for the trach (as the mouth and nose usually do), a compressor (incredibly noisy) to force in the humidified air, a suction machine, and another machine for lung care called a "nebulizer," along with the apnea monitor we had before. As the hour grew later, we grew increasingly desperate. We had to phone and ask which tubing went where and to complain that the humidifier ran out of water in about two hours. (Were we going to have to be up in the night, not for the baby but for this machine?) It struck us very forcibly that we had reached yet another new low in our hopes for the future; Katie needed all this equipment, it would be hard to look after her while seeing her fail to develop, and it looked like we would be on our own. When family called that night, we simply could not talk.

Helen Featherstone has written beautifully and wisely, drawing on the experiences of many parents, about the feelings such an experience can evoke: anger at fate, God, the baby and the situation; guilt mixed with anger at oneself, for it is hard not to feel responsible or at least not to feel singled out, as if one were guilty of a terrible sin; fear of the future, of what the child might do next, of one's own feelings; wild fantasies about somehow ending it all or escaping. We have had many of these feelings, and others which are equally impossible to discuss in polite society, on nights such as the ones I have described. Often the only thing that can lessen such grief and rage is to be able to share it with others.

GETTING TO KNOW OTHERS

Our first initiation into the "club" of parents like us came with classes we were expected to take before we could take Katie home for the first time—when she was about 10 days old. One class was on the apnea monitor, the other on CPR, or emergency life-saving. Most of the parents we met had babies whose only problem was premature birth. "Preemies" often require massive medical intervention in the first year of their lives, but in most cases, almost miraculously, they show no lasting serious ill-effects. Still, the parents of "preemies" were as scared as we were and, at that point, we could not be sure Katie was much worse off, even in the long term, than their babies. The anxiety, hurt and fear we all felt was deliberately heightened by our teachers; after all, as they told us, we were going to be on our own, in the middle of the night, with a baby's life at risk. We all had to demonstrate our knowledge almost as quickly as we acquired it. There was nervous laughter, but the atmosphere was extremely tense. The teachers could say everyone suffers some apnea—pauses in breathing—and all parents, at least, should know CPR, but you know perfectly well that you are in deep trouble when you are in those classes. We will always remember the father of twins who had trouble responding properly to a staged alarm. One twin was sicker than the other, but both would be at risk—did the father simply have too much anxiety to think straight? We were taught to let the alarm "beep" 10 times, while we watched the baby for a color change, to see if the baby corrected herself. One mother always rushed to shake the doll in front of her, representing her baby, without waiting for 10 beeps. "I can't help thinking the baby might die," she said.

In the long hospital stay, covering slightly more than the month of September, we met many parents. Those whose children had serious birth defects were most like us. One morning, Katie had seizures for the first time and Dr. B.'s partner, who was covering for him, had to take charge, ordering medications and sending Katie to LSU (Intensive Care) as a precaution. Laura was there without me, and another mother she had barely begun to know came to her in tears and hugged her. "I don't know why I'm crying," she said. "It's not even my baby." They laughed and cried together, and have stayed in touch ever since.

What can one say about the camaraderie among "special parents"? We meet in hospitals and doctors' waiting rooms, and as often as not, we introduce ourselves by giving a condensed version of our child's medical history. Often there are tears, yet there is a lot of laughter. I tend to think this is partly a reaction of relief. No matter how unfortunate we are, we would not trade places with other parents in distress; somehow, they seem at least as unfortunate as we are. Laura says this is too cynical and that it is simply that comradeship can cheer us up: for a moment at least, we are not alone, as we so often are at home. We know people in similar situations, and perhaps they can even help with stories and information. A hospital, where one can meet with other parents and professionals, can be a place to catch one's breath, ease the desperation a bit and gain new hope—especially if there is a good chance that medical treatment will bring real progress. Laura and I have not joined a parents' group, perhaps because we have been afraid of being the worst-off parents, but we are always amazed at meeting people who show strength and even cheerfulness in impossible situations.

HEALTH PROFESSIONALS

It seems right to deal next with the health professionals with whom one comes into contact. Most of the books by parents of special children say that "everyone has a horror story about one or more health professionals." We have no such stories. All the professionals we have met have done at least the jobs that are expected of them; many have sought ways to help us as best they can; and more than a few have gone well beyond the call of duty.

We have been especially impressed with Katie's doctors. They have taken long periods of time to talk to us when asked and have always taken the time to explain what they are doing. They have shown concern and respect for us, as well as great attention to Katie's needs. One example is the talking-to we got about nursing. As we prepared to take Katie home after her long hospital stay, we were urged to agree to have nurses come into our home. The subject came up at a big care conference which was supposed to deal with all of Katie's care. By this time, Katie's overall care was in the hands of pulmonologists, or respiratory specialists. (I sometimes call them "lung guys.") We dealt with several partners, but we eventually made Dr. W. Katie's primary doctor, and he presided at the meeting. Dr. W. has a tremendous bedside manner and has always been able to make us laugh in dark times. When I asked why we would need nursing, however, he became a bit stern, perhaps to dramatize his point. We think you need nursing, he said, because we have seen other families go through similar situations, and they have suffered, with or without nursing. We have seen stress, we have seen people unable to further their careers, we have seen families break up. Laura and I agreed to accept nursing; a few weeks later, it was unthinkable to be without it.

It was Dr. W. to whom we went recently to ask, among other things, about changing Katie's status to DNR—"Do Not Resuscitate" in a case where Katie cannot breathe on her own or suffers a drastic change in heart-rate. Dr. W. said he knew we had been through "agony," and that he was sure that a DNR order would now be among the acceptable options for us. When we asked him what he would do, he first said he had never been in our situation; we feared he was going to duck the question. Then he said he would do everything exactly as we had done it—waiting as long as we did and preparing for a DNR order now. We could not have asked for more support at this difficult time.

I must say something about the nurses we have had in our home, although it is hard to know what to say. They have relieved us of hours of difficult care; they have enabled us to sleep at night; often they boost our morale by the way they talk to Katie and seem to enjoy her. We have gone very quickly from being strangers to being almost family with some of them. It helps us, and makes our lives richer, just to be able to talk things over with them. They leave notes for each other, as we do for them, in a "communication book"; they usually end with a happy face, so when one of them has something like a warning to offer, she naturally uses an unhappy face. We know they will not keep coming forever, and we will miss them.

FINANCIAL SUPPORT

I should also say something about the financial support we have received. Our insurance, through my job as a college professor, has paid almost all the bills, and various government agencies have helped out with the rest. If this had not been the case, of course, we could not have afforded a fraction of the care Katie has received. It is up-to-date medical care which has allowed her to live so long, and very modern kinds of insurance and government benefits which allow for the bills to be paid. Everyone is concerned about the costs of health care and insurance in the United States, and it may be worth considering that in many ways Katie's case is not unusual: She required a lot of expensive care at a time when the eventual outcome, in terms of her health and quality of life, was very uncertain.

We often feel that in talking about our situation, it is hard to go beyond emphasizing the pain—above all, seeing all of one's hopes for a newborn child dashed over a matter of months. It is hard to describe this strange, isolated world we live in—what Edna Hong has called "Paindom"—to outsiders, and hard for them to understand. In the eyes of religious believers, I suppose, there are no outsiders, for such pain unites us all as suffering humanity under God. We always feel singled out and isolated, however, even from other "special" parents. We are suspicious of stories, written for a general audience, with a happy ending: either the child gets better, or the parents learn to accept the situation.

WE HAVE LEARNED

I am a teacher, so I'm inclined instead to take what Laura considers a too-academic approach and raise a teacher's question: What have we learned from our life with Katie, our life in the different world into which she had led us? Most mundanely, we have learned that medicine is not an exact science, and that this is especially true of neurology. In technical terms, for example, function in the brain cannot be inferred from structure. If part of the brain is missing or damaged, sometimes the function normally associated with that part does not disappear—the rest of the brain seems to adapt. Much more frequently, brain structure can appear normal to every existing test, while the expected function is missing; this is the case with Katie, for most of her brain looked fine at birth.

In a similar vein, but more significantly, we have learned that it is often hard to tell which babies are going to "make it," in almost any sense, and which are not. Any confident judgments about such matters should be treated with skepticism. Knowing what we know now, would we have wanted Katie to live these months? In a sense, of course not, but her diagnosis took time, and we have never felt it is for us to say her life is not worth living. We find ourselves envying parents of children with "milder" conditions, some of which can be detected before birth. Can such parents ever be sure it is better to end an unborn child's life by means of abortion? On the other hand, we may be better off than parents whose children are normal until a certain age and then are struck down in some terrible way. Often, no technological fix is offered in such cases; why should it be in others? This becomes both a personal matter for us, and a matter of principle, for we have both supported the pro-life cause, and many people would say we have now learned why abortion must be available in hard cases. I do not think this is true; Laura is less sure, especially because it would be so horrible to go through an experience like ours a second time.

Finally, we have learned a kind of patience, for we have tried hard to take whatever joy Katie can give us—and she has given us some. Arguably, our experience has made us and our marriage stronger, or made us more aware of our strength, and it has caused family members to rally around us in a way that has been very moving. If life were reducible to numbers and proportions, there would be no way of making these satisfactions, limited as they are, balance our terrible grief—but it is just possible that we human beings are not meant to think this way.

Lloyd W. Robertson lives with his wife, Laura, and their children, Katie, 4, and Benjamin, 2, in Northfield, Minnesota. He has recently completed a Ph.D. in Political Science at the University of Toronto, and has accepted a teaching position at St. Thomas University in Canada.

3

Helping Families Adapt Positively to Disability

Overcoming Demoralization Through Community Supports

*George H.S. Singer, Larry K. Irvin,
Blair Irvine, Nancy E. Hawkins,
Jack Hegreness, and Russell Jackson*

Researchers have reached three important conclusions about families of children with disabilities and chronic illness. First, most families adapt successfully to sharing a home life with a family member who has special needs. In fact, a majority of family members view their relatives with disabilities as positive contributors to the family and as sources of happiness (Summers, Behr, & Turnbull, 1989). Second, caring for a family member with a disability involves added daily stress that results in low morale for roughly one third of the families (Singer & Yovanoff, 1992). Finally, the right kinds of community supports for families can improve parental well-being and

The work reported in this chapter was funded by grant no. G008730149 between the Oregon Research Institute and the U.S. Department of Education, Office of Special Education and Rehabilitative Services (OSERS). The views expressed herein do not necessarily reflect those of the funders.

assist with positive adaptation (Singer & Irvin, 1991). This chapter briefly reviews the evidence for these three assertions and describes the Support and Education for Families (SAEF) model, a program that has assisted families to adapt successfully.

NEW PERSPECTIVES ON PARENTS OF CHILDREN WITH DISABILITIES

There is widespread perception in the popular culture as well as in the professional literature that being a parent or sibling of a child with a disability is, on average, an experience that is associated with sadness and stigma (e.g., Martino & Newman, 1974; Olshansky, 1970). Recently, researchers have challenged this notion (Singer & Irvin, 1991; Turnbull, Guess, & Turnbull, 1988; Turnbull & Turnbull, 1986). Behr, Murphy, and Summers (1992) developed the Kansas Inventory of Perceptions of Parents Who Have Children with Special Needs (KIPP) to measure cognitive adaptation to parenting a child with a disability. One of the scales on the KIPP measures perceptions of positive contributions to families of children with disabilities. In a validation study of the KIPP it was found that, on average, parents of these children agreed with statements about their children as sources of happiness. For example, a majority of parents agreed with statements such as:

My child is fun to be around.
My child is kind and loving.
My child is very affectionate.
The presence of my child cheers me up.
The presence of my child is very uplifting.
Because of my child I have many unexpected pleasures.

Approximately 85% of those who responded in the KIPP in one validation study expressed positive feelings such as these (Behr et al., 1992). Parents of children with disabilities also report that they learn important lessons in life from their family experience. An even larger percentage of the parents agreed with statements such as:

My child is responsible for my increased awareness of people with special needs.
I consider my child to be responsible for my increased sensitivity to people.
The presence of my child helps me understand people who are different.
Because of my child, I am more compassionate.

Because of my child, I learned about mental retardation.

Because of my child, my family is more understanding about special problems.

Because of my child, my other children have learned to be aware of people's needs and their feelings. (Behr et al., 1992)

Clearly, these are not the experiences of people who feel as if they are the victims of a tragedy or sufferers of chronic sorrow. Instead, parents learn from their experiences and form normal bonds of love and enjoyment with their children. However, this positive acceptance does not exempt parents from a variety of everyday stressors that are often experienced when their child has a disability.

SOURCES OF STRESS FOR
PARENTS OF CHILDREN WITH DISABILITIES

There is evidence that living with a child with a disability produces unusual stressors that can lead to fatigue and low morale in some families. These stresses appear to arise when a family has to alter its life-style to accommodate the needs of a family member who requires extra assistance and when these adjustments are difficult to maintain over time. Singer and Yovanoff (1992) conducted a meta-analysis of 17 studies comparing morale in parents of children with disabilities with parents of children without disabilities. They found that parents of children with disabilities generally had higher levels of demoralization than parents of children without disabilities. These studies also show that a *majority of parents of children with disabilities are not demoralized.* Singer and Yovanoff (1992) also examined the studies that used measures that yield a rough estimate of the proportion of parents who are at risk of depression. Across eight studies, they estimated that roughly 15% of parents of children without disabilities were at risk of depression compared with roughly 30% of parents of children with disabilities.

Many of the sources of stress for these families arise from reactions of others outside of the family and because of limitations on community resources. That is, the locus of the stress is not centered so much in the child as in the family's contacts with the community. The kinds of stressors that families encounter usually involve a complex mixture of family, child, and community factors that many believe can be remedied by providing the right mix of formal and informal support (Singer & Irvin, 1991). For example, financial worries are a source of stress for many families. It is increasingly common for infants with disabilities to spend weeks in a hospital neonatal intensive care unit before coming home. It is not uncommon for a family to owe $50,000 in medical bills before the baby even comes home. Birenbaum, Guyot, and Cohen (1990) found that children with severe mental retardation had average medical costs 10 times greater than children without disabilities. Currently over one quarter of all United States citizens do not have any form of health insurance (Davis & Rowland, 1990). The kinds of publicly financed medical care available to children with disabilities often entails extensive hassles. For example, eligibility for Medicaid waivers often entails multiple appeals and prolonged efforts. Also, private health insurance is often difficult for parents to obtain if they have a child with disabilities. People who are under chronic economic stress are more likely to experience symptoms of depression than people who are more comfortable financially. This relationship between money and depression is probably due to the fact that people with monetary difficulties experience more day-to-day hassles such as cars breaking down and bill collectors telephoning, along with fewer opportunities for recreation and enjoyable activities that cost money (Patterson, 1982). Other kinds of stressors also reside largely in the community; stigma and the resulting rejection by others, difficulties in obtaining child care, and aversive interactions with schools and hospitals can take a toll. They can also be remedied through the right kinds of social action.

Supports for Parents

Singer and Yovanoff (1992) summarized evidence from three studies that show that parental depression can be alleviated through the provision of certain kinds of supports. The interventions produced changes in parental depression that were equal to or greater than the average difference in levels of depression between parents of children with and without disabilities. In other words, there is emerging evidence that parents who are under severe stress can be assisted with the right combination of supportive provisions.

Several states in the United States now provide extra stipends to families of children with special needs. And many states have begun to develop an array of family support services to assist with other kinds of stressors (Dunst, Trivette, Starnes, Hamby, & Gordon, 1993). These efforts have to proceed without a research base to assist local communities in selecting interventions that are effective. In order to contribute data to the development of services, a series of studies to test various family support strategies was conducted. One promising package of support services has been a program called the Support and Education for Families (SAEF) project that was originally developed at the Oregon Research Institute (Singer, Irvin, Irvine, Hawkins, & Cooley, 1989).

Based upon a review of the literature and a series of focus groups with parents of children with multiple disabling conditions, it was decided that the research would focus on a combination of support services aimed at reducing parental stress. The package consisted of case management, respite care, parent-to-parent support groups, psychoeducational instruction in coping skills, behavioral parent training, and volunteers who took children to community activities.

Case Management Families of children with disabilities have a much greater need for a variety of formal services than do families of children without disabilities. These formal services may be provided by special education programs, medical clinics, respite care agencies, transportation agencies, technology centers, special recreation programs, insurance companies, and several different government agencies. Often these organizations have different eligibility requirements and each one usually requires the completion of a separate set of paperwork at critical junctures. Many parents describe the services system as a bewildering maze and list it as a source of stress (Harris & McHale, 1989).

One way to reduce parental stress and to increase appropriate service utilization is through well-designed assistance services, often called *case management*. This term is so widely used that it can mean any one of dozens of different roles and functions (Rothman, 1992). The kind of case management used in the SAEF model in particular has the following critical features: 1) the case management agency maintains an extensive library of information about formal and informal supports available in the community and gives central importance to linking parents to resources, 2) the agency prides itself on rapid response time, 3) the case managers are trained as good listeners who let parents take the lead in determining their own needs, 4) the case managers serve as advocates, 5) the case managers serve the same families over an extended period of time and develop a strong sense of rapport, and 6) the case managers are either parents of children with disabilities themselves or have had considerable life experience with persons with disabilities.

Self-Help The SAEF model brings parents together in groups and encourages them to support one another. It has a lot in common with the broader self-help movement, which has become increasingly popular in the United States since the 1970s. Self-help groups assist people with a variety of different challenges, including living with a family member who has a disability.

Researchers report several reasons why self-help groups are effective (Levine, 1988). These groups provide a wealth of experience and practical coping knowledge about specific problems. In most cases, professionals are not familiar with the 24-hour-a-day details of living with a child who has a disability, whereas other parents are intimately knowledgeable. Common experience makes it easier for parents to divulge personal concerns and to empathize with one another. Parenting a child with a disability can be an isolating experience because parents often feel that they are different and that their children are devalued. Other parents with similar experiences can often be more believable and easier to trust. The conditions for empathy are more readily created when people share common ground.

Furthermore, the structure of most self-help groups allows parents and siblings to both receive assistance and give it. Thus, there is a possibility of reciprocity and equality in the helping relationship. This reciprocal aspect of self-help organizations may reduce some of the threats to self-esteem that can arise in relationships between parents and professionals.

Finally, self-help groups provide a shared ideology that can provide members with a way of giving meaning to a difficult situation. One set of meanings that self-help groups provide to people who feel stigmatized is an alternative to the mainstream view that they or their children are devalued people. Thus, another function of parent-to-parent groups is to counter the negative societal views of persons with disabilities through the sharing of positive attributions about their children and their families.

Psychoeducational Instruction in Stress Management   The SAEF model also incorporates approaches to stress management that have been widely tested with people in many different stressful life circumstances (Woolfolk & Lehrer, 1984). The psychoeductional approach emphasizes the teaching of new skills. It contrasts, for example, with a psychodynamic approach, which centers more on an individual's private thoughts and feelings. In the psychoeductional approach, a group leader serves as a skills instructor or coach who explains, demonstrates, and guides group participants through the acquisition and practice of new coping skills that are derived from behavioral and cognitive-behavioral psychology (Hawkins & Powers, 1992; Singer, Irvin, & Hawkins, 1988). These skills are discussed in detail later in this chapter.

The most important aspect of stress management training is that it focuses primarily on the parent's needs. One of the basic principles undergirding the program is the idea that parents will be more successful in caring for a child with a disability if their own needs for relaxation and social support are being met. In this respect the SAEF model differs from many parent support programs that focus primarily on child-related issues. Parents participate in 10 weekly group sessions that last for 3 hours each. These meetings combine skills training with parent-to-parent support. Part of the time is spent discussing specific skills as well as fostering communication between the parents about common problems. At the end of the 10 weeks, parents are offered an additional class that focuses on parenting a child with special needs.

Behavioral Parent Training (BPT) In working with families, it was determined that a combination of parent-focused and child-centered approaches were needed. The primary source of stress for some parents was the challenge caused by their children's skill deficits or behavior problems. Prior research has found that parents of children with disabilities can be effective teachers of daily living skills and can also learn to successfully manage behavior problems that are sometimes associated with severe disabilities (Snell & Beckman-Brindley, 1984). Baker, Landen, and Kashima (1992) showed that parents who participated in a behavioral parenting class not only learned to teach their children daily living skills but also experienced lower stress levels as a result. A more detailed discussion of the content of these classes follows.

Respite Care Surveys of parents have repeatedly found that respite care services are one of the most requested and most valued support services (Apolloni & Triest, 1983; Salisbury & Intagliata, 1986). As part of the SAEF project parents were linked to a respite care agency that paid for child care on the evenings in which the group met. Parents who wished to make their own child care arrangements with extended family members and neighbors were encouraged to do so; in these instances, child care was paid for through the project.

Community Volunteers A further aim of the SAEF program is to increase community inclusion of children with disabilities and their families. Toward this end a program was established that consisted of student volunteers from a local college who took the children to integrated community activities on a weekly basis. The students were shown ways to interact with children with disabilities and were accompanied on their first outing with the children. Meetings were also conducted between the volunteers and parents in which the parents identified favorite activities for their children and gave the volunteers suggestions on how to get along with the children. Each volunteer originally made a commitment to visit the participating families once a week for a 6-month period; many stayed involved for a full year. In many cases, friendships developed between the volunteers and the families so that the volunteers were invited to dinners and on family outings as a kind of natural reciprocation for the volunteer's efforts. In a social validation study (Cooley, 1989; Cooley, Singer, & Irvin, 1989), many parents reported that they greatly valued the fact that the volunteers were working with their children out of a sense of personal commitment and friendship rather than as paid professionals. The fact that many of the volunteers developed genuine friendships with the children and their families was one of the aspects of the model that parents valued the most.

COPING SKILLS

This package of services has been tested by evaluating the combined effects of all services as well as their individual components. This series of studies has led to the belief that for many parents, stress management groups serve as a powerful part of intervention. In a recent study with parents of children with traumatic brain injuries (Singer, Glang, Powers, Nixon, & Cooley, 1992), it was found that the combination of a self-help group with instruction on stress management achieved significant reductions in parental depression. Adoption of the overall package of services is recommended, as evaluations have also shown that there is considerable variability regarding the particular services that parents prefer. Some parents attribute the majority of positive change to the behavior management class, others to the volunteer program, and still others to the contact with other parents. But if parents were given the choice of only one component to deliver, the study results suggest that the coping skills classes, with their emphasis on parent-to-parent support and stress management skills, would be the preferred component.

The stress management component of the SAEF model aims to teach a set of active coping skills that parents can apply to their daily lives. At the same time, the format of the class encourages parents to share with one another their experiences and strategies for coping with family stress. The classes cover the following skills: 1) self-monitoring, 2) progressive muscle relaxation, 3) relaxation in public settings, 4) monitoring and changing unproductive patterns of thinking, 5) finding meaning in difficult circumstances, and 6) utilizing social support.

Self-Monitoring

The SAEF program aims to teach self-monitoring skills by showing parents how to keep a diary of everyday stressors and successful coping efforts. Parents keep a daily diary during the 10-week class. The use of this diary helps participants to identify recurrent conditions that occasion stress reactions. This process of identifying recurrent stressors is a first step in problem-solving. Each week parents are asked to share any discoveries that they make as a result of keeping their diaries. When parents identify situations that are repeatedly distressing, they are coached to carry out problem-solving. Simultaneously, parents are encouraged to share empathetic understanding of the stressful situations and offer any advice that they have about coping with these problems.

For example, many parents identify their morning routine, when everyone must get ready for school and work, as a high stress time. One mother of a girl with cerebral palsy discovered from keeping a diary that such was the case for her. The morning was full of tasks that had to be completed in a short amount of time. An added stressor was her daughter's problem behavior, which consisted of resisting her mother's efforts to groom her. The child's cerebral palsy affected the use of her arms, making hairbrushing and toothbrushing difficult. With her mother in a hurry, the child would resist by tipping her head down and refusing to lift it. This situation often led to the mother yelling angrily or the daughter crying and kicking. When the mother described her difficult morning routine, other parents in the group admitted that they had experienced similar troubles. One father suggested that the mother ask the school teacher for help by including hairbrushing and toothbrushing in her educational plan. In this instance the mother was also assisted in setting up a picture chart for the child; it illustrated the child's morning routine in a step-by-step manner. The mother was also coached on how to use a simple token reward system to encourage her daughter to cooperate. The mother's subsequent diaries began to show clear improvement in the family's morning routine. This example shows how self-monitoring, coupled with sharing of common experiences with other parents and skills training in specific coping skills (in this case, behavior management skills), led to improvement in the quality of daily life.

It is important to note that the daily diary format includes a place for parents to note their successes. As the meetings progressed, parents had more of these achievements to share and were encouraged to recognize each other's accomplishments. This orientation toward solving problems and sharing solutions helps to build a kind of group spirit that itself appears to encourage further change. This milieu of mutual aid and encouragement is often described as a key component of self-help and it certainly has been an important part of the stress management groups.

Progressive Muscle Relaxation

The classes also teach progressive muscle relaxation (PMR) (Jacobson, 1938). There are many different relaxation procedures including meditation, yoga, diaphragmatic breathing, self-hypnosis, biofeedback, and autogenic training. Progressive muscle relaxation was selected because of its extensive research base and because of its wide use as an active coping skill. Instruction is preceded by an explanation of the importance of daily relaxation as a way to recover from stress and to become more resilient in the face of challenging circumstances. Progressive muscle relaxation is not insisted upon; parents are encouraged to share ways in which they currently recover from stress. It is likely that the repeated discussion of ways of taking care of oneself helps to create a social norm—an agreed-upon premise in the group that it is good for parents to take some time each day to care for themselves as well as for their family.

Teaching PMR involves modeling it and leading the group through a relaxation practice as part of each class. The group leader guides parents in alternately tensing and relaxing large muscle groups. Additionally, parents are taught to pair the relaxation with visualization of a pleasant scene. Parents are provided with tape recordings of the relaxation instructions and are asked to take these home to practice. Parents fill out self-report logs that indicate how often they practice and how they feel as a result.

After a few weeks of practicing the long form of progressive relaxation, parents are taught to utilize short forms of PMR as an active coping skill. Goldfried (1971) developed relaxation as an active coping skill by teaching people to use their own sensations of stress reaction as a cue to engage in brief forms of relaxation. When used in this way, PMR becomes a portable skill that parents can use in many different settings.

There are three parts to PMR as an active coping skill. First, parents learn a brief form of PMR that they can use in public. It consists of deep breathing and tensing and releasing a muscle group in a way that is not highly visible. For example, hunching the shoulders or making a fist and then opening the hand can serve as quick cues to relax. Second, parents are coached in monitoring their levels of tension during the day and to use their feelings of tension to prompt a relaxation response. In order to facilitate generalization, parents are encouraged to post unobtrusive visual cues in places that they frequent. For example, parents are provided with small stickers in the shape of circles for attaching to things such as the steering wheel of the car, the bathroom mirror, and the area above the kitchen sink. Parents are told to take a moment and check for any feelings of tension or other stress reactions whenever they see the stickers. If tension or agitation is present, they would then engage in a brief form of PMR. The parents usually have fun with these stickers. Several parents reported that they would like to stick them on their bosses' foreheads at work so they could teach themselves to relax whenever the boss was present.

Relaxation in Public Settings

Along with monitoring physical stress reactions, parents also are encouraged to pay attention to mental and emotional aspects of stress reactions. In this regard, they are asked to self-monitor their thoughts during situations that cause recurrent stress. The diary form they use provides a place to note each stressful situation and their thoughts during the stressful event. For example, one mother wrote, "My son tantrummed in the grocery store." In describing her thoughts about the situation, she wrote, "I must be a bad mother to have a child who misbehaves." Again, parents are urged to use each other as resources in finding alternative ways to think about such difficult situations. In this example, another parent responded by saying, "My son, who has autism, also misbehaves in town. I know how embarrassing it can feel. But I've let myself off the hook for his problems. I say to myself now when he acts up, 'I'll make it through this. It's not my fault, it's just that people with autism have trouble understanding how to behave sometimes.'" The group leader presents a discussion of cognitive coaching—the skill of noting how a stressor is being interpreted and consciously altering this interpretation. This discussion of cognitive coping leads to the next topic covered in the class, finding meaning.

Finding Meaning in Difficult Circumstances

According to cognitive coping theory (Summers, Behr, & Turnbull, 1989; Taylor, 1983), a significant life event such as giving birth to a child with a disability can challenge a parent's basic assumptions about vulnerability, fairness, and purposefulness. In resolving this encounter, many parents may arrive at a new perspective on life. The process of facing a dramatic divergence from the life that they expected leads many people to rethink some of their basic assumptions. As a result of this process, they arrive at a new sense of values and develop a sense of meaningfulness about the disability. Little is known about this cognitive coping process, although at least one investigation suggests that people can be helped with this process of cognitive coping through structured discussions about basic assumptions.

Monitoring and Changing
Unproductive Patterns of Thinking

Nixon and Singer (in press) reported on a cognitive-behavioral intervention to help parents who were experiencing high levels of self-blame and guilt regarding their children with severe disabilities. A set of guided discussions with a group of parents, it was found, led to a reduction in depression and guilt, and led to a change in attributions about the disability. Because cognitive adaptation is a key component of stress reduction, 1 of the 10 stress management sessions is devoted to a discussion of the larger meanings that parents give to the circumstance of living with a family member with a disability. In a number of the groups, this session has evoked some of the frankest and most emotionally charged conversations between parents; these discussions helped to cement a sense of group cohesion.

Utilizing Social Support

One session of the group is devoted to a discussion of the importance of social support. Parents are asked to respond to an assessment of different kinds of social support, the Provisions of Social Support Scale (Cutrona & Russell, 1987). It then serves as a basis for a discussion of the kinds of support that are available to parents from family, friends, professionals, and other community members. Parents are asked to consider their satisfaction with the amount of support available to them for different needs and to discuss some of the ways that they can develop new relationships or make greater use of available support that is unused in their network. The overriding result of the class is that it calls attention to the risk of social isolation and the importance of forming and maintaining viable support networks. Once again, the discussion supports a social norm, namely, that it is good for parents to take care of themselves through contact with people who are supportive. Simultaneously, the group serves as a supportive forum and parents are encouraged to stay in touch with one another outside of the meetings.

An important variant of the intervention that will be tested in an upcoming trial pairs veteran parents with new parents in classes. The parent-to-parent pairs are encouraged to make telephone contact at least once a week outside of the class. This variant of the model is designed to strengthen the self-help component.

BEHAVIORAL PARENT TRAINING (BPT)

The SAEF model also involves an 8-week BPT class that has been developed specifically for parents of children with severe and multiple disabilities. The classes have two primary aims: 1) to increase children's prosocial participation in family activities, and 2) to reduce coercive interactions between parents and children. The first aim is based upon research that indicates that home is the place where children without disabilities learn many daily living skills, ranging from cooking to recreation skills (Zill & Peterson, 1982). For children without disabilities these skills are taught informally through participation, observation, and coaching from parents and siblings during ongoing activities. That is, parents rarely give a child a lesson on how to use.the vacuum cleaner or how to make toast, but they may demonstrate and explain these skills in the course of housecleaning or preparing breakfast. This kind of naturalistic learning is more difficult when a child has severe disabilities. Many children with disabilities have difficulty in learning through observation and modeling; further types of assistance are often needed, such as physical prompts and additional rewards to motivate learning. In order to increase children's participation in daily family life, the BPT classes cover four topics: 1) partial participation, 2) reinforcement, 3) giving clear directions, and 4) using simple token systems.

The second aim of the BPT classes involves reducing negative interchanges in which parent and child each escalate the intensity of his or her own behavior in an effort to make the other person stop (Patterson, 1982). Such a conflict often occurs when a parent gives a directive to a child. To help prevent these kinds of confrontations, the classes cover these topics: 1) planned activity training, 2) giving directions and redirecting, 3) descriptive praise, and 4) the use of brief, nonseclusionary time-out.

Planned activity training (Powers, Singer, Stevens, & Sowers, 1992) has proven to be an extremely useful technique for many parents in the SAEF program. Planned activity training involves teaching parents to implement the following practices:

1. Identify times when the child needs to occupy himself or herself.
2. Give the child a choice of activities.
3. Get the child started at the activity.
4. Intermittently reinforce the child for engaging in the activity.

Powers et al. (1992) demonstrated that parents of children with severe disabilities could implement these steps in community settings as well as at home in order to reduce undesirable behavior and increase mutual enjoyment of activities.

EVALUATION DATA

The efficacy of the SAEF model has been studied by examining its individual components as well as its total package. Singer et al., (1988) found that the stress management class significantly reduced symptoms of anxiety and depression in parents. Singer, Irvine, and Irvin (1989) found that the behavior management class led to increases in positive parental interactions and to reductions in reported rates of undesirable behaviors. Two studies that used direct observation of children in home and community settings found that planned activity training was effective in reducing the undesirable behavior of children with severe disabilities at home and in community settings such as grocery stores, shopping malls, and churches (Powers et al., 1992; Singer & Singer, 1992). An evaluation of the entire SAEF model found that it led to reductions in parental depression, increased participation of children in community activities, and high levels of parent satisfaction with the program (Singer, Irvin et al., 1989). After demonstrating that the various components of the model are effective, it was then decided that the possibility of the model being replicated by others who were not part of the original development team should be determined.

In order to evaluate the efficacy of this package, parents were randomly assigned to either a waiting list group or a treatment group. Furthermore, in order to see that the model is replicable, treatment manuals were written and a group in another metropolitan area was asked to carry out the model. Changes in parental depression were measured as the key outcome variables. The first two waves were conducted by the program's authors, and the second by people whose only contact with the original model site involved reading treatment manuals. The subjects in this study were 67 parents of school-age children with severe disabilities. The outcome measure was the Beck Depression Inventory (Beck, Ward, Mendelson, Mock, & Erbaugh, 1961). A MANCOVA analysis revealed that both the original site and the replication site achieved significant results ($F = 5.76$, $df = 65$, $p = .002$). In each of the four waves of replication, the waiting list group either stayed the same or got worse while the treatment group improved. The MANCOVA also showed that the change in the groups could not be attributed to the particular location or the therapist who ran the program. The results strongly suggest that the SAEF model can be replicated effectively. Thus, there is reason to believe that a combination of family supports can reduce parental distress in those families who experience stress-related difficulties.

SUMMARY

The SAEF model is not meant to be a comprehensive family support service that can meet all of the problems that families present to service providers. In past experience with families it has been found that some families require much more intensive services. In order to meet these needs, the following kinds of intensive services were offered to families requesting them: 1) marital counseling, 2) in-home behavioral parent training, 3) treatment for depression, 4) counseling and referral for substance abuse, and 5) problem-solving and communication training for adolescents and their parents. It is believed that more intensive services are needed for families experiencing the severe disruptions that are typical of crisis.

It is also important to note that the model does not include political organizing and group advocacy. It is believed that joining together with others to promote common interests is itself an important element of effective coping in some cases. Consequently, family members are encouraged to become involved with local associations that advocate for services for persons with disabilities and their families.

The elements of the SAEF model described in this chapter appear to hold considerable promise for reducing stress-related demoralization in parents of children with disabilities and for improving the quality of family life.

REFERENCES

Apolloni, A.H., & Triest, G. (1983). Respite services in California: Status and recommendations for improvement. *Mental Retardation, 21,* 240–243.

Baker, B.L., Landen, S. J., & Kashima, K.J. (1992). Effects of parent training on families of children with mental retardation: Increased burden or generalized benefit? *American Journal of Mental Retardation, 96*(2), 127–136.

Beck, A.T., Ward, C.H., Mendelson, M., Mock, J.E., & Erbaugh, J.K. (1961). An inventory for measuring depression. *Archives of General Psychiatry, 4,* 561–571.

Behr, S.K., Murphy, D.L., & Summers, J.A. (1992). *User's Manual: Kansas Inventory of Parental Perceptions (KIPP).* Lawrence, KS: Beach Center for Families and Disability.

Birenbaum, A., Guyot, D., & Cohen, H. (1990). *Health care financing for severe developmental disabilities.* Washington, DC: American Association on Mental Retardation Publications.

Cooley, E. (1989). Community support: The role of volunteers and voluntary associations. In G.H.S. Singer & L.K. Irvin (Eds.), *Support for caregiving families: Enabling positive adaptation to disability* (pp. 143–158). Baltimore: Paul H. Brookes Publishing Co.

Cooley, E.A., Singer, G.H.S., & Irvin, L.K. (1989). Community volunteers as part of family support services for families with developmentally disabled members. *Education and Treatment in Mental Retardation, 24*(3), 207–218.

Cutrona, C.E., & Russell, D.W. (1987). The provisions of social relationships and adaptation to stress. In W.H. Jones & D. Perlman (Eds.), *Advances in personal relationships* (Vol. 1, pp. 37–67). Greenwich, CT: JAI Press.

Davis, K., & Rowland, D. (1990). *The crisis in health care, ethical issues— Uninsured and underserved: Inequities in health care in the United States.* New York: Meridian.

Dunst, C.J., Trivette, C.M., Starnes, A.L., Hamby, D.W., & Gordon, N.J. (1993). *Building and evaluating family support initiatives: A national study of programs for persons with developmental disabilities.* Baltimore: Paul H. Brookes Publishing Co.

Goldfried, M.R. (1971). Systematic desensitization as training in self-control. *Journal of Consulting and Clinical Psychology, 37,* 228–234.

Harris, V.S., & McHale, S.M. (1989). Family life problems, daily caregiving activities, and the psychological well-being of mothers of mentally retarded children. *American Journal of Mental Retardation, 94*(3), 231–239.

Hawkins, N., & Powers, L. (1992). *Stress Management Manual.* Eugene: Oregon Research Institute.

Jacobson, E. (1938). *Progressive relaxation* (2nd ed.). Chicago: University of Chicago Press.

Knoll, J., Covert, S., Osuch, R., O'Connor, S., & Blaney, B. (1990). *Family support services in the United States: An end of decade status report.* Cambridge, MA: Human Services Research Institute.

Levine, M. (1988). An analysis of mutual assistance. *American Journal of Community Psychology, 16*(2), 167–188.

Martino, M.S., & Newman, M.B. (1974). Siblings of retarded children: A population at risk. *Child Psychiatry and Human Development, 4*(3), 168–177.

Nixon, C., & Singer, G.H.S. (in press). Cognitive behavioral treatment of self blame and guilt in parents of children with disabilities. *American Journal of Mental Retardation.*

Olshansky, S. (1970). Chronic sorrow: A response to having a mentally defective child. In R.L. Noland (Ed.), *Counseling parents of the mentally retarded: A sourcebook* (pp. 49–54). Springfield, IL: Charles C Thomas.

Patterson, G.R. (1982). *Coercive family process.* Eugene, OR: Castalia.

Powers, L.E., Singer, G.H.S., Stevens, T., & Sowers, J. (1992). Behavioral parent training in home and community generalization settings. *Education and Training in Mental Retardation, 27*(1), 13–28.

Rothman, J. (1992). *Guidelines for case management: Putting research to professional use.* Itasca, IL: Peacock Publishers.

Salisbury, C.L., & Intagliata, J. (Eds.). (1986). *Respite care: Support for persons with developmental disabilities and their families.* Baltimore: Paul H. Brookes Publishing Co.

Singer, G.H.S., Glang, A., Powers, L., Nixon, C., & Cooley, E. (1992). *Stress management training for parents of children with acquired brain injury.* Unpublished manuscript, Hood Center for Caregiving Families, Dartmouth-Hitchcock Medical School, Lebanon, NH.

Singer, G.H.S., & Irvin, L.K. (1991). Supporting families of persons with severe disabilities: Emerging findings, practices, and questions. In L.H. Meyer, C.A. Peck, & L. Brown (Eds.), *Critical issues in the lives of persons with severe disabilities* (pp. 271–312). Baltimore: Paul H. Brookes Publishing Co.

Singer, G.H.S., Irvin, L.K., & Hawkins, N.J. (1988). Stress management training for parents of severely handicapped children. *Mental Retardation, 26*(5), 269–277.

Singer, G.H.S., Irvin, L.K., Irvine, B., Hawkins, N.J., & Cooley, E. (1989). Evaluation of communities-based support services for families of persons with developmental disabilities. *Journal of The Association for Persons with Severe Handicaps, 14*(4), 312–323.

Singer, G.H.S., Irvine, B., & Irvin, L.K. (1989). Expanding the focus of behavioral parent training. In G.H.S. Singer & L.K. Irvin (Eds.), *Support for caregiving families: Enabling positive adaptation to disability* (pp. 85–102). Baltimore: Paul H. Brookes Publishing Co.

Singer, G.H.S., & Singer, J. (1992). *Planned activity training and cross sibling generalization.* Lebanon, NH: Hood Center for Caregiving Families, Dartmouth-Hitchcock Medical School.

Singer, G.H.S., & Yovanoff, P. (1992). *Demoralization in parents of children with disabilities: A meta-analysis.* Unpublished manuscript, Hood Center for Caregiving Families, Dartmouth-Hitchcock Medical School, Lebanon, NH.

Snell, M.E., & Beckman-Brindley, S. (1984). Family involvement in intervention with children having severe handicaps. *Journal of The Association for Persons with Severe Handicaps, 9*(3) 213–230.

Summers, J.A., Behr, S.K., & Turnbull, A.P. (1989). Positive adaptations and coping strengths of families who have children with disabilities. In G.H.S. Singer & L.K. Irvin (Eds.), *Support for caregiving families: Enabling positive adaptation to disability* (pp. 27–40). Baltimore: Paul H. Brookes Publishing Co.

Taylor, S.E. (1983). Adjustment to threatening events: A theory of cognitive adaptation. *American Psychologist, 38,* 1161–1173.

Turnbull, A.P., & Turnbull, H.R. (1986). *Families, professionals, and exceptionality: A special partnership.* Columbus, OH: Charles E. Merrill.

Turnbull, H.R., Guess, D., & Turnbull, A.P. (1988). Vox Populi and Baby Doe. *Mental Retardation, 26,* 127–132.

Woolfolk, R.L., & Lehrer, P.M. (Eds.). (1984). *Principles and practices of stress management.* New York: Guilford Press.

Zill, N., & Peterson, J.L. (1982). Learning to do things without help. In L.M. Laosa & I.E. Sigel (Eds.), *Families as learning environments for children* (pp. 343–375). New York: Plenum.

Meet My Daughter, Annie

Nan D. Nelson

I don't want my daughter to be a preemie anymore. I don't care to discuss the subject with anyone, particularly strangers, ever again. This means that when we are at the supermarket and someone asks me how old she is, I will say she is five, almost six, and that's all I will say. This means that if someone asks me why one of her eyes is closed, I will say, "Because that eye doesn't work, but the other eye is just fine." And then Annie and I will continue on our way.

MY METAMORPHOSIS

Something remarkable has happened to me in the last few weeks. I have struggled to identify what it is all about, and now I think I know. When school started this year, Annie went off to a regular, ordinary elementary school near our house, within walking distance. Her class consists of 22 children, more boys than girls, most of them blond for some reason. The teacher is a handsome, tall woman with a soft voice and a way of getting kids in line that is nothing short of remarkable. Some parents find her unfriendly, hard to approach, but the kids, including Annie, love her.

The kindergarten experience represents the very first time Annie has been mainstreamed—that ominous, but welcome word meaning we are no longer nurtured by the Vision Program (Montgomery County, Maryland, Public Schools) as we were for three years. No longer is the classroom small and intimate with a vision-certified teacher and an aide, no longer does a notebook accompany Annie home every day with a gentle and thorough account of how she spent her day—the lesson plan, if she ate her lunch, if she was visited by a specialist. Now, it's all up to Annie to relay to me what she has done; so much of the time I am left in the dark. Like many children, she tends to keep her thoughts to herself about how she spends her time in school.

My metamorphosis occurred about two weeks into the school year, and several events contributed to it. Annie was playing with a doll, pretending to be the teacher. "One eye is different from the other. Can you tell the children why?" she said to the doll. I stepped softly into the game and asked her if that exchange had taken place at school. She shrugged and said nothing.

The second incident was learning that certain parents were asking around about Annie. Why was she different? Did she have some emotional disabilities along with a vision loss? I should point out that the latter questions occurred as a result of Annie throwing a tantrum in the playground one Saturday morning. Imagine that! A five-year-old getting angry.

And finally, there was the day Annie and I met up with a woman and a little girl at the same playground. The child was fair, small and very thin. My now well-trained eye spotted a preemie, but I said nothing to her mother. When the two girls began playing together, I asked how old she was, and the mother turned to me with a grave expression, lowered her eyes, and began The EXPLANATION. I call it that because for five years I drew in my breath, narrowed my eyes, and proceeded to explain, in grim detail, Annie's premature birth, from weight and length right down to time spent on a ventilator. The EXPLANATION. Complete with the harrowing account I felt I was required to give to perfect strangers, as though this information was due them. And all because of the simple question, "How old is she?" As this poor woman was rattling on about her child's medical history, I found myself sinking into a black hole, wishing she would stop telling me this story, and wishing that her little girl hadn't gone through so much agony.

MY NEW EXPLANATION

The EXPLANATION no longer fits. I look at my bright and talented little Annie with her joyful outlook, her determination to run as fast as other kids, to get across those monkey bars no matter what, and I realize that to trot out The EXPLANATION is doing her a great disservice. Clearly, she has a vision disability. She wears glasses. She is very, very fortunate that she can see. She fought so hard to get out of that intensive care nursery, and her father and I are terribly proud of her. We're proud of ourselves, too, for making it through such an ordeal. But no longer is Annie's battle, and ours, to be considered public information, to be our way of telling people who Annie is.

Unfortunately, unless people have been in similar circumstances, they cannot possibly understand some disabilities. Sadly, I have found that people exist who actually think in terms of perfection and are unable to appreciate the differences in others. Misinformed, ignorant and, I think, cruel, these are the adults who teach their children nothing about tolerance, kindness or admiration.

Annie will overcome the obstacles these people throw in her path. We will applaud her and all the other children who must add this unfortunate twist to an already complicated life ahead. But my job will be to stand by her and, when people want to know anything about her, I will tell them that she is five, almost six, and perhaps I'll add that she has a delightful sense of humor, she loves dolls, ballet, and her big golden retriever, Folly. This will be my New EXPLANATION, and it fits very nicely.

Nan D. Nelson holds a bachelor of fine arts degree from Philadelphia College of Art. She is a free-lance editor, writer, and graphics artist living in Bethesda, Maryland, with her husband Richard, and daughter, Annie, now age 8.

4

Family-Centered Case Management Practices

Characteristics and Consequences

Carl J. Dunst, Carol M. Trivette,
Nancy J. Gordon, and A. Lauren Starnes

The purpose of this chapter is to describe the findings and implications from an empirical investigation of case manager helpgiving practices and the consequences of different kinds of practices on a number of aspects related to family functioning. The data were collected as part of a national study of family support programs for persons with developmental disabilities as outlined in Dunst, Trivette, Starnes, Hamby, and Gordon (1993), and the reader is referred to this book for a fuller description of the larger investigation in general and the case studies specifically.

The study as a whole concerned the extent to which state and community-based human services program policies and practices

Appreciation is extended to Debbie Hamby for assistance in data analysis and Donna Basille for preparation of the manuscript.

The research reported in this chapter was supported in part by a grant from the U.S. Department of Health and Human Services, Administration on Developmental Disabilities (#90DD144). The views expressed in this chapter do not necessarily reflect those of the funder.

Much of the material presented by the authors of this chapter is also available in an expanded format in Dunst, C.J., Trivette, C.M., Starnes, A.L., Hamby, D.W., and Gordon, N.J. (1993). *Building and evaluating family support initiatives: A national study of programs for persons with developmental disabilities.* Baltimore: Paul H. Brookes Publishing Co.

were consistent with a set of principles that operationally defined family-centered intervention (Dunst, Johanson, Trivette, & Hamby, 1991). Principles are beliefs and elements that define or specify the bases of expectant behavior that is consistent with predetermined assumptions or ideals. More specifically, family support principles are statements of beliefs about how supports and resources ought to be provided so that they have competency-enhancing effects. Taken together, a particular set or combination of principles represents a *philosophy* about family-centered intervention policies and practices (Brewer, McPherson, Magrab, & Hutchins, 1989; Dunst, 1990; Johnson, 1990; Ooms & Preister, 1988; Shelton, Jeppson, & Johnson, 1987).

More than a dozen sets of family support principles can now be found in the family support program literature (see Dunst, 1990). An aggregation of these various sets of principles find that they can be conveniently grouped into six major categories (Dunst, Trivette, & Thompson, 1990). Table 1 shows these categories and lists the 12 principles that were used to evaluate case manager helpgiving practices and family–case manager transactions as part of the conduct of the case studies described in this chapter. Evaluatively, these principles provided one set of standards against which to judge the extent to which case manager practices showed a *presumption toward* "family-centeredness" in ways that were likely to support and strengthen family functioning (Dunst, 1990).

The authors have described elsewhere the relationship between case management practices and helpgiving behaviors (Dunst & Trivette, 1989), and how specifiable beliefs, attitudes, and behaviors that are both derived from family support principles (Dunst, 1990) and consistent with family-centered models and practices (Dunst et al., 1990) uniquely define a helping style that is different from other forms of helpgiving (Dunst, 1987; Dunst & Trivette, 1987, 1988; Dunst, Trivette, Davis, & Cornwell, 1988; Dunst, Trivette, & Deal, 1988; Dunst, Trivette, Gordon, & Pletcher, 1989). Others have made this distinction as well, especially in terms of how human services models that have unique paradigmatic features result in quite different assumptions about and implications for helpgiving practices (Brickman et al., 1982; Cohen, Agosta, Cohen, & Warren, 1989; Cowen, 1985; Danish & D'Augelli, 1980; Hartman & Laird, 1983; Hobbs et al., 1984; Katz, 1984; Moroney, 1986, 1987; Rappaport, 1981, 1987; Shelton et al., 1987; Singer & Irvin, 1989; Swift, 1984; Weissbourd, 1990; Zautra & Sandler, 1983; Zigler & Berman, 1983).

Both theoretical and empirical evidence from diverse but conceptually coherent fields of inquiry (see DePaulo, Nadler, & Fisher,

Table 1. Major categories and examples of family support principles

Category/characteristics	Examples of principles
Enhancing a sense of community: Promoting the coming together of people around shared values and common needs in ways that create mutually beneficial interdependencies	Interventions should focus on the building of interdependencies between members of the community and the family unit. Interventions should emphasize the common needs and supports of all people and base intervention actions on those commonalities.
Mobilizing resources and supports: Building support systems that enhance the flow of resources in ways that assist families with parenting responsibilities	Interventions should focus on building and strengthening informal support networks for families rather than depend solely on professional support systems. Resources and supports should be made available to families in ways that are flexible, individualized, and responsive to the needs of the entire family unit.
Shared responsibility and collaboration: Sharing of ideas and skills by parents and professionals in ways that build and strengthen collaborative arrangements	Interventions should employ partnerships between parents and professionals as a primary mechanism for supporting and strengthening family functioning. Resource and support mobilization interactions between families and service providers should be based upon mutual respect and sharing of unbiased information.
Protecting family integrity: Respecting the family's beliefs and values and protecting the family from intrusion upon its beliefs by outsiders	Resources and supports should be provided to families in ways that encourage, develop, and maintain healthy, stable relationships among all family members. Interventions should be conducted in ways that accept, value, and protect a family's personal and cultural values and beliefs.
Strengthening family functioning: Promoting the capabilities and competencies of families necessary to mobilize resources and perform parenting responsibilities in ways that have empowering consequences	Interventions should build upon family strengths rather than correct weaknesses or deficits as primary ways of supporting and strengthening family functioning. Resources and supports should be made available to families in ways that maximize the family's control over and decision-making power regarding services they receive.
Proactive human services practices: Adoption of consumer-driven human services delivery models and practices that support and strengthen family functioning	Service delivery programs should employ promotion rather than treatment approaches as the framework for strengthening family functioning. Resource and support mobilization should be consumer driven rather than service provider driven or professionally prescribed.

1983; Dunst & Trivette, 1988; Fisher, Nadler, & DePaulo, 1983; Nadler, Fisher, & DePaulo, 1983) indicate that different helpgiving models have quite different assumptions and presuppositions, which in turn are characterized by differential attitudes, beliefs, and behaviors. The extent to which different relationship-related helpgiving attitudes and behaviors varied among the case managers who participated in the case studies constitutes the focus of this chapter.

GENERAL APPROACH

Methodology

The case study methodology developed by Yin (1989) was employed as part of assessing a number of aspects of program practices and family outcomes. As investigators, the authors had no control over practitioner–family transactions yet were specifically interested in testing the hypothesis that program practices would have differential effects on family outcomes. According to Yin (1989), "*A case study is an empirical inquiry* that:

- investigates a contemporary phenomenon within its real life context; when
- the boundaries between phenomenon and context are not clearly evident; and
- multiple sources of evidence are used." (p. 23)

This kind of case study research employs designs that include five components: "(1) a study's questions; (2) its propositions, if any; (3) its unit(s) of analysis; (4) the logic of linking the data to the propositions; and (5) the criteria for interpreting the findings" (Yin, 1989, p. 29).

Study Questions The two primary questions that were posed as part of conducting the case studies were as follows:

- How and in what manner were case manager beliefs and practices linked to how services were rendered to families?
- How and for what reasons did different beliefs and practices produce like or unlike results among the families?

Study Propositions The two propositions that guided the conduct of the case studies were as follows:

- Helpgiving beliefs and practices that were consistent with and logically derived from family support principles would result in a greater incidence of family–practitioner transactions that showed a presumption toward being family-centered (Dunst, 1990).

- Beliefs and practices that showed a presumption toward being family-centered, compared to more professionally centered approaches to service delivery, would have the greatest positive influences on the behavior and functioning of persons with developmental disabilities and their families (Dunst et al., 1991).

Unit of Analysis The *transactions* between families participating in community-based human services programs and the case managers who worked with the families from these programs were the principal unit of analysis. Transactions were operationally defined in terms of both *quantitative* and *qualitative* measures of practitioner–participant relationships (see Dunst et al., 1993). These measures were used to make an assessment of beliefs and behaviors of the case managers that collectively defined their "helping" styles, whether the styles were related to practices that are either consistent or inconsistent with family support principles, and the extent to which case manager practices were related to family descriptions of the benefits and limitations of different kinds of helpgiving practices.

Linking the Data to the Propositions Pattern matching was used as the dominant method of analysis of both the quantitative and qualitative data. "Such a logic compares an empirically based pattern with a predicted one, . . and if the patterns coincide, the results help strengthen a case study's internal validity" and conclusions (Yin, 1989, p. 109). It was first established whether the practices used by the case managers were logically related to their helping styles, and then an assessment was made as to whether descriptions that matched practices consistent with family support principles were associated with better outcomes compared to practices that were not consistent with the intent of the principles.

Criteria for Interpreting the Findings Convergent and discriminant replication of the predicted findings across cases was the principle method used for determining the validity of the findings. The major criteria for interpreting the data were the extent to which the results replicated in ways consistent with the study propositions and hypotheses derived from family support principles.

Case Study Participants

The case study participants included 11 case managers employed by different community-based human services programs, and 22 families served by the case managers (2 each). The case managers were all from different states, with the selection of the states being based upon: 1) the *existence* and *type* of family support initiatives within the states, and 2) *geographic location* so that the different types of programs were roughly distributed evenly throughout the United States (see Dunst et al., 1993). The states were initially organized into three kinds of programs: 1) states with comprehensive family support programs, 2) states with family support initiatives, and 3) states without any formal type of family support initiative. The states were grouped in this manner based on findings indicating that this classification system best differentiated between different kinds of family support initiatives (see Dunst et al., 1993).

The case managers who participated in the case studies were selected by the program director in each community-based program or by his or her designee.

Table 2 shows selected characteristics of the case managers. Comparative analyses using either Kruskall-Wallis or Chi-square tests produced no significant differences between groups, indicating, on the average, that the case managers were much alike in each of the three types of programs.

Two families were selected from each of the programs by either the program directors or case managers. The latter were each asked to select a family whom they considered *typical* or representative of the majority of families served by their program, and one family whom they considered to be of *minority* status. Minority status (see Table 3) was generally based not on racial or ethnic background, but

Table 2. Selected characteristics of the case managers participating in the case studies

Case managers	Personal characteristics			Education		Years of experience as:	
	Race	Sex	Age range (years)	Degree	Discipline	Case manager	Human services worker
Family support programs:							
Case manager 1	White	Female	30–39	BA	Education	4	7
Case manager 2	White	Female	30–39	MA	Special Education	6	20
Case manager 3	White	Female	40–49	BA	English	2	2
Case manager 4	White	Female	30–39	BS	Child Development	3	4
Family support initiatives:							
Case manager 5	White	Female	20–29	BS	Social Work	1	2
Case manager 6	White	Female	30–39	MA	Special Education	2	7
Case manager 7	White	Female	30–39	BA	Early Childhood	1	2
Case manager 8	White	Male	40–49	BS	Psychology	2	2
No support initiative:							
Case manager 9	White	Female	40–49	MA	Education	5	5
Case manager 10	White	Female	30–39	BS	Education	6	6
Case manager 11	White	Female	40–49	BA	Sociology	5	17
Case manager 12	White	Female	40–49	AA	Elementary Education	1	5

Note: In one of the family support program states, two case managers were interviewed, one who worked with a typical family and one who worked with a family of minority status.

Table 3. Selected characteristics of the families participating in the case studies

Type of program	Demographic characteristics				Family classification		Characteristics of family member with disability		Length of family involvement with:	
	Family size	SES [a]	Monthly income (range)	Race [b]	Family type [c]	Determinant of minority status	Diagnosis	Age (years)	Case manager (months)	Community-based program (years)
Family support programs:										
Family 1	5	30	2,084-2,500	B	M	Race	Severe physical impairment	10	42	8
Family 2	5	24	1,667-2,083	W	T		Cerebral palsy	10	60	6
Family 3	4	27	1,251-1,666	W	T		Spina bifida	2	28	2
Family 4	4	47	2,501+	W	M	Foster family	Neuromuscular disease	4	12	2
Family 5	3	17	834-1,250	W	M		Autism	11	12	1
Family 6	4	32	1,667-2,083	W	T	Alternate primary caregiver	Werdnig-Hoffman Disease	3	9	1
Family support initiatives:										
Family 7	2	17	834-1,250	H	M	Disabled parent caregiver	Cerebral palsy	13	6	10
Family 8	4	11	2,084-2,500	W	T		Cerebral palsy	13	12	10
Family 9	3	17	2,501+	W	T		Mild mental retardation	32	25	11
Family 10	4	18	2,084-2,500	B	M	Foster family	Moderate mental retardation	40	25	5
Family 11	4	14	2,501+	W	M	Income	Down syndrome	17	6	1
Family 12	5	32	1,251-1,666	W	T		Cerebral palsy	5	15	2
Family 13	5	39	2,084-2,500	W	T		Holoprosencephaly	3	16	1
Family 14	4	32	2,501+	W	M	Single parent caregiver	Fragile X syndrome	18	15	1
No support initiative:										
Family 15	4	27	1,667-2,083	W	T		Cerebral palsy	13	18	11
Family 16	3	19	417-833	W	M	Single parent caregiver	Developmental delay	5	1	4
Family 17	3	17	1,667-2,083	W	T		Down syndrome	24	18	2
Family 18	2	11	417-833	W	M	Single parent caregiver	Severe mental retardation	60	66	11
Family 19	4	53	2,501+	W	M	Income	Down syndrome	2	30	3
Family 20	5	24	251-416	H	M		Down syndrome	11	11	1
Family 21	3	8	834-1,250	B	T		Moderate mental retardation	30	9	2
Family 22	4	58	2,501+	W	M	Income	Down syndrome	42	9	3

[a] Socioeconomic level computed using the Hollingshead (1975) Index.

[b] B = black, W = white, H = hispanic.

[c] T = typical family, M = minority status family (as specified by the case managers working with the families).

on other personal (e.g., income) and family (e.g., marital status) characteristics.

The descriptive and demographic characteristics of the 22 families are shown in Table 3. Either Kruskall-Wallis or Chi-square analyses of these data showed that the families in each of the three types of programs were, on the average, much alike on the majority of family characteristics measures. The only analysis that yielded a significant result was for the diagnostic variable. A greater proportion of persons with developmental disabilities in the family support program group had physical impairments as opposed to mental retardation as their primary disability, whereas the opposite was true for the diagnosis of persons with disabilities in the no family support initiative group.

Sources of Case Study Data

Three separate types of information were collected as part of the case studies in order to have multiple sources of evidence. The three major sources of data were: 1) *interviews* with the families and case managers, 2) *survey findings* from the case managers, and 3) *direct observations* of case managers and families. Complete descriptions of the particular kinds of information collected are described in Dunst et al. (1993).

The case study protocols used with both the case managers and the families were designed to obtain information about beliefs and practices that were either consistent or inconsistent with the family support principles (Dunst, 1990) that guided all aspects of the study (see Table 1). Two questions were asked in each of the six family support principles categories (enhancing a sense of community, mobilizing resources and supports, shared responsibility and collaboration, protecting family integrity, strengthening family functioning, and proactive human services practices) that correspond to the 12 major belief statements listed in Table 1.

Each of the case managers were interviewed separately about each family they served. The protocol questions asked the case managers to provide examples of practices in each of the family support principles categories from which a determination was made regarding whether the practices were consistent or inconsistent with the intent of the principles. Additionally, the case study material, together with both observations of the case managers and information from their surveys, were used to capture the unique aspects and defining characteristics of the helping styles employed by these practitioners.

The case managers also completed a survey about different aspects of how they viewed and worked with families. The surveys included a section that asked each case manager to indicate the extent to which he or she agreed that the 12 principles listed in Table 1 represented their beliefs concerning how families ought to be treated.

The case study questions used with the families elicited information about program and case manager practices that were either consistent or inconsistent with the family support principles. The protocol allowed for the potential elicitation of a range of descriptions (examples) of case manager/program practices in the six different family support principle categories as well as descriptions of the outcomes that were associated with different program and case manager practices. The data analyzed and reported below were restricted to family descriptions of practices and outcomes associated with the target program and/or case managers only. Descriptions of practices and outcomes that were provided by the families about services and resources obtained from other agencies and human services professionals are not included.

Case Manager Helpgiving Styles   The determination of each case manager's helping style was based on the aggregate information and data collected as part of the case studies and was used to ascertain whether: 1) there was adherence to family support principles as a belief system, 2) the case managers adopted and employed an empowering philosophy in interactions with families, 3) resource-based practices guided the ways in which the case managers worked with the families, 4) case managers used consumer-driven rather than professional-driven approaches to intervention, and 5) the behavioral descriptions and observations of case manager practices were consistent with the intent of family support principles. The defining characteristics of these aspects of case manager beliefs and practices were as follows:

- *Adherence to Family Support Principles*   The survey findings were used, in part, to establish the extent to which the case managers agreed or disagreed that the family support principles previously described and listed in Table 1 represented their *beliefs* about how families ought to be treated and how resources and supports ought to be made available to families. Additionally, both observations and family descriptions of case manager practices were used to corroborate what the case managers stated as their belief system and described as their methods of practice.

- *Enabling and Empowering Philosophy* The interview, survey, and observational data were collectively used to determine the extent to which the case managers: 1) treated the families as having existing capabilities as well as the capacity to become more competent, 2) were positive and proactive in their descriptions of and interactions with families, 3) employed strengths-based rather than deficit-oriented approaches to working with the families, and 4) created opportunities for the families to participate in interventions in ways that are consistent with family-centered practices (Dunst et al., 1991).

- *Resource-Based Approaches to Intervention* The aggregate data were used to ascertain the extent to which the case managers: 1) employed resource-based as opposed to service-based solutions for meeting family needs, 2) encouraged the use of both informal and formal sources of support and resources for meeting needs, and 3) employed responsive rather than prescriptive approaches to service and resource mobilization. Resource-based practices emphasize the use of a range of community resources and people for meeting needs as opposed to the entire or primary use of professional services.

- *Consumer-Driven Approaches to Intervention* The collective data from the case studies were used to assess the degree to which the case managers employed consumer-driven practices as opposed to practices that placed major emphasis on professional-centered decisions about what families need or ought to do. This aspect of the case managers' beliefs and practices permitted an assessment of whether a paternalistic stance was taken toward the families served by the programs and case managers.

- *Family-Centered Intervention Practices* All available information and data about the case managers were used to ascertain the manner in which professed and demonstrated beliefs, attitudes, opinions, and convictions were translated into *behavioral practices* that were either consistent or inconsistent with the intent of family support principles.

Reliability

Cohen's kappa was used to ascertain the reliability of the different measures of case manager practices and family outcomes (see Dunst et al., 1993). The median coefficients for the case manager practices and family outcomes were 0.89 and 0.85, respectively.

RESULTS

Case Manager Helping Styles

Five distinct helping styles were detected from the qualitative analysis of the data. The styles were roughly ordered on a continuum from those highly consistent with the intent of family support principles to ones highly inconsistent with the intent of the principles. The major features of each helping style (labeled as Styles A through E, respectively), as well as the behavioral characteristics of the styles, are briefly described next. (The case manager and family descriptions of practices described below have, in some cases, been altered to protect identities and maintain confidentiality but without changing the meaning or intent of the descriptions.)

Helping Style A   Style A was characterized by beliefs that constituted strong adherence to all the family support principles; adoption of a philosophy that was positive, proactive, and strengths-based; adoption of beliefs and practices that placed major emphasis on the mobilization of informal and formal supports and resources for meeting family needs; adoption of consumer-driven approaches to intervention; and behavioral practices that were almost entirely consistent with the intent of family support principles. Three case managers employed this particular helping style.

The case managers who employed Style A all agreed that the 12 family support principles that they were asked to rate constituted their beliefs regarding how families ought to be treated and how resources and supports should be made available to the families. This commitment was reflected, for example, in this statement made by one case manager:

> "The whole philosophy of our program is that the family decides what they need. Then we help the family tap into the resources necessary to meet their needs."

The adoption of and adherence to an enabling and empowering philosophy was equally apparent among all three case managers. As stated by one case manager:

> "It's my philosophy to look at family strengths and help the family use them as part of what we do. I don't like the word 'weakness'."

These three case managers all employed resource-based intervention practices that were predominantly consumer-driven. One case manager, for example, said:

"The family decides what (resources) they need and when they need them. My job is to help link the family with the resources."

In addition, case manager descriptions and observations of their practices indicated that all three individuals recognized the value of both informal and formal sources of support for meeting family needs, and placed major emphasis on broad-based approaches to mobilizing resources to meet these needs.

Both the descriptions and observations of case manager practices showed that nearly all transactions with the families were highly consistent with the intent of family support principles. The following are selected examples of practices used by the case managers:

"The family decides what they need and when they need it. We work our schedules around [that of] the family. We try to be as flexible as possible when a family's needs change."

"We have an honest and up-front relationship. We both feel we have a good partnership. After the family decides what they need, we sit down together and come up with a plan to access the needed resources."

"We [the staff] never push our beliefs on the family. We respect their decisions and maintain confidentiality about what the family shares with us."

"The family knows (it) has a lot of control and choices about what we do and when we do it. We also build on family strengths. During our interventions, we always try to build on the things families already do well."

Collectively, these descriptions constitute examples of both a family-centered philosophy and helping style that are considered the cornerstone of family resource programs (Dunst et al., 1990; Hobbs et al., 1984; Kagan & Shelley, 1987; Kagan, Powell, Weissbourd, & Zigler, 1987; Weissbourd, 1990; Weissbourd & Kagan, 1989; Zigler & Black, 1989) and empowering human services practices (Dunst, Trivette, & Deal, 1988; Dunst et al., 1990; Katz, 1984; Rappaport, 1981, 1987).

Helping Style B Style B was characterized by moderate to strong adherence to family support principles as a belief system and adoption of a philosophy that was generally consistent with a strengths-based approach to working with families. The characteristic of this style that differed from that of Style A was reflected primarily in terms of the resource-based practices adopted and employed in interactions with the families. Two case managers were characterized as having this style.

Both case managers generally agreed that the majority of family support principles represented their belief system, with only one exception. Neither case manager agreed that resources and support mobilization to meet family needs should occur in ways that are similar to how other families' needs are generally met in the community. This was reflected in different ways by each case manager. One case manager noted that the program staff evaluated the family's needs, shared their results with the family, and then recommended particular professional services that they thought ought to be used. However, as stated by one case manager:

> "Parents have the final say in what services and programs their child is enrolled in."

Similarly, the other case manager noted that:

> "The mother knows much better what her daughter's needs are and decides what services she gets from our program and when we provide the services."

Whereas the first case manager employed prescriptive practices in identifying needs and the second case manager employed responsive needs-identification practices, both emphasized primarily service-based solutions for meeting needs. And although families may have been given choices, the choices were primarily restricted to professional services provided by the programs and other agencies. This, by definition, constitutes a family-focused rather than a family-centered approach to working with families (Dunst et al., 1991).

The difference between Helping Styles A and B was clearly reflected in the behavioral descriptions of practices employed by the Style B case managers. On the one hand, there was a clear focus on professional solutions for meeting family needs; on the other hand, the case managers gave few or no examples of practices that were consistent with resource-based intervention practices. The emphasis on *professional-* and *service-based* solutions was noted in these statements:

> "We provide the mother with the information she needs, and we have the physical therapist and occupational therapist work with the family to teach them new things to do with their child."

> "The mother decided if she wanted the nutritionist to continue to make home visits. She decided it wasn't very helpful, so we discontinued this service."

In contrast, there were *no explicit* descriptions or observations of practices that were resource-based. In several instances, the practices ran counter to the intent of family support principles, as reflected in these case manager statements:

> "There really are not any community activities that we encourage the families to participate in."

> "We really don't encourage families to use informal supports (for meeting their needs)."

And in those instances where case managers gave examples that described informal sources of supports, the practices were minimally consistent with the intent of family support principles with respect to the broad-based mobilization of resources to meet family needs. For example, when asked for a description of a practice that built upon and strengthened informal support networks for meeting family needs, one case manager stated:

> "We certainly encourage that. I've seen the child at the grandparents' house and have been able to meet them personally and talk to them about what we do with their grandson."

In another instance, a case manager stated:

> "We encourage that kind of thing . . . like using respite care to relieve the stress the family has."

In both of these examples, the case managers stated that they used informal sources of support for meeting needs, but that the actual practices did not reflect an understanding of what it really meant to use personal social networks as sources of supports and resources for meeting family needs.

Helping Style C   Style C was characterized by weak to moderate adherence to family support principles as a belief system; adoption of a philosophy that is minimally consistent with a positive, proactive, and strengths-based approach to working with families; a major emphasis on service-based and professionally centered approaches to resource mobilization; and intervention practices that were only moderately consistent with the intent of family support principles. Two case managers employed this helping style.

The case managers who used Helping Style C adopted a belief system that was mostly deficit-oriented. Both case managers indicated that individual differences should be used as a basis for identifying and intervening with families and persons with disabilities, and that this should be done from a professional's and not a family's perspective.

There was less agreement by these two case managers (compared to the Style A and B case managers) that family support principles should guide intervention practices; in several instances, the case managers indicated that the principles ran counter to their beliefs. One case manager's intervention practices were guided by a belief that major emphasis should be placed on correcting dysfunctional behavior rather than building on strengths, and the other case manager indicated that persons with disabilities and their families should be treated differently from other families in their community. A deficit-oriented approach to working with families, to a large degree, uniquely defined the helping style of these case managers (see Zigler & Berman, 1983).

The role that the families played in deciding the services and resources that they received seemed less related to a case manager belief that families should be involved in making decisions, but rather appeared to be due more to the assertiveness of certain families. Both case managers worked with families who took a firm and self-assured stance toward the staff and the program, and in these instances the families were described as having control over decisions about what services were rendered. The following was a typical response:

> "The family has total control over whether their daughter participates in our program."

In contrast, the two families who were not assertive were not described as having choices and decision-making power. For example, one case manager noted that:

> "We pretty much decide what the family gets. We've never been questioned by the family."

Style C was also characterized as one that placed primary emphasis on service-based solutions to meeting family needs. As noted by one case manager:

> "We don't usually discuss or bother looking at informal sources of supports for meeting family needs. We'd rather use formal resources for doing so."

> "Most of the services that the family receives come from what we offer at our program."

Collectively, the beliefs, attitudinal stances toward families, and practices employed by these case managers reflected a negative or deficit-oriented approach to working with families, minimal emphasis on family-identified needs, and major emphasis on service-

based approaches to meeting staff-identified needs for families and
persons with developmental disabilities.

Helping Style D   Style D was characterized by moderate to
strong agreement with family support principles as a belief system
but *a lack of behavioral adherence to the principles,* adoption of
attitudes and beliefs that are inconsistent with an empowerment
philosophy, moderate to strong emphasis on professional-driven and
service-based approaches to meeting family needs, and a prepon-
derance of practices inconsistent with the intent of family support
principles. Two case managers were characterized as displaying this
style.

Both case managers generally indicated that most of the family
support principles guided the ways in which they worked with families, but their descriptions of practices and investigator observations
of practices often produced conflicting evidence. For example, one
case manager stated that the family's values are respected, but
added:

> "If my beliefs run counter to those of the family, I don't bother
> trying to change their mind because it's not worth the time and
> effort [since the family made up their mind about what they
> wanted]."

In this instance, the case manager did not respect the family's beliefs as reflected by the fact that she tried to change their mind, but
knew that the family's decision could not be changed.

There were two areas of beliefs that both case managers agreed
did not guide their practices. These concerned resource-based practices and the use of informal sources of support for meeting family
needs. Both case managers noted that building and strengthening
informal support networks was not a guiding principle.

The most telling aspect of Style D was the adoption of beliefs
and adherence to practices that were inconsistent with an empowering philosophy. In both cases, the families were seen predominantly
in a negative manner, were viewed as generally incapable, and the
case managers employed mostly deficit-oriented and paternalistic
intervention practices with the families. Consequently, it was not
surprising that the case managers assumed a stance toward the
families that clearly conveyed the message that the staff were the
experts who acted as if the families should be grateful for what
the program and the staff did for them. When asked for an example
of a practice that reflected a consumer-driven intervention, one case
manager said:

> "I, of course, know what is best for the family."

The other case manager felt that a mother wanted the program staff to make all the decisions. This seemed to be related to the fact that the staff conveyed the message that they were the experts who knew what was best for her child, which, by definition, is the major characteristic of a family-allied approach to working with families (Dunst et al., 1991). This case manager adopted an extremely paternalistic stance by assuming that the program staff had the authority to remove the child from the care of her parents. The case manager bluntly stated:

> "We (program staff) allow the child to remain in the care of the parents. We know that if we didn't provide them our services, the parents couldn't take care of the child."

The paternalistic, deficit-oriented stance of this helping style was also manifested in the nature of the relationships between the families and case managers. In all the case study material, the case managers either gave no examples of practices that were consistent with the intent of the principles in the shared responsibility and collaboration category, or when examples were given, they ran counter to the intent of the principles. For example, one case manager noted that:

> "It's a friendly [relationship], but there is not much exchange of information."

In this particular case, aggregated evidence pointed to the implicit assumption that the case manager did not consider the parent to be capable and certainly did not view the parent as a partner in the working relationship with the family.

Helping Style E Style E was characterized by a belief system that was mostly inconsistent with the family support principles; adoption of a strong paternalistic viewpoint toward families that was deficit-oriented and reflected a belief that families were generally not competent; a heavy emphasis on professional-driven and service-based approaches to meeting family needs; and practices that were almost entirely inconsistent with the intent of family support principles. Two case managers used this style.

Both practitioners who used this style disagreed with the belief (principle) that intervention practices should build on family strengths. Additionally, they did not agree with the belief that interventions should build upon and strengthen informal sources of support for meeting family needs, and one case manager strongly disagreed that resources and supports should be made available to families in ways that were flexible, individualized, and responsive to the needs of the family. The aggregate evidence from the case studies indicated that these case managers adopted predominantly professional-centered (Dunst et al., 1991) beliefs and practices in their interactions with families.

Neither of the case managers treated families in ways that are consistent with an empowering philosophy. In fact, the families were generally treated in a deficit manner and viewed as less than competent. Given the lack of beliefs about building on family strengths, it was not surprising that the case managers did not use strengths-based intervention practices. When asked to provide an example of how intervention practices built on family capabilities, one case manager stated:

"We don't really do that [build on family strengths]."

The paternalistic stance was also evident in other aspects of the case managers' work with the families. The following are examples of practices that reflected this stance:

"The parent knows where to come if she has a problem. The mother knows we have all the answers."

"I think our program has definitely been of benefit to the family. They really need our services."

The lack of use of informal sources of support for meeting family needs was apparent from several bits of evidence obtained during the case studies. In one instance, a case manager stated:

"We do not ask or encourage the family to use help from friends or relatives."

The other case manager gave a similar response:

"The family does this but we [the program staff] don't."

The emphasis on professionally driven and service-based solutions was reflected in both subtle and obvious ways by the practitioners employing this style. For example, one case manager noted, in response to the question asking for an example of how they promoted the use of normalized forms and sources of support, that:

"We put [the person with a disability] in a job coaching program [because] he needs to learn to work independently someday."

In a similar vein, another case manager stated, in response to the same question, that she:

"Gave the family the names of 'special' doctors in the community to see their child."

The particular style of these case managers was also reflected by the following kinds of descriptions and examples of intervention practices. The highly directive nature of one case manager's practices was reflected in the statement:

"I let the [caregiver] pick out clothes to buy for [the person with a disability]."

Aggregated evidence from one case manager indicated that she imposed her values upon the family; in response to a request for an example of a practice that minimized the intrusion of personal beliefs on a family, the case manager responded:

"That's an odd question. We don't [take into consideration the family's] views about their involvement with our program."

The above five sets of descriptions of the helping styles of the case managers provide qualitative evidence regarding the manner in which practitioner beliefs, attitudes, and convictions were related to family–case manager transactions. The pattern matching data analysis strategy indicated that Helping Style A, and its associated practices, was most consistent with the intent of family support principles, and that the empirically derived pattern of the helping style–practices–transactions of the Style A case managers coincided most closely with the predicted pattern derived from the hypotheses and study propositions. Additionally, the discriminant findings across helping styles showed that as one moved from Helping Styles A to E, the empirically derived patterns became progressively less consistent with the intent of family support principles. This was as expected based upon the assumptions that formed the underpinnings of the conduct of the case studies.

The aggregate descriptions of practices provided by the case managers with the families that were interviewed were used to independently rate, on a 5-point scale, the extent to which the practices varied along a continuum from highly inconsistent to highly consistent with the intent of each of the principles listed in Table 1. The sum of the ratings for the 12 principles was used as the measure of *degree of consistency* with the intent of the principles. A Spearman rank-order correlation between the consistency scores and the five helping styles (scored Style A = 5 to Style E = 1, respectively) was $r = 0.93$, $p < 0.001$, indicating that a considerable degree of covariation existed between the independent assessment of the case managers' helping styles and the qualitative classification of the beliefs, attitudes, convictions, and practices of the case managers.

Discussion   The above findings demonstrate that *the more consistent case manager practices were with family support principles,
the greater the practices showed a presumption toward being family-
centered.* The helping styles found most consistent with the intent of
family support principles were ones that have previously been found
to be competency-enhancing as opposed to protectionistic (Cowen,
1985; Danish & D'Augelli, 1980), empowering as opposed to usurpat-
ing (Dunst, 1987; Rappaport, 1981, 1987), and strengths-building as
opposed to dependency forming (Dunst et al., 1990; Moroney, 1987;
Swift, 1984). Additionally, these same helping styles have consistently been found to be related to a sense of control that one feels
and experiences as part of helpgiver–helpseeker exchanges (see De-
Paulo et al., 1983; Fisher et al., 1983; Nadler et al., 1983). To a large
degree, this sense of control constitutes a major outcome of family
support programs; namely, that families ought to have resources
provided to them in ways that are flexible, individualized, and responsive to their needs, and that these resources be made available
to families in ways that maximize their control and decision-making
power regarding the services they receive. The extent to which these
particular ways of responding to family concerns and needs were
related to differential outcomes among the families is examined
next.

Family–Case Manager Transaction Outcomes

Whether practices that are consistent with the intent of family support principles were related to better family outcomes compared to
practices that are inconsistent with the intent of family support
principles was ascertained by examining the family descriptions of
the effects they experienced as a result of different case manager
and program practices. It could be the case that different helping
styles are unrelated to the effects associated with each, and therefore it matters little as to how supports and resources are made
available to families. Consequently, empirically establishing the
conditional or unconditional relationships between helping styles
and their effects is of both theoretical and practical importance.

An aggregation of previous research examining the effects of
different kinds of helping styles points strongly to the fact that outcomes indeed differ as a functioning of particular kinds of helpgiving
attitudes, beliefs, and behaviors (see Brickman et al., 1982; DePaulo
et al., 1983; Dunst & Trivette, 1988; Dunst, Trivette, & LaPointe,
1992; Fisher et al., 1983; Nadler et al., 1983). Based upon the results
from previous investigations, it was hypothesized that better family
outcomes would be related to case manager helping styles that were
consistent with the intent of family support principles.

As part of the case study interviews with the families, each respondent was asked to give examples or describe situations of case manager and program practices in the six major categories of family support principles listed in Table 1. The families' descriptions of transactions obtained during the interviews together with investigator observations were used as a basis of classifying the practices as highly consistent, somewhat consistent, neither consistent nor inconsistent, somewhat inconsistent, or highly inconsistent with the intent of family support principles. The classification of the practices was done independently of, and without reference to, the families' descriptions of the outcomes that were associated with the different practices.

Following each description or example, the family was asked to describe the reaction they had or feelings they experienced as a result of the practice. The families' descriptions of the effects (outcomes) were classified as highly positive, somewhat positive, neither positive nor negative, somewhat negative, or highly negative. *Highly positive* outcomes were operationally defined as descriptions that included both positive feelings experienced by the respondent and specific reference to the characteristics of the practices that produced the reported effects (e.g., "I felt good having the decision about the resources I could have"). *Somewhat positive* outcomes were defined as descriptions that included positive feelings experienced by the respondent but no reference to the characteristics of the practices that were associated with the effect (e.g., "I really was happy about what happened"). *Somewhat negative* outcomes were defined as descriptions that included negative feelings only (e.g., "I was really upset about what they did"). *Highly negative* outcomes were operationally defined as descriptions that included both negative feelings and reference to the characteristics of the practices that produced the effects (e.g., "I was very angry that they didn't follow through on getting the information they promised"). Responses were classified as *neither positive nor negative* if they did not meet the criteria for any of the other four outcomes.

The outcome data were analyzed in two ways. First, a cross-tabulation analysis between the practices and outcome data was performed to ascertain if a trend existed that was consistent with the hypotheses and study propositions. Second, the "strength" of the relationship between the practices and outcome data was discerned by examining the qualitative description of the practices associated with the five different outcomes.

For each family, the case study methodology could have potentially elicited 12 different descriptions of program or case manager practices (total = 264 for the 22 families). About half ($n = 136$) of the family descriptions of practices were specifically made in terms of the case managers or the programs with which they were affiliated. The majority of these descriptions (73%) were classified as consistent with the intent of family support principles, whereas 21% were classified as inconsistent with the intent of the principles.

Table 4 presents the cross-tabulation results. The trend shows, with few exceptions, that practices consistent with the intent of family support principles were more highly associated with better outcomes compared to practices inconsistent with the intent of family support principles, whereas the opposite was the case for practices inconsistent with the intent of the principles.

Gamma (G), a measure of the relationship between two ordered variables, was used to statistically test the degree of covariation between the practices and outcome variables (Siegel & Castellani, 1988). The procedure yields a statistic equivalent to a correlation coefficient. The analysis produced a $G = 0.74$, $t(16) = 7.55$, $p < 0.001$, indicating a very strong relationship between the characteristics of case manager practices and the families' descriptions of effects associated with the practices. This result supports the study proposition that practices that were family-centered would be associated with more positive outcomes compared to effects associated with professional-centered practices.

Close examination of Table 4 shows that two major and two minor patterns to practice–outcome relationships were evident in the data. The *first major pattern* was between practices that are consistent with the intent of family support principles and positive outcomes. The *second major pattern* was between practices that are inconsistent with the intent of family support principles and negative outcomes. The *first minor pattern* was between practices that are neither consistent nor inconsistent with the intent of family support principles but nonetheless related to positive outcomes. The

Table 4.   Number and types of family outcomes associated with different case manager and program practices

Case manager/program practices	Family outcomes				
	Highly positive	Somewhat positive	Neither positive nor negative	Somewhat negative	Highly negative
Highly consistent with principles	11	27	2	1	0
Somewhat consistent with principles	10	42	6	0	0
Neither consistent nor inconsistent	1	6	1	1	0
Somewhat inconsistent with principles	0	1	0	6	1
Highly inconsistent with principles	0	0	0	11	9

second minor pattern was between practices that are consistent with the intent of family support principles and neutral outcomes.

Consistent Practices–Positive Outcomes Four different combinations of the two types of practices that were consistent with the intent of family support principles and the two different positive outcomes were found from the analysis of the data. A total of 90 family descriptions, or 66% of all the descriptions of practices and outcomes, were classified in this manner.

Inspection of the descriptions of practices classified as consistent with the intent of family support principles indicated that all the practices, to a large degree, showed a presumption toward being family-centered. All of the outcomes associated with the practices included self-attributions regarding the positive feelings or emotions that the respondents personally experienced as a result of the practices. The following are two of many examples of these types of case manager practices and family outcomes.

Case Manager Practice: "The program staff gave me total control in deciding what I need and when I need it. For example, when I needed to build a fence around my backyard so my daughter could play outside by herself, the staff encouraged me to spend the [cash subsidy] money in any way I wanted. It was nice to have the choice to spend it on buying the fence."

Family Outcome: "Knowing that I had the choice to spend the money to buy the fence felt really great. It was great that the staff cared enough to tailor their [practices] to meet my needs."

Case Manager Practice: "They always ask me what I need and I tell them. They never question [my requests]. For example, the staff say it's all right when I say there aren't very many people who can care for my child."

Family Outcome: "I felt good, supported, respected."

Inconsistent Practices–Negative Outcomes Four different combinations of the two types of practices and the two negative outcomes were found from the analysis of the data. A total of 27 family descriptions, or 20% of all the descriptions, were classified in this manner.

The practices that were classified as inconsistent ran counter to ones that were deemed family-centered, and in several instances, the practices were clearly paternalistic and usurped the families' roles in deciding their needs and the courses of action to meet needs. Negative attributions that were made by the families included a range of reactions both directed toward the case managers and felt by the respondents. The following are several examples of these types of case manager practices and outcomes.

> Case Manager Practice: "I can never get any respite care when I need it. They [the program staff] are never flexible. They want to do things around their own schedule. When I keep asking, their attitude is 'So what. Tough!'"

> Family Outcome: "I thought [the staff member] was just another nasty person I was going to have to deal with. I don't want to think this, but oh, what a bitch."

> Case Manager Practice: "When I made a decision to have my child cared for by someone else, the case manager did not respect my decision and tried to make me feel guilty about what I wanted to do."

> Family Outcome: "It [what the case manager did] made me feel guilty and like a bad person. It also made me mad because the case manager didn't really know what it was like to have to care for my child by myself all of the time."

Neutral Practices–Positive Outcomes   Seven, or 5% of all the family descriptions of practices, were classified as neither consistent nor inconsistent with the intent of family support principles but were nonetheless associated with positive outcomes. Four of the examples of practices classified in this manner were characterized by a common theme; namely, the case managers "taking care of things" for the families or their children with minimal family involvement in the intervention process. Close examination of the practices indicated that they constituted different forms of *noncontingent helping* (Brickman et al., 1982; Dunst, 1987). Noncontingent helping is characterized by doing for others, rather than teaching or enabling people to do for themselves, and is predicated on the belief that it does not matter how resources are rendered to people (see especially Dunst, Trivette, & Deal, 1988). Noncontingent helping, however, deprives people of the opportunity to play an active role in learning resource mobilization skills, and under certain conditions, creates helpseeker dependencies on helpgivers (Brickman et al., 1982). The danger of such helping is exacerbated by the fact that recipients of this type of help generally report positive influences, as the following two examples illustrate.

> Case Manager Practice: "The case manager told me she would enroll my child in school. She did, and everything worked out just like she told me it would."

Family Outcome: "It [the school] is great for my child. That made me feel great. Everything is great."

Case Manager Practice. "The case manager made the arrangements for my daughter to go to a social event. She also helped to get an apartment for my daughter."

Family Outcome: "I felt very good. That's what we wanted. She [case manager] made it happen without any problems."

To the extent that noncontingent helping produces positive feelings, this type of help is likely to be viewed as beneficial despite the fact that it may have long-term debilitating effects if it is repeatedly used by professionals to mobilize resources to meet the needs of help-seekers (Dunst, 1987). According to a number of investigators (see especially Dunst et al., 1989), noncontingent helping seems like "the right thing to do" but can lead the recipients of help to see their situations as beyond their capacity to handle effectively because professionals rather than themselves solved their problems.

Consistent Practices–Neutral Outcomes Eight, or 6% of all the family descriptions, were classified as being consistent with the intent of the principles but were associated with neutral outcomes. The family outcomes were classified as neutral because there were no self-attributions about feelings the respondents personally experienced as a result of the interventions. Rather, nearly all the descriptions of outcomes reported by the families had to do with feelings directed toward the case managers or other program staff. Close inspection of the data indicated that subtle messages were given to the families by the case managers that the professionals really controlled resource allocation, and the families ought to be thankful for any requests and decisions they were allowed to make. Available evidence from the aggregate data led to the conclusion that professionally centered control mechanisms were being employed, either intentionally or unintentionally, by the case managers.

Case Manager Practice: "Sometimes I need my child picked up early in the mornings and brought back late at night when I need to travel to [another city] for business. They [staff] are always willing to do whatever I need done."

Family Outcome: "It makes me feel grateful. I really feel that the staff are our good friends and care about us."

Case Manager Practice: "She [case manager] lets me decide myself about when my child goes to the center for services."

Family Outcome: "I feel grateful. I feel like I can talk to them
[staff] at any time."

Discussion   The results reported in this section demonstrated
that different types of case manager practices were differentially
related to family outcomes, and taken together provided considerable evidence that practices that showed a presumption toward being family-centered were associated with the greatest incidence of
positive outcomes compared to other types of practices. In the relatively few instances where patterns that did not coincide with predicted ones were found, close inspection of the aggregate data from
the case studies uncovered evidence that helped explain the perplex-
ing patterns.

Collectively, the data from the qualitative analysis of practices
associated with different types of family outcomes indicated that
family self-attributions that were positive in nature were more likely to be found when case manager and program practices were consistent with the intent of family support principles. The results add
to a burgeoning body of evidence demonstrating positive relationships between helpgiver behavior and helpseeker outcomes (Brickman et al., 1982; DePaulo et al., 1983; Dunst & Trivette, 1988;
Dunst, Trivette, Davis, & Cornwell, 1988; Dunst et al., 1989; Dunst
et al., 1992; Fisher et al., 1983; Nadler et al., 1983), where efficacious
outcomes are measured in terms of consumer satisfaction, enhanced
psychosocial health indicators, and self-attributions about the positive feelings one experiences from family–case manager transactions.

GENERAL DISCUSSION

The various sets of analyses presented in this chapter yielded con-
verging and corroborating evidence regarding: 1) the characteristics
of both different kinds of helping styles and family–case manager
transactions, and 2) the outcomes associated with different case
manager practices. The aggregated evidence supported the proposition that case manager helpgiving styles and practices that were
consistent with and logically derived from family support principles
would result in a greater incidence of family–case manager transactions that showed a presumption toward being family-centered
(Dunst, 1990). The reasons why family-centered practices were correlated with positive family self-attributions became increasingly
clear as the analysis of the case study data proceeded. Practices that
were characterized as family-centered were the ones that promoted

the involvement of families in all aspects of program practices. This was the case, to a large degree, because of the enabling and empowering practices used by the case managers, who recognized, built upon, and enhanced family strengths and capabilities. The case study results add considerably to what constitutes the key elements and defining characteristics of successful family support initiatives; namely, case manager beliefs, attitudes, convictions, and practices that were: 1) guided by an empowering philosophy, and 2) resource-based and consumer-driven, and truly placed the family in a pivotal role regarding all aspects of program and case manager practices.

Additionally, the outcome data supported the second study proposition regarding the relationship between family-centered practices and the positive influences such practices would have on family functioning (Dunst et al., 1991). Practices that were family-centered had the greatest positive influences on human services program participants because they were supportive of families, and were directly implemented in response to what families considered to be in their own best interests. In instances where practices were consumer-driven and resource-based, and when they were carried out in ways consistent with the intent of family support principles, families had the types of control that have been found to be associated with positive feelings of efficacy (see especially Dunst, Trivette, & Deal, 1988; Dunst, Trivette, Davis, & Cornwell, 1988; Dunst et al., 1989; Dunst et al., 1992).

Taken together, the data presented in this chapter provide considerable support for contentions made by family support program enthusiasts (Dunst et al., 1990; Kagan & Shelley, 1987; Singer & Irvin, 1989; Weissbourd, 1990; Weissbourd & Kagan, 1989; Zigler & Black, 1989) who have argued that the kinds of practices found consistent with family support principles should be, and indeed were found to be, related to a range of positive family outcomes compared to more professionally centered and paternalistic approaches to working with families.

REFERENCES

Brewer, E., McPherson, M., Magrab, P., & Hutchins, V. (1989). Family-centered, community-based, coordinated care for children with special health care needs. *Pediatrics, 83,* 1055–1060.

Brickman, P., Rabinowitz, V., Karuza, J., Coates, D., Cohn, E., & Kidder, L. (1982). Models of helping and coping. *American Psychologist, 37,* 368–384.

Cohen, S., Agosta, J., Cohen, J., & Warren, R. (1989). Supporting families of children with severe disabilities. *Journal of The Association for Persons with Severe Handicaps, 14,* 155–162.

Cowen, E.L. (1985). Person-centered approaches to primary prevention in mental health: Situation-focused and competence-enhancement. *American Journal of Community Psychology, 13,* 31–48.

Danish, S.J., & D'Augelli, A.R. (1980). Promoting competence and enhancing development through life development intervention. In L.A. Bond & J.C. Rosen (Eds.), *Primary prevention of psychopathology* (Vol. 4, pp. 105–129). Hanover, NH: University Press of New England.

DePaulo, B., Nadler, A., & Fisher, J. (Eds.). (1983). *New directions in helping: Vol. 2. Helpseeking.* New York: Academic Press.

Dunst, C.J. (1987, December). *What is effective helping?* Paper presented at the biennial meeting of the National Clinical Infants Program Conference, Washington, DC.

Dunst, C.J. (1990). Family support principles: Checklists for program builders and practitioners. *Family Systems Intervention Monograph, 2,* No. 5. Morganton, NC: Family, Infant and Preschool Program, Western Carolina Center.

Dunst, C.J., Johanson, C., Trivette, C.M., & Hamby, D. (1991). Family-oriented early intervention policies and practices: Family-centered or not? *Exceptional Children, 58,* 115–126.

Dunst, C.J., & Trivette, C.M. (1987). Enabling and empowering families: Conceptual and intervention issues. *School Psychology Review, 16,* 443–456.

Dunst, C.J., & Trivette, C.M. (1988). Helping, helplessness and harm. In J. Witt, S. Elliott, & F. Gresham (Eds), *Handbook of behavior therapy in education* (pp. 343–376). New York: Plenum.

Dunst, C.J., & Trivette, C.M. (1989). An enablement and empowerment perspective of case management. *Topics in Early Childhood Special Education, 8*(4), 87–102.

Dunst, C.J., Trivette, C.M., Davis, M., & Cornwell, J. (1988). Enabling and empowering families of children with health impairments. *Children's Health Care, 17,* 71–81.

Dunst, C.J., Trivette, C.M., & Deal, A.G. (1988). *Enabling and empowering families: Principles and guidelines for practice.* Cambridge, MA: Brookline Books.

Dunst, C.J., Trivette, C.M., Gordon, N., & Pletcher, L. (1989). Building and mobilizing informal family support networks. In G.H.S. Singer & L.K. Irvin (Eds.), *Support for caregiving families: Enabling positive adaptation to disability* (pp. 121–142). Baltimore, MD: Paul H. Brookes Publishing Co.

Dunst, C.J., Trivette, C.M., & LaPointe, N. (1992). Toward clarification of the mean and key elements of empowerment. *Family Science Review, 5*(1/2), 145–165.

Dunst, C.J., Trivette, C.M., Starnes, A.L., Hamby, D.W., & Gordon, N.J. (1993). *Building and evaluating family support initiatives: A national study of programs for persons with developmental disabilities.* Baltimore: Paul H. Brookes Publishing Co.

Dunst, C.J., Trivette, C.M., & Thompson, R. (1990). Supporting and strengthening family functioning: Toward a congruence between principles and practice. *Prevention in Human Services, 9*(1), 19–43.

Fisher, J., Nadler, A., & DePaulo, B.(Eds.). (1983). *New directions in helping, Vol. 1: Recipient reactions to aid.* New York: Academic Press.

Hartman, A., & Laird, J. (1983). *Family-centered social work practice*. New York: Free Press.

Hobbs, N., Dokecki, P., Hoover-Dempsey, K., Moroney, R., Shayne, M., & Weeks, K. (1984). *Strengthening families*. San Francisco: Jossey–Bass.

Johnson, B. (1990). The changing role of families in health care. *Children's Health Care, 19*, 234–241.

Kagan, S.L., & Shelley, A. (1987). The promise and problems of family support programs. In S.L. Kagan, D.R. Powell, B. Weissbourd, & E.F. Zigler (Eds.), *America's family support programs* (pp. 3–18). New Haven, CT: Yale University Press.

Kagan, S.L., Powell, D.R., Weissbourd, B., & Zigler, E.F. (Eds.). (1987). *America's family support programs*. New Haven, CT: Yale University Press.

Katz, R. (1984). Empowerment and synergy: Expanding the community's healing resources. In J. Rappaport, C. Swift, & R. Hess (Eds.), *Studies in empowerment: Steps toward understanding and action* (pp. 201–226). New York: Haworth Press.

Moroney, R. (1986). *Shared responsibility: Families and social policy*. New York: Aldine de Gruyter.

Moroney, R.M. (1987). Social support systems: Families and social policy. In S.L. Kagan, D. Powell, B. Weissbourd, & E. Zigler (Eds.), *America's family support programs* (pp. 21–37). New Haven, CT: Yale University Press.

Nadler, A., Fisher, J., & DePaulo, B. (Eds.). (1983). *New directions in helping: Vol. 3. Applied perspectives on help-seeking and receiving*. New York: Academic Press.

Ooms, T., & Preister, S. (1988). *A strategy for strengthening families: Using family criteria in policymaking and program evaluations*. Washington, DC: AAMFT Research and Education Foundation.

Rappaport, J. (1981). In praise of paradox: A social policy of empowerment over prevention. *American Journal of Community Psychology, 9*, 1–25.

Rappaport, J. (1987). Terms of empowerment/exemplars of prevention: Toward a theory for community psychology. *American Journal of Community Psychology, 15*, 121–148.

Shelton, T.L., Jeppson, E.S., & Johnson, B. (1987). *Family-centered care for children with special health care needs*. Washington, DC: Association for the Care of Children's Health.

Siegel, S., & Castellani, N.J. (1988). *Nonparametric statistics for the behavioral sciences* (2nd ed.). New York: McGraw Hill.

Singer, G., & Irvin, L. (Eds.). (1989). *Support for caregiving families: Enabling positive adaptations to disability*. Baltimore: Paul H. Brookes Publishing Co.

Swift, C. (1984). Empowerment: An antidote for folly. In J. Rappaport, C. Swift, & R. Hess (Eds.), *Studies in empowerment: Steps toward understanding and action* (pp. xi–xv). New York: Haworth Press.

Weissbourd, B. (1990). Family resource and support programs: Changes and challenges in human services. *Prevention in Human Services, 9*(1), 69–85.

Weissbourd, B., & Kagan, S.L. (1989). Family support programs: Catalysts for change. *American Journal of Orthopsychiatry, 59*, 20–31.

Yin, R.K. (1989). *Case study research: Design and methods* (2nd ed.). Beverly Hills, CA: Sage Publications.

Zautra, A., & Sandler, I. (1983). Life event needs assessment: Two models for measuring preventable mental health problems. In A. Zautra, K. Bachrach, & R. Hess (Eds.), *Strategies for needs assessment in prevention* (pp. 35–58). New York: Haworth Press.

Zigler, E., & Berman, W. (1983). Discerning the future of early childhood intervention. *American Psychologist, 38,* 894–906.

Zigler, E., & Black, K.B. (1989). America's family support movement: Strengths and limitations. *American Journal of Orthopsychiatry, 59,* 6–19.

5

Disability and Grief

From Tragedy to Challenge

Laurie E. Powers

Following genetic testing, a couple elects to carry to term their fetus who has Down syndrome. Another parent receives a telephone call at work and learns that his daughter has been injured in a serious accident. A third parent learns that, following months of concern and visits to professionals, her son is diagnosed with autism. Although the individual circumstances of these families are unique, each is touched by news that irrevocably changes their lives. It is their response to this change that provides the focus for this chapter—managing disability-related grief.

Relatively little has been written or discussed about the specific experience of grief among parents of children with disabilities. Chronic sorrow (Olshansky, 1962) and stage-based bereavement (Austin, 1990) represent two of the predominant models of bereavement in response to disability. The basis for understanding disability-related grief is primarily derived from the general grief literature, clinical observations of familial coping following the disablement of a member, and small-scale uncontrolled studies of parental reactions following the diagnosis of childhood disability or injury. The majority of writings specific to grief and disability have focused on familial response to life-threatening illness, most notably childhood cancer. Additional information has been provided by parents (e.g., Featherstone, 1980) who have eloquently shared their personal experiences of parenting children with disabilities.

Few controlled studies of familial bereavement following disability have been conducted, providing little opportunity to further sort out the responses experienced by parents and the differences between parents regarding the manner in which they confront the news about their children's disabilities or health challenges. Strategies to promote the clinician's ability to assist parents in managing their grief are also not well articulated or validated. The longitudinal, multifaceted, and sensitive nature of bereavement makes the design and implementation of such controlled studies difficult.

There continue to be widespread generalizations and misconceptions among professionals and the public regarding the nature and management of disability-related grief. For some, grief is regarded as a universal phenomenon—a necessary response on the part of families when they learn of the disability of a family member. Those family members who do not experience or demonstrate grief atypically are considered unusual, perhaps pathological. The parameters of what is grief and what is not grief are also not completely understood. As a result, those who express "grief-like" responses such as sadness or anger many years after learning of their children's disabilities are typically assumed to be experiencing either chronic sorrow or delayed grief reactions. Finally, clinical interventions to assist families to manage grief often follow a prescribed regimen associated with the clinician's perspective of effective grieving, with little attention devoted to understanding the contextual factors that contribute to a unique fabric of bereavement for each family member.

The topic of disability-related grief is also associated with sensitivity and controversy when considered in relation to current positive perspectives of disability. Theories that postulate the existence of grief or chronic sorrow in response to disability are sometimes regarded as promulgating the notion that disability is an inherently tragic event with an enduring negative impact on families. Yet, as is emphasized in this chapter, it can be through the validation and processing of grief that many family members shift their perspectives of disability from tragedy to challenge and opportunity.

The purpose of this chapter is to examine the nature of grief and interventions to facilitate grief management for families of people with disabilities and unique health needs, with emphasis on parental support. The chapter addresses the nature, timing, and duration of grief reactions, including a discussion of dysfunctional grief; factors that appear to affect the grief responses of family members; and potential strategies for professionals to use in assisting family members with grief management, from communication of facilitative values to specific intervention methods. Clinical, empirical, and anecdotal information is integrated within the discussion to both inform and correct conceptions about grief.

NATURE OF GRIEF

Grief as a Normal Response to Loss

Simply put, grief is a normal response to loss. Loss is typically perceived when the reality of life is changed in such a way as to make it less preferred than wanted or expected. Such is typically the case for families when a member is diagnosed with a disability or health challenge. The fact that loss is often experienced in response to the disability of a family member is, in part, reflective of predominant cultural norms that emphasize health and ablebodiedness as criteria for happiness and full acceptance within society. As such, a family may be disappointed because one of its members has not achieved this cultural ideal. For most families, the diagnosis of a member's disability more importantly precipitates perceptions of personal loss for the family and the member with the disability; loss of physical, sensory, or cognitive function for the member; loss of certainty about the future; and loss of confidence in the family's ability to support the member and prevent suffering (Kastenbaum, & Aisenberg, 1972).

For the family of a child with an acute disability, grief is often felt for the "original" child who is forever changed. Likewise, parents who give birth to a child with a disability often experience grief over their loss of the child without a disability whom they imagined having during pregnancy (Patterson, 1988). Regardless of the cause or type of disability, most families are faced with having to cope with the "loss of one child" while also coming to know and care for the "remaining child." Often the differences between the "original" child and the "new" child emerge over time, making this process of grieving and adaptation particularly complex and confusing for family members. Such is particularly the case for parents who are confronted with the chronic health challenges of their children. Often they manage through periods of health stability interspersed by health crises. For these parents, there is often little predictability in grief (Worthington, 1989). Because parents who experience illness or disability-related grief do not actually "lose their child," as in the case of death, and may not be able to point to a clear beginning to their loss, they and others in their lives may neither associate their reactions with grief nor validate the appropriateness of parental grief.

The diagnosis of a family member's disability is usually, though not always, accompanied by expressions of grief. Studies of bereavement and trauma indicate that approximately 70% of family members experience moderate to severe grief reactions (Sheldon, Cochrane, Vachon, Lyall, Rogers, & Freeman, 1981). A study of parents of children with Down syndrome found that the vast majority experienced chronic sorrow. However, there was great heterogeneity in the nature and intensity of grief responses (Damrosch & Perry, 1989). Thus, although the experience of identifiable grief is normative, it is not universal and there is no clear association between felt grief and adjustment to loss. There appears to be a subset of people who do not report significant grief responses and do not demonstrate difficulty accommodating the disability of their family members.

There is increasing evidence that suggests that the experience of grief is a biologically based response to loss observed in humans and animals (Darwin, 1872; Parkes, 1964). Grief is both associated with heightened risk for physical illness and impairment in specific neuroimmunological responses (Bartrop, Luckhurst, Lazarus, Kiloh, & Penny, 1977; Holmes & Masuda, 1974; Schleifer, Keller, Camerino, Thornton, & Stein, 1983). The reason for this association remains unclear. Some research suggests that pre-event health explains the relationship (Murrell, Himmelfarb, & Phifer, 1988). Other findings suggest that the level of self-care during bereavement may mediate physical response to loss (Powers, 1990). The experience of bereavement appears to be associated with an increased use of alcohol, tobacco, and tranquilizers; irregular sleep; and poor eating habits (Parkes & Weiss, 1983).

It is difficult to distinguish the nature of loss directly associated with the diagnosis of a family member's disability from the numerous secondary losses and stresses typically experienced in association with the disability. For many families, the presence of disability is associated with stressors such as loss of income, isolation from social support, marital strain, and little time for family recreation (Hobfoll & Parris Stevens, 1990; Patterson, 1988). As a result, family life can be completely overturned, with family members grieving the loss of their entire lives as they existed before the disability. A single mother recently shared a small portion of her life change:

> Since my child was born, basic parts of my life like taking a shower, getting enough sleep, and going shopping sometimes feel impossible to get done. I have to take a shower when he's at school. On the weekends, it's a lost cause unless someone can be with him. I have to go to bed after he falls asleep and get up before he wakes. During the night I listen to be sure he's asleep. As far as shopping goes, quick trips to a convenience store have to do most of the time.

Added disability-related demands typically precipitate family stress; however, it is often a lack of services, such as respite services, in-home medical support, financial assistance, and family support, that creates conditions in which families experience their stress as secondary loss. As is discussed later, the experience of such secondary losses both compounds initial grief reactions and impedes grief management for many families.

It is important to clarify that, although grief results from loss felt in response to the diagnosis of a family member having a disability, the experience of grief generally is not a sign of nonacceptance or devaluing of the family member with a disability. The focus of grief is typically on what is lost, not the family member with a disability who remains. This is a critical point for many families who worry that acknowledging their grief will be interpreted to mean that they do not love or want their member with a disability, particularly when normal grieving sometimes includes feelings of wishing the person with a disability could be replaced by the original or imagined member without a disability. Such feelings are normal and must be validated and understood as wishing that the disability, not the person, would go away.

Fabric of Grief Responses

There is no correct way to express grief. Although evidence suggests that bereavement is sometimes experienced in predominate phases, these phases are not uniformly identified by the expression of specific responses nor are specific reactions phase-limited (Bowlby, 1980; Leyn, 1976). For example, most family members experience an initial period of traumatic stress immediately following diagnosis or injury. During this phase, reactions of numbness, shock, disturbed sleep, and pangs of panic and despair usually predominate; however, individual family members vary in the extent to which they experience any one of these responses. Furthermore, although these reactions are also a normal part of later phases of grieving, they typically do not predominate. For instance, many parents report experiencing sadness years after their children have been diagnosed as having a disability. However, such feelings are typically not recurrent and occur in response to specific events that the parent associates with the original diagnosis. For some parents, later sadness may be triggered by hearing music from the time period during which their children were diagnosed, family birthdays, or taking their other children to the doctor. In each case, the pangs of sadness a parent experiences feel very much like his or her original reactions; however, the feelings usually do not impair the parent's functioning as completely or linger in the same way as originally experienced. As diagnostic news about disability is often delivered incrementally and changes based on new information, it is also normal for parents to cycle through phases and reactions repeatedly as they learn more about the realities of their children's differences.

In reality, the expression of grief is a very complex, personal experience that varies greatly from individual to individual. To some extent, how a person copes with disability-related grief can be predicted from understanding how he or she has coped with crisis and loss in the past (Frantz, 1981). Reflecting on reactions to loss and crisis such as moving away from friends, deaths of parents, or injuries to loved ones will often provide some clues about how one is likely to respond to the disability of a family member. However, in the case of the child-related loss, it is also clear that parents often report added distress (Miles, 1985).

The three dominant phases of grief can be characterized as traumatic stress, assimilation, and acknowledgment and integration.

Traumatic Stress

Traumatic stress usually occurs following injury or diagnosis and is often characterized by disbelief, episodic periods of intense distress separated by periods of numbness, disruption in sleep and eating patterns, intrusive memories of the event that caused the disability or the circumstances of diagnosis, and general feelings of disorientation and confusion. Although families who learn of their member's diagnosis may experience preparatory grief that makes this phase less intense over time, the receipt of definitive news almost always results in some shock, disorientation, and distress for family members. Such can repeatedly be the case for parents who experience major remissions and exacerbations in their children's health over time. It is through this emotional screen of traumatic stress that families must try to assimilate the meaning of the diagnosis and often make major decisions regarding treatment and service coordination. It is no wonder that some families report that, at the time of their children's diagnoses, they do not remember hearing much of what the physicians said and feel like they are in a dream state.

Amidst distress, it is also common for families to experience some relief when a diagnosis is finally conferred. Many families of children with disabilities are well aware that something is wrong with their children long before a diagnosis can be made. Receipt of definitive news that a child does indeed have a disability or health problem sometimes serves as vindication for parents who have searched for a valid explanation to make sense of their concerns.

Such is often the case for parents of children with behavior or learning challenges for which no immediate cause is known and for which parents are mistakenly held responsible.

During this initial phase, parents often use different strategies to manage and make sense of their experiences. Some focus their energies on gathering as much information as possible about the diagnosis. Others express anger about the incompetence of medical staff, questioning the accuracy of the diagnosis. Still others remain tearful and withdrawn, appearing shell-shocked by the news. Many parents demonstrate preoccupation with their child's prediagnostic state or their imagined picture of what their child should have been like if it were not for the disability. At the same time, parents often experience panic and helplessness regarding the comfort, unmet needs, and future of their child. In situations when the child is in health crisis or when very intense care demands are present, or other members of the family are in conflict or facing additional stress, parents often find themselves preoccupied with attending to immediate needs. During these periods, families typically report "going through the motions" without opportunity to, or capability of, experiencing feelings about what has happened to their children.

This period can be very frightening for other children in the family who often are not privy to information about their sibling's diagnosis, who witness the distress of their parents, and who have their daily routines disrupted. It is normal for children to demonstrate developmental regression, have nightmares, express anger at the disruption in their lives, and become afraid that something bad is going to happen to them or to their parents.

Assimilation

Typically, numbness gradually gives way to increased periods of restlessness and distress. Confusion also begins to dissipate, replaced by a sharper realization of the nature and extent of disability. It is this shift that usually marks movement into the second broad phase of grief. This phase, assimilation, is particularly difficult to characterize because family members often exhibit highly idiosyncratic, oscillating responses that are heavily influenced by personality and contextual factors. However, it is fair to say that this is usually the period during which families often experience their most intense reactions to both the loss of their hoped-for children and the emerging challenges associated with caring for their children with disabilities. This phase is also commonly identified by families as their most distressing period.

The experience of many different feelings and reactions is common. Although sadness and depression are generally thought to predominate, most families experience a variety of other reactions. For instance, parents may report feeling as if they have lost a part of themselves, sometimes experiencing associated somatic complaints. Although there is seldom a clear pattern of grief response among family members, specific individuals often demonstrate fairly predictable response patterns. For example, one father reported that, during the first few months after his son's accident, he had nightmares and felt "edgy" prior to every doctor's appointment. Following each appointment, he often felt very depressed and frequently expressed anger at his wife. His anger outbursts were often followed by periods of self-blame. To avoid those feelings, he got very involved in his job, a strategy that worked until the next doctor's appointment. As is discussed later, the identification of such individual patterns can both validate their presence as normal grief reactions and facilitate an important step in breaking a chain of responses that may not be useful or constructive.

Some families interpret the oscillations in their responses as signs of "craziness" and seek professional assistance. In reality, many families do experience symptoms that fit standard definitions for psychopathology (American Psychiatric Association, 1987; Kaplan, Grobstein, & Smith, 1976). Thus, under these circumstances periods of psychological impairment during the peaks and valleys of grief are normal. Examples of broad categories of bereavement responses are presented below, highlighting the heterogeneity of normal family reactions.

Hope   Although underemphasized, hope is perhaps the most important response to loss. Hope provides a perspective that sustains energy through hard times and helps parents define positive outcomes toward which they should reach. It is clear that hopefulness is a powerful and persistent response. For example, in her study of parents whose children died from cancer, Miles (1985) found that 29% remained confident that their children would survive until the time of their own deaths.

Hope is required for families to move ahead into an uncertain future. Such is usually the case for families who have a member with a disability, regardless of whether the disability is static, acute, or progressive. Often the nature of hope changes over time. Parents may begin by hoping the disability will go away. Over time, they may come to accept their child's disability and shift their focus toward preparing for their child's future. As grief becomes less predominant and parents have an opportunity to view their children's strengths and successes, the focus of their hopefulness often shifts further toward wishing that their children will be able to live as typically as possible.

It is this process of shift in hope that may be a good indicator of longitudinal family adjustment to disability. However, it is important to note that families usually hope for that which seems reasonably possible. Those families who have children with very significant challenges or who face many obstacles in supporting their children understandably have difficulty shifting their hope to outcomes that appear unreachable. Under these circumstances, lack of shift may be a strong sign that these families remain very unclear about what the future can bring.

Hope is associated with faith for many parents—faith in God, in physicians, in their children, in the help of others, or in their own strength (Frantz, 1981). Parents who are ordinarily religiously oriented may turn further to God for comfort and meaning. Parents who are not particularly religious may also find comfort in activities such as prayer. In contrast, parents who are ordinarily spiritually focused may drift away from their faith in God when confronted with the "unfairness" of their child's disability. Their estrangement may be temporary or permanent.

Anxiety and Restlessness Many parents report ongoing difficulties in concentrating, relaxing, sleeping, or maintaining organization in their lives. As a result, family members may be late for work or school and activities may not get completed. Parents or children may express atypical worries or a general sense of foreboding. Often families report they feel like "their wheels are spinning with nowhere to go." Disturbed sleep and nightmares remain common. Anxious feelings often become exacerbated when family members anticipate doing activities that somehow accentuate their loss: taking their child to a physician, providing disability-related care, having professionals come into their homes, and taking their children to the playground. Anxiety sometimes gets channelled into other activities such as intensive involvement in work or home projects, particularly for fathers. Sometimes the momentum of grief-related anxiety leads parents to consider making major life changes, such as selling the house, separating, moving away, or suddenly institutionalizing their child. Although making such changes often seems appealing and provides diversion from immediate discomfort, they are frequently associated with additional stress for families.

Depression and Apathy It is normal for family members to cycle through periods of fairly intense depression, loss of hope, and apathy. Through depression, many family members come to confront the reality of their loss. During depressive episodes, family members often withdraw, have difficulty mustering the energy to do even the most basic activities, and do not care whether these activities get done. Some parents even consider suicide. When asked if she was eating properly, a mother of a child with cytomegalovirus reported:

> Eating is way beyond where I'm at. Getting out of bed and brushing my teeth is an impossible effort. I know I'm supposed to do it, but it just doesn't matter. Lying in bed is easier. If I get up, I don't know what to do with myself. Nothing matters anyway except John. . . . He keeps me going.

For many parents, it is the care demands of their children with disabilities that push them to do activities in spite of their depression. As such, the needs of the child with a disability are often met while many other demands may be ignored (Perrin & Gerrity, 1984). This often especially affects the siblings of a child with a disability. To draw attention to their needs, siblings may misbehave, give gifts, or feign illness (Leyn, 1976). The presence of many demands and secondary stressors typically accentuates parental feelings of helplessness, despair, and depression. It is also common for parents to report concern that their despair is worsening over time. Although this can be a sign of dysfunctional grief, it often indicates the progression of a normal process during which despair seems to build until it precipitates the experience of other emotions. Over time, this oscillation of emotions gradually becomes less intense. As described by one mother, "It's like being on a roller coaster with no track."

Guilt   Guilt and self-blame are generally assumed to be widely experienced by parents of children with disabilities. While attributing a cause for the disability is important to most, recent evidence suggests that a large minority of parents are not preoccupied with understanding why their children have disabilities (Downey, Silver, & Wortman, 1990). Furthermore, parents who blame themselves or others for their children's disabilities appear more distressed. Although self-blame has been considered by some to be adaptive because it is a way for parents to explain the often unexplainable disabilities of their children, blaming oneself does not appear to be associated with subsequent reduction of distress. Furthermore, increase in distress does not predict self-blame, suggesting that self-blame is not a spillover response to extreme distress. Self-blame is in most cases a normative symptom of grief that is typically alleviated as distress lessens.

Guilt and self-blame can be expressed through a variety of direct and indirect behaviors. Most clear-cut is a parent's acknowledgment that he or she feels responsible for the child's disability. For instance, parents who give birth to children with genetically based disabilities may blame their "genetic weakness" (Patterson, 1988). Parents of children whose disabilities result from accidents sometimes report that they believe they should have been able to keep their children safe from harm. Parents who view their children's discomfort also tend to blame themselves for not being able to help. When the reason for disability is unclear, parents may relentlessly search for an explanation, expressing blame toward others or toward themselves. Such behavior can result in social isolation and self-destructive behavior (Leyn, 1976). Siblings, particularly younger children, often indicate that they think their brothers or sisters have disabilities because they wished it or did something bad.

In contrast to direct expression of self-blame, some family members express their guilt more indirectly. Parents may avoid or coddle the child with a disability, suddenly become involved in religious activities, blame their spouse, or withdraw. Children may punish themselves or run away from home. These behaviors are not necessarily associated with self-blame; however, their demonstration warrants considering guilt as a factor.

Parents generally deal with guilt in three major ways: recurrent self-blame, forgiveness, or refuting the irrational beliefs that typically underlie their guilt. Use of the latter strategies can result in reduced guilt (Nixon & Singer, in press). Recurrent self-blame may ordinarily diminish as distress recedes; however, this reaction can impair self-esteem and negatively affect a parent's relationship with his or her child. When confronting their guilt, parents often come to acknowledge that, although unable to protect their children from disability, they have tried their best to care for them. Through this process parents are required to confront the limitations and strengths of their humanness.

Anger and Irritability As already emphasized, experiencing the disability of a family member accentuates physical stress, feelings of helplessness, and fear. Under these circumstances, frustration, tension, irritability, and anger are normal responses that are directly expressed through pacing, crying, screaming, or outbursts at family members. While grief-related anger directed at the occurrence of disability is typical, much of the anger and frustration parents report is associated with their exposure to secondary stressors such as a lack of support services, incomplete access to information about their child's status, or financial strain.

Anger can be difficult for many family members to express directly because they fear hurting others, question that their reactions are unjustifiable or stupid, or fear recrimination. For example, it is normal for a family member to feel anger toward the disability, yet acknowledging this can lead to guilt if the member associates anger at the disability with anger at the child. Many parents also have difficulty expressing frustration at professionals because they worry that the professionals will respond by withdrawing care or labeling them as troublemakers. Indeed, some professionals do become threatened by parents' anger and respond by limiting parent access to information or asking other staff to run interference. In most cases, parents who express anger do so because they feel overwhelmed and unsupported. Assisting parents by providing nonpaternalistic validation for their feelings, access to information and decisions, and support for caring for themselves and their children can help them to deal with their anger.

Anger that is not expressed directly often gets expressed indirectly through criticism of oneself or others, withdrawal, fighting with one's spouse, or nightmares. These responses can lead to additional problems, such as marital discord and isolation from others. The direct expression of anger is critical for preventing the development of these problems. However, to prevent anger from becoming cyclic, it is critical that the source of anger be accurately identified and, as appropriate, corrective action be taken. For example, a mother described her relationship with her husband since their son's accident:

> I can't seem to help picking on him. I feel guilty when I do it, but I still keep it up. I criticize him for not helping, but when he does try to help, I yell at him for not doing it right. He doesn't talk to me anymore. I think he's afraid I'll yell.

This mother identified that most of her anger was due to a combination of inadequate sleep, lack of help caring for her child, and grief about no longer being able to keep her house clean in the way in which she was accustomed prior to her son's accident. Once she identified the reasons for her irritability, she was able to share them with her husband and together they approached the social worker to request additional help. As such, this couple was able to support one another and use her anger as a catalyst for trying to improve their situation.

In many cases, family members express anger when they feel helpless, guilty, or afraid. Often there is no immediate remedy for their distress; their child's disability won't go away, the future is uncertain, and feelings of responsibility linger. Furthermore, because family members usually process their grief differently from one another, it is common for tension to develop between couples and parents and children. Management of such tension is a critical predictor of long-term coping with disability in the family (Damrosch & Perry, 1989). Useful management strategies include identifying ways for family members to check in with one another on a regular basis for the purpose of communicating thoughts and feelings, establishing ground rules among family members for their support of one another, and providing opportunities for family members to spend non–disability-related time with one another.

Social Isolation It is normal for families to become socially isolated during the course of bereavement. Social isolation typically occurs during periods of depression or intense stress and, over time, as supporters gradually withdraw from the family because they feel helpless, afraid, or rejected. Although support from others is essential, enlisting such support often requires effort from affected families, particularly during periods of intense distress (Hobfoll & Parris Stevens, 1990). As expressed by one parent:

> My friends and neighbors really want to help, but when they come over they ask all kinds of questions that I just don't want to talk about . . . they mean well but when they say things like you're so lucky your other children are healthy . . . they just don't understand and I don't have the energy to explain.

Satisfaction with social support is an important predictor of adjustment to bereavement (Powers, 1990). Those families who perceive that they are receiving useful support without having to expend additional effort typically report less distress than families who are socially isolated. Because families often do not have the ability to ask for support or describe the kind of support they need, it often falls on those who want to help to reach out in those ways they think will be most helpful to families. For many families, useful assistance during intense periods of grief comes through practical supports like respite care, bringing meals to the hospital, or doing laundry. Some families also appreciate knowing that there is someone they can call who will just listen if they need to talk, or who will not feel hurt and withdraw if their calls to families do not always get answered.

Idiosyncratic Reactions In addition to the typical responses described above, family members often express their grief in very personal ways. For example, after learning that her son had muscular dystrophy, a mother expressed distress because her husband was not expressing any emotions about their son, instead spending most of his time working on a project in the basement. After several weeks and considerable marital tension, the father revealed that he had been spending his time in the basement carving a plaque for his son. Through this activity, the father found that he could express his grief in a manner that felt right for him.

Acknowledgment and Integration

The transition to the final phase of grief is usually marked by greater understanding and acknowledgment of disability, and integration of the child with a disability into an adapted family life. Periods of distress typically become more brief and gradually less intense, although it is common for parents to report that they experience "bad days" during which they feel grief as intensively as they did when their children were originally diagnosed. Grief management and parent–child bonding can be severely constrained by repeated hospitalizations and ongoing intervention by others. It is essential that parents be provided with normalized opportunities to be with, and care for, their children with disabilities. Through involvement in typical parenting, the self-esteem of parents will be enhanced, as will their perceptions of their children as typical children with challenges rather than children who are victimized by tragedy.

As grief recedes, it can be difficult for families to acknowledge that they are feeling better. For some, the shift to feeling better happens so gradually, interspersed by periods of distress, that it is difficult to detect or trust the permanency of the overall improvement. Many families find it hard to differentiate their grief-related stress from other life stress. Other family members are reluctant to acknowledge their grief is receding because they feel guilty or do not want others to interpret their acknowledgment as indicating that they are "back to normal." In truth, there is no "back to normal" for most families because they are forever changed as a result of their experiences with disability. Acknowledgment of this reality by others is an important method of communicating respect for the importance of such experiences for families. In contrast, using terms such as "recovering from grief," "accepting disability," or "returning to normal" may indirectly communicate lack of understanding of the permanent life change many families experience.

As families manage grief, they often begin to shift their perceptions of disability. In the beginning, the disability of a child is usually seen as a tragedy that will forever prevent the child and family from living a complete and happy life. During this time, the child is perceived as disabled first and a child second. Conversely, parents often view themselves as inadequate or abnormal which makes them fundamentally different from parents of children without disabilities. However, over time, many parents come to realize that their child is foremost a child who happens to have some differences that pose challenges. As such, they are normal parents who, in addition to normal parenting, will be faced with finding strategies to overcome their child's specific challenges. This shift in perceptions is important because it enables parents and children with disabilities to define themselves as normal people who can live typical lives. Additionally, it helps parents to focus their energies on identifying and finding ways to overcome challenges that become obstacles to their children's independence. As expressed by one parent of a child with cerebral palsy:

> I used to feel bad all the time because I thought my son's life would be ruined and it was my fault. Now I'm starting to see that in most ways he's like any other kid . . . he can't do some things like walk or speak, but he loves music, being with other kids, and likes to do things by himself . . . he gets around with his wheelchair and we're working on getting him a communicator to make talking easier. We've just started to think that maybe someday he will get a job he likes and live on his own . . . maybe he'll even find the right girl and get married. It's hard sometimes, but we're all trying our best and hopefully it will work out.

As parents confront their grief and the other challenges involved with their children's disabilities, they may also discover that they possess personal strengths and resilience that they did not formerly recognize. Many parents find out that they are competent advocates, good decision makers, and effective organizers. Parents may also realize that, through their experiences, they have opportunities to clearly define their own personal values in ways that many parents of children without disabilities cannot. As such, they feel better prepared to make decisions that are consistent with their values. The identification and acknowledgment of such strengths can be a valuable tool for parents to build their self-esteem and resilience as they manage their often-demanding lives.

Time Course of Grief

The time course of grief has received much attention in the non–disability-related literature. Studies suggest that the grief dominates life for at least 1–3 years for most people who experience loss (Vachon et al., 1982; Zisook & Schuchter, 1985), with approximately 25% experiencing recurrent distress after 2 years. Grief in response to the death of a child is often more intense and lasts longer (Miles, 1985). A "typical" time course for disability-related grief is not well-understood and, in fact, often has no clear start or end. It is likely that the trauma of experiencing disability within the family is associated with a comparable period of dominant grief. In fact, because the diagnosis of disability-related loss often emerges over time and is associated with many secondary losses, it is reasonable to expect that the experience of grief may normally be prolonged or episodic for some families, especially those who are dealing with chronic, unpredictable health challenges (Worthington, 1989). It is important to emphasize that there is likely to be large variation in the time course of grief across families, just as there is great diversity in the nature of grief expression.

In some sense, management of loss is a lifelong experience, requiring ongoing recognition that life will never be the same and that grief-related responses will reemerge from time to time throughout life for most families. Recycled responses are often stimulated by transitions for the family, health and developmental changes in the child, additional losses, and secondary stressors.

Normal lifelong family responses sometimes take the form of chronic sorrow—intermittent feelings of grief that may include recollections of experiences associated with original loss and be stimulated by current stressors and developmental transitions. These experiences are common for most parents, including those who have very positive views of their children with disabilities and themselves. Most often the experience of chronic sorrow is not a sign of ongoing despair for the child.

Although triggering experiences may lead to expressions of grief-like responses, family reaction may also be unrelated to the original grief event or current feelings about the child with a disability. For many families, coping with disability-related challenges constitutes normal stress that results in periodic emotional ups and downs. Thus, "a bad day" can include feelings of distress related to a current problem that may or may not be combined with recollection of the sadness felt by a parent when his or her child was diagnosed as having a disability. It is critical that supporters maintain their perspective of the complexity of family responses to avoid unnecessarily labeling families as experiencing "problems" such as unresolved grief based on simplistic notions about how they believe families should respond.

Responses functional for families during one period of grief may impede their adaptation in other periods (Patterson, 1988). For instance, enmeshment with a child during her initial health crisis may impede parents from feeling comfortable with affording the child opportunities for independence following health stabilization. It is inevitable that this type of conflict will occur, prompting families to reconsider the usefulness of their reactions and shift them accordingly. When families question the helpfulness of their responses, it is important to emphasize both the validity of their original reactions and their abilities to modify their responses to accommodate new life circumstances.

Dysfunctional Grief

If grief is truly a very individual experience with little predictable organization of responses, the question arises as to the nature of pathological grief. As alluded to earlier, the judgment that a person is experiencing pathological grief must be filtered through an understanding of the normal nature of grief. That the majority of families demonstrate some psychiatric symptomology and many seek out psychiatric care (Binger, 1984; Kaplan et al., 1976) during bereavement suggests that some responses ordinarily considered pathological are normal during bereavement. However, it is clear that some people have extraordinarily difficult experiences in integrating their losses. To understand their difficulty often requires moving beyond straightforward definitions of pathology to considerations of functionality and dysfunctionality of grief. The following discussion suggests four broad strategies for identifying circumstances in which grief may be dysfunctional.

The most important determinant of whether grief is functional or dysfunctional is the family member's own assessment of distress and his or her ability to manage life demands. Parents are the best judges of their status, even under circumstances during which they report great uncertainty about how well they are doing. Often if provided with information about the parameters of normal grief and validation of their ability to assess how they are doing, parents will be able to differentiate "feeling terrible but maintaining" from "feeling terrible and unable to manage." Of course, both the parameters of what parents experience and definitions of acceptable life management change as a function of time since injury and diagnosis and the presence of secondary stressors. Shortly after diagnosis or following exposure to additional major stress, such as job loss or rehospitalization of a child, "life management" may merely mean being able to care for basic physical needs, with most other activities put on hold. During noncrisis periods, effective management is often reflected in parental ability to modulate performance of disability-related and "regular" life activities in a way that enables fulfillment of most essential life roles. Coping patterns that respond to both family needs and personal needs appear to be associated with better outcomes (McCubbin & Patterson, 1983).

A second strategy for evaluating the functionality of grief involves observing the extent of the shift in grief responses that a parent reports. As mentioned earlier, grief is usually characterized by many different reactions that recycle and catalyze one another over time. For example, feelings of anger may blend into feelings of depression, which may lead to intense reflection by a parent about whether he or she can effectively deal with what has happened to his or her child. This type of response shift is dynamic and indicative of momentum for coming to terms with what has happened. Parents may report they feel better or worse; what is certain is that there will be continual change. If a family member ceases to experience this type of response shift and experiences stagnant impairment in his or her ability to function across life domains, the member's grief may become dysfunctional. When this happens, a family member may report feeling stuck or unable to move beyond experiencing a specific response or pattern of responses. Marital discord may also be evident and may indicate rigidity in the ways partners are able to respond to and support one another.

A third strategy for assessing functionality is observing the extent to which, over time, parents report that their reactions are becoming less intense and overwhelming. Although responses are normally recycled and intense responses occur throughout bereavement, most family members find that recycled responses are less intense than original responses, and that intense responses do not endure as long when experienced later in bereavement. Deviation from these normal patterns may signal that a family member is experiencing dysfunctional grief that requires specific attention.

A final determinant of dysfunctional grief is the presence of a severe psychological disability, such as major depression or post-traumatic stress disorder that is experienced outside of normal grief-related sequelae. Although periods of major depression are normal during grief, prolonged episodes with associated gross impairment in daily functions and/or detailed suicidal ideation often signal atypical distress that warrants some type of intervention. Likewise, other symptoms such as chronic intrusive disability-related memories, recurrent nightmares, or persistent startle responses may suggest that grieving has moved beyond typical parameters.

Factors that Influence Grief Experiences

Grief responses are heavily influenced by factors such as gender, age, concurrent stress, and the nature of the disability.

Gender   It is clear that most men manage grief differently than most women. One study of the reactions of parents to their children's experience of mental retardation revealed that most of the fathers exhibited steady, time-bound adjustment, whereas most of the mothers reported grief patterns characterized by more chronic distress interspersed with crises (Damrosch & Perry, 1989). Mothers were also more likely to express negative affect than fathers, although the majority of both mothers and fathers reported experiencing chronic sorrow. When rating their satisfaction with different methods of professional help, fathers were more likely to report that strategies such as encouraging parents not to dwell on their situation and to be strong were most useful, whereas mothers rated as most useful strategies such as encouraging the expression of sadness, allowing demonstrations of weakness, and providing positive feedback.

Given their different styles of grief management, it is critical that spouses employ methods to keep their communications open and maintain mutual respect for one another's differences (May, 1992). When communication and mutual respect are in place, couples are able to help each other explore their feelings and identify ways to manage feelings that are useful and not destructive to the integrity of the family. For example, one father reported that he stayed at work late because he "couldn't take" seeing his wife upset all the time. When she became upset, he felt helpless and very sad. Over time, his wife became angry because he was not available to help out at home and hurt because he did not reach out to comfort her. As a result of talking with one another about their reactions, this couple discovered that the mother needed permission to be upset and did not expect the father to make her feel better. They also realized that his staying away from home was not an indication that he did not care; rather, it was the only way he knew to manage his own feelings of guilt and sadness without feeling his wife's pressure to disclose. As a result of their discussion, they agreed that the best way to support each other was for the father to come home on time and be available to help out, with both agreeing to try not to rescue or pressure one another's feelings.

Age The child's, parent's, and family's ages at diagnosis or injury are an important predictor of family adaptation (Damrosch & Perry, 1989; Newbrough, Simpkins, & Mauer, 1985; Sutkin, 1984). Familial adaptation is generally more adversely affected the younger the child, parents, and family. Disability and injury at birth or to a very young child is considered perhaps the most unfair and abnormal event that can happen to families. Feelings of absolute shock and unfairness felt by most parents faced with this situation may exacerbate their grief reactions. Likewise, many young parents are not prepared to deal with the emotional and practical demands imposed by disability or injury to their children, and many newly organized families do not possess the maturity to weather such a crisis. An exception to heightened risk as a function of youth is the case in which older parents give birth to a child with care demands that exceed their strengths and physical capacities.

Concurrent Stress As suggested throughout the preceding discussion, the presence of secondary stressors is the most critical determinant for grief management and family coping (Cowen & Murphy, 1985). Unfortunately, exposure to concurrent stress is the norm for most families of people with disabilities. Child care demands often require much time and energy (Foster & Berger, 1985). As a result, the work and family management lives of parents must be rearranged. Often it is the mother who quits her job to stay at home with the child. This often results in both role-redefinition stress for her and loss of income for the family. When one parent reduces work time, the other parent is often required to expand employment to make ends meet. As a result, there is less opportunity for parents to spend time together, parental roles become increasingly rigid, and marriages are at heightened risk for tension and discord (Patterson, 1988). Attention to the needs of siblings and opportunities for families to participate in family-focused recreation are also impaired. Premorbid marital conflict, health and poverty, and the experience of additional losses usually make managing grief and disability even more difficult (Stroebe & Stroebe, 1987). It is important to emphasize that such concurrent stressors are often not inherent to disability and most appear primarily as a function of lack of family access to services and supports.

Nature of Disability The experience and management of grief appears to be affected by the type and course of disability. In general, parental grief is exacerbated when a child is diagnosed with multiple disabilities, with adaptation to mental retardation being particularly difficult for many families (Cummings, 1976; Fewell, 1986). Parental grief is also exacerbated and prolonged when children experience disabilities or illnesses of chronic, unpredictable course, and in cases in which children have high technology support needs (Kohrman, 1991; Worthington, 1989). It is likely that disability-specific differences in parental responses are, in part, reflective of socially defined stigmas associated with various disabilities (Wolfensberger, 1972). It is likely that disability-specific differences in grief responses will become less prominent as societal views regarding appreciation and support of diversity become increasingly embraced.

STRATEGIES TO FACILITATE GRIEF MANAGEMENT

It is clear that grief is a normal and functional response to disability for most family members. The expression and management of grief is a very personal experience during which families may receive support from other family members, friends, and professionals. Strategies to facilitate family coping with specific issues that may or may not be grief-related, such as self-blame and marital discord, are presented elsewhere in this volume. This section focuses on basic perspectives and specific strategies helpful for the promotion of grief management by family members.

Basic Perspectives

There are three broad perspectives regarding grief, disability, and coping that are necessary for the provision of helpful support to family members coping with grief-related disability.

Grief as a Normal Response to Disability When a family member seeks professional assistance for disability-related distress, it is essential that the clinician assess, label, and validate for the member the potential role of grief in his or her reactions. As described earlier, many parents confronted with the disabilities or health problems of their children do not recognize that they may be experiencing grief because no objective "death" has occurred. Many often experience fear and confusion because they have no clear explanation for their feelings of disorientation, mood swings, anger at family members, or inability to function at normal levels. It is essential that clinicians recognize that grief reactions are normal responses to disability and provide families with information about grief that helps them place their responses in context. This requires clinicians who support families to have accurate information regarding the nature and progression of disability-related grief, including the normal idiosyncratic course of bereavement and potential signs of dysfunctional grief reactions.

Family-Centered Approach to Support Believing that families are capable of knowing what is best for them and communicating this trust is essential for the empowerment of families (Dunst, Trivette, & Deal, 1988). When a family member experiencing disability-related grief seeks assistance from others, he or she has often reached a point of serious distress and distrust of his or her capacity to manage life. To effectively assist the family member, it is critical that the clinician both believe and communicate to the family member that he or she is capable of self-assessment and self-management.

This can be accomplished by telling the person that, although he or she currently feels confused and distrustful of his or her capacities, the clinician knows that he or she is capable of figuring out what he or she needs to do to feel better and doing it. The clinician's role is to provide information, feedback, and suggestions, with treatment planning conducted in partnership with the family. Although it is a reality that some families are currently not able to manage their lives, clinicians must believe that, if provided with support and resources, these families have the potential to manage effectively.

Disability as Challenge   If a clinician believes that disability is inherently tragic, she or he should not work with families affected by disability. It is normal for parents, when initially affected by the disability of their children, to regard their circumstances as tragic and their children as tragic figures who will be forever limited. When these parents seek support, it is important that clinicians both validate their current feelings of tragedy and gradually provide families with additional perspectives of disability as an event that poses unique challenges but need not ruin a child's or family's life and can be a positive force. This can be accomplished by providing families with information about the supports and opportunities available to people with challenges and by assisting families to sort out and strategize solutions for specific challenges faced by their children. Such information and assistance must be provided at the appropriate time with respect for the family's current focus and processing of grief. However, presenting positive perspectives on disability to families is ultimately essential for their creation of new visions and hopes for their children.

Specific Strategies

There are several specific strategies that clinicians and other supporters can use to assist families with disability-related grief management.

Let Families Tell Their Stories   Perhaps the most important strategy for processing loss is having an opportunity to tell others about the experience. Telling one's story of loss enables a person to outwardly acknowledge the change, begin to process the meaning of the change, and receive validation from others. Most families who experience the disability or illness of their children have few opportunities to tell their stories of the events that comprise their losses. This is because families are often required to immediately shift their attention to caring for their children and often have few people available to validate the fact that, even though their children remain, they have experienced real loss. When families are provided with opportunities to tell their stories, they often do it in great detail. For many, such opportunities provide their first chance to explore and sort out what happened to them and their children. Usually, families become less focused on their stories as they are able to create clear pictures of their experiences.

Help Families To Identify and Process Unresolved Issues As parents recall their experiences, they often identify feelings and issues that remain unresolved. For instance, one mother related that she continued to feel very angry at a doctor who consistently left her daughter's hospital room every time the mother expressed sadness. Another parent reported that he continued to feel guilty because he had yelled at his son before his accident. Once aware that these issues were important and unresolved, both parents were able to identify ways to gain closure. The mother decided to return to the hospital and explain to the doctor that remaining with a person when he or she is distressed is important and provides comfort. The father decided to share his guilt with his wife, who provided support and assured him that his yelling did not cause their son's accident. He also wrote and mailed to himself a note in which he acknowledged his guilt and requested forgiveness. Identification and resolution of such unfinished business is critical for effective processing of grief.

Help Parents Who Choose To Process Loss Through Ritual Throughout the world, deaths of family members are often accompanied by rituals such as funerals and prescribed bereavement periods. Rituals provide opportunities for families to acknowledge the importance of their loss and receive validation from others. Although much of the ritual associated with bereavement has been minimized in America, it is clear that acknowledging loss through ritual is important for productive grief management (Osterweis, Solomon, & Green, 1984).

When a child experiences a serious illness or disability, often there is no analogous formal mechanism for families to mark their loss. Yet, it may be important for families to have some kind of opportunity to acknowledge the major change in their lives and have it validated.

The intention of ritual processing of loss is not to devalue the child with a disability or reinforce negative views of disability. Rather, the purpose is to provide a context for families to personally process their change so that they may be better able to move forward in welcoming their child with a disability.

Such an opportunity can be created by assisting families who find this strategy helpful to identify personal rituals that they can complete to mark their loss. Families may choose to pass on to another child a bicycle that their child won't be able to ride, light a candle for that part of their child they have lost and say goodbye, rearrange their child's room to signify that a change has occurred, or make a list of those expectations for their child that they believe are lost and share it with others.

Which specific activity a family chooses is not important. What is important is that, if desired, families have methods by which to acknowledge their loss through the activity and share their acknowledgment with others in a way that the family finds comfortable. For some families, identifying an integrated ritual for saying goodbye to those aspects of their children they have lost and welcoming their "new" child is possible. However, many families first need to have an opportunity to acknowledge their losses before they are prepared to process their new gifts.

Help Families To Modulate Their Activities   Effective grief management seems to require that families have opportunities for both expression of disability-related grief and engagement in regular life activities (Powers, 1990). Achieving such modulation can be difficult for various reasons. For some, grief is experienced as an overwhelming experience that makes other life activities difficult. For others, the expression of grief is uncomfortable and focusing their attention on other issues and activities appears easier. Still others report that expressing their grief is difficult because they do not want to upset others, especially their children with disabilities. Additionally, most families are realistically overwhelmed by demands and focus more energy on getting done what they can rather than modulating their efforts.

Modulation of involvement in grief-related activities and other life activities, although difficult, is important and can be accomplished through a variety of strategies. One such strategy involves assisting a family member in identifying opportunities for comfortable expression of grief during his or her normal day. For instance, one mother who was worried about crying in front of her child decided that the best place to shed her tears was in the shower. Before dinner each evening, following what was usually a stressful day, she took a warm shower during which she released feelings that had built up. By making time for her feelings, this mother reported feeling less tense and better able to share the evening with her family. Identifying opportunities for comfortable processing of grief is important, even for those family members who do not think they need such opportunities. This is because grief often surfaces spontaneously and can be suppressed if opportunities for processing thoughts and feelings are not available.

A second modulation strategy is sometimes useful during periods when there is no opportunity to express grief-related feelings, such as a meeting at work or at the grocery store with the kids. This strategy involves learning to manage feelings when they surface by "noting" them while not focusing on them. For example, when feeling a pang of sadness during a meeting, a parent reported that she learned to acknowledge the feeling of sadness and then gradually shift her attention back to the meeting. After the meeting, she took time during lunch to process her sadness with greater focus. Of course, there were situations during which acknowledging her feelings and then shifting her attention back to her current activity did not work for this parent. When that happened, she gave herself permission to take a break from work by going to the rest room, writing a poem, or taking a brief walk. However, she returned her focus to work as soon as she felt she had found a way to take the edge off the intensity of her feelings. Finding comfortable ways to use this strategy often takes practice for parents who either think they should not shut off their feelings or worry that by acknowledging feelings they might lose control.

A third modulation strategy involves making a personal commitment to try to continue performing specific life activities even though one is distressed. For some parents who are highly distressed, such a personal commitment might focus on getting dressed each morning. For others, continuing to go to work, even if part-time, or maintaining some family activities such as reading to the children before bedtime or going out to dinner once a week becomes the focus of commitment. Using this strategy can be difficult for families whose lives have been completely disrupted by disability. However, finding a way to preserve some level of normality is essential in ensuring that family members do not become swallowed by their distress or isolated from one another. Clinicians can be of assistance by helping families to explore their current levels of modulation and to identify ways to achieve balance in their management of grief, disability-related activity demands, and regular life activities. Many families also benefit from specific acknowledgment that they cannot do everything and from discussion of strategies for prioritizing demands and focusing on one issue at a time.

Promoting Self-Care

When overwhelmed by disability-related grief and practical demands, it is common for family members, particularly parents, to neglect taking care of themselves. For many, regular meals become suspended, sleep is disrupted, and smoking and drinking gradually increase. It is clear that a lack of self-care is an important predictor of distress and functional impairment for families facing loss (Powers, 1990). As such, it is important that families receive support for both monitoring their levels of self-care and identifying strategies to promote their self-care. This can be accomplished through routine check-in with families regarding their eating, sleeping, and substance use patterns, assisting them to identify strategies they might try to enhance their self-care, and contracting with them to encourage their use of such strategies. Families may use a variety of strategies to facilitate their self-care, including getting additional respite assistance, letting friends and neighbors who want to help know that providing meals would be appreciated, buying cigarettes by the pack instead of the carton, temporarily removing liquor from the house and taking a walk instead of drinking, or listening to relaxation tapes before bedtime. Specific strategies must be acceptable to each family member, realistically taking into account his or her unique preferences and needs.

Help Families To Maintain and Develop Support Networks   Social support is perhaps the single most important buffer against distress and promotional force for well-being (Blaney & Ganellen, 1990). Because many families become socially isolated following the diagnosis of their children with disability or illness, they often benefit from efforts to help them both reinstate their naturally occurring supports and establish additional social connections. Reestablishing links with family and friends is often difficult for families who feel abandoned, and supporters who avoid contacting families because they do not know how to help or are uncomfortable with disability. Assisting a family member to express, in person or through a note, that a friendship is important without saying or doing anything different to be helpful is one strategy to promote reconnection. Helping a family member to identify and provide relevant and positive information about disability to family and friends is another useful strategy, as is encouraging the family member to integrate discussion of his or her child into ordinary conversations, even though supporters may initially appear uncomfortable.

Facilitating new social connections, particularly to other parents of children with disabilities, can also be helpful (see Santelli, Turnbull, Lerner, & Marquis, chap. 2, this volume). Many families are glad to be referred to Parent to Parent or other self-help organizations, welcome being provided with names and phone numbers of other families in their communities who have children with disabilities, or enjoy participating in support groups with other parents. Facilitating parent involvement in such activities often requires more than mere referral, especially when parents are experiencing significant distress and do not have the energy to proactively reach out. Sometimes parent involvement can be facilitated by arranging, with parent permission, for another parent or a representative of a parent organization to make the first contact. Parents may also need help to make practical arrangements to give them time to meet with other parents. Generally it is helpful to first identify a parent's interest in meeting other parents, and then to explore how such a contact could be arranged and what type of supports the parent needs.

Facilitate Development of New Meanings Many people who are faced with unpredictable, negative life events express a need to sort out or understand the meaning of their experience (Antonovsky, 1987). They may search for meaning through involvement in formal religion, informal spiritual investigation, or just spending time thinking about the meaning and impact of their experience on their lives. Meanings are most useful when they both explain what happened (even if the explanation is that the disability was a random event), and suggest ways for the family member to accommodate to the event (Weisner, Beizer, & Stolze, 1991). For example, a father may interpret his child's disability as a test of his parental commitment and, as a result, decide that it is important for him to spend additional time with his child. Another parent may view her child's disability as a prompt to become more aware of others with challenges and express interest in helping others. Still another parent may decide that his child's disability is a punishment and seek forgiveness through religious practice.

That many families search for meaning is normal. It is also a reality that some families adopt meanings that promote their accommodation and relieve distress, while others subscribe to meanings that increase their distress and adjustment. As such, it is appropriate for supporters to offer to help families explore their personal meanings for their children's disabilities, to identify the accommodations that are suggested by those meanings, and to explore the helpfulness of those accommodations. For example, a clinician might help the guilt-ridden parent described above to explore what he believes he is being punished for doing, how his child's disability punishes him for those transgressions, and whether or not seeking forgiveness through church activity is helping. Through such a discussion, this parent may come to substitute new meanings for his child's disability and, ultimately, feel less guilty.

Finding understanding for events such as the disability or illness of children is very difficult. Sometimes, clinicians can help families to identify their personal meanings and choose accommodations that facilitate their coping and provide comfort. To be helpful, it is critical that clinicians resist both imposing their own meanings for disability on families and judging the utility of meanings family members adopt without reference to how well families believe their interpretations work for them.

Help Families To Cope with Periods of Exacerbated Distress   As already described, disability-related grief may become exacerbated during transitions, other family crises, or other events that prompt parents to reflect on their children's disabilities. Supporters can assist families by acknowledging that periods of exacerbated distress are normal and by helping family members to both anticipate events that may provoke distress and identify strategies to manage distress. For instance, one parent of a child with a disability reported that she usually experiences sadness at the beginning of each school year. During August, one of her supporters reminded this mother of her pattern, and they both brainstormed strategies the parent could use to manage any sadness that developed. One of the strategies she identified was going out to lunch with another parent of a child with a disability on the first day of school. This strategy provided her with opportunities for distraction from her sadness through a fun lunch and discussion of her feelings with a friend whom she felt would understand.

Promote Skill-Building   Managing disability-related grief is a challenging process that requires patience, support, and strategies. In the context of managing their grief, parents may welcome and benefit from learning specific skills, such as stress management, problem-solving, and marital communication strategies. Often clinicians are reluctant to propose sharing such skills with grieving parents, whom they view as overwhelmed and unable to integrate additional information. This is sometimes the case; however, if specific strategies are presented in the context of a parent's current experiences and felt needs, they may prove helpful. For example, if a parent reports feeling overwhelmed with demands, a clinician might offer to provide some time-management tips. If the parent is interested, the clinician may assist the parent in developing a list of personal priorities and resources to help him. The clinician and parent might then rehearse strategies for enlisting help and saying no to additional requests for time.

Emphasize Strengths of Families   By far, one of the most important and helpful supports for families experiencing disability-related grief involves pointing out and reinforcing their personal strengths. Many families of children with disabilities feel unprepared, incompetent, and helpless. They are also typically surrounded by well-meaning people who are also focused on searching for solutions to their challenges. Yet, throughout their struggle most of these families demonstrate, but have not acknowledged, intense love and concern for their children and families, quick acquisition of new skills, perseverance, and adaptability. Without minimizing their felt distress, it is important to acknowledge the many strengths and capabilities that family members exhibit as well as those of their children with disabilities. It is normal for families to minimize such acknowledgments because they feel overwhelmed by what is not going well in their lives and are devoting most of their attention to solving problems. When family members minimize their capabilities, it is sometimes helpful to stop them and restate appreciation for their strengths. Some families may also benefit from periodic redirection of their attention to acknowledge their capabilities and efforts.

SUMMARY

The experience of grief in response to the disability or health problem of a family member is a normative, highly individualized experience. Although distressing, the processing of grief has the potential to create opportunities for self-reflection and the development of strengths that can provide new impetus for personal growth and appreciation of self and others. Such opportunities can be highlighted and facilitated by caring friends, family members, and professionals who honor the capabilities and challenges of families and offer assistance in a manner that reflects their respect.

REFERENCES

American Psychiatric Association. (1987). *Diagnostic and statistical manual of mental disorders* (rev. 3rd ed.). Washington, DC: Author.

Antonovsky, A. (1987). *Unraveling the mystery of health: How people manage stress and stay well.* San Francisco: Jossey-Bass.

Austin, J.K. (1990). Assessment of coping mechanisms used by parents and children with chronic illness. *Maternal and Child Nursing, 15,* 98–102.

Bartrop, R.W., Luckhurst, E., Lazarus, L., Kiloh, L.G., & Penny, R. (1977). Depressed lymphocyte function after bereavement. *Lancet, 1,* 834–836.

Binger, C.M. (1984). Psychological intervention with the child cancer patient and family. *Psychomatics, 25,* 899–902.

Blaney, P.H., & Ganellen, R.J. (1990). Hardiness & social support. In B. Sarason, I. Sarason, & G.R. Pierce (Eds.), *Social support: An interactional view* (pp. 297–318). New York: John Wiley & Sons.

Bowlby, J. (1980). *Attachment and loss, Vol. 3. Loss: Sadness and depression.* New York: Basic Books.

Cowen, M., & Murphy, S. (1985). Identification of postdisaster bereavement risk predictors. *Nursing Research, 34,* 71–75.

Cummings, S. (1976). The impact of the child's deficiency on the father: A study of fathers of mentally retarded and of chronically ill children. *American Journal of Orthopsychiatry, 46,* 246–255.

Damrosch, S.P., & Perry, L.A. (1989). Self-reported adjustment, chronic sorrow, and coping of parents of children with Down syndrome. *Nursing Research, 38*(1), 30.

Darwin, C. (1872). *The expression of the emotions in man and animals.* London: Murray.

Downey, G., Silver, R.C., & Wortman, C.B. (1990). Reconsidering the attribution–adjustment relation following a major negative event: Coping with the loss of a child. *Journal of Personality and Social Psychology, 59,* 925–940.

Dunst, C.J., Trivette, C.M., & Deal, A.G. (1988). *Enabling and empowering families: Principles and guidelines for practice.* Cambridge, MA: Brookline Books.

Featherstone, H. (1980). *A difference in the family: Living with a disabled child.* New York: Basic Books.

Fewell, R. (1986). A handicapped child in the family. In R. Fewell & P. Vadasy (Eds.), *Families of handicapped children* (pp. 3–34). Austin, TX: PRO-ED.

Foster, M., & Berger, M. (1985). Research with families with handicapped children: A multilevel systemic perspective. In L. L'Abate (Ed.), *The handbook of family psychology and therapy* (Vol. II, pp. 741–780). Homewood, IL: Dorsey Press.

Frantz, T.T. (1981). *When your child has a life-threatening illness.* Bethesda, MD: Association for the Care of Children's Health.

Hobfoll, S.E., & Parris Stevens, M.A. (1990). Social support during extreme stress: Consequences and intervention. In B. Sarason, I. Sarason, & G.R. Pierce (Eds.), *Social support: An interactional view* (pp. 454–481). New York: John Wiley & Sons.

Holmes, T.H., & Masuda, M. (1974). Life change and illness susceptibility. In B.S. Dohrenwend & B.P. Dohrenwend (Eds.), *Stressful life events: Their nature and effects* (pp. 45–72). New York: John Wiley & Sons.

Kaplan, D.M., Grobstein, R., & Smith, A. (1976). Predicting the impact of severe illness in families. *Health Social Work, 1,* 72–82.

Kastenbaum, R., & Aisenberg, P. (1972). *The psychology of death.* New York: Springer.

Kohrman, A.F. (1991). Medical technology: Implications for health and social service providers. In N.J. Hochstadt & D.M. Yost (Eds.), *The medically complex child* (pp. 3–13). New York: Harwood Academic Publishers.

Leyn, R.M. (1976). Terminally ill children and their families: A study of the variety of responses to fatal illness. *Maternal–Child Nursing Journal, 3,* 179–188.

May, J. (1992). Loss and grief: The paradox of pain. *The National Fathers' Network Newsletter, 2*(2), 5–9.

McCubbin, H.I., & Patterson, J. (1983). The family stress process: The double ABCX model of family behavior. In D. Olson & B. Miller (Eds.), *Family studies review yearbook* (pp. 87–106). Beverly Hills: Sage Publications.

Miles, M.S. (1985). Emotional symptoms and physical health in bereaved parents. *Nursing Research, 34*(2), 77–81.

Murrell, S.A., Himmelfarb, S., & Phifer, J.F. (1988). Effects of bereavement/loss and pre-event status on subsequent physical health in older adults. *International Journal of Aging and Human Development, 27,* 89–107.

Newbrough, J.R., Simpkins, C.G., & Mauer, M.A. (1985). A family development approach to studying factors in the management and control of childhood diabetes. *Diabetes Care, 8*(1), 63–71.

Nixon, C., & Singer, G.H.S. (in press). Cognitive behavioral treatment of self-blame and guilt in parents of children with disabilities. *American Journal of Mental Retardation.*

Olshansky, S. (1962). Chronic sorrow: A response to having a mentally defective child. *Social Casework, 434*(4), 190–194.

Osterweis, M., Solomon, F., & Green, M. (Eds.). (1984). *Bereavement: Reactions, consequences and care.* Washington, DC: National Academy Press.

Parkes, C.M. (1964). Effects of bereavement on physical and mental health: A study of the medical records of widows. *British Medical Journal, 2,* 274–279.

Parkes, C.M., & Weiss, R.S. (1983). *Recovery from bereavement.* New York: Basic Books.

Patterson, J.M. (1988). Chronic illness in children and the impact on families. In C.S. Chilman, E.W. Nunnally, & F.M. Cox. (Eds.), *Chronic illness and disability* (pp. 69–107). Beverly Hills: Sage Publications.

Perrin, E.C., & Gerrity, P.S. (1984). Development of children with a chronic illness. *Pediatric Clinics of North America, 31,* 19–31.

Powers, L.E. (1990). *Cognitive–behavioral factors in adjustment to bereavement.* Unpublished doctoral dissertation, University of Oregon.

Schleifer, S.J., Keller, S.E., Camerino, M., Thornton, J.C., & Stein, M. (1983). Suppression of lymphocyte stimulation following bereavement. *Journal of the American Medical Association, 250,* 374–377.

Sheldon, A.R., Cochrane, J., Vachon, M., Lyall, W., Rogers, J., & Freeman, S. (1981). A psychosocial analysis of risk of psychological impairment following bereavement. *Journal of Nervous and Mental Disease, 169,* 253–255.

Stroebe, W., & Stroebe, M.S. (1987). *Bereavement and health: The psychological and physical consequences of partner loss.* New York: Cambridge.

Sutkin, L.C. (1984). Introduction. In M.G. Eisenberg, L.C. Sutkin, & M.A. Jansen (Eds.), *Chronic illness and disability through the life span* (pp. 1–19). New York: Springer.

Vachon, M., Sheldon, A.R., Lancee, W.J., Lyall, W.A., Rogers, J., & Freeman, S. (1982). Correlates of enduring stress patterns following bereavement: Social network, life situation and personality. *Psychological Medicine, 12,* 783–788.

Weisner, T.S., Beizer, L., & Stolze, L. (1991). Religion and families of children with developmental delays. *American Journal on Mental Retardation, 95,* 647–662.

Wolfensberger, W. (Ed.). (1972). *The principle of normalization in human services.* Toronto, Ontario, Canada: National Institute on Mental Retardation.

Worthington, R.C. (1989). The chronically ill child and recurring family grief. *Journal of Family Practice, 29*(4), 397–400.

Zisook, S., & Schuchter, S.R. (1985). Time course of spousal bereavement. *General Hospital Psychiatry, 7,* 95–100.

Grieving Is the Pits

Donna Lea Johnson

Grieving is the pits!

Complications during birth caused brain damage to our son, Eric, leaving him disabled. His doctors told us he was disabled before he even came home from the hospital, so the grieving process started the day he was born. Still stunned with the news, my husband and I didn't want to believe it could be true. The denial stage worked overtime. I didn't realize it then, but the grieving process had begun. No doubt about it, grieving is the pits!

DENIAL—ANGER

Denial soon gave way to anger. I was so mad! Not just at the fact that I had a child with a disability—I was mad at everything . . . the weather, friends, doctors (really mad at doctors), our health insurance carrier (this anger was totally justified) and the dog (and I don't even own one)! I wondered if I were going nuts. I was downright ugly at times. While I hated being angry, I couldn't seem to control it.

Eric's physical therapist kept reassuring me that anger was a normal, healthy stage in the grieving process, as long as I didn't beat my children or hurt myself. "Find ways to vent the anger," she'd say. That made me mad too. Grieving is the pits!

GUILT

After I had been angry with everything and everyone I knew, and even some I didn't know, along came guilt. My mind was invaded with guilt feelings for not bringing a normal and healthy baby into the world. The whole motherhood thing is a basic, fundamental part of my feelings of worth as a woman. Logically, I can tell you I did all the "right" things to produce a normal and healthy baby; however, what does logic have to do with it? Guilt does not respect logical thinking. When guilt seemed to overtake me and I dwelled upon it, my emotions went crazy. I'll bet you can guess what came next . . . depression. Grieving is definitely the pits!

DEPRESSION

It's so depressing to be depressed. I like to have fun and when depression first assaulted me, I tried to fight it by having "fun." The only problem was, I couldn't find anything fun about having a child with a disability.

It was about this time when Eric started getting labeled: cerebral palsy, epilepsy, vision problems, etc. It seemed that every part of my life had changed. I had to quit my full-time and part-time job because most of my afternoons were spent taking Eric to doctors' and therapy appointments.

It was also at this time that I learned a lot of specialists are cold, rude jerks who seem to compete with each other to see who can upset a mom the most by being as blunt and negative as possible. Some of Eric's doctors delighted in using words they were reasonably sure I'd never heard in my entire life. I guess they felt they had succeeded when I was not only upset but felt ignorant as well. There were, however, a few compassionate doctors who more than made up for the rude ones.

Now, I'm a reasonably intelligent person, but I can honestly say I never really knew what cerebral palsy was, or a myoclonic seizure, or what side of the brain did what. My husband and I educated ourselves and asked a lot of questions. Gradually knowledge and understanding of Eric's problems replaced the mystery.

And then, just when I thought I knew and understood Eric's various labels, I learned I needed to abbreviate! So now Eric has "CP," he goes to "PT," and he takes "meds." Aren't you impressed? Using the abbreviations made me feel like I was on the inside of some sort of special group. I was. Some of the neatest people I have ever met in my entire life either have children with disabilities or have chosen a profession where they work with children with disabilities.

I think this is when the finality of Eric's problems hit home. I had to come to terms with the fact that I would never be able to "fix" Eric. No amount of money or medicine will change the damage to Eric's brain. He will always be disabled. Coming to terms with this was very hard and very depressing and seemed to take too long. Once again, I was reassured that depression was a normal and necessary stage of the grieving process and that it would pass. Oh, grieving is the pits!

ACCEPTANCE?

With the final stage of acceptance mysteriously lurking out there somewhere, I have tried on numerous occasions to find it. I've tried to trick myself into thinking I'm there. Sometimes the depression would lift and I would begin to feel pretty good. And then gradually I caught myself sneaking peeks of Eric and feeling joy.

Sometimes watching him would actually make me smile. I noticed I wasn't sad every time I looked at him. Finally, I can say I'm not sorry he's my son. . .

As some of the hurt gradually went away, I figured I was through grieving. I just knew I had arrived. Acceptance was here! It's funny now, but I remember as early as Eric's first birthday telling Eric's speech pathologist that I was done with the grieving process. She smiled a knowing smile and said, "I'm glad to see you're coping well right now, but please remember it normally takes about three years to get through the entire process." Not me, I thought, I've done it. I'm ready to move on with my life. Less than one month later I was depressed again. Isn't grieving the pits?

The last two years have been spent on the depression roller coaster. I dip real low and just when I can't stand it any longer, I start to rise up above it. Up and down. Up and down. The lows are not quite as low now, and I think the highs are getting a little bit higher and lasting for longer periods of time.

The last really bad depression was Eric's third birthday. I remembered what one of Eric's therapists told me about the grieving process usually taking three years. I guess I thought I could wave a magic wand when Eric turned three and be finished with the grieving process. No such luck. When the realization hit me that I wasn't finished grieving in the allotted three years, I really got depressed. Grieving is the pits!

ACCEPTANCE, WHEN?

What now? Sometimes I wonder if I'll ever find the acceptance stage. It's as if acceptance is playing hide and seek with me. Just when I think I've found it, it turns out to be a shadow. I think acceptance is a lot like heaven. In my heart I believe unquestionably that heaven exists. But where is it? I've never actually seen it or met anyone who has. Beyond a shadow of a doubt, I know it exists.

Acceptance is something like that. I know it's out there . . . somewhere. Other parents of children with disabilities have found it. It exists, and someday I'm going to find it. When I do, I wonder if I'll recognize it. Will it be like a flash of lightning across the sky, bold and obvious? Or will it be subtle like a gently blowing wind that isn't noticeable until I really stop to take notice? I look forward to the day I realize I've found it. In the meantime, I'll keep on grieving . . . and it's the pits!

Donna Lea Johnson lives with her husband, Alan, and her two sons, Christopher, 10, and Eric, 6, in Sand Springs, Oklahoma. She is currently running a desktop publishing business out of her home, in addition to freelance writing and selling Mary Kay Cosmetics. Johnson and her husband have also taught a class on "Reaching Out to the Disabled and Their Families." She is happy to report that the grieving process has wound down.

6

Counseling in the Health Care Relationship

A Natural Source of Support for People with Disabilities and Their Families

W. Carl Cooley and John B. Moeschler

Physician, healer, shaman—human societies have long supported roles for counselor therapists in the promotion of health and well-being. Such counselors were traditionally chosen and trained as ones with wisdom and insight into the combination of spiritual, somatic, and environmental factors associated with feeling ill or well. Though "curing" in the sense of eradicating disease has always been a part of the healer's role, assisting the individual's re-achievement of balance with society and nature and his or her reempowerment were given equal if not greater importance in many societies.

The advent of complex technology-based interventions and a scientific approach to ill health, however, has interfered with the effectiveness of physicians as counselors, but has not reduced the importance of this role. Modern Western medicine has become so focused on curing and preventing disease that many physicians have never developed skills in caregiving, amelioration, or support when a "cure" is not likely. The relationships that caregivers have with their clients have been changed by other societal and economic trends as well. Issues regarding liability and financial limitations have placed unnatural constraints on the professional–client interaction. Moreover, the language of modern medicine has evolved into a vocabulary of pathology and disease that molds and pervades the physician's attitudes and behavior around human variation. As a result, contemporary physicians may regard persons experiencing disabilities only as patients "suffering" from incurable conditions for whom the physician has no effective role to play.

This chapter's discussion of the counseling roles of physicians for individuals with disabilities and their families is aimed at the other counseling professionals who use this book. It is hoped that the contents of this chapter will help professionals of other disciplines understand potential counseling and support roles that physicians may play. This understanding may enhance opportunities to collaborate in support of individual families and to share information about methods of intervention. The purpose of this chapter is not to reexamine the failings of physicians in the support of persons with disabilities and their families, but to review ways in which counseling and support by physicians may add to the coping, enrichment, and well-being of individuals and families. This positive approach is aimed at characterizing best practices as they are embodied, or could be embodied, in the health care provider–patient relationship. The various physician roles and levels of care are reviewed as contemporary arenas for counseling interactions. Newer models of holistic, community-based, family- and patient-centered care, and nonhierarchical partnerships between physicians and patients are discussed. Counseling is addressed both as an aspect of direct physician care and as a separate, more formal intervention in its own right. Specific occasions for counseling by physicians of individuals with disabilities and their families are addressed. The chapter concludes by discussing possible ways in which the training of health care professionals and the organization of health care services could improve the effectiveness of health care providers as counselors and supporters.

ROLES OF PHYSICIANS

There are aspects of the traditional physician role that are common to the role of healer in all societies. The healer has access to a body of knowledge and methods and is credentialed by society with the privilege of using his or her knowledge on behalf of the society's members. Most healers are invested with powers based on the society's beliefs. These powers include direct treatment, access to resources for further treatment and consultation (gatekeeper role), interpretation and dissemination of information, and support and advocacy. In the prescientific era and in less technologically complex societies, the healer's powers were spiritually based and strongly dependent on the society's beliefs whereas the contemporary Western physician exercises control over the utilization of science and technology on behalf of his or her patients. Professional mystique plays a less important role in investing the healer's actions with the power of belief and now may serve only to mystify or confuse (Barnlund, 1976; Emanuel & Emanuel, 1992). Paternalism and professional mystique must be replaced by clarity of language, roles, and attitudes for the physician to be an effective counselor to individuals and families. The modern physician must combine an analytic, problem-solving approach to care with an awareness of the power of the mind and spirit to affect outcomes. Now, however, it is not the mind and spirit of the healer, but rather that of the patient, that must be respected and empowered.

The expansion of medical knowledge and the evolution of its technology have engendered a process of specialization within health care. Medical services have been stratified into levels as primary, secondary, and tertiary care. Care has also been divided geographically between that which is regionally or medical center-based and that which is part of the patient's own community. Traveling to a medical center has generally come to represent the pursuit of more specialized (i.e., tertiary) levels of care. Unfortunately, in our technology-oriented society, the belief that specialization is synonymous with excellence has resulted in a tendency toward fragmented, center-based health care. Even within specialized areas of interest, such as pediatric endocrinology, lie more layers of categorical care—for example, the pediatric endocrinologist who specializes only in the care of persons with diabetes or with thyroid disease. While individuals with severe disabilities often benefit from the care of specialists with narrow but highly developed expertise, their total care cannot simply be the sum of services provided by a team of specialists. Such specialists may provide important counseling and support during specific events or treatments such as an operation or establishing medical control over seizures. However, the surgeon or the neurologist is not well-positioned to provide holistic support for the person with complex health care needs or to facilitate necessary family and community support for well-being and growth after or between health-related crises.

The primary physician (pediatrician, internist, or family practitioner) or other health care provider (nurse practitioner, physician's assistant) is the only source of care required by many people. The person with a disability or with complex health care needs requires primary care as a "medical home" from which more specialized care "away from home" may be arranged, interpreted, and incorporated into the person's overall health plan (Delbanco, 1992; Martin, 1985; Sia & Peter, 1990). The primary care medical home becomes the focus of coordination, of attention to the person and his or her family as a whole, and of support (Sia, 1992). As such, the primary care provider is in the best position to provide counseling support for individuals with disabilities and chronic illness and their families. Only the primary care provider is positioned to know the health care issues in the context of the whole person and the person in the context of the family and the community. The primary physician or health care professional is accessible and provides continuity that is often missing from tertiary medical center encounters.

In this setting, counseling may be embedded in direct medical care as, for example, empathetic inquiries about past and current issues during checkups. Or, counseling may be a separate endeavor—for example, behavioral training methods for parents who experience stress due to a child's difficult behaviors (Singer, Irvin, & Hawkins, 1988). Counseling about specific treatments and discussion of controversial therapies, such as facilitated communication for autism or vitamin therapy for Down syndrome, may also occur more easily in the primary care setting, where less emphasis is placed on a single standard practice or procedure.

In summary, the traditional role of the physician as the provider of direct care services (e.g., prevention, diagnosis, or treatment of ill health) is changing. Health promotion provides a more positive and less reactive approach to caregiving. With the explosion of new information and technology in the health care field and the evolution of specialization, primary physicians can no longer "know everything." As a consequence, primary physicians' efforts beyond direct care into such areas as counseling, advocacy, service coordination, and information dissemination are growing in importance. At the same time, consumerism has led to a demand for these services and a growing expectation of a balanced partnership in which there is equality of information and decision-making power between clients and professionals.

Counseling Interventions at the
Diagnosis of a Disability: The Informing Process

The diagnosis of a disability in a child may occur as an unanticipated event, such as the diagnosis of Down syndrome in a newborn.

The diagnosis may also occur as the confirmation or culmination of suspicions by parents that their child is not developing in a typical fashion. Finally, the diagnosis may occur following a traumatic event, such as an automobile accident or a serious illness that has altered the developmental course of a child. Often there is no diagnosis, but simply the evidence that development has been seriously affected by unknown causes. In all of these instances, there is clear evidence that "how they were told" has an important impact on the adjustment of a family to disability in one of its members (Wolfensberger, 1978).

The informing interview, as "breaking the news" about a disability is sometimes called, is much more than a transmission of new information about a child or family member. It is an occasion that demands all the elements of humanistic focus inherent in a counseling relationship. As a counseling opportunity, there are also standards of "best practice" for passing on such news that have been established through a combination of professional experience and feedback from families. Furthermore, the informing interview is actually an ongoing process over days, months, or perhaps years in which the implications of new and old information are subjected to continual review and reevaluation. This process supports families in their endeavors to find and maintain balance in their lives, which now include a family member with a disability. It is also a process that might be carried through by several different professionals. What begins as a diagnosis by a geneticist or a developmental pediatrician may be followed through on over time by a family's primary physician.

Although there are some descriptions of the informing process by thoughtful professionals, much of this work was based on a more or less pathologic model for the way in which families react to the news that they have a member with a disability. In such models, families were expected to behave in certain ways while passing through a series of stages, such as shock, anger, and denial, eventually experiencing some form of chronic stress or depression (MacKeith, 1973; Ohlshansky, 1962). Families were made to fit the current model, so that a family who made a rapid adjustment was viewed as exercising denial rather than coping in a favorable manner. Not until the late 1970s were families questioned about the informing process regarding what was helpful and what was not.

Cunningham, Morgan, and McGucken (1984) examined the reactions of 59 families to the disclosure that their newborns had Down syndrome. Over half of the sample expressed some form of dissatisfaction with the process; similar results have been reported in other studies (Gayton, 1974; Pueschel & Murphy, 1976). Common complaints reported were parents being told separately, being told belatedly, or being told in an abrupt or insensitive manner. Other parents complained that the interview was conducted as a teaching opportunity for students or by someone with whom they were unfamiliar or in whom they had little confidence. One might argue that no informing interview can be a positive experience and that these parents' concerns simply reflected their projected anger about the news itself. However, Cunningham et al. (1984) went on to study the use of a "model service" of "breaking the news" at several hospitals. This "model service" was developed based on complaints and concerns raised by families (Cunningham et al., 1984). The model included such practices as presenting the diagnosis to both parents together, doing so with the baby present and valued as a person, ensuring privacy during and after the interview, and providing easy access to support, information, and follow-up. The "model service" was compared with the experiences of families at hospitals providing a routine approach to the informing process. All of the families receiving the "model service" were satisfied with the process, and, in fact, "the positive attitude and confidence expressed . . . was particularly striking" (p. 37). Of the families in the control group receiving routine services, only 20% expressed satisfaction with the informing interview.

Clearly there are "best practices" for bearing news concerning a child's disability that provide useful guides to professional behavior. Many variations on such methods have been described (Kaminer & Cohen, 1988; Myers, 1983). Informing interviews and their follow-ups constitute emergencies that have priority over most everyday demands of professional practice. A physician assuming the awesome responsibility of informing parents about a child's disability must be emotionally prepared and be undistracted by other issues. He or she must be well-informed and must either be ready to answer questions or willing to help find the answers. A good bearer of such news proceeds with patience and acceptance, with directness and honesty, using understandable language. Listening ability is combined with tolerance both of emotions and of nonacceptance of the news at hand.

The most important elements in the informing process are a high regard for its importance for the family and a commitment by the professional to understand his or her own attitudes and beliefs about disability. It is ironic, and sometimes tragic, that this important counseling interaction is entrusted to physicians because physicians generally tend to hold more pessimistic and often inaccurate beliefs about the future for infants with disabilities when compared to other helping professionals such as social workers, psychologists, or educators. Wolraich (1980) used a survey method to present helping professionals, including physicians, with birth scenarios involving infants with Down syndrome, spina bifida, and unspecified conditions likely to cause varying degrees of mental retardation. Subjects were asked to predict skills and abilities in adulthood (prognostic beliefs) for the hypothetical newborns. Physicians consistently predicted lower levels of functioning and more restrictive living situations when compared to professionals in other fields. Fortunately, recent replication of earlier studies by the same investigators has demonstrated notable improvements in the attitudes and beliefs of physicians over a 10-year period (Wolraich, Siperstein, & O'Keefe, 1987).

In addition to the tenor and the structural aspects of the informing process, there are content elements that are important to its counseling aspects. Though families remember a variable amount of information from the initial informing interview, the importance of accurate information about their child's condition may be instrumental to their adjustment and to planning for financial and support needs. Such information may help families to redefine their visions of disability in a more positive way. It also is part of the groundwork for families to establish actions they can take or choices they can make to benefit their children. For example, a child with cerebral palsy may benefit from careful pediatric orthopedic care, ongoing physical therapy, and the use of orthotic devices. Though unhappy that their child needs such interventions, the family may welcome the opportunity to take specific action on behalf of their child. This helps with the reacquisition of a sense of control over events that is often lost when a diagnosis is imposed on a family member.

The informing process is also an opportunity to offer connections to a variety of other information and support resources. The most important of these for many families is the parent-to-parent connection with others who have been through the same experiences. This is not only a source of pragmatic tips that only families who are living through day-to-day experiences can provide, but a profound source of support for many families. Other parents can share reassurances that they have had similar feelings of despair that eventually passed or that they, too, felt guilty about wishing their child might not survive. The presence of another parent is a physical embodiment of the fact that families live through such traumas and carry on with their lives. In addition to parent-to-parent connections, the informing process can help link a family to groups of parents including support groups at the local level and advocacy and information groups at the regional or national level.

All families have coping strategies. Some have active and effective strategies, and others have less successful means of coping. Some families have been challenged more vigorously than others by past experiences. The informing process is an occasion to review how families have coped with stress in the past. Some families require information and reading material, while others need a place for tears, or prayers, or hugs. Most families will require a variety of supports. Usually, different members of a single family will have different coping strategies. In some cases, they may not be familiar with each other's coping methods under severe stress. The physician should attempt to identify a family's natural supports, such as extended family, friends and neighbors, and church, and be sure that connections to these supports are established and not disrupted or preempted by professional sources of support (i.e., social workers, therapists).

Finally, the informing process includes the beginning of a new relationship between a family and a physician. This relationship may in fact be a new one, or it may be one in need of redefinition in the new context of a family member with a disability. As such, it is an important opportunity for the physician to be a model for the family by showing that the member with a disability is welcome to the same kind of care and attention as other family members. This might include holding and cuddling a newborn and referring to him or her by name, careful attention to the use of positive descriptors about the child to balance discussions of disability and challenge, and a review of routine health care issues as they would apply to any individual of the same age. It is also a chance to review the physician's and the family's expectations about the role that the physician will play as a source of support for the family. The physician should make clear his or her philosophy of practice with regard to the balance of power and decision making in the physician–family relationship. Furthermore, in the case of older individuals with disabilities, the physician's goals for the direct doctor–patient relationship should be reviewed. Such expectations and goals may vary widely enough that serious but avoidable misunderstandings occur. A specialist also needs to clarify his or her philosophy about care and treatment goals for a person with a disability. Specialists need to define their role as distinct from that of the family's primary physician. Families may need to consider other resources or a different physician if there is a wide philosophical gap between the family's expectations and those of the physician.

Counseling Interventions After Diagnosis

The diagnosis of a disability in a child may be a single, discrete, and incontrovertible event such as the diagnosis of Down syndrome in a newborn. More commonly it is a protracted process that may or may not end in a specific diagnosis. This process may begin with intensive medical intervention following an event such as a serious head injury or a baby's premature birth. Under such circumstances, parents' hopes and energies are often devoted to supporting themselves and their child through what may be regarded by them as a traumatic but time-limited challenge. The prospects of long-term sequelae and additional diagnoses such as cerebral palsy, sensory impairment, or seizure disorder are understandably of less importance when a child's survival remains in the balance. Health care providers in a counseling role for such families must remain in touch with the family's current agenda and priorities of concern. Assumptions about what a family may or may not be "ready to hear" can and should be avoided by using the family's current concerns as a point of departure. If a child in an intensive medical care setting already shows clear evidence of significant neurologic impairment, then this represents diagnostic information about which an informing process for parents is needed. However, if the medical conditions of a child simply place him or her "at risk" for altered development or for neurologic complications, care must be taken to connect such information with parental questions about prognosis or outcome and to avoid confusing "risk" with "certainty."

In other circumstances, children with less complex medical needs may fail to develop at an expected rate or according to typical patterns. The realization that such a child's development is different usually emerges over time. Such developmental differences may become apparent in the context of developmental surveillance (Dworkin, 1989) during well-child care or may present themselves as a parental concern brought to the attention of primary health care providers. Whatever their origin, when such concerns are raised, counseling about the possibility of the child having a disability should be initiated. Traditionally, the goal of counseling in this context would be to provide information and clarify confusion in order to help families adjust and make decisions. However, with a longer and more proactive viewpoint, counseling should be one part of a system of supports that empowers parents to handle a new, often confusing, and sometimes frightening situation. In the instance where the developmental concerns are raised by the physician, parents must be made aware of the concerns promptly and honestly, know what observations caused the concerns, and hear suggestions about possible next steps both diagnostically and therapeutically. Parents also must be able to dispute such observations and participate in decision making regarding interventions. However, when developmental concerns are raised by parents, they require the same respect and response as tests and observations conducted by professionals. In fact, as a means of developmental screening, parental observations have been shown to be among the most accurate (Glascoe, Altemeier, & MacLean, 1990). Failure to take parental concerns seriously will not only undermine the partnership between parents and health care providers, but will result in the real possibility of overlooking a problem for which timely investigation and intervention are indicated.

When it becomes clear that a child's development is significantly altered, but no immediate, specific diagnosis is made, the question of cause remains unanswered. Pursuit of a diagnosis has a number of dimensions that affect the responses of health care providers. First, as a purely health-related issue, if there are possible causes that are curable or amenable to amelioration with medical interventions then further investigation may be in the child's best interests. Such possibilities need to be discussed with the child's parents and pursued promptly. Second, and of equal importance, are the various reasons that pursuit of a diagnosis may benefit a family's coping with their child's disability. Many families feel the need for a frame of reference for their child's disability, including a name to attach to the problem, other families to contact, information to examine, and visions of the future to formulate. Moreover, the pursuit of a diagnosis helps some families reestablish a sense of control or mastery over their family's and their child's destiny (Summers, Behr, & Turnbull, 1989). The process may rule out nagging feelings such as guilt that a disability was due, for example, to a medication taken during pregnancy or to exposure to lead in the mother's or child's environment. Some families may feel the need to satisfy themselves that several experts agree about the nature of a child's disability or agree that all currently available, reasonable diagnostic steps have been taken. It is an important area of counseling support for the primary physician to help families think through their needs to "find the cause" for their child's disability and to provide them access to additional opinions and reasonable medical tests. Interactions around the pursuit of a diagnosis are important opportunities for the development of a nonhierarchical partnership between the health care provider and the family. The physician's comfort with honestly saying "I don't know" helps to reinforce the notion that some questions may not be answerable. Moreover, it serves to humanize the physician and equalize the relationship between physician and family. It is important and appropriate for the family to share ownership and acceptance of a decision to end the pursuit of a diagnosis, or to begin it again in the face of new information or concerns later on. Continued effort to find a diagnosis is also a potential area of advocacy by physicians on behalf of families when there are systemic obstacles, such as managed care practices (e.g., HMOs), to some diagnostic resources or to obtaining second opinions.

Whether a child has a specific diagnosis or has a condition for which the cause is undetermined, the primary health care provider has a series of roles to play. These roles are interdependent and form the fabric of continuity in the relationship between the health care provider and the individual experiencing a disability or the individual's family. The major roles include direct care, coordination of care, informing and counseling, and advocacy (Fenichel, 1992). Though the usual encounter with a health care provider is prompted by a "direct care" need, all such encounters provide opportunities for counseling, advocacy, and coordination of care. Furthermore, in the case of individuals with complex needs, visits purely for the purpose of counseling or for the coordination of care are useful alternatives that are not always utilized. For example, the parents of a child with severe disabilities and challenging behaviors might benefit from a visit to his or her physician, without the child present, to provide time for discussion that is free of distractions or interruptions.

Whatever the reasons for encounters in a primary health care setting, each encounter is an occasion for ongoing support. This is accomplished through direct statements and indirectly through professional practice and example. Primary health care providers play a crucial role for many individuals and families in establishing and sustaining a positive vision of the future. This develops both through direct discussion of the future and through interactions along the way. When a physician's office welcomes family members with disabilities naturally and warmly and provides all of the typical aspects of health care, such as concerns for privacy and appreciation of accomplishments, it serves as an example of acceptance for both the person's family and for the community to follow. Health care providers should also support a vision of independence and inclusion. This not only pertains to encouraging and advocating for inclusion within family, educational, and community settings, but acknowledging the individual's need and right to independent treatment in the health care setting and in the community at large. Counseling in which visions of the future are discussed may also include more practical matters, such as information about guardian-ship, financial planning, and health insurance needs.

Primary health care encounters are natural opportunities to review the impact of a family member's disability on family life. It is an occasion to support and reinforce as natural a life-style as possi-ble. This may include efforts to monitor with the family the extent to which interventions will be intrusive for the person with a disability. Although intended to be helpful and supportive, service systems (e.g., health care, early intervention, family support) have a tenden-cy to portray themselves to families as crucial and necessary sup-ports, leaving families with little choice but to acquiesce to every demand and expectation. While all such formal service systems may have important roles to play, some families may need assistance in sorting out how much of which services they really require. In some instances, such formal supports may get in the way of a family's normal coping strategies and natural sources of support (Cooley, 1992b).

A truly holistic approach to a family's health in the context of a family member with a disability includes inquiries into the well-being of other family members. In the pediatric setting, attention is usually focused on the child with a disability and on the mother, who is most often present at office visits. Fathers may have different but profoundly important coping strategies and processes of adjust-ment, some of which may create added stresses for the family as a whole. Siblings' needs also must be addressed in counseling discus-sions, with intervention provided when needed.

Primary health care providers must recognize signs of stress, depression, or demoralization in family caregivers. They should be knowledgeable about typical sources of chronic stress for families such as behavior issues, sleep disorders, and financial worries (Pahl & Quine, 1987) and inquire specifically about them. A repertoire of useful suggestions or a knowledge of referral resources for address-ing these areas of stress are obviously as important as being aware of the stressors themselves. For example, would a child's sleep prob-lems be more clearly understood, and therefore possibly treated, if a formal sleep study was performed? Or could sleep problems be medi-cally related to obstructive sleep apnea or a nocturnal seizure dis-order?

Counseling Interventions During Transitions

Primary health care in its preventive orientation involves a health-promoting relationship over time. It should have a life span perspec-tive for all individuals. Among the myriad events that constitute the life experience of a person or family are many transitions. Such transitions can be archetypal and shared by all members of a society (e.g., birth, puberty, marriage, parenthood, death) or they may be artificial, arbitrary, or imposed as a result of a family member's disability (e.g., transitions from one service system to another, from periods of health to periods of illness, or from home care to hospital care). Transitions share common themes around which counseling is sometimes needed and, as such, anticipatory counseling can sometimes be provided as well. Transitions imply a move into a realm where new rules may apply, where new people will be involved, and where new language or jargon will be used. For families, transitions herald a new loss of mastery and a possible struggle to regain control and balance in their lives. Transitions often force a reliving of painful past transitions. Many parents reexperience feelings that were felt at the time of their child's diagnosis or see the need to readdress the correctness of a diagnosis at each transition. Transitions, such as going to school or finishing school, may highlight the differences between what a person with a disability does and what other individuals do at the same time in life.

A person's health may undergo transitions such as the onset of new concerns (e.g., seizures in a child with cerebral palsy) or occurrence of a major intervention such as surgery. A person's condition may change to a terminal stage, such as with muscular dystrophy or AIDS, where death is the next transition. Health care providers need to be prepared to deal with these changes not only for their implications in terms of new forms or levels of health care, but for their potentially profound symbolic and psychological importance to individuals and families.

The transitions of life (puberty, adulthood, etc.) have health care implications for everyone. For individuals with disabilities and their families, they often raise special concerns that are brought to the attention of health care professionals. The physical, hormonal, psychological, and social changes of puberty affect all individuals and all families of adolescents. These typical life events may have the same impact on individuals with disabilities, but this impact may be misinterpreted due to the disability. Issues of sexuality have a profound impact on all emerging adults and on those around them; this is not changed by the presence of a disability. Family members of adolescent females may become acutely concerned about a mixture of issues related to sexuality, including fears about exploitation, sexual behaviors, and pregnancy. Some parents raise the issue of sterilization in a naive attempt to find security from these worries. Health care providers must be knowledgeable about the rights of persons with disabilities in this regard, but be sensitive to the need for parents to discuss their concerns and address their anxieties with more appropriate interventions.

Transition to adulthood provides a new opportunity to re-address the health care provider's support of independence, the individual's right and need to leave home, and the family's obligation to begin to "let go." This is a painful and frightening transition for many parents that is often heightened in the case of a child who has required extra care and attention, who has survived medical crises, and who will continue to need some level of support in the community. In the present world of services and opportunities for adults with disabilities, this may be a transition from a rich and familiar daily routine of school attendance to a potentially less satisfying and, at the very least, less familiar life-style in the adult community. There may be periods of depression and demoralization for the person with a disability that his or her primary health care provider can recognize or anticipate in order to implement helpful interventions. Adulthood means dealing with issues such as mature and possibly intimate relationships, marriage, and parenting for the person with a disability, all of which may be areas for which counseling in the context of primary health care may be welcome. Finally, issues of aging apply both to the individual and to his or her parents, who may remain the individual's primary advocates in life if not also primary caregivers. Health care professionals play important roles in assessing the aging process, its impact on functional capacities, and the emergence of age-related complications such as Alzheimer-type dementia, for which adults with Down syndrome are at increased risk (Cooley & Graham, 1991).

Counseling Interventions about Choices

The occurrence of a chronic illness or disability in an individual or a family member is never a matter of choice. In many cases the impact of such an event on a family so undermines their sense of mastery and control that confident decision making must be relearned. The complex choices about tests, treatments, educational programs, and behavioral interventions confronting individuals and families are often made more confusing by unfamiliar jargon, disagreement among professionals, and tangential issues such as funding, eligibility requirements, and an irrational service system. Yet the successful adaptation of many families hinges to some degree on their ability to regain a sense of mastery over their lives (Cooley, 1992a).

Physicians and other health care professionals are well-positioned to facilitate the process of reempowerment for a number of reasons. First, they may be among the first involved with the family following the diagnosis of disability or disease, since most complex or severe disabilities are usually identified by physicians (Palfrey, Singer, Walker, & Butler, 1987). Second, much of the initial decision making may take place in a medical environment involving laboratory tests, brain imaging studies, consultation with medical subspecialists, and possibly medical or surgical treatments. Third, primary care professionals may have a prior relationship of trust with a family on which to build in the event that a family member has a disability. Finally, the family may perceive or believe that physicians possess knowledge and power that, when shared in a decision-making partnership with the family, will help to restore the family's self-confidence.

Counseling interactions between health care providers and individuals with disabilities or their families that involve choices or decision making are crucial opportunities. Professional behavior that supports a hierarchical, paternalistic relationship will not foster family strength and self-determination and will undermine the evolution of the family's partnership with other professionals. For example, parents of children with disabilities may be confused about how much time and energy to invest in therapeutic or educational interventions for their child that on the one hand may appear to enhance the child's progress but on the other hand disrupt natural family life on a daily basis. Individual therapists may feel strongly that their particular area of intervention is too important to be diluted or excluded. Knowledgeable primary health care providers may be able to help parents find a balance between a realistic intervention program and the provision of a natural family life-style for all family members. Part of this process involves the reinforcement of a family's confidence in their instincts and beliefs as valid considerations in the face of multiple treatment and intervention recommendations from professionals.

For individuals with complex health care needs for which extended hospitalization was, until recently, the standard practice, choices about the timing, safety, and practicality of home-based care are important occasions for counseling support of families by health care providers. The health care professional's knowledge about the risks and benefits of home- versus hospital-based care and his or her judgment about the individual's readiness to leave the hospital must be balanced with respect for the family's opinion on these issues and belief in its readiness to manage health care needs at home. In the course of a long hospitalization, many parents acquire or can be taught nursing and technical skills needed for care at home. The family's caregiving skills can be supplemented by home nursing services and other technical supports, which have grown in sophistication and complexity during the 1980s. Primary health care providers must not only be ready to support a family's choice about home-based care, but to support the provision of that care in the community. Helping families move from a vulnerable sense of dependence on hospital-based professionals and "high-tech" equipment to a confidence in their own strengths and their communities' resources and in the value of the family member's reintegration into that community is a natural counseling role for the primary health care provider.

Physicians may also be involved in profoundly important choices about the future that some families may confront. Among the most common choices for the parents of a child with a disability involve decision making about subsequent pregnancies. Parents must have the opportunity to consider and discuss accurate information about recurrence risks in cases of prenatally determined conditions. They must identify their concerns about family size and the positive role of siblings in the life of a child with a disability and on the family. As the era of prenatal diagnostic testing evolves in complexity, parents must have an unbiased source of current information and support for their decision making regarding such testing. Finally, for a few parents, the caregiving demands of a child with a disability may feel intolerably heavy. It is important for such a family to have access to a clear, nonjudgmental arena in which to air these concerns and consider possible caregiving alternatives. If informal and formal sources of family support in the community are insufficient to offset the real or perceived needs of the family, then counseling about specialized foster care, shared parenting, and/or adoption could begin in the primary health care setting.

As much as decision making and reempowerment are closely related, a family's decision-making powers are not unlimited. For example, as mentioned previously, a family acting in what they feel are their child's best interests cannot make a choice for sterilization of a child with a severe disability. Even more fundamentally, parents are not free to deny life-saving medical interventions to an infant born with a disability such as Down syndrome or spina bifida based on misinformed assumptions about pain and suffering or quality of life (Lantos, 1987; United States Commission on Human Rights, 1989). When parents raise questions about such choices, an occasion for thoughtful, frank, and well-informed counseling on the part of health care professionals presents itself. The outcome of such counseling may ultimately strengthen a family's ability to cope and carry on, but should never do so at the expense of the rights and well-being of the individual for whom decisions are being considered.

COUNSELING ROLES AND THE TRAINING OF HEALTH CARE PROFESSIONALS

As implied in the introduction to this chapter, modern physicians and other health care professionals may not be completely trained or prepared for the counseling roles described in the remainder of the chapter (Goodman & Cecil, 1987). Until recently, medical school and postgraduate medical training has tended to emphasize the technical aspects of care and to perpetuate an understanding of chronic illness and disability in a frame of reference that is pathology- and deviance-oriented. Such an orientation regards disability as irrevocably negative and does not easily find the vantage point of strengths and assets for individuals or families. Medical education must enlarge upon its efforts to alter this orientation in order to make purposeful any further efforts to provide training in counseling about disability-related issues (Desguin, 1988; Guralnick, Bennett, Heiser, & Richardson, 1987). If students learn about Down syndrome, for example, from an apparently current genetics textbook (Nora & Fraser, 1991) that characterizes persons with Down syndrome as "Mongoloids" for whom institutionalization is still a consideration then their ability to understand the need to support and empower the parents of a newborn with Down syndrome will be severely impaired. On the other hand, if instruction about Down syndrome includes presentations by parents and individuals with Down syndrome, the student is left with a lasting impression of people and families leading natural, "regular" lives (Cooley, in press).

Assuming that there is emphasis on positive, inclusionary attitudes and language about disability during medical training, time must be devoted to practical training about interviewing and counseling methods that extend to the issues experienced by persons with disabilities. This training must inevitably include and value the direct input of those individuals and their families. Postgraduate training programs must continue to incorporate a curriculum of disabilities, appropriate interventions and services, and rights and values. In addition, as some model programs are doing, trainees should have direct experience away from the health care setting in communities and homes in order to face day-to-day issues and concerns for persons with disabilities (Cooley, in press). Such experience also allows trainees to see that "normalcy" and routine are part of the lives of all families. Medical students and other trainees must be exposed to the literature of family studies and, in particular, to recent research examining family strengths as coping resources as well as common stresses that are identified by families (Singer & Irvin, 1989). Since individuals with severe disabilities or complex health care needs may continue to require support and services from a variety of professionals, health care providers need training in the roles played and methods used by other professionals and in skills needed for enhancing communication and mutual respect across disciplines.

SUMMARY

Individuals with disabilities of all types and severities now live with their families or in homes of their own in the community. They are increasingly likely to play an age-appropriate role in community life whether as fully included students in public school or as members of the competitive work force. The delivery of health care services to individuals with disabilities must correspondingly become more community-based and more accessible to families. Fragmentation of care in highly specialized clinics within distant tertiary medical centers that exclude the involvement of primary health caregivers does not allow for a useful counseling role by health care professionals. When the principles behind the notion of "comprehensive, family-centered, culturally sensitive, community-based care" (Brewer, McPherson, Magrab, & Hutchins, 1989) become fully supported as the standard for health care organization, such a counseling role can grow in effectiveness and importance.

REFERENCES

Barnlund, D.C. (1976). The mystification of meaning: Doctor–patient encounters. *Journal of Medical Education, 51,* 716–725.
Brewer, E.J., McPherson, M., Magrab, P.R., & Hutchins, V.L. (1989). Family-centered, community-based, coordinated care for children with special health care needs. *Pediatrics, 83,* 1055–1060.
Cooley, W.C. (1992a, June). *The ecology of family support.* Paper presented at the First International Congress on Serving Children With Special Health Care Needs in the Community, Washington, DC.
Cooley, W.C. (1992b). Natural beginnings—unnatural encounters: Events at the outset for families of children with disabilities. In J. Nisbet (Ed.),

Natural supports in school, at work, and in the community for people with severe disabilities (pp. 87–120). Baltimore: Paul H. Brookes Publishing Co.

Cooley, W.C. (in press). Residency training programs in developmental disabilities. In R. Darling & M. Peter (Eds.), *Families, physicians, and children with special health care needs: Collaborative medical education models.* Boston: Greenwood Press.

Cooley, W.C., & Graham, J.M. (1991). Down syndrome—an update and review for the primary pediatrician. *Clinical Pediatrics, 30,* 233–253.

Cunningham, C.C., Morgan, P.A., & McGucken, R.B. (1984). Down's syndrome: Is dissatisfaction with disclosure of diagnosis inevitable? *Developmental Medicine and Child Neurology, 26,* 33–39.

Delbanco, T.L. (1992). Enriching the doctor–patient relationship by inviting the patient's perspective. *Annals of Internal Medicine, 116*(5), 414–418.

Desguin, B.W. (1988). Preparing pediatric residents for the primary care of children with chronic illness and their families: The chronic illness teaching program. *Zero to Three, February,* 7–10.

Dworkin, P.H. (1989). British and American recommendations for developmental monitoring: The role of surveillance. *Pediatrics, 84,* 1000–1010.

Emanuel, E.J., & Emanuel, L.L. (1992). Four models of the physician–patient relationship. *Journal of the American Medical Association, 267*(16), 2221–2226.

Fenichel, E. (1992). *Promoting health through Part H.* Arlington, VA: National Center for Clinical Infant Programs.

Gayton, S.F. (1974). Down syndrome: Informing parents—a study of parental preferences. *American Journal of Diseases of Children, 127,* 510.

Glascoe, F.P., Altemeier, W.A., & MacLean, W.E. (1990). The importance of parents' concerns about their child's development. *American Journal of Diseases of Children, 143,* 955–958.

Goodman, J.F., & Cecil, H.S. (1987). Referral practices and attitudes of pediatricians toward young mentally retarded children. *Developmental and Behavioral Pediatrics, 8,* 97.

Guralnick, M.J., Bennett, F.C., Heiser, K.E., & Richardson, H.B. (1987). Training future primary care pediatricians to serve handicapped children and their families. *Topics in Early Childhood Special Education, 6*(4), 1–11.

Kaminer, R.K., & Cohen, H.J. (1988). How do you say, 'Your child is retarded'? *Contemporary Pediatrics, May,* 36–49.

Lantos, J. (1987). Baby Doe five years later: Implications for child health. *New England Journal of Medicine, 317,* 444–447.

MacKeith, R. (1973). The feelings and behaviour of parents of handicapped children. *Developmental Medicine and Child Neurology, 15,* 524.

Martin, E.W. (1985). Pediatrician's role in the care of disabled children. *Pediatrics in Review, 6*(9), 275–281.

Myers, B.A. (1983). The informing interview: Enabling parents to "hear" and cope with bad news. *American Journal of Diseases of Children, 137,* 572.

Nora, J.J., & Fraser, F.C. (1991). Autosomal chromosomal anomalies. In J.J. Nora & F.C. Fraser (Eds.), *Medical genetics: Principles and practice* (3rd ed., pp. 29–35). Philadelphia: Lea & Febiger.

Ohlshansky, S. (1962). Chronic sorrow: A response to having a mentally defective child. *Social Casework, 43,* 190–193.

Pahl, J., & Quine, L. (1987). Families with mentally handicapped children. In J. Orford (Ed.), *Treating the disorder, treating the family.* Baltimore: Johns Hopkins University Press.

Palfrey, J.S., Singer, J.D., Walker, D.K., & Butler, J.A. (1987). Early identification of children's special needs: A study of five metropolitan communities. *Journal of Pediatrics, 111,* 651–659.

Pueschel, S.M., & Murphy, A. (1976). Assessment of counseling practices at the birth of a child with Down syndrome. *American Journal of Mental Deficiency, 81,* 325.

Sia, C.C.J. (1992). Medical home and child advocacy in the 1990s. *Pediatrics, 90*(3), 419–423.

Sia, C.C.J., & Peter, M.I. (1990). Physician involvement strategies to promote the medical home. *Pediatrics, 85,* 128–130.

Singer, G., Irvin, L.K., & Hawkins, N.J. (1988). Stress management training for parents of severely handicapped children. *Mental Retardation, 26,* 269–277.

Singer, G.H.S., & Irvin, L.K. (1989). Family caregiving, stress, and support. In G.H.S. Singer & L.K. Irvin (Eds.), *Support for caregiving families: Enabling positive adaptation to disability* (pp. 3–25). Baltimore: Paul H. Brookes Publishing Co.

Summers, J.A., Behr, S.K., & Turnbull, A.P. (1989). Positive adaptation and coping strengths of families who have children with disabilities. In G.H.S. Singer & L.K. Irvin (Eds.), *Support for caregiving families: Enabling positive adaptation to disability* (pp. 27–40). Baltimore: Paul H. Brookes Publishing Co.

United States Commission on Human Rights. (1989). *Medical discrimination against children with disabilities.* Washington, DC: U.S. Government Printing Office.

Wolfensberger, W. (1978). Counseling the parents of the retarded. In A.A. Baumeister (Ed.), *Mental retardation: Appraisal, rehabilitation, and education.* London: University of London Press.

Wolraich, M.L. (1980). Pediatric practitioners' knowledge of developmental disabilities. *Journal of Developmental and Behavioral Pediatrics, 1,* 147–151.

Wolraich, M.L., Siperstein, G.N., & O'Keefe, P. (1987). Pediatricians' perceptions of mentally retarded individuals. *Pediatrics, 80,* 643–649.

7

Reducing Self-Blame and Guilt in Parents of Children with Severe Disabilities

Charles D. Nixon

Most parents make healthy adjustments to the reality that their child has a disability, but many parents who do not make adaptive adjustments experience excessive self-blame and guilt (LaBorde & Seligman, 1983). In one survey, one third of parents blamed themselves for their child's disability (Bristol & Schopler, 1984). And parents of children with disabilities seem to experience more guilt than parents of children without disabilities. From a sample of mothers experiencing major depressive disorders, Breslau and Davis (1986) found that depressed mothers of children with disabilities experience significantly more guilt than depressed mothers of children without disabilities.

Nixon and Singer (1993) have reviewed the literature that indicates the maladaptive impact of excessive parental self-blame and guilt. Guilt and self-blame in parents of children with disabilities are associated with depression, helplessness, hopelessness, and low self-esteem. Guilt and self-blame in parents of children with disabilities are also believed to disrupt parental attachment to the children, effective parenting, healthy family systems, the sexual relationships of the parents, and the ability of the parents to take care of

The study presented in this chapter was funded by grant no. H023T80013-90 between the U.S. Department of Education and the Oregon Research Institute. The opinions expressed herein do not necessarily reflect those of the funders.

their own needs. It is the judgment of those who work with parents of children with disabilities that a reduction of parental self-blame and guilt would be therapeutic.

TYPES OF SELF-BLAME AND GUILT

Using research (Miles & Demi, 1986) and clinical observations, Nixon (1989) has identified three kinds of self-blame and guilt that apply to parents of children with disabilities. The assessment of these three types of self-blame and guilt is important because each requires different types of interventions.

Causation Guilt

Causation guilt is related to the parents' belief that they contributed to the cause of their child's disability in some way. Many parents of children with disabilities conduct an extensive search to discover the cause of their child's disability, and many of them conclude that they have contributed somehow to their child's disability (Tennen, Affleck, & Gershman, 1986). Featherstone (1980), the mother of a child with a disability, says that it makes intuitive sense to make causal, self-blaming attributions:

> Our children are, as I have said, wondrous achievements. Their bodies grow inside ours. If their defects originated in utero, we blame our inadequate bodies or inadequate caution. (p. 73)

Parents believe that if they had taken better care of themselves (e.g., eliminating trips, sexual intercourse, alcohol, and stress), their child would not have been born with a disability. Kaiser and Hayden (1984) described the causal guilt of mothers:

> In fact, most expectant mothers worry at some point about the possibility of giving birth to a handicapped child. It is just not possible for them to hear all the warnings about what they should and should not do during pregnancy without considering what might happen if they slip up. The message our society gives to pregnant women is that if they do all the right things, the baby will be fine. . . . The converse, of course, while rarely stated, is certainly implied. It is not difficult to understand some of the origins of the deep guilt feelings often experienced by such mothers and their intense need to know what caused the handicap. (pp. 291–292)

Parental Role Guilt

Parental role guilt is related to the parental belief that the parent has failed to live up to self-expectations and societal expectations in the overall parent role. Parents, especially mothers, are judged in our culture as being totally responsible for the outcome of their children (Featherstone, 1980). Parents judge themselves as failures and guilty because they "should" have been able to prevent harm to their child (Miles & Demi, 1986). Parents feel that their child's "maximum developmental progress" depends on them, and they therefore blame themselves for any free time not spent with the child (Wright, Granger, & Sameroff, 1984). Featherstone (1980) relates the reaction of one mother of a child with a disability:

> Lucy Forrest says that every time she sees Christopher lying on the living room floor she thinks, "Gosh, I'm terrible. I really ought to stop this (whatever she is doing) and play with him." (p. 78)

The parental role also requires that parents should always have feelings of warmth and love toward their newborn children, but like all parents, parents of children with disabilities sometimes have ambivalent feelings (Wright et al., 1984). Parents of children with disabilities ultimately cannot live up to these ideal roles and therefore experience parental role guilt.

Moral Guilt

Moral guilt is related to the parents' belief that the child's disability is punishment or retribution for violating a moral, ethical, or religious standard. Moral guilt is related to characterological self-blame, which involves people interpreting a negative event as a deserved punishment for past deeds; this leads to helplessness, low self-esteem, and depression (Janoff-Bulman, 1979). Bristol and Schopler (1984) found that some of the parents interviewed did make statements implying that their child's disability was a punishment for some past deed. This is the reaction of one mother whose child and sister-in-law both had Down syndrome:

> So, when Lisa was born, my first reaction was that I was being punished because I wasn't charitable enough in my own heart toward my sister-in-law. In order to make me into the person I should be, I had been given a child with Down syndrome. Now this is a terrible burden to put upon yourself, but this was my initial feeling in the hospital. I worked with this feeling for a long time. (Roberts, 1986, p. 196)

Darling and Darling (1982) observed that before the birth of a child with a disability, parents often have the same negative attitude about children with disabilities that are harbored by the general public. When a child with a disability then enters their lives, they are shocked into dealing with these negative attitudes. These previous negative feelings could be the source of moral self-blaming and guilt, as was the case with the mother quoted above.

COGNITIVE APPROACH TO SELF-BLAME AND GUILT

How self-blame and guilt are understood will determine and shape clinical interventions. In the intervention described in this chapter, self-blame and guilt are understood cognitively as the outcome of how people think about, interpret, and explain negative events. For example, these are the guilt feelings of one mother within a year after the birth of her child with a disability:

> I felt a lot of guilt because I worried about Geoff living at home for the rest of his life. I needed to accept the fact that at some point in time he would live someplace else. He would eventually be someone else's concern. I needed to face that, in order to lose that black cloud, that oppressed feeling. But, at the same time, it brought on guilt because, as his mother, I should love him enough to take care of him the rest of his life, right? Another side of my guilt was that I felt, in a way, that because of the nature of Geoff's brain damage, because his placenta had separated early and caused oxygen distress, that I had let my child down—that my body had somehow betrayed him by letting that happen. And if I couldn't "do it all" and be Supermom, I was still letting him down. (Roberts, 1986, p. 204)

This mother interpreted the birth of her child with a disability as a "betrayal," and she interpreted her behavior and feelings about the birth as failing to live up to her own exacting standard of parenthood. Other parents interpret the birth of a child with a disability as a special gift or calling in life. It is the cognitive interpretation or explanation of the event that leads parents to experience self-blame and guilt.

WHY PARENTS BLAME
THEMSELVES FOR THEIR CHILD'S DISABILITY

Beck (1967) proposed that a negative view of oneself, of the world, and of the future forms a triad that leads to depression and self-blame. Not only do people feel inadequate, but they blame themselves for their inadequacies and failures. Beck believes that people tend not to be accurate information processors, and he has spent much of his time identifying cognitive distortions that lead to needless self-blame, guilt, and depression.

The Cognitive Therapy of Beck (Beck, Rush, Shaw, & Emery, 1979) proposed that changing and restructuring automatic thoughts, cognitive distortions, and negative schema would reduce self-blame and guilt. Automatic thoughts or images are appraisals of specific situations and are reflexive, involuntary, irrational, and usually lacking in awareness. Geoff's mother said that she had "let my child down," which is an automatic thought that mothers experience at the birth of a child with a disability.

Cognitive distortions involve the thinking process by which a person comes to a particular appraisal. For example, Geoff's mother said, "I should love him enough to take care of him the rest of his life, right?" "Shoulds" can be cognitive distortions that create unrealistic and rigid standards that lead to self-blame and guilt. Holon and Beck (1979) have identified six cognitive distortions: personalization, polarized thinking, arbitrary inference, overgeneralization, selective abstraction, and magnification. Burns (1980) has identified 10 cognitive distortions, which are listed in Table 1, and calls personalization the greatest source of self-blame and guilt. Personalization is the tendency to relate events to oneself even when there is no connection; that is, to blame oneself for a negative outcome over which one had no control.

Finally, schemata consist of stable patterns of cognitions that can affect a broad range of cognitive judgments. Geoff's mother was trying to live up to the schema of the "Supermom," which require that mothers always be giving, patient, kind, and loving. Schemata can filter and interpret all information and therefore can maintain irrational, self-blaming attributions and guilt feelings.

According to cognitive therapy, one reason why people excessively blame themselves is that they are programmed to do so because of negative and distorted cognitions. Some parents were global self-blamers before the birth of a child with a disability, and their child's disability simply intensified their self-blame and guilt. For these parents, cognitive restructuring of automatic thoughts, cognitive distortions, and dysfunctional schema would be very effective in reducing their self-blame and guilt.

Since the early 1980s, researchers in attribution theory have done extensive research into self-blaming attributions (explanations). One of their major discoveries was the extent to which people apparently blame themselves irrationally for negative events. Much of the research has focused on the self-blame that occurs after *one* traumatic event. Some people make self-blaming attributions for negative events over which they have no control. Self-blaming attributions have been expressed by victims of rape (Janoff-Bulman, 1979), persons with cancer (Timko & Janoff-Bulman, 1982), and parents of infants with perinatal complications (Tennen et al., 1986). Attribution therapy and research has tried to explain why people irrationally blame themselves.

According to attribution theory, people very often ask "Why?" in an attempt to find the cause of negative events that occur in their

Table 1. Examples of cognitive distortions

1. *All-Or-Nothing Thinking.* You see things in black-and-white categories. If your performance falls short of perfect, you see yourself as a total failure.

2. *Overgeneralization.* You see a single negative event as a never-ending pattern of defeat.

3. *Mental Filter.* You pick out a single negative detail and dwell on it exclusively so that your vision of all reality becomes darkened, like the drop of ink that discolors the entire beaker of water.

4. *Disqualifying the Positive.* You reject positive experiences by insisting they "don't count" for some reason or other. In this way you can maintain a negative belief that is contradicted by your everyday experiences.

5. *Jumping to Conclusions.* You make a negative interpretation even though there are no definite facts that convincingly support your conclusion.
   a. *Mind Reading:* You arbitrarily conclude that someone is reacting negatively to you, and you don't bother to check this out.
   b. *The Fortune Teller Error:* You anticipate that things will turn out badly, and you feel convinced that your prediction is an already-established fact.

6. *Magnification (Catastrophizing) or Minimization.* You exaggerate the importance of things (e.g., your mistake or someone else's achievement), or you inappropriately shrink things until they appear tiny (your own desirable qualities or the other fellow's imperfections). This is also called the "binocular trick."

7. *Emotional Reasoning.* You assume that your negative emotions necessarily reflect the way things really are: "I feel it, therefore, it must be true."

8. *Should Statements.* You try to motivate yourself with "shoulds" and "shouldn'ts," as if you had to be whipped and punished before you could be expected to do anything. "Musts" and "oughts" are also offenders. The emotional consequence is guilt. When you direct "should" statements toward others, you feel anger, frustration, and resentment.

9. *Labeling and Mislabeling.* This is an extreme form of overgeneralization. Instead of describing your error, you attach a negative label to yourself. "I'm a loser." When someone else's behavior rubs you the wrong way, you attach a negative label: "He's a louse." Mislabeling involves describing an event with language that is highly colored and emotionally loaded.

10. *Personalization.* You see yourself as the cause of some negative external event for which you were not primarily responsible.

From Burns, D. D. (1980); *Feeling good: The new mood therapy* (p. 40). New York: New American Library. Reprinted by permission.

lives (Heider, 1958). This pursuit of causal explanations enables people to organize the changing events of their lives and to perceive the world as stable, predictable, and controllable.

Parents have a need to explain their child's disability, but they experience significant ambiguity surrounding the birth and care of their child. When they are told that their child has a disability, they want to know the cause even though the cause may be unknown or ambiguous and the information and diagnoses they receive can be wrong, incomplete, or conflicting (Bristol & Schopler, 1984). Wortman (1976) has reviewed the research indicating that causal ambiguity is so aversive that people are willing to give a self-blaming explanation rather than no explanation. Because of this ambiguity, parents may make extensive searches for the cause, and this endless searching can lead to self-blaming explanations (LaBorde & Seligman, 1983; Tennen et al., 1986).

This need for a controllable, predictable world can take different forms. Wortman (1976) reviewed research suggesting that excessive self-blame may reflect a desire to gain some perceived control over a negative event ("I caused the event, and I won't let it happen again"). Blaming oneself may be more tolerable than concluding that no one knows who is to blame and/or that the person is living in a chaotic world in which negative events occur at random. Parents of children with disabilities may blame themselves in order to maintain some sense of perceived control.

The need for a predictable world also can be found in the hindsight effect (Janoff-Bulman, Timko, & Carli, 1985). The assumptions that people make about their world is called their *assumptive world.* People have an orderly and predictable assumptive world that they protect by projecting their present knowledge of a negative event to the past; they then blame themselves for not predicting and preventing the event. Many parents of children with disabilities replay all the events of the pregnancy and delivery and then blame themselves for not having predicted the presence of their child's disability. In the "victim" field of research, invulnerability is believed to be part of people's assumptive worlds, and when a negative event shatters that assumption of invulnerability, people blame themselves in order to maintain their belief in a safe, orderly world (Perloff, 1983). Parents of children with disabilities (especially those considering having another child) may blame themselves in order to maintain their belief in their own invulnerability and their belief that the world is a safe place. Another expression of this need for a predictable, orderly, controllable world can be found in the need to believe that the world is just (Lerner & Miller, 1978). If parents believe in a world in which people deserve what they get and get what they deserve, they may blame themselves for their child's disability in order to preserve their belief in a just world.

The common theme in these cognitive distortions is that some people are willing to blame themselves in order to maintain their predictable, assumptive worlds, over which they have a sense of personal control. Parents' assumptive worlds are often shattered when they learn that their child has a disability. One way for parents to rebuild a world that is controllable, predictable, orderly, safe, and just is to take the blame. The clinical goal is to help parents rebuild their assumptive world so that they can feel safe and in control again without resorting to self-blame.

Attribution theory explains excessive self-blame and guilt in a more positive way than cognitive therapy—parents self-blame in order to rebuild and maintain their view of the world as controllable, predictable, and safe. Some parents do not experience excessive self-blame and guilt before their child's disability, but they do experience excessive self-blame and guilt related to the disability.

COGNITIVE STRATEGIES AND TECHNIQUES

Cognitive therapy (Beck et al., 1979) was developed for people who are cognitively programmed to globally blame themselves whenever a negative event occurs. Cognitive therapy describes some specific cognitive restructuring strategies and techniques to help such people by changing automatic thoughts, cognitive distortions, and dysfunctional schema. Attribution therapy makes some important contributions to strategies for parents who blame themselves for their child's disability only.

The three types of self-blame and guilt (causal, parental role, and moral) and the two levels of scope (global self-blaming, self-blaming about the child's disability only) can be interacted to create a 2-by-3 grid of six distinct situations (see Figure 1). Each of these six situations requires different cognitive strategies and techniques.

CAVEAT ABOUT COGNITIVE STRATEGIES

It is obvious that parents do not fit neatly into the six kinds of parental self-blame that have been described. Parents will usually have characteristics of two or more categories. The organization of the cognitive-behavioral strategies around these six kinds of parental self-blame is an attempt to help the reader to begin the process of developing clinical strategies in particular cases. However, these

Causal self-blame	Parental role self-blame	Moral self-blame	
Global causal self-blame	Global parental role self-blame	Global moral self-blame	Global self-blame
Disability-related causal self-blame	Disability-related parental role self-blame	Disability-related moral self-blame	Disability-related self-blame

Figure 1. Six kinds of self-blame experienced by parents of children with disabilities

categories of self-blame and clinical strategies should *not* be used in a rigid way.

Global Self-Blame—Causal Guilt

The parent who experiences global self-blame and causal guilt will globally attribute any negative outcome to something that he or she did wrong. The birth of a child with a disability easily fits into this preexisting pattern of self-blame and leads to causal searches after which the parents (especially the mother) will conclude that they caused their child's disability (stress, diet, working too close to the child's birth, etc.). After the birth of a child with a disability, this kind of pattern will lead parents to blame any negative outcome for their child on themselves. The following cognitive strategies apply to the parents.

First, parents are taught a *cognitive theory of emotions*. This theory states that people's feelings are the result of their beliefs and interpretations of events in their lives. A simple illustration is effective in demonstrating this theory (Burns, 1980):

$$Event \rightarrow\rightarrow\rightarrow Interpretation \rightarrow\rightarrow\rightarrow Feelings$$

Many people see themselves as victims of their feelings and believe that their feelings just happen and are out of their control. This cognitive theory of feelings empowers parents because it increases their perceived control over their feelings. The reaction of many parents is that it never occurred to them that they had some control over their feelings.

Parents are also taught about automatic thoughts, cognitive distortions, and dysfunctional schema, and how these distorted ways of thinking can lead to self-blame, guilt, and depression. A list of cognitive distortions, such as the one in Table 1, is given to parents. With the use of concrete examples, parents understand how

against these ideas that lead to destructive self-blame. The realistic goal is not for parents to eliminate all cognitive distortions, but to reduce them enough so that they can see things in a new way.

The fifth strategy is *formal cognitive restructuring*. If self-monitoring, reality testing, and challenging does not change cognitive distortions, then they need to be restructured. Self-talk not only needs to be challenged, but new, more adaptive self-talk must be substituted in its place. For example, "shoulds" are one of the ways that parents can personalize negative events in their child's life. The "should" is the bridge that connects the negative event to the parents' actions. Parents are often told that they "should" spend a certain amount of time every night doing therapeutic exercises with their child. Parents often find these exercises burdensome and disruptive of parent–child interactions, but if they do not do them, they can become a cause of their child's lack of development. Once "shoulds" are brought into awareness and challenged, parents can be taught to say "I prefer" instead of "I should" (Kranzler, 1974). Substituting "I prefer" is not just challenging a "should," but it is also restructuring the way people think and understand themselves and the world. "I prefer" expresses the belief that the parents are in control of their lives and their feelings and are not victims of "shoulds." Implicit in "I prefer" is the idea that one can choose not to do certain things. "I prefer" also expresses the idea that one's preferences are as valid as other people's preferences. One parent who learned this skill said to the professionals who worked with her son with cerebral palsy, "I prefer not to do the exercises at home. I prefer that we find another way to provide these exercises for my child."

Summary Example of Cognitive Strategies   "Should" statements are pervasive, and detrimental effects of "shoulds" can easily be understood by parents. "Should" statements usually consist of unattainable expectations that lead to feelings of failure and guilt. Parents are especially prone to "shoulds." "Should removal" techniques, which demonstrate all the strategies that are used to change cognitive distortions, consist of the following:

1. *Cognitive Theory of Emotions*—Use the cognitive theory of emotions to become aware that "shoulds" are interpretations of events that shape our feelings.
2. *Monitor*—Count the number of "should" statements during a prescribed period of time.
3. *Reality Test*—List all the "should" statements for 1 day and say them all at once in order to realize that one is imposing on oneself unattainable expectations.

4. *Challenge*—Ask "Why should I?", which exposes automatic thoughts and cognitive distortions behind the "should" statement. Challenge the feeling: "Just because I feel I should do something doesn't mean it is what is best."

5. *Restructure*—Substitute "It would be nice if" and "I wish I could" for "shoulds." Kranzler (1974) suggests substituting "I prefer" for "I should." "Is this something I should do or something I prefer to do?"

Global Self-Blame—Parental Role Guilt

The parents who experience parental role guilt not only have a global pattern of blaming themselves for any negative event that occurs to their child, but they also attribute the negative event to being a "bad parent." These parents feel overly responsible for their children, and they believe that they are failing to live up to expectations concerning the parental role. The strategies are similar to the strategies used with global, causal self-blame. The difference is that parents experiencing global parental role guilt will have to do some cognitive restructuring of the parental role. The following are strategies for these parents.

Parents must be taught the *cognitive theory of emotions*. The strategies to teach this understanding of emotions can be found on pages 183–186.

Parents are then asked to *monitor* negative feelings, automatic thoughts, and cognitive distortions (see page 184). Any attempt to change self-blame and guilt in parents can be undermined if a parent is saying to himself or herself several or even hundreds of times a day, "I'm a bad parent." This self-monitoring is an important way of assessing automatic thoughts and cognitive distortions related to the parental role.

Reality-testing the cognitive distortions related to parenting is the next step. One parent in therapy overgeneralized by saying that she was a bad parent because she was always yelling at the children. She monitored her yelling and discovered that she had many pleasant experiences with her children each day and that her yelling occurred at stressful times, such as getting the children off to school and at dinner time. She cognitively restructured her yelling in the following conclusion: "I yell at the children because I'm stressed." She then worked with the counselor on ways to reduce the stress before school and at dinner time.

Guilt-producing cognitions need to be *challenged* by parents. Cognitive distortions must be challenged at the level of self-talk, and parents are asked to dispute negative automatic thoughts about their parenting by saying, "I'm a good parent" or something similar. Parents are also asked to list some of the things they do for their children such as feeding them, doing the laundry, telling bedtime stories, hugging them, and so forth. After each of these activities that contribute to their child's welfare, parents are asked to say something positive about their parenting. Some parents find this positive self-talk very difficult. One parent who tuned into her self-talk found she was unable to compliment her parenting:

> I found that I went a whole week without being able to say anything nice about my parenting. I knew then something was wrong. I looked a little closer and saw all the negative things I was saying about myself as a parent. Then I started saying nice things to myself about my parenting. It was hard, but I started.

One mother of a child with a disability monitored her self-talk and discovered that she was saying to herself, "I shouldn't feel this way." She was feeling tired, depressed, and in need of a respite from her child, and she was blaming herself for these feelings. When she became aware of this self-talk, she was able to conclude that there was nothing wrong with her desire for some rest.

Cognitively restructuring the parent's understanding of the parental role is often necessary. For example, parents are asked to describe the social expectations of parenthood. They usually generate a long list of qualities that describe a "perfect" parent. When these qualities are listed, parents may discover that *no one* can live up to these expectations, which are found to be unrealistic. Parents are therefore prepared to change their parenthood schema by developing alternative conceptualizations of parenthood.

Alternative conceptualizations (Beck et al., 1979) compete with existing parenthood schema. Often, creating an alternative conceptualization for a schema like parenthood is difficult. One strategy is to discover people in the parents' lives who model an alternative conceptualization of parenthood, but people may not have those kinds of models in their lives. Another strategy is to have the counselor describe alternative conceptualizations of parenthood, but many times parents have difficulty understanding and visualizing the alternative parenthood schema. One alternative that has been helpful for parents has been the conceptualization of the "good-enough parent" (Bettelheim, 1987). This concept is inherently vague, but it communicates to parents the idea that the responsibility of parents is not to be perfect but to give their children enough of the good things on which they can build their lives. It communicates to parents that there are limits even to parental responsibility.

Global Self-Blame—Moral Guilt

Parents experiencing global self-blame and moral guilt not only globally personalize the negative events that their children experience but go beyond attributing these negative experiences from being "bad parents" to being "bad people." Parents believe that all the negative events in their lives are a punishment for some past sin and that they consequently deserve such a punishment. Moral guilt is also called characterological self-blame and is closely related to depression. It is also the most difficult kind of self-blame and guilt to change.

The cognitive strategies of self-monitoring, reality-testing, and challenging are effective with causal guilt and parental role guilt, but they are not as effective with moral guilt. If self-monitoring discovered that a parent was saying in self-talk, "I deserve everything bad that happens to me," reality-testing and challenging may not be effective because of the parent's belief that he or she deserves to be punished. It is very difficult to convince parents that their moral self-blame and guilt is irrational, and any attempt to change the parents' belief is often resisted. For example, the double standard that is often seen in global self-blamers can be challenged. The double standard for moral self-blamers is the belief that one deserves to be punished for his or her own mistakes but others do not. Bringing this double standard into awareness will sometimes help parents reject the belief in deserved punishment, but many times they will simply acknowledge the irrationality of the double standard and still maintain this belief. Moral self-blame and guilt often need to be cognitively restructured first before they can be reality-tested and challenged.

If the blame is attributed to the character of the parent, then the parent can feel powerless and helpless. The central clinical goal of reducing moral self-blame is to change the attribution from character to behavior. Just as parents are encouraged to label a child's behavior as good or bad but not label the child good or bad, so parents are encouraged to switch their self-blaming attributions from their character to their behavior. One strategy is to ask parents if they intentionly caused the negative events in their lives. If they conclude that there was no intentionality, their actions can be reconstructed as bad judgment or mistakes.

Moral and characterological self-blame are closely related to depression, and if the negativity and depression are severe enough, self-blame will have to be addressed as part of a more general treatment for depression. The clinical goal is to interrupt the depressive, self-blaming cycle. For example, people stop doing enjoyable things when they are depressed (Lewinsohn & Libet, 1972). Having parents schedule pleasant events in their lives can help reduce self-blame by disrupting the depressive cycle. If the parent believes that he or she does not deserve to experience pleasant events, there could be some resistance. But having experiences that bring enjoyment can also challenge the belief that a lack of pleasure in life is a punishment for past sins.

The depression of many parents is related to the stress of parenting a child with a disability. Parents who are experiencing global, moral guilt can become helpless in the face of the overwhelming demands. Changes in environment and in routine that can reduce stress empower the parent and challenge the belief that this overwhelming stress is unchangeable and deserved. Parents are often helped by structuring the family routine so that expectations are clear and limited. Blocks of time are scheduled so that children receive special time with their parents, but time is also scheduled so that parents can be away from their children to do their desired activities. If parents can follow through on this kind of scheduling, the idea of deserved punishment will be challenged by this "deserved" time for the parents.

Other strategies to reduce negativity and depression can be used. Using any of the cognitive techniques to reduce negative automatic thoughts, cognitive distortions, and dysfunctional schema can reduce negativity and depression. Behavioral techniques used to provide respite and increase social support are helpful. Depressed people feel strange and different, so normalizing their experience and feelings is important. The clinical goal is to reduce the depression enough so that the moral self-blame can be restructured into behavioral self-blame, which leads to a reduction in the depression and to a more positive cycle.

Disability-Related Self-Blame—Causal Guilt

Parents who experience disability-related self-blame and causal guilt did not have a pattern of blaming themselves before having children with disabilities. It is usually mothers who believe that they did something that contributed to their child's disability. The parents have had all of their assumptions about the world shattered, and they are trying very hard to make sense of what happened to their child. The parents search for a cause of their child's disability and conclude that they did something that led to their child's disability. Parents believe that a stressful vacation, diet, sex late in the pregnancy, genetic deficiency, mixed feelings about the pregnancy, or any number of other things caused their child's disability.

The parents' belief that they somehow caused their child's disability can be reality-tested and challenged. The reality-test consists of checking the factual basis for this belief. Physicians and other medical professionals might be able to give expert information that shows that the parents did not cause the disability. These beliefs concerning causality can also be reality-tested and challenged by family and friends. One mother believed that she caused her child's disability because she did not get enough rest during her pregnancy. Family and friends reminded her of all the times she had carefully gotten the rest she needed during her pregnancy, and she reported feeling less guilty.

Reality-testing for this disability-related, causal self-blame is not always effective because for many parents the alternative to not believing they caused the disability is to believe that it was due to chance, which is very aversive to parents. An alternative meaning for their child's disability needs to be substituted for the conclusion that the world is a place where meaningless, negative events occur at random. Featherstone (1980) describes how each parent must find the meaning of his or her child's disability for him- or herself:

> As we learn that our child's difference need not entirely define us, we begin to fit it into the images we already have of ourselves and our lives. For we ourselves create the meaning of an event—even as important an event as a disability. We are the ones who decide how to weave this thread into the larger design. Out of the many possible ways we might use it, we choose one or two. To one parent the message of a disabled child is: "Life is harsh, but I am tough enough to survive." To another the disability says: "Everything I touch seems to wilt." (p. 222)

Here are two common meanings that parents give to their child's disability:

> Sometimes God lets things happen to us so we can learn a lesson. This is His way of talking to us. Maybe He is telling us we have to work for worthwhile things. I don't think God gives us more than we can do. He selects us to do these things because He knows we can do them. (Melton, 1968, p. 153)

> Because of Ellie I became a different person. A better person. (Featherstone, 1980, p. 228)

If parents believe they have in some way caused their child's disability, the factual basis for that belief can be reality-tested and challenged. But if the parents maintain their belief that they contributed to their child's disability in the face of the facts, the counselor should avoid getting into an argument about what is factually true. Some parents cannot eliminate this belief until they have some kind of meaning and understanding of their child's disability to replace the self-blaming explanation. The counselor cannot give a meaning for a child's disability, but a counselor can affirm meanings that are adaptive. Many times these attributed meanings have a point of view that is foreign to the counselor. But any meaning that allows the parents to rebuild and restructure their world as predictable, safe, and meaningful without the need for excessive self-blame and guilt can be validated by the counselor.

Disability-Related Self-Blame—Parental Role Guilt

Parents who experience disability-related self-blame and parental role guilt had a realistic view of parenthood before they became the parents of a child with a disability. They may have non–guilt-producing relationships with their other children but experience excessive self-blame and guilt in relation to their child with a disability. These parents are often seen as model parents because they are active in advocating for and obtaining services for their child. But in fact many of these parents are overly responsible for their child, and their view of parenthood for a child with a disability is unrealistic. These parents feel that they are required "to do everything possible for their child," "to maximize the developmental potential of their child," and "to be 100% responsible for their child." These parental requirements are absolute ideals that set parents up for self-blame and guilt when they fail to live up to these unrealistic expectations. According to this distorted view, a parent of a child with a disability must be a "Superparent."

This concept of Superparent is a social ideal that seems to be imbedded in most people's thinking. Many parents are able to maintain more realistic views of parenthood until they are confronted with their child's disability. Then this social ideal kicks in and controls the thinking of the parents in relation to their child with a disability. The cognitive distortions imbedded in this unrealistic social ideal can be identified by "shoulds," as in, "Parents should be perfect," or "Parents should always be patient." One strategy to help parents identify these cognitive distortions related to the parental role is to ask parents to complete this sentence stem: "Parents should. . . . ." "Should removal" techniques described previously could then be used.

One reality-testing technique is to ask parents if they would do things differently. Many times they evaluate their reasons for their decisions and discover that they would not change their actions. For example, one mother felt guilty that her family had not moved to another school district that had better special education services. After evaluating her decision, she realized that she had very good reasons (the impact on the rest of the family) for her decision and would make the same decision again, and she then reported that she felt less guilty.

Reattribution (Beck et al., 1979) is an important way to challenge and restructure the Superparent schema. For example, one of the important sources of *parental role guilt* for parents is the belief that they are 100% responsible for the development of their child with a disability. Since the goal of counseling would not be to eliminate the concept of parental responsibility, this belief in 100% responsibility will need to be restructured. Reattribution is a cognitive restructuring technique that consists of "deresponsibilizing" parents so that they accept part of the responsibility for events but not 100% of the blame. In reattribution, parents are asked to list all the people who have some responsibility for the development of their child (e.g., the child, the other parent, doctors, therapists, teachers, extended family). Then the parents are asked to give a percentage of the responsibility that they bear. Since they have just listed a number of other people who carry some of the responsibility, they usually describe their responsibility as less than 100%. Even if they reduce their percentage of the responsibility to 90%, this is a significant restructuring, for they now view themselves as sharing responsibility for their child's well-being. Reattribution may prepare parents to restructure their parenthood schema from Superparent to "good-enough parent."

Often a parental statement will not appear to be irrational and guilt-producing, but the meanings behind the statements can be cognitive distortions and contribute to self-blame. For example, a parent might say, "I would like some time away from my child." This is not an unreasonable desire or a guilt-producing cognitive distortion, but the meaning given by the parent to that statement ("I don't love my child") could be. The desire to have some respite from the child can be restructured to mean that if the parent gets some rest, then he or she will be more loving.

The attribution therapy technique of normalization is an effective cognitive restructuring technique for parental role guilt. The question that is asked of the parent is, "What would any reasonable parent have done in your situation?" If the actions of the "reasonable parent" and the actual parent are similar, the parent's actions can be normalized, which reduces self-blame and guilt. The counselor can also normalize by validating the feeling of the parents as normal. Klass (1990) believes that "permission-giving" reduces guilt by giving people permission to have certain feelings that provoke guilt. This permission-giving can take the form of direct endorsement ("Parents are just human") or therapist-provided information ("Most parents feel that way"). But the most effective form of normalization is social comparison with other parents of children with disabilities.

The effectiveness of social comparison as part of a group treatment is discussed later in this chapter.

Disability-Related Self-Blame—Moral Guilt

Parents experiencing disability-related self-blame and moral guilt believe that their child's disability is a punishment for some past sin. These parents can usually identify a particular transgression in the past that makes them subject to such a "punishment." The transgression can be related to sexuality, such as promiscuity, having a baby out of wedlock, or having an abortion. It can be associated with legal and life-style issues, such as using and selling drugs or "wasting" one's life. It can be connected to treating other people badly, such as family, friends, or people who are "different."

Moral self-blame is characterological self-blame and is more detrimental to psychological well-being than causal self-blame, which focuses on behavior. As already stated, one constant clinical goal for moral self-blame is to help people change their attributions of self-blame from their character to their behavior. For example, moral self-blame can be restructured into "mistakes" or "bad judgments," which are forms of behavioral self-blame. Once the moral self-blame has been restructured as behavioral self-blame, it can be reality-tested and challenged. One mother whose child suffered from fetal alcohol syndrome illustrates this clinical strategy.

> I finally realized that I did not intentionally harm my baby. I was addicted, and I didn't know what I was doing. I made a mistake, and I'm going to do everything possible to make it up to my baby, but I am not a terrible person.

In most cases the cause of a child's disability is not known, but even in this case where the mother clearly harmed her child, the mother found it therapeutic to accept responsibility for her actions but not to condemn herself as morally guilty.

Even though this kind of moral self-blame is related only to a child's disability, it can lead to a negative, self-blaming cycle. It has been noted by parents and other observers that after the birth of a child with a disability, parents tend to become more socially isolated. For many different reasons, friends and family withdraw their social support. For a parent who is experiencing moral guilt and self-blame, this withdrawal of social support is confirmation that the parent has a stigma and deserves to be isolated. Parents blame themselves for this withdrawal of social support, and in this social situation irrational ideas such as the belief that they deserve to have a child with a disability grow. The self-blaming leads to deeper depression, which leads to more withdrawal of social support, which in turn leads to more depression and self-blame.

The lack of support from a spouse is especially painful. One mother could think of only one reason why her husband did not help with the care of their child with a disability: He blamed her for their child's disability. In counseling he could not convince her that he did not blame her. She finally blurted out that if he loved her and did not blame her, he would help her care for their child. She specifically asked for help during the most stressful time of the day for her—bedtime. The husband began to take responsibility for putting the child to bed, and the mother's depression and self-blame was reduced. The husband's support allowed her to say, "My husband doesn't believe I deserve these overwhelming demands, and I don't believe it either."

This depressive, self-blaming cycle can be disrupted by increasing social support. Helping parents reconnect with their social support networks can be very important in preparing parents to look at their self-blame differently. Parents sometimes discover that they are not being blamed by others, but others have stayed away because they felt awkward and did not know how to help. Family and friends must be made to realize that it is not their responsibility to remove the pain for the parents and that they should continue being there for them.

There is always one part of many parents who self-blame that doesn't believe that all the negative events in their lives are a deserved punishment for past sins. It's the part that doesn't believe that they intentionally hurt their child. It's the part that doesn't believe that they deserved to be treated differently than others. It's the part that doesn't believe that they deserve to meet all the demands of their child alone. For these parents, the goal is to get in touch with that part of themselves and challenge this irrational belief that negative events associated with a child with a disability are deserved punishments.

HOMEWORK

Homework is important in developing skills such as self-monitoring, reality-testing, and challenging and restructuring automatic thoughts, cognitive distortions, and dysfunctional schema. Homework assignments ask parents to monitor and write down their cognitive distortions and then to challenge these cognitive distortions with a rational, positive statement about themselves. Parents are given simple forms with column headings such as "Stressful Event," "Negative

Feelings," "Automatic Thoughts," "Cognitive Distortions," and "Rational Response." Burns (1980) gives examples of many different forms that can be used.

Many parents have difficulties doing this self-monitoring. The self-talk of some parents is so far out of awareness that they are unable to readily obtain it. Some parents claim that they simply do not understand the concept of "self-talk," which seems to be too abstract an idea for some concrete-thinking parents. Time must be spent examining concrete situations found in these parents' lives and helping them to discover their self-talk in those situations ("When you are getting the children off to school and nothing is going right, what do you think to yourself?").

Many parents live such stressful lives that they find it difficult to find the time to self-monitor. The amount of time for self-monitoring can be negotiated with parents; even 15 minutes during stressful moments of the day can be very insightful. Other parents will claim to not have done the self-monitoring homework, but what they often mean is that they did not write it down. In discussions about their experience during the last week, it becomes apparent that they have been doing some self-monitoring.

The primary goal is to have parents practice and reinforce skills they have learned. Other important goals of homework are to bring cognitive distortions into awareness and challenge them, to disrupt the reinforcing patterns of cognitive distortions, and to reinforce the parents' belief that they can have some control over their thoughts and feelings.

THE IMPORTANCE OF GROUP TREATMENTS

All the strategies to reduce self-blame and guilt in parents that have been described can be used in a group format. Parents will not receive as much individual attention to their problems, but group treatments of self-blame can better provide the opportunity for social comparison than individual treatment can. The basic principle of social comparison theory is that our comparisons with others affect how we feel about ourselves (Festinger, 1954). There are social comparisons that can have a negative impact on parents of children with disabilities. Comparing themselves with parents of a "miracle" child who has overcome his or her disability or with parents of children without disabilities increases self-blame and guilt (Featherstone, 1980). Comparing themselves with other parents who have children with disabilities and who are extremely depressed and overwhelmed increases the negativity directed at themselves and their situation. But social comparison is very helpful when parents compare themselves with parents in similar situations. This means that in selecting parents for a treatment group, the severity of their child's disability should be in some similar range. It also means that parents who act as if they have no problems with their child's disability or who are extremely depressed and overwhelmed should not be selected for the group.

Social comparison reduces self-blame and guilt in parents in ways that are similar to the strategies previously described in this chapter. Whereas parents often see information-giving from people who have not gone through the same experiences as controlling and demanding, they will accept information from parents who are in a similar situation (Thoits, 1986). Reality-testing information, facts, and assumptions of parents that contribute to self-blame and guilt by means of social comparison is very effective.

Negative beliefs, such as "I'm a bad parent," can also be reality-tested by social comparison. Social comparison gives parents important information about how they are doing as parents because they can compare themselves to other parents. Social comparison restructures the belief to "I'm a bad parent compared to other parents like me." Most parents compare themselves with other parents and conclude that they are doing about as well as other parents are in their situations. Social comparison therefore normalizes their experiences as parents and reduces the feeling that they are strange and isolated. For example, many parents experience a shrinking of their social support network, and they blame themselves for the loss: "What is wrong with me?" But when they hear other parents talking about how their family and friends backed off from them, their experience is normalized and they are able to say, "It's not just me." One single mother of a child with a disability said this about her support group:

> The other moms filled a very real need. And I found I could talk about bad feelings like resentment and even a sort of dislike toward my disabled son, and they had similar feelings. We helped each other and cried together and took our kids out together, so that we didn't feel like the only ones who had a disabled child. That really helped. (Stagg & Catron, 1986, p. 285)

In a group of parents who are in similar situations, almost anything can be normalized. In one treatment group, parents trusted one another enough to share humorous stories about their children. But these stories were not about cute little things their children had done, but about feces and spit and thrown food. As they laughed with one another, their sense of humor was normalized: They weren't the only ones who thought these things were funny.

Social comparison sometimes is the most effective strategy for reducing self-blame and guilt. For example, a parent described how she felt very guilty because her son with a disability periodically got out of the house and roamed the streets. The mother had brought in locksmiths and had the most sophisticated locks available installed. She had taken every reasonable precaution, but her son still discovered creative ways to get out of the house. Reality-testing by telling her that she had taken every reasonable precaution did not help to reduce her self-blame and guilt. But having other parents describe how their children had run out into the street, got lost at the mall, or climbed onto the roof did seem to help. Social comparison was more effective than reality-testing in reducing self-blame and guilt. Parents can validate the feelings and experiences of other parents in ways that no one else can.

Group treatment and social comparison also enhance other strategies. The goal of self-monitoring is to emphasize cognitive distortions that lead to self-blame. In a group treatment, the shared experiences of one parent will stimulate awareness in another parent. The group format also provides an opportunity to challenge the double standard of many parents: the application of standards and rules to themselves that they would never apply to other people. After a group exercise of determining the percentage of responsibility for their children, one mother said, "You (other parents) are not 100% responsible for your children, but I am." Her irrational overresponsibility had already been challenged, so no one in the group challenged it further. But a few weeks later, she said that she had changed her mind about being totally responsible for her child.

Parents must find their own meanings for their child's disability, and no one can provide a meaning for them. But in groups of parents in similar situations, parents share the meanings they have given to their child's disability. It is not surprising that some parents choose a meaning from this "menu" of meanings provided by the group of parents. This is another example of what group counseling can provide that individual counseling cannot.

STUDY

A research study was conducted to measure the intervention effect of a 5-week class on self-blame and guilt in parents of children with severe disabilities (Nixon & Singer, 1993). Each session was 2 hours in length. The following is a brief outline of a 5-week group intervention for self-blame:

Week 1: Cognitive model of emotions
Week 2: Strategies to deal with cognitive distortions of parents
Week 3: Cognitive distortions related to issues of control
Week 4: Explaining negative events
Week 5: Parental role and self-blame

Fifty-eight parents were randomly assigned to treatment and control groups. Thirty-four mothers (18 in treatment and 16 in control) completed the Situational Guilt Scale (Klass, 1983, 1987) pretreatment and posttreatment. By an analysis of covariance, the difference in scores on the Situational Guilt Scale at posttest for the treatment (257.1) and control (285.9) groups were significant (alpha = .05). The treatment was therefore successful in reducing self-blame and guilt in parents of children with severe disabilities. The conclusion of the study was that not only were the cognitive therapy strategies successful in reducing self-blame and guilt, but social comparison also contributed greatly to this reduction. A manual of this treatment can be obtained from the author at 2610 Windsor Circle East, Eugene, Oregon 97405.

SUMMARY

For parents of children with disabilities, self-blame and guilt are related to an assortment of problems, such as helplessness, that interfere with effective parenting. This chapter has identified the different types of self-blame and guilt that parents experience and has identified cognitive strategies that are helpful in reducing these negative thoughts and feelings. This therapeutic process encourages parents to become involved in making changes, and parents learn that they are not helpless but can actively take steps to change self-blame and guilt. The ultimate goal of these strategies is to empower parents as individuals so they can become more effective parents.

REFERENCES

Beck, A.T. (1967). *Depression: Clinical, experimental, and theoretical aspects.* New York: Hoeber.
Beck, A.T., Rush, A.J., Shaw, B.F., & Emery, G. (1979). *Cognitive therapy of depression.* New York: Guilford Press.

Bettelheim, B. (1987). *A good enough parent: A handbook on child-rearing.* New York: Alfred A. Knopf.

Breslau, N., & Davis, G.C. (1986). Global stress and major depression. *Archives of General Psychiatry, 43*(4), 309–314.

Bristol, M.N., & Schopler, E. (1984). A developmental perspective on stress and coping in families of autistic children. In J. Blacher (Ed.), *Severely handicapped young children and their families: Research and review* (pp. 91–141). New York: Academic Press.

Burns, D.D. (1980). *Feeling good: The new mood therapy.* New York: New American Library.

Darling, R.B., & Darling, J. (1982). *Children who are different: Meeting the challenges of birth defects in society.* St. Louis: C.V. Mosby.

Featherstone, H. (1980). *A difference in the family: Life with a disabled child.* New York: Basic Books.

Festinger, L. (1954). A theory of social comparison processes. *Human Relations, 7,* 117–140.

Heider, F. (1958). *The psychology of interpersonal relations.* New York: John Wiley & Sons.

Hollon, S.D., & Beck, A.T. (1979). Cognitive therapy of depression. In P.C. Kendall & S.D. Hollon (Eds.), *Cognitive-behavioral interventions: Theory, research, and procedures* (pp. 153–203). New York: Academic Press.

Janoff-Bulman, R. (1979). Characterological versus behavioral self-blame: Inquiries into depression and rape. *Journal of Personality and Social Psychology, 21,* 161–177.

Janoff-Bulman, R., Timko, C., & Carli, L.L. (1985). Cognitive biases in blaming the victim. *Journal of Experimental Social Psychology, 21,* 161–177.

Kaiser, C.E., & Hayden, A.H. (1984). Clinical research and policy issues in parenting severely handicapped infants. In J. Blacher (Ed.), *Severely handicapped young children and their families: Research and review* (pp. 275–317). New York: Academic Press.

Klass, E.T. (1983). *Guide to the use of a situational self-report measure of guilt.* Unpublished manuscript, Hunter College, City University of New York.

Klass, E.T. (1987). Situational approach to assessment of guilt: Development and validation of a self-report measure. *Journal of Psychopathology and Behavioral Assessment, 9*(1), 35–48.

Klass, E.T. (1990). Guilt, shame, and embarrassment: Cognitive-behavioral approaches. In H.L. Leitenberg (Ed.), *Handbook of social and evaluation anxiety* (pp. 385–414). New York: Plenum.

Kranzler, G. (1974). *You can change how you feel.* Eugene, OR: Author.

LaBorde, P.R., & Seligman, M. (1983). Individual counseling with parents of handicapped children: Rationale and strategies. In M. Seligman (Ed.), *The family with a handicapped child: Understanding and treatment* (pp. 261–284). San Francisco: Harcourt Brace Jovanovich.

Lerner, M.J., & Miller, D.T. (1978). Just world research and attribution process: Looking back and ahead. *Psychological Bulletin, 85,* 1030–1051.

Lewinsohn, P.M., & Libet, J. (1972). Pleasant events, activity schedules, and depression. *Journal of Abnormal Psychology, 79,* 291–295.

Melton, D. (1968). *Todd.* Englewood Cliffs, NJ: Prentice Hall.

Miles, M.S., & Demi, A.S. (1986). Guilt in bereaved parents. In T.A. Rando (Ed.), *Parental loss of a child* (pp. 97–127). Champaign, IL: Research Press.

Nixon, C.D. (1989). *The treatment of self-blaming attributions and guilt feelings in parents of severely developmentally disabled children.* Unpublished doctoral dissertation, University of Oregon, Eugene.

Nixon, C.D., & Singer, G.H.S. (1993). A group cognitive behavioral treatment for excessive parental self-blame and guilt. *American Journal of Mental Retardation, 97*(6), 665–672.

Perloff, L.S. (1983). Perceptions of vulnerability to victimization. *Journal of Social Issues, 39*(2), 41–61.

Roberts, M. (1986). Three mothers: Life-span experiences. In R.R. Fewel & P.F. Vadasy (Eds.), *Families of handicapped children: Needs and supports across the life span* (pp. 193–220). Austin, TX: PRO-ED.

Stagg, V., & Catron, T. (1986). Networks of social supports for parents of handicapped children. In R.R. Fewell & P.F. Vadasy (Eds.), *Families of handicapped children: Needs and supports across the life span* (pp. 279–295). Austin, TX: PRO-ED.

Tennen, H., Affleck, G., & Gershman, K. (1986). Self-blame among parents of infants with perinatal complications: The role of self-protective motives. *Journal of Personality and Social Psychology, 50,* 690–696.

Thoits, P.A. (1986). Social support as coping assistance. *Journal of Consulting and Clinical Psychology, 54,* 416–423.

Timko, C., & Janoff-Bulman, R. (1982). *An attributional model of coping with breast cancer.* Paper presented at the annual meeting of the American Psychological Association, Washington, DC.

Wortman, C.B. (1976). Causal attributions and personal control. In J. Harvey, W. Ickes, & R.F. Kidd (Eds.), *New directions in attribution research* (Vol. 1, pp. 23–52). Hillsdale, NJ: Lawrence Erlbaum Associates.

Wright, J.S., Granger, R.D., & Sameroff, A.J. (1984). Parental acceptance and developmental handicap. In J. Blacher (Ed.), *Severely handicapped young children and their families: Research in review* (pp. 51–90). New York: Harcourt Brace Jovanovich.

8

The Self-Esteem Parent Program

Quantitative and Qualitative Evaluation of a Cognitive-Behavioral Intervention

Bonnie Todis, Larry K. Irvin,
George H.S. Singer, and Paul Yovanoff

Since the early 1980s, opportunities for persons with disabilities to be included in societal roles have multiplied. However, some children with disabilities are denied access to those avenues that lead toward positive life careers and are put at risk of experiencing failure and social rejection in home, at school, and in community environments (Cruikshank, 1976; Lindemann, 1981). Success in these settings requires a combination of skills and attributes that are often referred to collectively as *self-esteem, self-efficacy,* or *mastery motivation.* Singer and Irvin (1988) have developed a model, based on Harter's model of mastery motivation (Harter, 1981), that describes the dynamics whereby some children acquire a generalized positive orientation toward achievement and striving, whereas others become discouraged and avoid opportunities and challenges. Ac-

The study reported in this chapter was funded by grant no. H023T80013-90 from the U.S. Department of Education, Office of Special Education and Rehabilitative Services. The views expressed herein do not necessarily reflect those of the funder.

cording to this model, mastery motivation is learned through a process of opportunities to act and repeated behavioral action paired with reinforcement for success. Learned helplessness, which is the opposite of mastery motivation and is characterized by passivity, avoidance, self-denigration, and internalization of devalued social status, is also a learned behavioral disposition. Children who are denied opportunities to experience success, who are punished for attempts that yield less than perfect results, or who encounter repeated failure may acquire a general passivity or resistance to task performance.

Singer and Irvin (1988) have conducted a 4-year research project to test this model. Specifically, they have concentrated on identifying the factors in home, school, and community environments that contribute to the development of high self-esteem or to learned helplessness of school-age children with physical disabilities. The results of these studies, based on quantitative and qualitative data from children and adults with disabilities, their families, and their educators, support the importance of environmental characteristics in the development of self-esteem in this population.

In addition, children with high self-esteem had parents with authoritative rather than authoritarian or permissive parenting styles. These three styles or patterns of family interaction have been delineated by Baumrind and her colleagues (Baumrind, 1971, 1973; Baumrind & Black, 1967) and have been shown to be differentially related to academic and psychosocial outcomes (Dornsbusch, Ritter, Liederman, Roberts, & Fraleigh, 1987; Steinberg, Elemen, & Mounts, 1989). Authoritarian parenting is characterized by a high degree of parental control, emphasis on obedience and respect for authority, and discouragement of give and take. Permissive parents are tolerant toward the child's impulses, use as little punishment as possible, make few demands for mature behavior, and allow considerable self-regulation by the child. Authoritative parenting exhibits the following elements: high, appropriate standards for the child's behavior; firm enforcement of these standards, using commands and sanctions when necessary; encouragement of the child's independence and individuality; open communication between parents and children; and recognition of the rights of both parents and children (Dornsbusch et al., 1987). Several specific factors were found to be critical to fostering children's self-esteem: having opportunities to make choices, being responsible for self-care and household tasks, participating in leisure activities, interacting with peers, practicing assertiveness, learning to cope with difficult situations and accept the consequences of one's actions, and having parental advocates who teach self-advocacy skills (Irvin & Todis, 1992).

In the third and fourth years of the project, a cognitive-behavioral intervention was developed to teach parents of children with physical disabilities and mild cognitive disabilities some practical ways to use these findings. The aims of the intervention were: 1) to raise parental awareness of the importance of self-esteem; 2) to identify environmental and psychological barriers that prevent children from participating in environments and activities that foster self-esteem; 3) to help participants to modify attitudes and beliefs, parenting practices, home environments, and family activities in order to overcome these barriers; and 4) to demonstrate that such an intervention would increase child behaviors that are associated with the development of high self-esteem. By providing information about the relationship between parent behavior and child self-esteem, the intervention prompted parents to consider and act on cognitive representations of effective parenting as fostering progressively increasing child autonomy rather than controlling and protecting the child.

This chapter describes the quantitative and qualitative outcomes of the field test of the intervention. Qualitative parent evaluations and data from quantitative measures are consistent in notable respects, in spite of the difficulty in measuring some of the outcomes and the small number of participants in the intervention study.

METHOD

Participants

Participants were recruited through a public school serving children with physical disabilities in preschool through Grade 5. The school social worker distributed consent to contact forms to parents of children between the ages of 6 and 12 with little or no cognitive disability but who have moderate to severe physical disabilities. Approximately 20 forms were distributed; seven families responded, requesting more information. Of these, three families participated in the intervention groups.

Participants were also recruited through two local hospitals serving children with physical disabilities. Fliers describing the program were posted and hospital staff distributed consent to contact forms to interested parents. Two participating families, one whose children were home-schooled and another from a nearby state, learned about the program in this way.

Families who had previously participated in the self-esteem project were also invited to attend. Of the 16 families who had completed measures, interviews, and observations related to children's self-esteem, 11 had children who met the criteria for participation in the parent intervention program (i.e., between the ages of 6 and 12 and with little or no cognitive disability). One family had moved, one declined to participate, and two were unable to attend because of schedule conflicts. The field test of the intervention, therefore, included seven families who had previously participated in the self-esteem project, three families recruited through the public school, and two who learned about the program through a hospital clinic.

Eight of the families were represented by mothers, both in the measures that were collected and in class meetings. Of these, three were single parents. Two families were represented by fathers, neither of whom was a single parent. One couple attended most class meetings together. One child was represented by his maternal grandmother and his stepmother, who attended all class meetings together.

Participants were randomly assigned either to an initial intervention or a wait-list group. The five families in the initial group, including three families who had previously participated in the project, one family whose child was recruited through the school, and one family recruited through the clinic, met weekly for 6 weeks in January and February 1992. The intervention procedures were then repeated with the wait-list group in March and April. In order to accommodate as many participants as possible, the wait-list group met in two sessions, one in the afternoon and the other in the evening. This group consisted of four families who had previously participated in the project, two whose children attended the school, and one who was recruited through the clinic.

In general, the division of the participants into groups was designed for the convenience of the participants and to produce small groups for weekly meetings to enhance and maximize program effects. The original intention was to evaluate program effects with data from both treatment and wait-list groups. But, as is detailed later, because there were only five to eight participants per group, data from both groups were combined in order to evaluate preintervention–postintervention differences.

Although all participating parents had children in the same age group with physical disabilities and normal cognitive functioning, the families were surprisingly heterogeneous. The severity of disability ranged from mild (weakness in one limb) to severe (ventilator dependent); family size ranged from one to seven children, with three of the larger families having several adopted children with disabilities; family socioeconomic status ranged from blue-collar to high upper-middle class; and parenting styles included authoritarian, authoritative, and permissive approaches.

MEASURES

At both preintervention and postintervention occasions, each participant completed five written forms and two interviews. These are described below.

Quantitative Data

Written Measures   These included the Family Information Form, the Modified Parent Expectation Questionnaire, the Child Improvement Questionnaire, the Self-Esteem Parent Program Questionnaire, and a social validation measure.

The Family Information Form is a 16-item questionnaire about family income and education, number and ages of family members, and the disabilities of the target child.

The Modified Parent Expectation Questionnaire (PEQ) (Powers, 1992) is a 39-item measure consisting of two subscales. The first subscale, which consists of 29 items, assesses the extent to which parents expect their children to participate in household and social activities, to cope with difficult situations, to behave assertively and appropriately, to engage in self-advocacy, and to discuss their disabilities. The second subscale includes 10 items for which the parent rates his or her ability to help the child in each of the content areas covered by the instrument. In both subscales the parent circles the appropriate response on a 4-point Likert scale, ranging from a little (1) to a lot (4). The PEQ has a reliability coefficient alpha of .93 on the child subscale and .90 on the parent subscale (Powers, 1992).

The Child Improvement Questionnaire (CIQ) is adapted from the CILC Scales by DeVellis, DeVellis et al. (1985). Using a 5-point Likert scale, parents indicate whether they agree, disagree, or are undecided about 27 statements concerning why children with disabilities do or do not change or make progress. The underlying constructs are the extent to which respondents are oriented to locus of control as external or internal regarding the progress of the child with a disability.

The Self-Esteem Parent Program Questionnaire was developed by project staff to measure three types of changes related to program objectives: 1) how *important* the factor is, 2) *how well the child performs* in that area, and 3) the *parent's ability to help the child* in that area. The questionnaire consists of 22 questions related to the themes presented in the parent classes: choice and responsibility, leisure activities, peer interaction, assertiveness, coping, parent advocacy, and self-advocacy. This approach to evaluation is a social validation strategy (Wolf, 1978) in which perceptions of the significance of program goals and the *perceived* effects of the program are documented from the perspective(s) of those who are directly affected by it.

Additional Social Validation Measure   When parents had completed the intervention, an additional social validation measure was included in the packet with the other written measures. For each of the six class topics, parents were asked to rate the extent to which they had seen a change in their child's behavior that they attributed to their own participation in the intervention program. Change was rated on a 4-point Likert scale: no change (1), a little more (2), somewhat more (3), and a lot more (4). Parents were also asked to list specific changes in each area that were directly related to the program. The form also included a 12-item satisfaction/acceptability rating of various technical aspects of the program, such as program content and format, presentation, and scheduling.

Interviews   Two measures—an adaptation of the Landman Parent Interview (Landman, 1978) and an activity checklist—were administered in a face-to-face interview format. The Landman Interview was adapted from a measure used in a dissertation study to assess parent protectiveness and expectations (Landman, 1978). In the adaptation of the Landman Parent Interview, parents were asked to indicate whether their children engaged in activities such as staying home alone, talking on the phone, getting around the community, or spending the night at a friend's house. If the child had not done an activity, the parent was asked if the child could do such activities if given the opportunity. For both questions, the parent was also asked to rate the level of assistance that is or would be required for child performance (0 = none, 4 = maximum).

The Activity Checklist is an adaptation of a measure by Sowers (1982). For the purposes of this study, the checklist consisted of four sections: participation in household activities, participation in leisure activities, involvement with peers, and self-care activities. In the first three sections, parents were asked to indicate the frequency of the child's participation in specific activities, the level of assistance required, and with whom the child had done the activity. For self-care activities, only the level of assistance and the person providing assistance were recorded. Parents' comments and qualifying remarks related to each question were also recorded and incorporated in the qualitative data set.

Qualitative Data

The project coordinator, who was one of the intervention class facilitators, kept a detailed log of class meetings and telephone calls to class participants. The log contained descriptions of class activities and discussions, parent comments or suggestions presented in class, and strategies and experiences that parents shared with each other. It was also used to record the impressions of the two class facilitators regarding parents' responses to the class content and activities, the impact of various features of the program, and ideas for improving the class format and interactions.

The telephone call log recorded participants' comments, both positive and negative, about other participants and about the meetings in general, the ways by which parents had implemented ideas presented in class, and parents' reports of the impact of the implementation. In the log of the second intervention group, the project coordinator also noted differences between the first and second intervention in terms of participant response to the program or to the materials.

The class log was prepared on a computer and was analyzed as described in the data analysis section below. The comments from the social validation measure of child changes attributed to parent participation in the program were also entered into a computer file and qualitatively analyzed.

PROCEDURES

All participants completed the first round of the measures, excluding the additional social validation measure, prior to implementation of weekly group meetings.

The groups met at the school for children with physical disabilities through which recruitment of participants for the study had occurred. Meetings were held in the faculty lounge, in one of the classrooms, or in the cafeteria in the late afternoon or evening when children and staff had left.

Description of Intervention Program

The intervention was titled "Something To Grow On." In each of the six weekly lessons a theme related to developing feelings of competence and self-esteem was presented and discussed. These themes were: developing independence through choice and responsibility, participating in leisure activities, interacting with peers, being assertive, coping with tough situations, and advocacy skills for parents and self-advocacy for children. The themes had emerged from previous interviews with adults who grew up with disabilities and who are now personally and professionally successful and from interviews and observations in families in which children with disabilities have high self-esteem.

The themes were presented in the order listed above and built upon each other. Thus, choice, responsibility, and participation in leisure activities with family and with peers were presented early and were discussed and encouraged throughout the entire 6 weeks within the context of each week's theme. Assertiveness was presented as most usefully learned in conjunction with the preceding activities and as a component of the skills that follow, effective coping and advocacy. Coping with difficult situations such as teasing, failure, disappointment, and rejection was treated as a normative childhood experience when children are appropriately engaged in leisure activities with peers. Self-advocacy was also presented as a logical outcome when children have been encouraged to be autonomous, to participate in integrated activities, to assertively manage their own care, and to cope with difficult situations effectively.

Class Format   The class format was based on the authors' previous experiences in conducting groups for parents of children with disabilities. Several parent interventions on various topics including stress management and behavior management have been developed and field-tested (Singer & Irvin, 1990; Singer, Irvin, & Hawkins, 1988; Singer, Irvin, Irvine, Hawkins, & Cooley, 1989). Meeting weekly for several weeks for about 1 1/2–2 hours for a combination of presentation, discussion, and activities has proven both feasible and effective for parents of children with disabilities, particularly if a child care stipend is provided. Each class was introduced with a videotape presenting the week's theme. In each video, some of the adults who participated in the interviews told about their experiences related to the theme of the week, and parents of children with disabilities shared their concerns and strategies. The on-camera interviews were interspersed with narration highlighting the important points for parents to remember, with footage of children engaged in activities related to the theme and with still photos of the adult interviewees when they were children.

Following a brief discussion of the ideas presented in the video, the group leader discussed the importance of the week's theme and its relationship to self-esteem. Much of this information was also contained in a manual provided for each parent or couple. For each lesson the manual contained a review of the important points presented in the video, in-class activities designed to stimulate discussion of the current theme, and worksheets for planning ways to implement activities related to the theme during the coming week.

Throughout the meeting, discussion among parents and between parents and the group leader was encouraged. Parents were invited to share their experiences related to the week's topic, to offer suggestions, and to ask for advice. Following the video and group discussion of the weekly theme, parents worked individually or in small groups to plan ways to incorporate ideas related to the theme into their family activities. Parents were encouraged but not required to role-play interactions that they felt might be problematic or that required the use of new skills with their children or with professionals. At the end of each class, each parent or couple presented a plan for the coming week that targeted activities related to the current theme. Beginning in Week 2, before the video, each parent or couple reviewed for the group how their planned activity was carried out and what their child's response was.

In answering participants' questions and addressing their concerns during class discussions, the group facilitators encouraged parents to reframe the parenting role from protection and caregiving to structuring the environment to present opportunities for growth and appropriate challenges. The difficulty some parents experienced in altering their parenting approach was normalized by the facilitators, who emphasized that all parents find it challenging to balance their responsibility to protect their children from harm with the equally important responsibility of guiding them toward independence.

In all six class meetings, the facilitators encouraged parents to consult with their children about their preferences in activities and their concerns related to the various class themes. Role-plays were presented that illustrated the effectiveness of several techniques in helping children talk about their feelings, as were helpful responses parents can make that develop children's problem-solving skills and ability to cope effectively with difficult situations. To use the recommended communication techniques, some parents needed to reframe their parenting role from authoritarian to authoritative; other parents need to provide support rather than solutions and directives.

During each week between classes, staff members telephoned parents. The original intention of the telephone calls was to prompt parents to implement their planned activities and to help them to remove barriers to those activities. However, parents had often carried out their planned activity before the calls were made and often had other related activities to report. The telephone calls, therefore, became opportunities to reinforce parents for their efforts and to remind them of the next class meeting.

After the 6-week intervention, all participants again completed all written measures and the two interviews. All data were then analyzed to evaluate program effects, as described below.

DATA ANALYSIS

Quantitative Data

Quantitative measures were scores from the instruments described in the quantitative measures section. The Parent Program Questionnaire produced scores of Importance, Child Capability, and Parent Ability to Assist for four different subscales—assertive, appropriately assertive, coping, and advocacy—as well as scores for Total Importance, Total Child Performance, and Total Parent Ability to Assist. The Activities Interview produced five scores regarding the number of daily activities in Play, Chores, Peer/School, Peer/Home, and Peer/Community domains, and an additional score for assistance required in Self-Care. The Parent Expectation Questionnaire produced two scores—one of parent expectations for child participatory behavior and the other of parents' perception of their ability to help their children participate. The Child Improvement Questionnaire produced two scores—one of extent of internal orientation to locus of control and the other of external orientation to locus of control. The Landman Parent Interview produced three scores—number of activities performed, assistance required, and parent perception of child capability.

Data analyses of quantitative measures included analysis of means and standard deviations for preintervention and postintervention measures, and of differences between preintervention and postintervention measures for both groups combined. The effect size statistic (Cohen, 1988) was used to determine the significance of preintervention and postintervention differences. Effect size can be defined colloquially as "the degree to which the phenomenon is present in the population" (Cohen, 1988, p. 9). In more statistical parlance, the effect size is the difference in means expressed in units of the population standard deviation. Thus, an effect size of 1.0 is interpreted as a difference of 1 population standard deviation between two means. This approach is the method of choice when the sample size is so small that the power to detect differences that may indeed exist is extremely low to nil. Because the total initial $N = 13$, and because the intervention was field-based where "the influence of uncontrollable extraneous variables makes the size of the effect small relative to these" (Cohen, 1988, p. 25), the analysis of effect sizes was more appropriate than typical F or t tests of significance of differences. Cohen (1988) suggests that effect sizes of .20 are "small" (1% of variance accounted for), those of .50 are "medium" (6% of variance accounted for), and those of .80 or higher are "large" (14% of the variance accounted for). These criteria were used for determining significance of effect sizes in the analyses.

Qualitative Data

The class logs were entered into a computer program, the Ethnograph (Seidel, Kjolseth, & Seymour, 1985), for coding and sorting. This text editor permits categorization, sorting, and rapid retrieval of text-based data. The Ethnograph was used to search the data files by code category to identify recurrent patterns and themes running through the data and to formulate tentative theories grounded in the data (Glaser & Strauss, 1967).

The logs and comments were searched again for data that either supported or refuted the theories. Memos outlining the theories and supporting them with specific incidents and comments from the data were distributed to staff for discussion. The revised memos provide the basis of the qualitative results section below.

RESULTS

Quantitative Measures

Preintervention Measures of Importance   Social validation results regarding the importance of the content focus of the intervention program documented that participants uniformly regarded all areas of the content as highly important. As Table 1 shows, mean ratings of Importance for the four domains and total were all near the highest rating possible with very low variability on a scale ranging from 1 ("very") to 4 ("little or none").

Locus of Control Orientation   Results from the Child Improvement Questionnaire demonstrated that, as a group, participants in the intervention clearly were oriented more toward an internal locus of control than toward an external one. The average of pre-intervention and postintervention measures of "internal" orientation was 3.76 with a standard deviation of .43, while the average score for

Table 1.   Self-Esteem Parent Program Questionnaire ratings of importance

| | Mean | | SD | |
	Pre	Post	Pre	Post
Total	1.23	1.22	.251	.313
Appropriate	1.17	1.18	.224	.273
Assertive	1.26	1.22	.298	.281
Coping	1.32	1.25	.389	.447
Advocacy	1.20	1.25	.350	.635

"external" orientation was 2.27 with a standard deviation of .44 (on a scale of 1–5, with 1 being "strongly disagree," 5 being "strongly agree," and 3 being "undecided"). On the internal subscale, participants were nearly 2 standard deviations away from "undecided" on the "agree" side, while on the external subscale, they were the same distance away from "undecided" on the "disagree" side. The effect size associated with this mean difference was $d = 1.70$, which is more than double the magnitude of Cohen's criterion of .80 for "large" effects. Participants clearly expressed beliefs that their child's growth and development could be affected by their actions and decisions to use specific other resources. No differences were apparent between preintervention and postintervention measures of either orientation, documenting that participants' orientations regarding locus of control were not influenced by the intervention program.

Preintervention/Postintervention Comparison   The means and standard deviations for preintervention and postintervention measures from all quantitative instruments are presented in Table 2, and preintervention and postintervention effect sizes for all measures are presented in Table 3. Using Cohen's (1988) criteria for interpreting effect sizes, notable results of the intervention are: one "medium" and one "large" effect in both subscales of the Parent Expectation Questionnaire; two "large," one "medium," and one "small" effect in four of the six subscales on the Activities Interview; "medium" effects in all three of the scales from the Landman Parent Interview; and four "large" effects, one "medium" effect, and two "small" effects in 7 of the 10 measures on the Parent Program Questionnaire. The negative signs result from the scales used in some of the measures; a "better" rating receives a higher score value. As a result, when posttest gains occur, posttest means are higher than at pretest, and a negative difference is apparent when the posttest mean is subtracted from the pretest mean to calculate the effect size.

Table 2. Esteem parent intervention preintervention/postintervention measures

Instrument	Mean		SD	
	Pre	Post	Pre	Post
PEQ				
Child capability	3.28	3.37	.358	.315
Parent capability	3.17	3.34	.426	.283
S-E Program Questionnaire				
Total				
Child performance	1.94	1.81	.490	.358
Parent assistance capability	1.78	1.70	.366	.387
Appropriate				
Child performance	2.09	1.70	.807	.470
Parent assistance capability	1.68	1.71	.425	.502
Assertive				
Child performance	1.99	1.81	.650	.479
Parent assistance capability	1.82	1.74	.443	.437
Coping				
Child performance	2.11	2.05	.653	.534
Parent assistance capability	1.88	1.75	.531	.403
Advocacy				
Child performance	1.90	2.00	.516	.471
Parent assistance capability	1.75	1.55	.486	.369
Landman Interview				
Child activities	7.27	7.64	2.80	3.60
Assistance required	1.50	1.60	.72	.95
Child capability	2.09	2.28	.62	.721
Activity Interview				
Play activities	3.26	3.65	1.753	1.785
Chore activities	3.89	4.37	2.781	3.200
Peers in school	2.76	2.51	0.964	0.865
Peers at home	1.01	1.05	0.981	0.944
Peers in community	0.03	0.04	0.059	0.089
Self-care assistance	1.81	1.63	1.124	0.946

Thus, negative signs are appropriate for the effect sizes on the Parent Expectation Questionnaire, for all subscales on the Activities Interview except for Self-Care, and for all scores from the Landman Parent Interview. Positive signs are appropriate for the Self-Care measure from the Activities Interview and the Self-Esteem Program Questionnaire, because "better" scores receive lower score values. Thus, when improved posttest ratings are subtracted from pretest scores on these measures to calculate effect sizes, the difference remains positive. Overall, 16 of the 22 effects examined met Cohen's criteria: 7 effects were "large," 6 were "medium," and 3 were "small."

Table 3. Preintervention/postintervention effect sizes for quantitative measures

Instrument	Child performance	Parent ability to assist
Parent Expectation Questionnaire		
Child	−.66	
Parent	−.95	
Activities Interview		
1. Play	.48	
2. Chores	−1.00	
3. Peer/school	1.19	
4. Peer/home	−.24	
5. Peer/community	.03	
6. Self-care	3.87	
(assistance required)		
Landman Parent Interview		
Child activity	−.38	
Assistance required	−.59	
Child ability	−.61	
Parent Program Questionnaire		
Total	1.34	.75
Assertive	1.51	.27
Appropriate behavior	1.21	−.18
Coping	.38	.45
Advocacy	−.26	.35

Additionally, approximately 60% of the possible effects were "medium" ("visible to the naked eye") (Cohen, 1988, p. 26) to "large" ("grossly perceptible") (Cohen, 1988, p. 27).

Qualitative Analyses

Two types of themes emerged from the analysis of the qualitative measures: 1) those that pertained to most participants and could be regarded as general themes, and 2) those that pertained to and helped define subgroups of participants.

    General Themes All participants except one rated the videos "excellent" or "good" in terms of both content and presentation. The participants became interested in the adults with disabilities and parents of children with disabilities and requested additional information about their disabilities and their present circumstances. This desire for additional information seems to have derived both from development of an interest in the video participants, who were sharing a great deal of personal information, and from a desire to compare their own children's situations with those depicted in the video and perhaps to extrapolate some predictions for their future development. Several parents said that it was interesting to hear adults with disabilities reflect on how their parents' attitudes and behaviors had affected their development, and that it made them wonder what their children would say about them in the future.

Comments made by parents in the videos often stimulated class discussions in which class participants cited personal experiences to either concur or disagree with the comments of the parents in the video. For example, one mother commented that she concurred with the mother in the video, who complained that she was tired of people staring at her daughter and her wheelchair and sometimes asked them to stop staring. A father in the same class responded that since he has "three kids in wheelchairs being pushed by three other kids who are shorter than the chairs," he expects the family to generate such attention. He sees part of the family's role as educating the public to the needs of and accommodations for people with disabilities.

A frequent comment from parents was that the class made them aware of the importance of small, daily interactions and subtle aspects of parent–child communication. In early class discussions parents often referred to significant anticipated events that they were expecting to change their children's attitudes and behaviors. These events involved being included in public school in 2 years, getting a motorized wheelchair in 6 months, settling in to the adoptive family over a number of years, and going through puberty. Over the course of the intervention, parents noted positive changes in their children as a result of much smaller events and adjustments in parenting practices.

The emphasis on reframing the parenting nurturing role from protection to building child autonomy prompted many parents to reorder their parenting priorities. One mother, a nurse who reported that she "nagged" her daughter about the types and amounts of fluid the child would consume each day, turned those choices over to her daughter. She chose to place a higher priority on developing her daughter's ability to make decisions and informed choices than on her own concerns about nutrition. The mother addressed her concerns by supplementing the girl's diet with vitamins and minerals and by engaging in positive self-talk to reassure herself about her daughter's health and the adequacy of her fluid intake. Other parents' shifts from overprotective or authoritarian roles to roles in which they structured their children's environment to promote independence and self-esteem are described below.

Themes by Subgroups Ratings of child behavior change attributed to parental participation in the intervention are presented in

Table 4 by item and by participant. Parents reported the greatest child behavior changes in the areas of responsibility for chores and self-care and in using assertive behavior.

These ratings indicated that different levels of child behavior change were attributed to the intervention by different subgroups of participants: some indicated little change, some noted moderate change, and others reported considerable change. Qualitative data from the class log and from written comments were consistent with the ratings, and further documented how participants in the program could be considered to represent three subgroups characterized by different preintervention parenting styles and different responses to the intervention as well as different degrees of child behavior change related to the intervention. These subgroups included: 1) parents who were already aware of and implementing most of the strategies presented in the intervention and thus who were characterized by little child behavior change, 2) parents who were characterized by moderate levels of child behavior change and some degree of preintervention parental overprotection, and 3) parents who were characterized by high ratings of child behavior change and preintervention authoritarian parenting. The subgroups were not entirely distinct from one another, and areas where themes transcended subgroups or where other factors predominated over ratings of child behavior change are described below.

Participants 2, 3, and 7 attributed little child behavior change to the intervention. (Although Participant 11's rating was the same as Participant 7's, other data indicated that Participant 11 is more properly associated with another subgroup.) Participant 2 was the only participant in the intervention who did not indicate in written or spoken comments that the program was effective to some degree in raising awareness of parent behaviors that affect the child's self-esteem, in affecting parenting behaviors, and/or in changing child attitudes and behaviors. This parent's child was deaf in addition to having cerebral palsy, and she often stated during class meetings that she felt the presence of this additional disability made her child's case unique and that the examples and suggestions offered were of little benefit to her. She also stated that she had already tried most of the strategies discussed in class and had found them ineffective or too costly in terms of time and energy. The other two parents in this subgroup (Participants 3 and 7) indicated that little change had occurred in their children's behavior or activities as a result of the class, but that this was because they had already done extensive reading and parent training in the area of self-esteem and were already implementing most of the communication and interac-

219

Table 4. Parent intervention social validation measure ratings of perceived child changes attributable to program

Item	Participant #													
	1	2	3	4	5	6	7	8	9	10	11	12a	12b	Total
Chores/self-care	1	1	1	3	2	1	0	2	3	2	2	2	1	21
Leisure	0	0	0	1	2	0	0	0	0	3	1	—	0	7
Peers	1	0	0	1	0	1	1	1	0	0	1	—	0	6
Assertive	0	0	0	4	1	2	0	1	3	3	1	—	1	16
Coping	1	0	0	1	0	1	0	2	3	0	0	1	1	10
Self-advocacy	—	0	0	1	1	0	1	1	3	—	0	1	—	8
Parent advocacy	2	0	0	1	—	2	2	1	—	1	2	1	1	12
Total	5	1	1	12	6	7	4	8	12	9	7	5	4	

tion strategies discussed in class. They expressed appreciation of the opportunity to review effective parenting practices, exchange ideas with other parents, and participate in a parenting "refresher" course that focused on self-esteem issues.

The parent of the child with the most severe disabilities (Participant 11) had characteristics in common with this subgroup in that he was aware of parenting behaviors that affect child independence and self-esteem. He indicated, however, that his child showed moderate gains in the target areas as a result of the intervention. In class discussion this parent stated that he was using the class as a motivator to set up technological environmental controls that had been purchased before his participation in the intervention program, to institute parenting practices that had been previously discussed but not implemented, or to reinstitute procedures that had been successfully used in the past.

The six other participants, who attributed low to moderate child behavior change to the intervention, exhibited attitudes associated with some degree of overprotectiveness prior to the intervention. They were a somewhat homogeneous subgroup within the larger group since most of their children had mild physical disabilities. Participants 1, 5, 6, 7, 8, 12a, and 12b (a grandmother and a stepmother) indicated that the intervention had made them aware that they were communicating with their children as if they were at an earlier developmental level and held behavior expectations for them that were inappropriately low. For these parents, the intervention program pointed out age-appropriate expectations in each of the target content areas. Class discussions then helped them determine to what degree, if any, the child's disability should be a factor in modifying those expectations. Comments during and after the intervention program indicated that these parents began to reframe their role from controlling and protecting their children to structuring the environment to provide the child with opportunities to experience independence. For example, Participants 12a and 12b had assumed the role of protecting their grandson/stepson from his fears associated with being in a car accident that had killed his mother and resulted in his disability. Through the intervention they reported becoming aware of the relationship between child self-esteem and independence and responsibility, and they began to require the boy to sleep in his own bed and to go upstairs unaccompanied by an adult. This child and the other children of these six parents were reported as responding positively and enthusiastically to being given a greater say in family discussions and a greater responsibility for self-care, household chores, and decisions about how to spend leisure time. Some parents in this group were careful to point out that, although they had not seen changes in their child's behavior in a particular area, they nonetheless felt that the intervention had had an effect. As one participant wrote regarding her son's interaction with other children:

> No change in interaction but [the program] made me more aware of [the] importance of peers/friends and of "letting go" somewhat so that he can interact more independently and be "like other kids."

A common response in this group of parents was that the examples of protective or dependency-producing behaviors mentioned by the facilitators or by other parents resonated with their own family situations. As one participant put it, "It's like you've been reading our mail!" She also said that the examples of protective behaviors given in class "tweaked" her awareness of similar behaviors in which she was engaging with her son. Examples of parent behaviors that were common in this group, in which the children ranged in age from 7 to 12 years, were cutting a child's food, selecting his or her clothing, and combing his or her hair. Interestingly, the examples given by facilitators and other parents were not always entirely congruent with the behaviors parents identified as being similar to their own situations. This indicated that parents generalized information offered in class to their own situations. For example, the facilitator mentioned brushing hair out of a child's eyes as a parent behavior that encourages the child and others to view the child as dependent. One participant related this to her daily battles with her 12-year-old son to get him to comb his hair to her specifications and began to permit him to comb his hair the way he wanted.

In their narrative comments on the Social Validation Questionnaire and in class, these parents also highlighted their previous lack of information about parenting in general and about being the parent of a child with disabilities in particular. They spoke and wrote of the intervention "shaking [them] out of bad habits," "making [them] aware of mistakes," and offering "creative ideas for modifying" the home environment and parent–child interactions.

The three parents (Participants 4, 9, and 10) who rated their children highest in degree of behavior change attributable to the intervention were, at preintervention, highly directive and authoritarian in their parenting and communication styles. Two of these parents were also initially the most resistant to suggestions for modifying their own and their children's behaviors. They argued that their children were "too disabled," that they had too many other children, that adaptive equipment was too expensive, or that instituting the changes would complicate their family life. The facilitators' response to this "Yes, but . . ." parent style was to acknowledge the difficulty of changing even small behaviors and communication style features, to validate the parents' rights to hold different views from those presented in the intervention program, and to encourage but not require parents to try to apply suggestions discussed in class to their home situations. Invariably these participants responded by trying a modification at home, even if they had insisted that they would not. Often these parents saw positive results from their experiments. In other cases they indicated that the experience was interesting but that they preferred to put their energies into making changes in other areas.

The three authoritarian parents were often so pleased with their families' responses to the changes they made that they generalized the class suggestions to other problem areas. For example, Participant 4, the mother of a 6-year-old, initially rejected every suggestion offered in class for expanding her daughter's leisure activities and peer interactions, citing transportation problems, the fact that her husband was out of town, the expense involved, and conflicts with other children's schedules. In spite of her objections, she did arrange for her daughter with disabilities to go with two older siblings to the grocery store. This outing was so successful that in the same week she rearranged her schedule to allow her daughter to attend a birthday party and invited a friend to come over to play with her. After these positive experiences, which occurred in the second week of the intervention, this parent was open to suggestions for adaptive equipment, communication strategies, and integration possibilities that she had vehemently rejected in the first week. This parent's changed attitude toward the importance of peer interaction was apparently maintained even 2 months postintervention; her daughter invited the daughter of another participant, who was dependent on a ventilator, to her birthday party.

During the 6 weeks of the intervention, this participant also made arrangements to place her daughter in an inclusive school setting a year earlier than planned and over the objections of personnel in the self-contained setting. This decision was based primarily on recognition of the importance of social integration and appropriate expectations for her daughter's development, and of factors in the self-contained setting that were contributing to her social isolation and potential learned helplessness. This parent tended to mention modifications that she had tried in an offhand manner, particularly if they were ideas that she had previously rejected. The facilitators responded in a similar manner, expressing support for the change and pleasure at the child's positive response, and giving credit for positive outcomes to the parent and not to the intervention.

Another participant generalized suggestions from class less readily than others, but nevertheless tried specific strategies that met with some success. This participant was a father who did not permit children to speak at the dinner table unless addressed by an adult, and who was proud of the rigid family structure and of the fact that his children were isolated as much as possible from peer influences. He was disturbed by his son's passivity and his slow pace, and attributed these characteristics to his son's early years in an orphanage in India. Although this father objected to most suggestions for interventions, he did provide his son with additional opportunities for choice, individual attention, and training in and encouragement of assertiveness. He reported that, as a result, his son whined less and was more assertive. He began to relate his authoritarian parenting practices to the difficulty that an older daughter who did not have a disability had encountered when she went to college. Unable to cope with life in a dormitory, where she was faced with many choices and had no authority figure to tell her what to do, she had left school and returned home frightened and demoralized. The father commented that he could see the value of giving children practice in making choices and decisions. This participant also confronted some of his attitudes toward disability in the course of the intervention. He began to include his son in activities such as basketball games that had previously been considered appropriate for only the father and his sons without disabilities.

Participant 9, who was authoritarian with an abrasive interaction style, initially reported extreme stress and conflict with her daughter in regard to getting ready for school in the morning. She tried a calmer, more respectful communication style and gave her daughter responsibility for setting her own bedtime. The morning situation resolved itself immediately, and the mother reported that her daughter communicated more openly and was more affectionate and receptive to parental requests. This parent also applied the suggestions for teaching assertiveness to children to her own communication style, with the result that she was less demanding and aggressive in her interactions with adults as well as with her own children.

Summary The primary theme emerging from the qualitative data is that most participants become aware of simple and subtle aspects of daily life that positively or negatively affect child self-esteem, and modify their parenting practices to varying degrees based on this information.

One subgroup, consisting of parents who were already aware of much of the material presented in the intervention program, made few modifications and gave low ratings of child behavior change attributable to the intervention.

A second subgroup, consisting of parents who at preintervention were overfunctioning to some degree as protectors and nurturers for their children with disabilities, learned that these parenting roles might interfere with the development of their children's self-esteem and might actually be fostering dependency. This group reframed the parenting role and redirected their energies to create opportunities for their children to face appropriate choices, responsibilities, and challenges. These parents thus shifted their cognitive representation of effective parenting from protection to striking a balance between protection and support of child independence and development. They reported low to moderate ratings of child behavior change.

The parents in the third subgroup, who had described their use of authoritarian parenting practices prior to their participation in the intervention program, also reframed the parenting role, but in a slightly different way from the protective group. These parents also began to see their role as providing opportunities for their children to become increasingly more competent and independent, but this required them to see themselves as less in control of the details of their children's lives. They recast their parenting role as structuring the environment to provide safe, appropriate opportunities for children to have more choice and control.

CONCLUSIONS

The quantitative data on locus of control and on importance of program content areas documented that the participants may have been predisposed to be accepting of the approach and content of the intervention. The clear pattern of the number and magnitude of significant effect sizes on the quantitative measures suggests that the intervention did produce positive changes in parent perceptions of child performance, particularly in the areas of assertiveness, chores, and self-care; parent expectations for child behavior; and parent perceptions of their ability to assist their children to meet those expectations. Smaller effects were noted in the frequency of child play activities, child and parent effectiveness as advocates, and parent ability to assist in the areas listed on the Program Questionnaire. The medium effect sizes on the three scales from the Landman Interview suggest that the program may have assisted parents in permitting their children to engage in activities that involved a degree of risk (e.g., spending the night at a friend's house or going to camp), to provide less assistance for those activities, and to have greater expectations for their children's ability to perform those activities.

Additionally, the pattern wherein approximately 60% of the effects examined on quantitative preintervention and postintervention measure were "large" or "medium" adds strength to the interpretation that the intervention indeed had some positive effects on participants. This consistency in the quantitative results was supported and clarified to some extent by the themes that emerged from the qualitative data. Taken together, the quantitative and qualitative results argue in favor of doing more focused studies to determine how the intervention procedures and the outcomes are related.

The qualitative data also indicated that most parents found value in the intervention. Parent ratings of child behavior change attributable to the program showed the greatest gains in the areas of chores and self-care, assertiveness, and coping (see Table 4). Parents also gave higher ratings to their own abilities to be advocates for their children as a result of the intervention program. In general, the qualitative and quantitative data taken together support the conclusion that the cognitive-behavioral intervention produced changes in parent perceptions and parent and child behavior.

The greatest child behavior changes on both the qualitative and quantitative measures occurred in the areas of responsibility for self-care, chores, and child assertiveness. Parents often indicated that their children had been wanting to take more responsibility for hygiene, grooming, and household chores, but that to maintain "quality control," this had not been permitted. By emphasizing reframing of parental role from caregiver to facilitator of child independence, the intervention program appeared to assist parents to regard turning over responsibility for self-care to their children as a way of fostering self-esteem rather than as an abdication of their own duties. It was also relatively easy for parents to implement changes in this area, and to note changes in the child's need for assistance in each activity since the activities were ones that, out of necessity, were engaged in frequently.

It was also easy for parents to detect changes in child assertiveness. Parents were highly motivated to decrease demanding or manipulative child behaviors, and the intervention program provided very specific strategies and correction procedures for instructing their children to be assertive in ways that were respectful and non-demanding. The intervention also encouraged parents to reframe assertiveness and persistence as positive child qualities, so that higher postintervention ratings of child assertiveness may reflect parent reevaluation of their children's persistent behavior as well as changes in the ways children made requests.

One outcome of the intervention seemed to be that parents became more aware of the relationship between increasing autonomy in childhood and adult independence. In the Landman Parent Interviews, completed before the intervention, parents had high expectations for their children's *adult* independence, but did not seem to be shaping independence through appropriate risk-taking in the present. The preintervention and postintervention effect size scores on this measure indicate that there was a moderate tendency at postintervention to permit children to engage in activities that involve some risk.

The qualitative data are helpful in understanding some puzzling features of the quantitative data. A ceiling effect may have been operating in the areas of leisure activities and peer interactions. It should also be noted that the intervention program was conducted in the winter and early spring, when recreational opportunities were restricted. Parents may have perceived a contradiction between turning over responsibility to the child for many aspects of functioning, while at the same time setting up opportunities for the child to interact with peers. Parent comments also indicated that there had not been time to note child behavior changes in these areas but that the change in parent awareness and attitudes would eventually lead to greater child social integration.

Narrative comments on the Social Validation Questionnaire were helpful in accounting for the small effect size for child performance and the apparent absence of effect in parent ability to assist in the area of coping with difficult situations, as measured on the Self-Esteem Parent Program Questionnaire. The intervention curriculum and video presented teasing, social rejection, and disappointment as normative events that children routinely encounter and that may prove to be valuable, albeit painful, learning experiences. Strategies such as cognitive reframing and positive self-talk were provided to help children face such situations rather than avoid them. Parents indicated that although little change was apparent between pretest and posttest, they felt that their children's coping skills would develop over time. Narrative comments also suggested that the effect of the intervention program was to make parents more confident that their children could cope effectively on their own, rather than to give parents a sense that they could help their children cope. It should be noted that on the Parent Expectation Questionnaire, which registered large preintervention and postintervention effect sizes on both the child and parent subscales, many of the items addressed the extent to which children should be expected to cope with different types of difficult or challenging situations.

One section of the Activities Interview, interaction with peers at school, showed large effect sizes in a negative direction. That is, parents indicated that their children's interactions with peers at school were more infrequent postintervention. It is possible that after the discussions on integrated activities and advocacy for inclusion, parents had higher standards for the quality of the children's peer interactions at school. As one mother said, "He has lunch and recess with the other kids, but they never talk to him, so I would say he has zero interactions."

The degree and type of change was highly individual across this heterogeneous group of participants. Parent response and assessment of child behavior change was influenced by the degree of the child's disability, preintervention parenting style, previous parent training, and other factors. Authoritarian parents perceived the greatest changes in their children's behavior, while parents who tended to be mildly to moderately overprotective attributed moderate child behavior change to the program. One possible explanation for this may be that these parents were already convinced of the importance of parental intervention to produce positive outcomes for children and were predisposed to take an active role in all aspects of their children's development. This explanation is supported by the scores on the Child Improvement Questionnaire and the ratings of importance on the Self-Esteem Parent Program Questionnaire. Another explanation might be that since these parents were making significant, often difficult changes in their own behavior, they may have been expecting corresponding changes in their children. A preintervention measure of parenting style and attitudes might be helpful in prioritizing services to parents. Such a measure would also help to determine whether degree of parent attitude and behavior change influences parents' perceptions of child behavior change.

The differential effects of treatment depending on a variety of factors argues for allowing parents to select the areas that have most salience for them rather than requiring them to put equal effort into making modifications in each area. The child's developmental level and priorities will also have an influence on the choices that parents make about the changes they wish to make in their families. It is important to point out that whether or not those conducting the intervention see participants as constituting a homogeneous group in terms of dimensions related to their research interests, participants in an intervention such as this are likely to see themselves as different from each other on a number of subtle dimensions, and to react to the intervention accordingly.

REFERENCES

Baumrind, D. (1971). Current patterns of parental authority. *Developmental Psychology Monographs, 4,* 1–103.

Baumrind, D. (1973). The development of instrumental competence through socialization. In A. Pick (Ed.), *Minnesota symposium on child psychology* (Vol. 7, pp. 3–46). Minneapolis: University of Minnesota Press.

Baumrind, D. (1978). Parental disciplinary patterns and social competence in children. *Youth and Society, 9,* 239–276.

Baumrind, D., & Black, A.E. (1967). Socialization practices associated with dimensions of competence in preschool boys and girls. *Child Development, 38,* 291–327.

Cohen, J. (1988). *Statistical power analysis for the behavioral sciences* (2nd ed.). Hillsdale, NJ: Lawrence Erlbaum Associates.

Cruikshank, W.M. (Ed.). (1976). *Cerebral palsy: A developmental disability.* Syracuse, NY: Syracuse University Press.

Devellis, R., Devellis, B., Revicki, D.A., Lurie, S.J., Runyan, D.K., & Bristol, M.M. (1985). Development and validation of the Child Improvement Locus of Control (CILC) Scales. *Journal of Social and Clinical Psychology, 3,* 308–325.

Dornsbusch, S., Ritter, P., Liederman, P., Roberts, D., & Fraleigh, M. (1987). The relation of parenting style to adolescent school performance. *Child Development, 58,* 1244–1257.

Glaser, B.G., & Strauss, A.L. (1967). *The discovery of grounded theory: Strategies for qualitative research.* Chicago: Aldine.

Harter, S. (1981). A model of mastery motivation in children: Individual differences and developmental change. In S. Collins (Ed.), *Minnesota symposium on child psychology* (Vol. 14, pp. 215–255). Hillsdale, NJ: Lawrence Erlbaum Associates.

Irvin, L.K., & Todis, B.J. (1992). *School-based factors related to development of self-esteem in children with physical/neuromotor disabilities.* Unpublished research proposal submitted to U.S. Department of Education.

Landman, S.H. (1978). *A study of the relationship between parental overprotectiveness and the achievement of selected life skills among mildly retarded adolescents.* Unpublished doctoral dissertation, University of Oregon, Eugene.

Lindemann, J.E. (1981). Cerebral palsy. In J.E. Lindemannn (Ed.), *Psychological and behavioral aspects of physical disability* (pp. 117–145). New York: Plenum.

Powers, L. (1992). *Parent Effectiveness Questionnaire.* Eugene: Oregon Research Institute.

Seidel, J.V., Kjolseth, R., & Seymour, E. (1985). *The ethnograph*. Littleton, CO: Qualis Research Associates.

Singer, G.S., & Irvin, L.K. (1988). *Development of positive self-perceptions and mastery orientation in children with multiple disabilities*. Contract No. H023T80013 between the U.S. Department of Education and the Oregon Research Institute, 1988–1991. Eugene: Oregon Research Institute.

Singer, G.S., & Irvin, L.K. (1990). Supporting families of persons with disabilities: Emerging findings, practices, and questions. In L.H. Meyer, C.A. Peck, & L. Brown (Eds.), *Critical issues in the lives of people with severe disabilities*. Baltimore: Paul H. Brookes Publishing Co.

Singer, G.H.S., Irvin, L.K., & Hawkins, N.E. (1988). Stress management training for parents of severely handicapped children. *Mental Retardation, 26*(5), 269–277.

Singer, G., Irvin, L., Irvine, B., Hawkins, N., & Cooley, E. (1989). Evaluation of community-based support services for families of persons with developmental disabilities. *Journal of The Association for Persons with Severe Handicaps, 14*(4), 312–323.

Sowers, J. (1982). *Validation of the weekly activity interview*. Unpublished doctoral dissertation, University of Oregon, Eugene.

Steinberg, L., Elemen, J.D., & Mounts, N.S. (1989). Authoritative parenting, psychosocial maturity, and academic success among adolescents. *Child Development, 60,* 1424–1436.

Wolf, M. (1978). Social validity: The case for subjective measurement, or how applied behavior analysis is finding its heart. *Journal of Applied Behavior Analysis, 11,* 203–214.

9

Cooperative Family Problem Solving

An Intervention for Single-Parent Families of Children with Disabilities

Marilyn S. Shank
and
Ann P. Turnbull

The number of single-parent households has risen dramatically in the United States since the 1970s. According to the U.S. Bureau of the Census (1990), the number of male householders with no spouse present and with children under 18 increased 70% from 1980 to 1988. Female householders with no spouse present increased 15% during the same period. In 1970, 12% of children under 18 were living with their father or mother only; however, by 1988 this percentage had increased to 24%. The ratio of single-parent to non–

Development of this chapter was supported in part by Cooperative Agreement H133B80046 from the National Institute on Disability and Rehabilitation Research, U.S. Department of Education and by grant no. H029D00094, U.S. Department of Education. The opinions expressed in this chapter are solely those of the authors and no official endorsement from the Department should be inferred.

The authors gratefully acknowledge Sherry Borgers, Frances Clark, Samuel Green, Mary Ross Moran, Douglas Murphy, and Richard Simpson for their assistance.

single-parent homes is even higher among minorities than across the population as a whole. Statistics from 1988 revealed that 19% of children who are white, 30% of children who are Hispanic, and 54% of children who are black reside in single-parent homes. Although no percentages have been identified in the literature for the number of children with disabilities who are living in a single-parent home, if the figure of 24% is used as an estimate, approximately 1 million children with disabilities resided in a single-parent household during 1988. Therefore, the issues confronting single-parent families of children with disabilities warrant attention by service providers. However, no programs specifically targeting such families were found in the literature.

DEVELOPMENT OF AN
INTERVENTION PROGRAM FOR SINGLE PARENTS

In developing a program for these families, avoiding the stereotype of the single-parent household as a "broken home" was a high priority. Reid (1985) pointed out the following benefits of single parenthood:

> relief from marital conflict, increased self-esteem derived from one's competence in managing work and family matters, greater autonomy and independence, opportunities for increased self-growth, and closer relationships with children. (p. 263)

Likewise, Hanson (1986) found that many single-parent families were not necessarily less able to manage problems than other family types. However, Hanson also acknowledged that single "parents and children can be helped to improve their communication skills and broaden their social support systems" (p. 131).

Although the potential strengths of single-parent families were recognized, single-parent families of children with disabilities can face even greater stressors than two-parent families of children with disabilities (Beckman, 1983; Vadasy, 1986). Vadasy (1986) quoted a parent who illustrates the sense of isolation experienced by many of these single parents:

> When I was divorced, the group of parents we worked with and saw frequently seemed to step back. It was almost as if they were afraid it would happen to them, and they'd be faced with raising their handicapped child alone. It was easy to give support when it was a problem we had in common. (p. 236)

Another single parent described herself in this way:

> Tired. Lonely. Isolated. This is how it was as a single parent, raising three children, one of whom was disabled. I fell asleep crying, many

nights, because I did not have a partner to share the daily responsibilities and problems of raising Katherine . . . I was both father and mother, trying to meet the emotional needs of all three children, working a forty-hour week, dealing with emergencies, Katherine's therapy schedule, and afterschool homework and activities of her brother and sister. (Barnes, 1986, p. 47)

These vignettes illustrate the magnitude of responsibilities confronting single parents of children with disabilities.

Family Problem Solving

One of the difficulties faced by single parents, including those with children with disabilities, is family problem solving. Borduin, Henggeler, Hanson, and Pruitt (1985) concluded that single-parent families may need more problem-solving skills because of additional stressors and lack of support. In another study (Hannum & Mayer, 1984), single parents generally exhibited more instances of conflict, less constructive problem solving, less authoritarian control, less organization, more disagreement, and more noncompliance on the part of their children than two-parent families. Blechman and McEnroe (1985) concluded from their research, which revealed poorer performance on a problem-solving task by single-parent families, that "an adult may work harder in the presence of another adult, and communicate more fully" (p. 436). Furthermore, children from father-absent homes have also been found to have poorer problem-solving skills (Stanley, Weikel, & Wilson, 1986). Hence, an intervention for family problem-solving might benefit single-parent families of children with disabilities.

Such a program, as envisioned, would encourage single parents to work together with their children, including the child with a disability, to determine appropriate solutions for family problems. Bass (1989) suggested that cooperative learning, a technique that emphasizes having students work together to learn skills and solve problems, would be useful in families. She stated that cooperative activities could be used by families to enhance: 1) decision making, 2) resource interdependence, 3) recognition of cooperation, 4) reward interdependence, and 5) division of labor interdependence. It was speculated that teaching these skills could empower single-parent family members to work together to solve problems.

RESEARCH PARTICIPANTS

The subjects for the intervention were recruited from three suburban school districts in eastern Kansas and from organizations for parents of children with disabilities. Efforts were made to solicit volunteers by leaflets that briefly described the study and asked for participation by single-parent families of children with learning disabilities, behavior disorders, mild to moderate developmental disabilities, or physical disabilities. The communiques included a form that parents could return to request more information and a brief application.

The 19 parents who requested more information were mailed an application, and a consent form enclosed with the application explained the program in more detail. Stipends of $15 for preassessment and postassessment and $12 for each session attended were offered as incentives.

The only criteria that were used for family inclusion in the study were: 1) that a school-age child in the family was currently receiving services due to a disability; 2) that the single parent, at a minimum, had visitation rights with the children; and 3) that the child had enough verbal communication skills to be able to participate at some level in a problem-solving interaction.

Follow-up letters were sent and a telephone call was made to each of the parents after enough time had elapsed for receipt of the application to address question or concerns and to encourage prompt return. All 15 of the parents (2 men, 13 women; 2 African-Americans, 13 Caucasians) who completed an application, except one, met the criteria stated above and were invited to participate in the study. The one parent who completed an application but did not meet the criteria was a former single parent of a child with a disability who wrote to express her concerns about the need for special programs for single parents and to offer any assistance she could provide.

Ten of the 14 parents (1 man, 13 women; 1 African-American, 13 Caucasians) attended Cooperative Family Problem Solving (CFPS) at least once. Of those 10, 6 were considered completers (those who attended at least three of four sessions or two sessions and a catch-up session). In addition, two of the three parents who originally said they could not participate in CFPS and were invited to the catch-up session attended. Two other parents dropped out of the program. One left the program because of other family commitments, and the other stopped coming because "the timing was not right" and the program's format of discussing problems with strangers was too stressful for her. Demographics for the completers are detailed in Table 1.

Assessment

Several procedures for assessing participant progress in developing target skills were developed. The single parents and their children

Table 1. Demographic characteristics of CFPS completers (*N* = 6)

Characteristic	*n*
Parent's age	
30–39	2
40–49	4
Parent's sex	
Male	5
Female	1
Marital status	
Divorced	6
Custody status	
Primary	4
Joint	2
Race	
White, non-Hispanic	6
Income	
Under $15,000	3
$26,000–$40,000	3
Education	
High school	1
2 years college	1
College graduate	3
Graduate school	1
Child's age (with disability)	
6–8	2
9–11	2
12–15	2
Child's sex	
Male	5
Female	1
Child's disability	
Learning disability	2
Behavior disorder	2
Physical disability	2
Developmental disability	1
Child's position in family	
Oldest	0
Middle	1
Youngest	2
Only child	3

who were over the age of 12 completed the Family Assessment Device (FAD) (Epstein, Baldwin, & Bishop, 1982; Miller, Epstein, Bishop, & Keitner, 1985) at preintervention and postintervention. Each family was also videotaped at preintervention and postintervention as they worked to solve a family problem. These videotapes were then analyzed using the Beavers Interactional Competence Scale (BICS) (Beavers, Hampson, & Hulgus, 1990). A third instrument developed for the program was administered postintervention to ascertain consumer satisfaction. Furthermore, the single parents were interviewed after the intervention, and anecdotal records were maintained throughout the intervention. In the current work, the results of the interviews and anecdotal records are discussed. The statistical findings are also mentioned, but the reader is cautioned that interpretation of those results is limited by the small sample size. The full scope of this study, including a survey that was conducted after the intervention to determine how recruiting parents for training programs such as CFPS can be more successful, is found in Shank (1992).

The Intervention

The participants attended a 5-week intervention titled Cooperative Family Problem Solving (CFPS) that met on Saturday mornings for 2–3 hours, yielding more than the 12 hours that Giblin (1986) specified as the minimum for change to occur as a result of family training (see Figure 1). The format of the intervention included techniques that have been associated with cooperative learning.

According to Johnson, Johnson, Holubec, and Roy (1984), the responsibilities of the teacher in cooperative learning include: 1) specifying objectives; 2) making decisions about grouping; 3) explaining the purpose, structure, and activities to participants; 4) monitoring effectiveness of the groups and facilitating group skills; and 5) evaluating group progress. These responsibilities were carried out by the session leader throughout the intervention.

The four skills needed by participants in cooperative learning—forming, functioning, formulating, and fermenting—were developed during the intervention (Johnson et al., 1984). Thus, during the forming stage, the parents were: 1) divided into two groups, 2) provided with an activity to foster getting acquainted, and 3) told to encourage everyone in their group to participate in the sessions to follow. To enhance group functioning as other opportunities for discussion occurred during the initial phase of the intervention, the session leader circulated among the groups and gave direction, encouragement, clarification, elaboration, empathy, and suggestions as appropriate.

After the first week, the single parents participated as one group. As the group began to function well, the parents were encouraged to formulate cooperative skills by asking the members to: 1)

Schedule

Session	Week	Time	Content
Session 1	Week 1	1 1/2 hours 9:30–11:00 Break	9:30–9:45 Program guidelines/get acquainted activity 9:45–10:20 Goal setting 10:20–11:00 What is the problem?/To think about
Session 2	Last half of Week 1; First half of Week 2	1 1/4 hours 11:15–12:30 1 1/4 hours 9:30–10:45	11:15–12:30 WE CAN strategy 9:30–9:45 Review 9:45–10:15 WE CAN strategy role play 10:15–10:45 WE CAN strategy group-generated problems/to think about
Session 3	Week 2	Break 1 1/2 hours 11:00–12:30	11:00–11:40 Four phases of group cooperation 11:40–12:00 Positive interdependence 12:00–12:30 Plan a fun activity/to think about
Session 4	Week 3	1 3/4 hours 9:30–11:15 Break	9:30–10:15 Who owns the problem? 10:15–10:55 5 rules for listening/to think about 10:55–11:15 Catch-up or supplemental activity
Session 5	Week 3	1 hour 11:30–12:30	11:30–11:50 Add to resources 11:50–12:05 Discussion of resources 12:05–12:30 Concerns about teaching WE CAN to children
Session 6	Week 4	2 1/2 hours 9:30–10:30 Break 11:00–12:30	9:30–9:40 Icebreaker 9:40–10:20 Role play of WE CAN by groups 11:00–11:30 Rich relative role play 11:30–12:00 Using WE CAN to solve a family problem 12:00–12:30 Closure activity

Figure 1.   Schedule of activities for Cooperative Family Problem Solving.

take responsibility for the progress of each of the members in developing the skills, 2) summarize participant contributions, and 3) seek elaboration from members. Finally, to encourage the groups to ferment during the third and fourth weeks, it was suggested that the group: 1) distinguish disagreement among members, 2) synthesize different ideas in the group into a single position, 3) extend member contributions, 4) ask questions about member responses, and 5) test solutions against reality (Johnson et al., 1984).

For each topic in the CFPS intervention, descriptions and examples of the component skills were given and the parents were provided with opportunities to practice the skills in a cooperative group. The group gradually progressed from discussing problems presented in fictional vignettes to discussing personal family problems (Switzer, 1985). Written homework was not assigned because of the hectic schedules of single-parent families and the concern that homework is perceived as a task associated with the intervention and, therefore, does not promote generalization (Foster, Prinz, & O'Leary, 1983). However, the parents were encouraged to think about specific skills that had been presented in the session and how these skills could be applied. At the beginning of each session except the first, the parents were asked to discuss any opportunities they had to try the skills learned in previous sessions.

The following topics were presented to the single parents during the Cooperative Family Problem Solving intervention.

Defining Problems in Terms of Unmet Goals   The need to clearly define the problem has been specified by Bradford and Stein (1984). Therefore, Session 1 (1½ hours) of the intervention encouraged the parents to begin thinking about problems by answering three questions (see Figure 1). First, *what is the problem* (Koberg & Bagnall, 1974)? Second, *why is it a problem* (Brody, 1982; Covey, 1989; Janis, 1982)? Third, *how can the problem be stated so that I know when it is solved* (Bradford & Stein, 1984; Clark, Striefel, Bedlington, & Naimen, 1989; Moss, Falloon, Boyd, & McGill, 1982; Nezu, Nezu, & Perri, 1989; Stonewater, 1980)? Emphasis, therefore, was placed on examining problems according to principle-based goals (Covey, 1989) and stating problems behaviorally. Participants had opportunities to practice the skills individually and in groups.

Using a Problem-Solving Strategy   Twelve steps for problem-solving were derived from a literature review:

1. Accept that a problem exists (Koberg & Bagnall, 1974).
2. Find a relaxed, quiet atmosphere for discussion (Schroder, Casadaban, & Davis, 1988).
3. Describe the problem in behavioral terms (Bradford & Stein, 1984).
4. Inhibit action until a decision is made (Thomas, 1977).
5. Consider personal and family values and objectives that relate to the problem (Brody, 1982; Covey, 1989, Janis, 1982).
6. List solution options (Janis, 1982).
7. Search for relevant information and expert opinion (Janis, 1982; Parnes & Harding, 1962; Thomas, 1977).

8. Evaluate positive and negative consequences and specify how each option coincides with family and individual goals and objectives (Clark et al., 1989; Covey, 1989).
9. Decide on the preferred option (Reese, 1986; Stonewater, 1980).
10. Plan implementation strategies (Schroder et al., 1988).
11. Practice and then implement the solution (Bradford & Stein, 1984; Clark et al., 1989).
12. Evaluate whether the proposed solution was successful, and, if necessary, choose another option (Bradford & Stein, 1984; Nezu et al., 1989).

Because a lengthy, involved strategy for problem-solving has been shown to be difficult for parents to master (Schroder et al., 1988), the 12 steps derived from the literature were collapsed into the following mnemonic strategy (WE CAN), which was taught to the parents during Session 2 (3 hours) of the intervention:

What is the problem? Parents were encouraged to use the skills they learned in Session 1 of the intervention when they first encountered a problem (Koberg & Bagnall, 1974).
Evaluate options. Brainstorming and evaluating the pros and cons of each option in terms of principle-based goals were taught (Janis, 1982; Parnes & Harding, 1962; Thomas, 1977).
Can anyone help? Participants were taught the importance of seeking relevant information and resource persons during the decision-making process (Janis, 1982; Parnes & Harding, 1962; Thomas, 1977).
Agree or agree to disagree. The necessity of valuing the perspectives of all members and attempting to reach consensus on a problem were stressed (Clark et al., 1989; Covey, 1989; Janis, 1982; Reese, 1986).
Notice the results. This element of the problem-solving strategy included: 1) determining a plan of action, 2) carrying out the plan, and 3) evaluating the results (Bradford & Stein, 1984; Clark et al., 1989; Janis, 1982; Moss et al., 1982; Nezu et al., 1989; Schroder et al., 1988).

The groups practiced using the WE CAN strategy to solve problems presented in fictional vignettes and with family issues suggested by the parents (see Figures 2 and 3 for curriculum samples).

Enhancing Family Cooperation Session 3 of the intervention (1½ hours) encouraged family unity in problem-solving. The four skills needed by participants in cooperative learning—forming, function-

I. What is the problem?

WE CAN!

W hat is the problem?	**C** an Anyone help?
E valuate options.	**A** gree or agree to disagree.
	N otice the results.

A. Describe (Write the problem in a sentence.)

Bill's kids' fussing gets on his nerves.

B. Defend (Why is it a problem? Explain in terms of unmet goals.)

Bill wants to be a good father for his children. When they fuss, he feels like he hasn't done a very good job with them.

Bill wants to be able to be known as a productive person at work. When his kids have been fussing, he has a hard time concentrating at work.

Bill wants his kids to treat other people, including each other, with respect.

C. Detail (Restate the problem so you know when it will be solved. Consider what was going on before, during, and after the problem.)

What's going on before the problem started?

Bill comes home from work, puts his feet up, and begins to read the paper.

What behaviors do you notice when the problem occurs?

The children begin to argue. Usually, the children argue over unfinished chores and what to watch on TV.

What are the results?

Bill talks to the kids about their behavior and sends them to their rooms. Then he talks to each of them about their behavior. After that, he's tired and grouchy and the evening's ruined.

Figure 2. The first component of the WE CAN strategy with examples. (Image part of the ClickArt Series by T/Maker Co.; reprinted by permission.)

ing, formulating, and fermenting—were described to the parents, and an explanation of how their participation in a problem-solving group had prepared them for Session 4 of the intervention was provided. They were asked to discuss in their groups, using the WE CAN strategy, how these four skills could be applied to family problem solving. Then the groups discussed, again using the WE CAN strategy, how goal interdependence, task interdependence, resource interdependence, and reward interdependence could be developed in the members' families.

As a cooperative activity, parents—using WE CAN for a third time—planned a social activity to take place before the next meeting. This activity provided them an opportunity to "notice the results" at the beginning of the next session. In addition, parents were encouraged to establish family meetings on a weekly basis. The parents brainstormed possible topics to include in the meetings as well as possible solutions for obstacles encountered.

Resolving Family Conflict Session 4 of the intervention (2 hours) was devoted to establishing skills for resolving conflict. This session stressed the need to identify who owns the problem (Bryant, 1989; Eden, Jones, & Sims, 1983) and to allow the owner to take responsibility for the solution. Moreover, the participants learned five rules for listening (adapted from Covey, 1989; Feldman, 1985):

Think about:

1. What the speaker wants
2. How the speaker feels
3. What you can say to let the speaker know you understand
4. How you can help the listener know what you want and feel
5. How you both can win or how you can agree to disagree

The groups practiced the skills by role-playing family scenarios that were suggested by the members.

Locating Resources During Session 5 (1 hour) of Cooperative Family Problem Solving, the families also discussed how those problems that cannot be solved (Bryant, 1989) can be managed successfully by locating helpful resources. The group used the WE CAN strategy to determine possible resources for coping with problems that had been deemed unsolvable by the members. The parents received a bibliography of resources and were given an opportunity to brainstorm additions to the list.

Reviewing the Skills An additional 2-hour session that allowed the families to discuss and practice the skills learned previously was conducted between Sessions 5 and 6. This session also served as an opportunity for parents who could not attend one or more meetings

WE CAN!

W hat is the problem?
E valuate options.
C an Anyone help?
A gree or agree to disagree.
N otice the results.

II. Evaluate Options

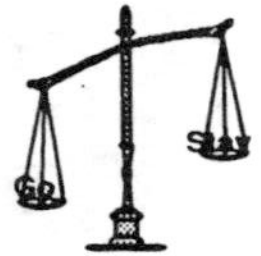

Brainstorm all possible solutions. Then go back and list pros and cons for each.

Solution *Tell the kids no TV in the evenings*	**Solution** *Dad waits till kids go to bed to read the paper*	**Solution**
Pros *Kids won't fuss about TV* *Kids will probably spend more time on homework* **Cons** *Kids will probably fuss about something else* *Kids will be angry with Dad*	**Pros** *Dad can control kids' behavior more* *Dad spends more time with kids* **Cons** *Dad feels he needs a break after working all day* *Kids won't learn self-control*	**Pros** **Cons**
Solution	**Solution**	**Solution**
Pros **Cons**	**Pros** **Cons**	**Pros** **Cons**

Figure 3. The second component of the WE CAN strategy with examples. (Image part of the ClickArt Series by T/Maker Co.; reprinted by permission.)

to learn some of the missed skills. Three families who had originally expressed interest in the intervention but who had been unable to attend because of family crises were invited to this overview session; two of the three parents attended.

Another focus of this session was to encourage the parents to discuss any concerns they had about teaching the WE CAN strategy to their children during the final session. The parents again used the WE CAN strategy to plan another social activity for themselves and their children to take place before the last session.

Practicing the Skills as a Family   For the last session (Session 6, 3 hours) of the intervention, the children with disabilities and their siblings came with the parents. Parents introduced their children to other members of their cooperative group. As an icebreaker, each family was given a large sheet of paper and markers. On one half of the paper they drew pictures of activities that everyone in the family enjoyed doing, and on the other half, each member drew activities that he or she enjoyed but no one else in the family enjoyed. These pictures were then shared with the other families.

The session leader explained the purposes of the meetings and the WE CAN strategy to the children. The parents then modeled the WE CAN strategy to the children by assuming family roles and solving a problem presented by the instructor.

Subsequently, each family formed its own group and discussed one vignette and one family problem using the strategy. The group leaders provided support to the families as needed by circulating among them while they practiced the skills. All the participants came together at the end of this session and problem-solved, using the WE CAN strategy, how they could continue to provide support for each other after the intervention.

RESULTS

Although the Family Assessment Device (FAD) and the Beavers Interactional Competence Scale (BICS) were administered pre-intervention and postintervention, interpretation of the results is limited by the small sample size. Some participants seemed to make greater gains on the BICS than others and to perceive more improvement as measured by the FAD after the intervention period. Those who made and perceived the greatest gains had consistently reported throughout the intervention that they were trying out the skills at home and had entered the program looking for solutions to family problems. Some families may have experienced disruption

(Giblin, 1986) as they attempted to apply the new skills, especially in the context of a videotaped setting. Moreover, extenuating circumstances could have contributed negatively to the performance of two of the families.

Of the four subscales on the BICS that were determined a priori to relate to the intervention (goal-directed negotiation, clarity of expression, unresolved conflict, and empathy), empathy yielded a significant difference. Thus, the cooperative learning format of the intervention might have developed this skill. Certainly, replication with a larger sample is warranted.

The FAD comprises six subscales: problem solving, communication, roles, affective responsiveness, affective involvement, behavior control, and general functioning. Significant differences were noted in roles and general functioning from preassessment to postassessment. When the parents' scores were calculated with the scores from adolescents who participated with their parents, problem solving also yielded a significant difference.

The family roles subscale has special relevance to the intervention because many of the statements in that subscale relate to the distribution of household responsibilities, a major concern that many of the single parents expressed throughout the intervention. Perhaps, then, these parents see a practical application of problem solving to family chores.

Another subscale of interest was behavior control. Participants and adolescents who scored high on this scale during preassessment tended to score less on postassessment while participants and adolescents who scored lower initially tended to score higher during postassessment. This phenomenon might correspond with comments made during postassessment interviews by parents who were originally high on this score. They indicated that they no longer felt a need to "control everything and everybody" and were giving their children more opportunities for self-control.

Correlations between preassessment and postassessment scores of the parents on subscales of the BICS and FAD were determined to ascertain how the parents' perceptions related to the videotaped evaluators' perceptions. The goal-directed negotiations subscale on the BICS was correlated with the problem-solving subscale of the FAD, and the global health-pathology summary scale of the BICS was correlated with the general functioning subscale on the FAD. The results suggest that the parents were more accurate in their perceptions of family problem solving and general functioning after the intervention. Therefore, the intervention might help parents to become more self-aware. However, the study would have to be replicated with a larger sample size before any conclusions could be made with confidence. More information about the statistical results, including charts of individual family performances on the FAD and BICS, are found in Shank (1992).

After the intervention was completed, interviewers asked the completers, attenders, and nonattenders 14 questions about: 1) reasons for attendance and nonattendance, 2) their opinions about the content of the sessions, 3) whether they had actually seen changes in their families as a result of the intervention, and 4) the most desirable time in the family life cycle for participation in CFPS. Along with two questions about nonattendance, the parents who did not attend any sessions were asked to describe programs they would like to see developed for parents.

Perceptions of Program Content

All completers and one-timers were asked the following:

1. Was CFPS what you thought it would be?
2. What did you like most about CFPS?
3. What did you enjoy least?
4. What could we leave out of CFPS?
5. What should we add to CFPS?
6. How could the program be made better?
7. Would you recommend the program to a friend?

Overall, responses to program content were positive. Most of the parents said CFPS was what they thought it would be. One commented that the program was "all that I thought it would be and then some more." Another parent stated that she came to the program open-minded, with no preconceived ideas. One parent indicated that she thought there would be more discussion of parents' personal problems, but that the format was good because "it made us learn how to resolve our problems and how to cope with our problems."

When asked what they liked most about the program, most parents immediately mentioned learning the WE CAN strategy. The steps were a "useful tool," according to one parent. "The first thing you think of whenever something comes up is the WE CAN formula." Another stated, "I think it's a neat idea. . . . It's something we've already used." One parent said she liked working out problems with this different approach:

> I kind of needed that because I just had . . . over the years gotten to where I didn't even try to think of a different way to handle [my child] . . . This gave me some different ideas, different perspective.

One-timers mentioned "trying out a couple of things that seemed like a great idea," especially talking to children about problems. A completer said that having the children come to the last session was useful and "I'm not sure that it would have been effective without that." Another one-timer said she liked the plan for solving problems but needed to "get into the material more."

Goal-setting was particularly important for one parent. In her words, she "hadn't thought much about personal goals" despite previous training.

Several parents mentioned the importance of learning about resources. One specifically mentioned the usefulness of the bibliographies that were provided.

Additionally, the social component was an important facet of the program for many parents. Several mentioned the importance of hearing how other parents were dealing with problems. One parent stressed the importance of recognizing the roles people play in groups such as CFPS and then transferring that idea to roles that each family member, including the child with a disability, play in the family team. Another mentioned that other people's willingness to communicate and talk was helpful to her. A third parent also emphasized that contacts with other parents and personal conversations with the instructor were helpful.

Personal and Family Changes Resulting from CFPS

Participants, including one-timers, indicated changes that had occurred personally and in their families as a result of attending CFPS. "The changes are in me now," according to one participant, "and I have this tool. When something comes up I'm very quick to talk to [my child] and we talk about the number of options that we have." She added that she was not so "tunnel-visioned" now. Two others said that they were applying the WE CAN strategy to their personal problems and not only to their family problems. One commented that she no longer made decisions as impulsively, but instead finds herself "sometimes even waiting it out."

Several others alluded to the importance of weighing pros and cons during problem solving. One said, "I think subconsciously we really . . . go through the process and define what is really the problem . . . rather than just trying to do a quick-fix thing." A similar comment by a parent included discussion of "fixing the long instead of the short aspect of a problem." A parent who had already been using some problem-solving techniques realized that she was "not doing things too bad."

One parent articulated that the program changed her whole attitude about how to address family problems:

> I used to think [the problem] was mine and it's not necessarily mine. It's ours, so I'll say to them, "How can we fix this?" It's going to change our family a lot.

In a similar vein, a parent described feeling less of a need to "control everything and everybody" and that making each person responsible had become important.

Some parents, including a one-timer, emphasized that having family meetings was a change they had implemented for their families. Family meetings, according to one parent, "helped us come together as a family more than we were before." A parent pointed out that the family was meeting at least once a week and that they had distributed household chores. A change for one parent was including the entire family instead of dealing individually with a child when a problem arose.

Three parents specifically mentioned their relationships with their children with disabilities. One said she had not realized her child could participate in problem solving and had found out differently. A one-timer said she was trying to communicate more with her child with a disability, understand her point of view, and not just say, "This is the way we're going to do it." A completer said,

> It's a slow process [changing responses to a child with a disability] when you've been reacting a certain way for years. It's helped me probably more than it has [my child] right now. . . . Yeah, we've been doing a lot better. . . . By the time school starts this fall, I look for . . . us to be different, and [my child] will be a different kid, too.

This parent had also mentioned at the last intervention session that her child's teacher had asked about what had happened at home to contribute to the positive changes the teacher had noticed in the child.

Ideal Time for Program Delivery

Parents were asked when they thought the best time to deliver CFPS to families would be, considering both how soon after a parent learns about a child's disability and the ages of the child and his or her siblings. Most parents thought that families should wait at least 6 months to a year after diagnosis before participating in CFPS, although a completer thought the training would be valuable "as soon or shortly after they find out." One commented, however, "Let it sink in and let them have some trial and error before you introduce

something like this." This statement was reiterated by a one-timer
who stated that after a year the shock of learning that one's child
has a disability wears off. Another thought that at that point, parents might be ready to work on problems associated with the disability. A completer recommended that parents be given a list of groups
they could join when their child is diagnosed and "let them pick their
own. That would have been good instead of going all those years with
literally nowhere to turn." At the time of diagnosis, according to a
one-timer, parents primarily need information about what to expect.
A different completer said that some parents would appreciate an
opportunity to attend CFPS soon after learning the diagnosis and
others would benefit more a few years later. However, according to
this completer, all should be given options when told of the diagnosis.

A few parents indicated that the type of disability of the child
and the ages of all children in the family were important considerations. One said that she thought children under 8 years of age or
those who had trouble communicating might not be able to participate as much. Another said she thought some children with more
severe disabilities might never be able to benefit. A completer said
that the age of the child did not matter, and one said that her young
adolescent, a sibling, had enjoyed the training and that an upper
limit should not be placed on program participation.

Other Comments

When asked if they had other comments about the program, several
completers spontaneously mentioned that their group planned to
continue meeting for social and academic reasons. During the last
session, the parents used the WE CAN strategy to determine how
they could provide support for each other after the sessions were
finished. They formed an organization, Single Parents with Exceptional Children (SPEC), that has met several times since the intervention was completed. One completer commented that the group
was planning to develop its own newsletter. Another parent mentioned how much she had enjoyed the social activity (pizza party)
that had been planned by the group during one of the sessions and
how much she was looking forward to their ongoing meetings.

Two nonattenders indicated that they might be able to participate if the program was offered again. Also, completers and one-
timers commented:

"I enjoyed the class I attended and learned a lot."

"I'm glad you guys are doing this."

"It was very beneficial."

"I enjoyed this very much, and I'm glad I did it. It was a growing kind of thing."

SUMMARY

On the basis of comments made by participants during interviews, several general conclusions can be drawn about participant perceptions of the nature and frequency of CFPS. First, participants apparently found the program useful and all indicated that they had incorporated at least some of the ideas presented in the intervention into their family problem-solving routines. However, most also expressed concern about session length and frequency, asking that a more concise program be delivered in the future. Despite the training sessions being too long, participants did express a desire for the social opportunities that the group afforded them to be continued. Thus, they formed their own support group during the last session.

COMMENTARY

Several themes emerged from the postassessment interviews regarding program participation, program content, and program outcomes for participants. Each of these themes is discussed in some detail.

Program Participation

The importance of social support from the program was stressed by attenders and nonattenders alike. The obvious attraction of the idea of the program being for single parents who could provide support for each other validates the need for separate programs for these parents. Therefore, the social component of an intervention for single parents must be expanded and emphasized as much as possible. Furthermore, parents will need to perceive that they have support from the instructor and the other participants as they confront obstacles to attendance during the intervention. Schraft (1980) recommended that parents with leadership skills be recruited for an initial session. To expand Schraft's suggestion, these parents could do more than assist with recruiting other parents; each of them could serve in an ongoing capacity as a support person for an individual member. Hence, the value of the veteran parent should not be underestimated.

Another issue relating to parental participation is the conflictual nature of attending such a program for parents who are under-

going or have recently undergone personal crises that were perceived as overwhelming. One, for example, expressed concern about
"overcounseling." Participants confirmed the problem of "too much
too soon" when they discussed the importance of not having the
program for those who had recently become parents of a child with a
disability because these parents needed time to "let it sink in." Instead, the participants recommended that these parents be given
emotional support, resources, and options for group participation
when they are ready. For single parents, not only should the instructor be concerned about the recency of the diagnosis of disability, but
also how recently the parent was separated, divorced, or widowed.

Because many single parents will experience personal and professional stressors that cause them to be unable to participate in all
sessions, creating opportunities to participate in catch-up sessions
or to receive instruction on missed skills from the instructor or another participant is essential. Expecting perfect attendance by single parents of children with disabilities at a more-than-one-time
intervention is unrealistic; many will not have a support person to
help them when a crisis or time conflict occurs.

Program Content

Interview comments suggested that parents were satisfied with the
content of the program. One parent expressed being attracted to the
program because of its emphasis on cooperation, but most appeared
to be attracted to the idea of learning how to problem-solve with
their families more effectively. Apparently, they found the WE CAN
strategy to be a "useful tool" that was readily applicable to everyday
situations. Thus, giving single parents a strategy to use with their
families seems to be a practical way to deliver skills, although more
research into whether a strategy approach is applicable to other
areas of family living is needed. The recommendation by one participant that parents be given a list of vignettes to use to teach the
strategy to their children during family meetings, especially in the
initial stages of the intervention, could be helpful. The suggestion
made by another parent to allow families to watch and discuss videotapes of themselves problem solving is also worthy of consideration as a technique to improve family skills related to the intervention.

Program Outcomes

Participants commented on changes in their families and in their
personal lives that directly relate to the two primary foci of the
intervention: cooperation and problem solving. Some said that their

relationship with their child with a disability had changed as they began to view the child as being able to contribute to problem solving. Many specifically mentioned starting family meetings and encouraging their children to cooperate in solving problems. Thus, an intervention such as CFPS appears to be able to influence how single parents view their families and their ability to work together to solve problems. Additionally, willingness on the part of these single parents to make changes that they perceived as beneficial to their families despite competing demands argues for a salutogenic perspective, which focuses on health rather than dysfunction (Antonovsky & Sourami, 1988), when working with these families.

IMPLICATIONS FOR FUTURE INTERVENTIONS

The comments of the parents during the interview suggest that CFPS can be improved to facilitate attendance. The following changes will be incorporated in future interventions:

    1. The first meeting will be a social activity and a planning meeting. Announced in the brochure, single parents of children with disabilities will be invited to attend if they think they might be interested in the intervention. The session will include get-acquainted activities, and the WE CAN strategy will be briefly explained. Light refreshments will be served and babysitting will be provided. Parents will be invited to sign up for the intervention program at the end of the meeting. Veteran parents will describe the program and the benefits they received from attending.

    2. Parents indicating an interest in the program will be interviewed. Those parents who are experiencing unusual personal or family stressors (e.g., having only recently become a parent of a child with a disability, having just become single) might want to utilize other resources (a list will be provided by the interviewer) immediately and attend the program at a later time. Parents who seem likely to benefit from the program will be given consent forms to sign, and will be asked to develop, before they come to the first session, a list of family problems they hope to see resolved in the near future, hopefully increasing their motivation for family change.

    3. Partners will be assigned at the first session of CFPS. In case one partner misses a meeting, the other will call and explain what was missed. Veteran parents will also be enlisted to help parents develop skills that they missed. Most CFPS completers commented in their postassessment interviews that the frequent review of previous content during each session caused them to have a casual attitude about attending all the sessions. Therefore, videotapes of

previous sessions will be made available to parents for checkout.

4.   The program will still run for six sessions, with the last session providing an opportunity for children to participate in problem solving with their parents. During the fifth session, parents will be asked to share concerns they have about bringing their children to the last session. Parents will also be involved in planning the final session, with recommendations requested from each parent for making the session enjoyable and practical for her or his family. However, each session will start at 10:30 A.M. instead of 9:30 A.M. and last for 2 instead of 3 hours. Lunch will be provided at 12:30 P.M. to give the participants opportunities for socialization. Participants will be instructed that lunch might be a good time to brainstorm ideas for solving family problems.

5.   Babysitting will be provided and problem solving training will be offered concurrently for children and adolescents during the first five sessions.

CONCLUSION

> Instead of labeling these [single-parent] families as dysfunctional, it would appear to be more productive to approach the single-parent family as one that has unique stresses and is, therefore, more likely to benefit from primary and secondary prevention techniques focusing on decreasing some of the problem areas. (Feldman, Manella, & Varni, 1983, p. 166)

Feldman et al. summed the primary purpose of Cooperative Family Problem Solving: to assist single parents of children with disabilities in learning some practical skills that would allow them to cope more effectively with the magnitude of stressors frequently encountered by this population. A secondary purpose was to provide single parents with opportunities for socialization. Cooperative Family Problem Solving appeared to be well-received by the majority of participants and all program completers. Some completers appeared to benefit more than others, but all perceived at least some improvement in the two components of the intervention: family cooperation and family problem solving. Difficulty in recruiting single parents for the program appears to be related more to personal stressors and time conflicts rather than to a lack of interest in participating in the training program. That participants appeared to value the intervention, however, suggests that the socialization and skill-development needs of this population should not continue to be overlooked. As one single parent who completed CFPS commented, "Just bringing us together I thought was very important for me."

REFERENCES

Antonovsky, A., & Sourami, T. (1988). Family sense of coherence and adaptation. *Journal of Marriage and the Family, 50,* 79–92.

Barnes, K. (1986). Surviving as a single parent. *The Exceptional Parent, 16*(3), 47–49.

Bass, M.B. (1989). The cooperative family. *The Pointer, 33*(2), 39–42.

Beavers, W.B., Hampson, R.B., & Hulgus, Y.F. (1990). *Beavers Systems Model manual: 1990 edition.* Dallas: Southwest Family Institute.

Beckman, P.J. (1983). Influence of selected child characteristics on stress in families of handicapped infants. *American Journal of Mental Deficiency, 88*(2), 150–156.

Blechman, E.A., & McEnroe, M.J. (1985). Effective family problem solving. *Child Development, 56*(2), 429–437.

Borduin, C.M., Henggeler, S.W., Hanson, C.L., & Pruitt, J.A. (1985). Verbal problem solving in families of father-absent and father-present delinquent boys. *Child and Family Behavior Therapy, 7*(2), 51–63.

Bradford, J.D., & Stein, B.S. (1984). *The ideal problem solver: A guide for improving thinking, learning, and creativity.* New York: W.H. Freeman & Co.

Brody, R. (1982). *Problem solving: Concepts and methods for community organizations.* New York: Human Sciences Press.

Bryant, J. (1989). *Problem management: A guide for producers and players.* New York: John Wiley & Sons.

Bureau of the Census. (1990). *Statistical abstract of the United States, 1990* (110th ed.). Washington, DC: U.S. Government Printing Office.

Clark, H.B., Striefel, S., Bedlington, M.M., & Naimen, D.E. (1989). A social skills development model: Coping strategies for children with chronic illnesses. *Children's Health Care, 18*(1), 19–29.

Covey, S.R. (1989). *The seven habits of highly effective people.* New York: Simon & Schuster.

Eden, C., Jones, S., & Sims, D. (1983). *Messing about in problems: An informal structured approach to their identification and management.* New York: Pergamon Press.

Epstein, N.B., Baldwin, L.M., & Bishop, D.S. (1982). *Family Assessment Device.* Providence, RI: Butler Hospital.

Feldman, L.B. (1985). Integrative multi-level therapy: A comprehensive interpersonal and intrapsychic approach. *Journal of Marital and Family Therapy, 11*(4), 357–372.

Feldman, W.S., Manella, K.J., & Varni, J.W. (1983). A behavioral parent training programme for single mothers of physically handicapped children. *Child Care, Health, and Development, 9,* 157–168.

Foster, S.L., Prinz, R.J., & O'Leary, K.D. (1983). Impact of problem-solving communication training and generalization procedures on family conflict. *Child and Family Behavior Therapy, 5*(1), 1–23.

Giblin, P. (1986). Research and assessment in marriage and family enrichment: A meta-analysis study. *Journal of Psychotherapy and the Family, 2*(1), 79–96.

Hannum, J.W., & Mayer, J.M. (1984). Validation of two family assessment approaches. *Journal of Marriage and the Family, 46*(3), 741–748.

Hanson, S.M.H. (1986). Healthy single parent families. *Family Relations, 35,* 125–132.

Janis, I.L. (1982). Decisionmaking under stress. In L. Goldberger & S. Breznitz (Eds.), *Handbook of stress: Theoretical and clinical aspects* (pp. 69–87). New York: The Free Press.

Johnson, R.T., Johnson, D.W., Holubec, E.J., & Roy, P. (1984). *Circles of learning: Cooperation in the classroom.* Alexandria, VA: ASCD.

Koberg, D., & Bagnall, J. (1974). *The universal traveler: A soft-systems guide to creativity, problem-solving, and the process of reaching goals.* Los Altos, CA: William Kaufman, Inc.

Miller, I.W., Epstein, N.B., Bishop, D.S., & Keitner, G.I. (1985). The McMaster Family Assessment Device: Reliability and validity. *Journal of Marital and Family Therapy, 11*(4), 345–356.

Moss, H.B., Falloon, I.R.H., Boyd, J.L., & McGill, C.W. (1982). Strategies of behavioral family therapy in the community treatment of schizophrenia. *International Journal of Family Psychiatry, 3*(3), 289–299.

Nezu, A.M., Nezu, C.M., & Perri, M.G. (1989). *Problem-solving therapy for depression.* New York: John Wiley & Sons.

Parnes, S.J., & Harding, H.F. (Eds.). (1962). *A source book for creative thinking.* New York: Charles Scribner's Sons.

Reese, R.M. (1986). *Teaching individual and group problem solving to adults with mental retardation.* Doctoral dissertation, University of Kansas, Lawrence.

Reid, W.J. (1985). *Family problem solving.* New York: Columbia University Press.

Schraft, S.P. (1980). Working with parents in rural communities. In R.R. Abidin (Ed.), *Parent education and intervention handbook* (pp. 489–515). Springfield, IL: Charles C Thomas.

Schroder, K.H., Casadaban, A.B., & Davis, B. (1988). Interpersonal skills training for parents of children with cystic fibrosis. *Family Systems Medicine, 6*(1), 51–68.

Shank, M. (1992). Cooperative family problem solving: An intervention for single-parent families with a child who has a disability. *Dissertation Abstracts International, 53,* 08A. (University Microfilms No. 92–38, 703)

Stanley, B.K., Weikel, W.J., & Wilson, J. (1986). The effects of father absence on interpersonal problem-solving skills of nursery school children. *Journal of Counseling and Development, 64*(6), 383–385.

Stonewater, J.K. (1980). Strategies for problem solving. In K.E. Eble & J. Noonan (Eds.), *New directions for teaching and learning: Fostering critical thinking* (Vol. 3, pp. 33–57). San Francisco: Jossey-Bass.

Switzer, L.S. (1985). Accepting the diagnosis: An educational intervention for parents of children with learning disabilities. *Journal of Learning Disabilities, 18*(3), 151–153.

Thomas, E.J. (1977). *Marital communication and problem solving: Analysis, assessment, and change.* New York: The Free Press.

Vadasy, P.F. (1986). Single mothers: A social phenomenon and population in need. In R.R. Fewell & P.F. Vadasy (Eds.), *Families of handicapped children: Needs and supports across the life span* (pp. 221–252). Austin, TX: PRO-ED.

A New Beginning

Valerie Bateman

There is never a good way to find out that your child has a permanent disability. But some of the ways are considerably worse than others. I was told seven years ago that my son, Brandon, would never walk, talk, run, jump, play, or even know that he existed in this world. In other words, I was told to take Brandon home and love him, nothing more. Needless to say, I did take him home, but I did much, much more.

I began making phone calls to agencies to obtain information and assistance for myself and for my child. Little did I know that this was the onset of the breakup of my marriage and that I would eventually be raising my child all alone.

Bringing Brandon home was the beginning of countless hours, days, weeks, and years of physical therapy, occupational therapy, speech therapy, special preschools, doctors, hospitals, clinics, and the list goes on and on. My days were spent driving all over town to obtain services for Brandon and my nights were spent planning for the next day.

It seemed that as more time passed, my husband and I began to grow further and further apart, each afraid to let the other know the pain we felt in our hearts. In addition, my husband became obsessed with Brandon's disability. Whenever we went out socially, it was his sole topic of conversation, and it was the same at home. Of course, affixing the blame depends on who is telling the story. We finally reached a point where I had to choose between my marriage and my child. It was unfortunate when it happened, but I had to go with what I believed in. I made my decision to leave.

SINGLE PARENTING

I am now what is known as a "single parent," which nowadays is not so unusual. It is slightly more difficult, however, when you are the single parent of a child with a disability.

From Bateman, V. (1992). A new beginning. *Exceptional Parent* (Third Annual Mobility Guide), pp. 44–46. Copyright © 1992 by Psy-Ed Corporation; reprinted by permission.

My first task was to obtain a job. After finding one, my search for a day-care program began. No one wanted the added responsibility of caring for a child with cerebral palsy. After contacting 36 day-care facilities, I stumbled across an excellent program that accepted Brandon with open arms. It was definitely the answer to one of my many prayers. Putting him in a regular day-care setting was the best thing I have ever done for him. He has learned to be "just one of the kids." Everyone likes him and shows tremendous interest in helping him be the best that he can be.

I believe that setting realistic goals and priorities are the two most important factors in surviving single parenting. After my divorce, I gave myself five years to have a stable job, a home for us, and somewhat happy lives. It has only been three years but already I have a stable job, a home and, believe it or not, overall happiness and security. I feel that setting goals and striving to reach them also gives you the drive it takes to make it in this world.

SIBLING ISSUES

Brandon has a sister who is five years old. Lindsey was born healthy (another prayer answered). I never thought I could manage to raise two children on my own, but I am doing it. Not that there isn't a hitch now and then, but still, in all, I AM DOING IT!

Finding time for Lindsey is one of my on-going priorities. I never want her to feel that she is not as important to me as Brandon is or that his needs are greater than hers. Watching her grow has been one of the greatest joys of my life. She does everything with such ease. Although she is my youngest, she is sometimes my strength. In the beginning of our new lives, my children were the only reasons I cared to survive. I thought they really needed their mother; but the truth is, *I* needed *them*—and still do.

YOUR EMOTIONAL RIGHTS

Being a single parent gives you many rights, rights which you probably have never thought of. This is an area I feel I must address: single parents not as parents, but as people. It is all too common for parents to be so totally caught up in the daily pressures and priorities of meeting the needs of a child with a disability that they forget they, too, are human beings with needs. If you do not remember to be human you cannot help your child to become more so. More than other parents, you need to stay in touch with yourself and constantly reaffirm your humanity by exercising your rights, whenever necessary.

These are some of the rights we parents have as people:

- *Cry.* Parents have the right to cry. Don't hold in all that fear, hurt and anxiety. It helps to let it out—cry, yell, scream. It's nothing to hide or be ashamed of: You are not the only one who hurts.
- *Talk to others.* They can tell you that this, too, will pass.
- *Grieve.* It is okay to grieve. There is a time for grief, and it is necessary.
- *Learn to accept.* I would say that the agony passes as you give up the dreams and accept the reality of your child, whatever it is. You will gradually begin to enjoy each gain the child makes and take pleasure in whatever he or she can do. That's the world of acceptance. It's not necessarily a bad world. It's just that getting there is so very hard. Know that we all hurt at first and it doesn't seem like things will ever be the same, and in a way they won't. Now after three years, I laugh at jokes, I still work out, I enjoy my friends, my life goes on, and I'm enjoying it!

  I do still cry sometimes and feel so incredibly alone: lying awake at night wondering when the heartache and sadness will be lifted from my life; needing someone to help make decisions; and so desperately wanting someone who can understand all the feelings inside of me. My emotions are so complex at times that I do not understand most of them myself.
- *Allow others to care about you.* During difficult times, lean on your family and friends. For the first year, I didn't allow anyone to get close to me. I felt numb, unable to feel—it was the safest way to protect myself from feeling alone and hurt and angry. Don't make my mistake. Let others in and more importantly—let them help you and be with you.

  A bit of a hard shell still remains with me, but now I am able to feel again. It is not bad to have any kind of feelings or even a combination of them. Feelings are not bad or good; it is what you do about them that's important. Though anger is acceptable, understand that you must not allow it to possess and destroy you. You will discover friends, family and others who will accept your anger because they have shared it, and who will listen and accept your feelings because they accept you.
- *Do things for yourself.* You must make yourself happy before you can work on the happiness of others. I was always told that true happiness comes from within, and finally I know what that really means.
- *Take time away from your child once in a while.* Get away from everything, alone or with a friend, for a few minutes a day, a week or

whatever you feel is best for you. You'll be surprised at how it will change your perspective on caring for your child.

- *Relax.* Feel confident that you can look back at some future time and know that no one could have done more.

Finally, but most importantly, remember the one right that distinguishes you from other parents and bonds you to others like you, other parents of children with disabilities—the right to *never* give up. You have the right to believe in miracles, great and small, and the right to make them happen.

Valerie Bateman is a legal assistant in Mobile, Alabama, and the single mother of Brandon, 9, who has cerebral palsy, and Lindsey, 6. Bateman has spoken on single parenting the child with a disability to various local support groups. She is willing to speak to other interested groups and can be contacted at her office in Mobile at (205) 433-3131.

10

Help for Troubled Marriages

Jacqui Lichtenstein

The purpose of this chapter is to describe a method for working with couples who are experiencing relationship difficulties and who have children with disabilities. The chapter addresses issues of marital discord, communication, problem solving, negotiation, and managing conflict. In this chapter the process of behavioral marital counseling is explained, beginning with assessment and its importance and continuing with goal setting, skill introduction and development, support for feelings and emotional struggles, and the creation of a mutual frame of reference for meeting life's challenges. The clinical approach used falls into the broad category of behavioral marital therapy and draws on the rich and creative clinical traditions in that field. In addition, the chapter describes interventions and constructs that draw from other theoretical orientations and clinical experiences that enrich the process and allow the therapist to engage the couples in intensely personal ways.

LIFE CYCLE CHANGES

Marriage or being part of a committed relationship is an integral part of many people's lives. Our culture suggests that marriage, or its equivalent, is the ideal way to live; two people become committed to one another, available to provide support, nurturance, love, sex, and comfort in times of stress and challenge. The difficulties of man-

The research reported in this chapter was funded in part by grant no. G008730149 between the U.S. Department of Education and the Oregon Research Institute. The views expressed herein do not necessarily reflect those of the funders.

aging life's tasks on financial, physical, emotional, and spiritual levels are shared. Historical studies of family life suggest the idea that marriage meets individual needs, promotes personal happiness, and provides a safe haven for child-rearing. These ideas have been dominant in Western society for many centuries.

In reality, marriage or commitment to a relationship is a major developmental step that requires individuals to adjust on both intrapersonal and interpersonal levels. The experience of being married is such that individuals must confront their idealized images of self and partner and test them against a background of work and responsibility (Arond & Pauker, 1987). This may involve letting go of some expectations and clarifying and resolving others. It may be that the process of falling in love removes the couple from the world and allows them to focus on and see only one another. Marriage is a social convention that propels the couple back into a social world in which idealized images come up against reality in profound ways. The process of adjusting, understanding, and becoming a two-person unit in a way that meets the needs of the individuals involved and the responsibilities they choose to assume becomes the process of couple definition and development. For some couples, this process is a natural and organic flow of discovery and adaptation. Together they create a joint reality and perspective within which they flourish and support one another. For other couples, this process is a challenging and confusing road that requires work and, on occasion, outside assistance.

Just as marriage presents significant developmental challenges to individuals, the addition of a baby presents significant developmental challenges to the marriage. Marriage partners face many unexpected changes in their relationship as couples when they have children. Both men and women report shifts in their relationships with parents, friends, and co-workers, more traditional division of roles than either expected, and an increase in conflict when they have a baby (Cowan & Cowan, 1989). In addition, the more marriage partners feel their experience in transitioning to parenting roles to be different and the more conflict increases, the more the couple's overall satisfaction declines (Cowan & Cowan, 1989).

The addition of a child produces tremendous change and challenge to the marriage relationship, calling forth effort, resources, personal maturity, and relationship and communication skills. When the arrival of a child introduces additional factors, such as coping with the unexpected and different, the degree of challenge may increase dramatically. The birth of a baby with a severe disability deeply challenges the couple and their resources. Role differences can be further exacerbated; caregiving routines are often more complicated, time-consuming, and stressful as they are so essential to the infant's physical survival. These experiences combine to exert tremendous pressure on some couples.

For some couples with children with severe disabilities, the stresses they face do not differ greatly in content from those faced by families of children without special needs; rather, the breadth or degree is intensified. The inclusion of a child with a disability in a family poses challenges for the family; the specific difficulties of the child shape and influence the lives of those around him or her. Particular problems are encountered—practical issues, such as time, money, physical effect, and emotional energy; and psychological issues, such as adjustment, adaptation, and acceptance—that require creative responses from the family. When a child has a disability, the mismatch between child and parental expectations and behavior may be high; feelings of grief, denial, and profound disappointment are often experienced by the parents as they mourn the loss of the healthy baby they had hoped for (McCollum, 1984). Various feelings may interfere with the couple's ability to support one another through the adjustment process. Fears of hurting or overburdening an already stressed partner may keep couples from reaching out to one another. Difficulty processing and expressing anger at oneself, others, or fate can also work to keep couples apart.

Studies examining marital satisfaction and adjustment suggest that the presence of a child with a disability has a significant impact on the marital relationship (Benson & Gross, 1989). Studies differ with regard to whether the impact is positive or negative. Much of the literature reports decreased marital satisfaction, poor communication, financial problems, and sexual difficulties. Other studies find greater cohesiveness and satisfaction within the marital relationship. The inconsistent nature of the findings may be due in part to methodological flaws, poor measurement, and lack of appropriate controls (Benson & Gross, 1989). The differences may also reflect coping abilities and skills development that assists a couple in the process of adaptation to, and integration of, difficult life events and stress.

The information in the literature suggests that families of children with disabilities do experience greater stress than similar families of children without disabilities. However, the data suggest that the picture is a complex one and the relationship between increased stress and dysfunction is neither clear nor always negative. Kazak and Marvin (1984) found that families of children with disabilities responded to very real stresses and, on the whole, adapted to them in ways that were functional. These families were different from families of children without disabilities, and the differences placed the families at higher risk for dysfunction or problems. Despite these risk factors, they found the families that they studied to be resilient and adaptive in the face of extra challenges.

By contrast, some of the literature on marital relationships suggests that families of children with disabilities are more vulnerable to marital conflict and divorce. Featherstone (1980) suggests that the child's disability attacks the fabric of the family in four ways: 1) by creating powerful emotions in both parents, 2) by acting as a symbol of shared failure, 3) by reshaping the organization of the family, and 4) by being a potential for conflict. Work done with families of children with disabilities has shown that numbers 1 and 3 were especially significant. Number 3, the reshaping of family organization, has been true in all the families with whom the author has worked. The nature of the disability and the caregiving required have often had profound influences on the families. Number 1, the creation of powerful emotions in both parents, has been true for some families. On several occasions it was true for one parent, but not for the other. This difference in experience raised issues that were critical for parents to discuss and understand in order for them to communicate well and support one another. This difference in perception was frequently tied to number 4, potential for conflict. Conflict was often seen when there was limited or ineffective communication. Number 2 was not seen in the study that is outlined in this chapter nor in the author's other clinical work. It may be that this is less an issue than was previously suspected, or that by the time children are a little older, parents have effectively worked through these feelings.

Bristol, Gallagher, and Schopler (1988) examined the relationship between the marital relationship and parental adjustment to young children with developmental disabilities. They found that the strongest predictor of adjustment was harmony in the marital relationship. Specifically, harmony consisted of convergence between spouses' expectations of each other and the reality of what they provided. Mothers and fathers were asked to identify the role that their spouse would ideally play in providing emotional support and instrumental support. They also asked parents to report on what kinds of emotional and practical help their spouses actually provided on a daily basis. When there was a large discrepancy between what spouses hoped to receive from each other and what they actually received, there was evidence of maladjustment in the parental role. These findings suggest that the extra caregiving demands of raising a child with a disability require spouses to have a clear understanding of each other's expectations. Furthermore, this study suggests that couples must have good communication and problem-solving skills when there is a discrepency between the kind of support they desire from each other and what they actually receive. One well-documented approach to helping couples to communicate and problem-solve is behavioral marital therapy (Jabobson & Gurman, 1986).

BEHAVIORAL MARITAL THERAPY

Several excellent articles and treatment manuals are available regarding behavioral marital therapy (BMT). Thus, the following discussion emphasizes some of the themes that have arisen in using BMT with parents of children with severe disabilities.

For couples who are experiencing increased marital conflict and dissatisfaction, BMT can be a tool that offers assistance in improving the quality of the marital relationship, communication, and problem-solving skills. These improvements, in turn, reduce stress on the family and assist the parents in increasing their satisfaction with other personal and family roles.

In order to study the utility of BMT with parents of children with disabilities, marital counseling services were offered to couples who defined themselves as experiencing marital distress, and who had a child with a disability. For several couples, their initial assessment of the source of distress regarding the parenting of a child with a disability turned out to not be the case, while for others that was a critical issue. BMT was the treatment offered to assist the couples who experienced marital dissatisfaction.

The process of BMT involves the application of a specific scientific methodology to the treatment of distressed couples (Bussod & Jacobson, 1982). The theoretical underpinnings of BMT are derived from social exchange and social learning theory. Each of these theories describes a comprehensive model of intimate relationships that helps to explain the multidimensional character of marital distress. Internal events or perceptions about one's partner and one's relationship are central in the formulations of social exchange theory. Social learning theory examines the ratio of rewarding and punishing behaviors that determine the quality of people's daily lives.

Studies described in the BMT literature have empirically identified several general deficits as common problems experienced by distressed couples. Some of these deficits have to do with the way couples perceive and interpret one another's behavior. In distressed couples, one partner is more likely to make negative attributions about the other partner's behavior, more likely to focus on the negative side of the other's behavior, and more likely to distort perceptions of the other. In addition to these negative cognitive patterns, distressed couples are more reactive to negative events and become more distressed than untroubled couples when disagreements arise. They are more likely to reciprocate immediate negative behaviors and to use aversive control strategies with one another. They are more likely to have impaired communication and conflict resolution skills. Furthermore, they are likely to experience less enjoyment from their relationship as time passes, a process known as reinforcement erosion (Bussod & Jacobson, 1982).

In a general sense, BMT can be understood as a process that helps partners to obtain more benefits from their relationship by increasing positive behaviors and interaction. Because each couple is both classic and unique in their presentation of distress and discord, BMT has emphasized multidimensional assessment methods to assist in gathering a careful and comprehensive picture of a couple and their situation. The assessment process in turn leads to and facilitates the formulation of a treatment plan that addresses the couple's strengths and weaknesses at both the content level (behavioral exchanges) and the process level (communication skills). The assessment emphasizes the dyadic nature of the current problems and assists the couple in challenging dysfunctional cognitions and appraisals.

Treatment within BMT generally contains several components. One component is behavioral exchange (BE) techniques. BE creates an increase in positive marital exchanges and builds on the rewarding/reinforcing experiences that the couple shares. BE aims to enhance the couple's quality of life at home. Typically, in the BE component of therapy, couples agree to increase the number of positive interactions and enjoyable experiences that they provide each other.

The second component in BMT treatment is communication and problem-solving training (CPT). CPT focuses on teaching process-interaction skills, particularly those involved in conflict resolution, during sessions. CPT is understood as a preventive approach, a way to make the skills part of the couple's repertoire to be used at any time they are needed.

Communication training as a unique component involves learning speaker skills (using "I" statements, describing specific behaviors in specific situations, sticking to the present), and listener skills (active listening, summarizing the partner's remarks, checking one's accuracy, asking open questions, giving positive feedback) (Hahlweg, Revenstorf, & Schindler, 1984). The core skills in communication include reciprocal self-disclosure of feelings, attitudes, and thoughts and accepting the speaker's words. These skills help couples to avoid blaming, criticizing, and sidetracking one another (Hahlweg et al., 1984). The focus on problem-solving training assumes that the couple's lack of skills at generating change within the relationship is an important antecedent of marital distress (Margolin, 1982). Distressed couples who lack these communication and problem-solving skills tend to wreak havoc on their relationships and repeat ineffective, nonproductive strategies. The natural inclination for most people seems to be to do more of the same behavior, regardless of whether or not it is useful. In many cases behaviors are most often repeated when they are least effective.

Problem-solving training, as a distinct component, teaches the couple to define their problems in specific terms, to generate possible solutions, to evaluate the solutions, and to negotiate agreements on implementing particular solutions (Jacobson, 1977; Jacobson & Margolin, 1979). The couple also learns to pay attention to conditions that impede or facilitate collaborative problem-solving discussions.

Communication/problem-solving training (CPT) as a joint program component combines the skills of both areas. CPT teaches partners with a problem to voice grievances in a positive manner, to acknowledge their role in the maintenance of the problem, and to express their feelings and their complaints clearly and in specific behavioral terms. Partners who are on the receiving end of a complaint learn to use active listening skills, paraphrasing and reflecting, and nondefensive acceptance of the partner's perception (Jacobson & Margolin, 1979). After these skills are learned, the couple is then able to address specific issues.

In BMT, couples work on their problems by first dealing with relatively simple problems that are not highly charged with emotion or laden with past history. As the couple becomes more skilled in resolving these kinds of problems, the therapist helps them to move on to identify and tackle larger themes that divide them. Examples of these larger themes are discussed later.

The therapist's role in BMT is an active and directive one, advocating for the relationship rather than for either individual. The therapist's role provides structure to the therapy experience so that the sessions create an environment that is conducive to active and constructive participation on the part of the couple (Margolin, 1982). This requires the establishment of a collaborative spirit that lets the couple know that they are on the same team.

Within the BMT model the therapist also functions as an instructor. To assist couples with the learning of new interactional skills and definitions, the behavior therapist uses a combination of direct instruction, corrective feedback, and behavioral rehearsal (Jacobson, 1977). It is the responsibility of the therapist to monitor and control the pacing of treatment so that both partners of the couple are successful in the process of learning and mastering new skills. The therapist's responsibility extends to the need to maintain an awareness of short-term skill building with the integration of long-term goals for change, which may include presenting problems or other issues identified in the process of treatment.

INTERVENTION

In the study described later in this chapter, intervention was divided into three phases. The first phase included the collection of baseline data and assessment. This means that during and after baseline measures are taken, session time is used to introduce the couple to the therapeutic process and to set the stage for therapeutic change by building positive expectancies and trust.

The process of assessment was slow and thorough. The needs of the family with regard to marital problems and the emotional and practical realities of raising a child with a particular disability are often complex and intricately interwoven. The tendency of one parent to step back from the other in an attempt to avoid burdening an already overextended partner was seen frequently. It also appeared that the process of withdrawing was perceived by the other as not helpful or was not interpreted in the way in which it was intended.

Understanding the behaviors in question, their consequences in the relationship, and the intentionality of the doer was very important with regard to developing intervention strategies. In these couples, as with all couples, the *why* of behaviors, the presumed goal or intent, was critical in effecting change. Until couples were clear and convinced that the desired intent was backfiring and causing difficulty rather than alleviating it, their commitment to change tended to be rather minimal. If (and when) this understanding took place, it served to create a process of motivation and tempo of change that was exciting for the couple and the therapist. The reality of creating this kind of a framework for recognizing and understanding the problem grew out of a detailed and comprehensive assessment.

Content of the assessment sessions included: a brief discussion of current difficulties, an explanation of the special needs of the child, an historical review of difficulties, a developmental history of the relationship, history of the child and the experience for the family, a descriptive picture of daily interaction and relevant reinforcers, exploration of time alone and together, shared activities, positive experiences with one another, and the generation of a list of possible topics for the 5- to 10-minute negotiation sessions.

Time was taken during assessment sessions in order to gain an understanding of why and how the couple had chosen to enter into treatment at this time in their relationship; who, if anyone, had taken the lead in pursuing help; and the reaction of the other partner to this suggestion and process. In general, it appears that one partner tends to take the lead in this process and either willingly or unwillingly brings his or her mate along. Time is initially taken to understand this process and address feelings and reactions, and this seems to facilitate future work. Whether this was useful in building a collaborative spirit or whether it gave the partner who did not actively choose to participate time to get used to the idea and verbally express doubts and concerns is not clear.

The nature of assessment was such that initial information about the couple and their current difficulties was sought both in their own words and descriptions and in behavioral terms from the beginning. Descriptive phrases such as "unsupportive," "uninterested in the children," and "unhelpful with the child with a disability" were pursued with questions that asked for specificity. Sometimes this took the form of asking for additional information about duration, frequency, and intensity, and asking for a concrete example.

The second topic addressed in assessment was the particular needs of the child with a disability. The experiences of these families are very much shaped by caregiving routines. Understanding the demands on the family with regard to their child's physical, emotional, educational, and therapeutic (i.e., occupational therapy, physical therapy, speech therapy) needs was very important in forming a picture of their lives and the energy and resources that would be available to help in changing patterns and behaviors.

The treatment phase of intervention began with the therapist sharing specific feedback with the couple. The feedback session provided an opportunity to build a case for the creation of a positive framework for change and to establish a mutual point of reference. The information learned from the forms and the assessment sessions enabled the therapist to present the couple with feedback about the strengths of the relationship and the problem areas, and with the couple's help, to generate a treatment plan to address the issues. Each treatment plan tends to include five general tasks:

1. To learn effective strategies for solving problems
2. To put the couple in touch with their abilities to influence one another in a positive manner
3. To focus on effective communication in situations other than formal problem-solving interactions
4. To assist partners in reinforcing good communication patterns and styles with one another
5. To develop a unified policy on handling the child(ren)

The treatment also addresses specific issues that were unique to given couples.

The feedback session also includes a process whereby the therapist and the couple develop a way to track, change, and attend to the development of efforts and new interactional patterns in the relationship.

The treatment phase continued with the introduction of specific communication skills. These skills, which were defined and practiced in session, included: active listening, paraphrasing, reflection, pinpointing, modality checking, and making effective opening statements. Pinpointing skills, a particularly pivotal part of the intervention, included the following: using "I" statements, being positive, being specific, and staying in the present. The introduction and development of other skills hinge on the couple's ability to effectively integrate and use these ideas. The amount of session time spent on this phase differs for each couple.

The final aspect of treatment was the introduction and practice of problem solving. In this phase the couple addresses issues from their lives using the skills, new information, and therapist support to attempt to resolve differences or create new patterns and responses to challenging situations.

Clinical Examples

This section offers examples of aspects of the intervention process and how it worked for four particular couples. These couples were seen over a 3-month period for a single-subject study of behavioral marital therapy with couples whose children had disabilities. Each couple consisted of two biological parents and at least one child with a moderate to severe disability. Couples filled out self-report forms pretreatment and posttreatment, including the Beck Depression Inventory (BDI) (Beck, Ward, Mendelson, Mock, & Erbaugh, 1961), the Dyadic Adjustment Scale (DAS) (Spanier, 1976), and the Parenting Stress Index (PSI) (Abidin, 1983).

The marital therapy for these couples followed the procedures that have been briefly listed previously. (Interested readers should obtain treatment manuals [Jacobson & Margolin, 1979; Weiss & Perry, 1979].) In addition to the skill-training procedures that are detailed in these manuals, therapy also involves nonspecific processes such as building a sense of rapport, active listening, and helping the couple to conceptualize their relationship problems. The theoretical constructs were tied to the presenting problems or the stumbling blocks that the couples encountered along the way. In the following discussion, some of these themes are emphasized in order to help the reader better understand some of the challenges faced by these families. It is important to keep in mind that each session centered around behavioral skill training and that the themes that are described below arose in the context of skill training. Without the essential backbone of skill-training exercises, the attention to relationship themes would not have provided the couples with practical ways of alleviating conflict and increasing mutual pleasure.

COUPLE A

Couple A had two boys, ages 13 and 2½. The younger boy had Down syndrome and serious heart complications. The parents entered treatment because of concerns over poor communication, emotional distance, and general unhappiness with their relationship. Their issues were very specific. The wife wanted more from her husband—more interaction, more attention, more awareness on his part. The husband was not sure if he wanted to give what was asked, nor was he sure that he was capable of doing so, particularly on a long-term basis. During the assessment process if became clear that these issues, the wife's desire for more and the husband's reluctance to comply, were longstanding. The couple had sought therapy in the past and both felt that no gains had been made. Efforts to develop behavioral strategies were met with responses such as, "That doesn't work for us," or "We have already tried things like that."

After discussing these experiences it was clear that efforts at change carried a heavy load from the past. This understanding was defined with the couple and presented in a theoretical framework as a "climate of passive hopelessness where historical distress pervaded all attempts at change," and was discussed explicitly with the couple. The couple was challenged to stay consciously in the present whenever possible and to identify for themselves and each other when they slipped into past issues and distress. The couple and the therapist agreed that all hope for useful change needed to be grounded in the present. Behavioral listening and problem-solving strategies were taught as one way to avoid falling back into the sense of hopelessness associated with past failures.

The spiritual and psychological understandings and interests of this couple gave meaning to these somewhat vague concepts. To some degree both partners, the wife in particular, were interested in the idea of personal growth and change and believed in a "higher self." These understandings supported the couple, particularly the wife, in remembering to stay with the present and not drag in past problems. The construct, historical distress intruding into the present and creating a sense of passive hopelessness, was noted to be useful to the couple at the 3-month follow-up check.

At the follow-up session this couple assessed the intervention as useful in creating a sense of hope for them by offering specific skills and styles that were of assistance in avoiding old and destructive patterns. Issues remain for this couple, particularly around intimacy, but they express positive feelings about working on them.

COUPLE B

Couple B had three children: a 5½-year-old boy with a rare genetic disorder similar to Tay-Sachs disease, a 3-year-old girl, and a 5-month-old boy. One week prior to beginning treatment, the couple learned that their youngest child did not have this disorder. Five years before, the couple lost their oldest daughter to this disease following a long and arduous struggle to meet her health needs. The course of the disorder is such that the child develops along normal lines until about 2½ or 3 years of age, then seizures and other complications develop and the child loses skills significantly. As the disorder progresses, feeding needs and daily care become extremely demanding. Concerns with adequate nutrition, respiratory infections, and specialized medical needs are a part of every week. The couple entered treatment because of concerns over poor communication, personal depression on the part of both parents, and a general feeling of helplessness in the face of their child's disorder.

Issues for this couple seemed to stem from feelings of helplessness and discouragement in the face of overwhelming circumstances. Additional complications were encountered during treatment due to external life events. The condition of the 5½-year-old deteriorated, the father's stepfather died, and relatives moved in for 3 weeks, crowding an already full house.

This couple entered the study with specific issues as well. Working on these issues appeared to relieve distress on the part of the husband, but did not do much for the wife. She seemed to respond more when the construct of "shyness" was introduced. Shyness was defined as a pervasive feeling that limited the couple's ability to share pain and deep feelings, as a fear that no one was there, and as a sense of profound isolation. The introduction of this construct provided support for the wife in talking about the deep pain and isolation she still felt in relation to the death of their daughter 5 years before and her impending fears and anxieties about the deterioration and loss of their son. In response, the husband related his feelings from the time of their daughter's death and from other situations where he too felt that no one was there. Session time was used to discuss the feelings and pain around the death of their older child and the distance that developed between the parents since that time.

In the process of addressing these issues, the wife also discussed some painful experiences with her father and explored the implications that she felt they had for her. As the husband listened to her and supported her in this process, she expressed a greater feeling of safety and security in the marriage. The husband's responses and increased ability and desire to listen were very important to both of them in this process.

Both husband and wife were able to affirm that they wanted the other to be there during the hard times and that they wanted to be there for each other. It was at this point that therapy seemed to move forward for the couple as a unit, despite intense circumstantial hassles. In the sessions both spouses talked about the need to separate themselves from their families of origin and the historical feelings of isolation and pain that they carried. They affirmed their desire to do things differently for themselves and their children.

At the follow-up session, the couple assessed the intervention as being extremely helpful to them. The ability to trust one another with important feelings and to talk together more freely brought about a sense of increased closeness and positive feelings in their relationship. The couple chose to continue treatment on an intermittent basis every 4–5 weeks, making use of the booster sessions. The couple wanted to continue to deal with issues around the deteriorating condition and impending death of their 5½-year-old child.

COUPLE C

Couple C had three boys: a 5-year-old boy with Down syndrome, a 4-year-old boy, and a 6-month-old boy. The couple entered treatment because of concerns over poor communication, frequent fights, ensuing periods of silence, and feelings of general unhappiness. Special circumstances for this couple included significant scheduling complications and difficulty in defining and clarifying the main issues in the relationship. Child care, health problems, and work commitments made scheduling sessions particularly difficult.

Over the course of the sessions it was difficult to determine what was really the pressing issue that caused the fights and limited the couple's attempts at communication. Historically, the husband was the talker in the couple, while the wife was silent and disapproving, withdrawing from conflict and then blowing up when she could stand it no longer. Temporary progress was made with interrupting this pattern, but it could not stand up to the big issues in the relationship. Issues such as time away for the wife, the husband helping out more at home, relationships with her family, and his drinking continued to result in unproductive stalemates. The construct offered to the couple was the difficulty of working toward change when there was no common definition of the problem. Session time was used to understand the efforts that did not work and to be clear why that was the case. This was helpful for a period of time, but again it could not stand up to real stress in the relationship.

A critical issue for this couple was the wife's belief that the husband did not understand the reality of caring for the child with a disability. The husband did not share her perception; he felt that he knew the efforts involved. During the final three sessions the wife began to talk about the emotional and personal pain that she felt because her child had a disability. She tried to explain the feelings connected with her sadness and loss with regard to this child, not the day-to-day difficulties. The husband had great difficulty in supporting her with these feelings. He just did not experience the situation in the same way. The wife expressed feelings of hopelessness and discouragement in the face of his lack of understanding and retreated from talking with him.

At this point the wife discussed her desire to seek individual treatment to deal with her feelings and concerns. The husband was supportive of this and encouraged her to seek assistance for herself. Agreement was reached to terminate the marital work. The wife's decision to enter individual therapy was an important step in freeing the couple from feelings of hopelessness and discouragement. At follow-up they reported doing better and indicated their appreciation of the skills and information they had received.

COUPLE D

Couple D had two children, a 5-year-old girl with cerebral palsy and a 3-year-old boy. The girl also had seizures and had very limited language and communication skills. She would have periodic bouts of screaming and unexplained discomfort at night that was upsetting to and demanding on the parents.

Special circumstances for this couple included the suicide of the husband's father, the emotional needs of his mother and sisters following this event, and the special needs of their child with regard to seizures and sleep problems.

This couple was clear upon entering treatment that they were satisfied with their relationship but felt that they would like to improve their communication. They used the intervention sessions to develop and practice communication skills, which they then used at home. The wife voiced a concern about the husband being distant and withdrawn when he was upset or angry. She wanted him to express his feelings more. The husband wanted more assistance from the wife with regard to household responsibilities. He wanted her to be more productive with her time at home with the kids, as he felt he was.

A significant factor for this couple was the different way they viewed their child's disability. For the wife the child's problem was a distressing situation that was part of their reality. She was able to delight in her child's gains and deal with problems as they came up. For the husband, the child's disability was a tragedy, one that influenced every aspect of their lives. He appreciated the gains his child made, but he suffered a great deal over her limitations and the restrictions these imposed on the family. The husband was disappointed in himself that he felt this way and tended not to share these feelings with his wife. This increased the distance between them and sometimes confused the wife as to why he was upset or unhappy.

This couple began treatment with the desire to achieve better communication. For the wife this meant being able to approach her husband and ask about his feelings; for the husband this meant sharing his feelings with his wife and asking her directly for help.

In the intervention sessions the couple discussed this issue and the husband's tendency to retreat with these feelings and their relationship to childhood issues for him. The husband's experiences of growing up with an alcoholic father and of his father's suicide were an important focus in the treatment. Discussing these issues was not easy for the husband, but the wife wanted to understand what he was feeling and how she could be of help. The very process of talking about the feelings challenged the husband's pattern of retreating with his feelings.

The theoretical construct that was introduced for this couple was described as "fear of burdening one another." In an effort to spare the other person pain or distress, each person was settling for distance and isolation. The experience of distance and isolation from one another was a source of distress to both husband and wife. They each saw that there were benefits to being more direct and expressive with one another. The process of achieving this was more difficult for the husband; he had to look at aspects of his past and his family. Some progress toward this was made in the sessions, but the husband was clear that he only wanted to go so far with it. The understanding was helpful to him and served as a reminder that he could ask directly for support and/or practical help. The construct was useful to the wife as she no longer saw herself as responsible for his moods or his distancing behavior. She became more able to reassure him that she could deal with his feelings and sadness and became more patient in the process. Both the husband and the wife considered themselves as benefiting from the intervention and described the communication techniques as helpful in circumventing old patterns.

Evaluation

In order to evaluate the effectiveness of BMT for these four couples, both self-report measures of marital satisfaction were administered and direct observation assessments of the couples' behavior were conducted. The self-report measures used were the Marital Happiness Scale (Azrin, Naster, & Jones, 1973) and the Beck Depression Inventory (Beck et al., 1961). In order to determine whether the couples learned new skills in communication and problem-solving, they were videotaped during negotiation sessions before, during, and after the therapy. These videotapes were coded using the Marital Interaction Coding System (MICS). This code measures the extent to which couples cooperate, use aversive or positive interactions, and generate or fail to generate solutions to problems.

A detailed description of the measurement and outcomes of this study is shown in Lichtenstein (1990). To summarize the findings briefly, the data show that all four couples demonstrated an increase in their communication and problem-solving skills and decreased conflict during negotiation. Three of the four couples showed a decline in self-reported depression. The one couple who had higher levels of depression at the end of the treatment was reeling from the suicide of a family member. Three of the four couples also rated their marriages as happier and more satisfying after the treatment.

RESEARCH CONCLUSIONS

Behavioral and verbal feedback from the couples indicated a positive response to therapy. All of the couples involved in the study came for therapy regularly, family member health and babysitting conditions being favorable. The health of both the child with a disability and of the mother were factors in regard to rescheduling some meetings. Couples discussed greater levels of satisfaction due to the ability to bring up sensitive or difficult topics even when the ensuing discussion was hard and unpleasant. The fact that the couples agreed to come for therapy seemed to work as permission to talk more and/or to make the need to communicate a valid concern.

Over the process of therapy certain assumptions in the field were observed to be in effect. Couples with children with more severe disabilities, those requiring greater amounts of care, experienced more stress. Improving the communication in the relationship, while helpful, did not change the reality of having a child with a disability. Couples in which one partner had great difficulty in accepting the child's disability suffered emotional pain that could not be lessened by support or discussion.

The data obtained from each of the couples demonstrated the usefulness of behavioral marital therapy with regard to interrupting old patterns of behavior and communication. The process of learning communication skills tended to create a climate of self-awareness and reflection with regard to one's language, tone, and intention. It was almost impossible to attempt to be positive, specific, and focused in the present without noticing one's tendency to not do those things. Each partner saw, if only for a few moments, the role he or she played in setting up ineffective communication patterns. The speaker, as he or she struggled to change, noticed this difficulty and, either independently or with the therapist's help, drew the connection between the difficulty and the responsibility he or she could assume in solving communication problems. The process of doing this often included humor and surprise as well as awareness and struggle for the speaker. Unsuccessful attempts at practicing communication skills were an important part of the learning process; these were extremely instructive as they allowed each individual to realize the effort required to communicate in a different manner.

SUMMARY

In this chapter BMT is described and used as a method for working with couples who are experiencing relationship difficulties and who have children with disabilities. Emphasis is placed on the skills-based aspects of BMT and the need for an in-depth assessment that clarifies, for the therapist and the couple, the specific nature of the problems they are experiencing. Within this context, the unique situations and challenges facing each couple are understood and validated. The need for increasing relationship benefits, communication skills, and problem-solving abilities is addressed in a manner that respects the timing and needs of each couple. In addition, metaphors or descriptions are developed to assist each couple in creating a framework of understanding that ties the skills and information together in a cohesive and personalized process.

REFERENCES

Abidin, R. (1983). *Parenting stress index manual.* Charlottesville, VA: Pediatric Psychology Press.

Arond, M., & Pauker, S.L. (1987). *The first year of marriage.* New York: Warner Books.

Azrin, N.A., Naster, B.J., & Jones, R. (1973). Reciprocity counseling: A rapid learning-based procedure for marital counseling. *Behavior Research and Therapy, 11,* 365–382.

Beck, A.T., Ward, C.H., Mendelson, M., Mock, J., & Erbaugh, J. (1961). An inventory for measuring depression. *Archives of General Psychiatry, 4,* 561–571.

Benson, B.A., & Gross, A.M. (1989). The effect of a congenitally handicapped child upon the marital dyad: A review of the literature. *Clinical Psychology Review, 9*(6), 747–758.

Bristol, M.M., Gallagher, J.J., & Schopler, E. (1988). Mothers and fathers of young developmentally disabled and nondisabled boys: Adaptation and spousal support. *Developmental Psychology, 24*(3), 441–451.

Bussod, N., & Jacobson, N.S. (1982). Cognitive behavioral marital therapy. *The Counseling Psychologist, 11*(3), 57–63.

Cowan, P.A., & Cowan, C.P. (1989). Marital relationship, parenting style, and the child's development at the age of three. *Voprosy–Psikhologii, 4,* 110–118.

Featherstone, H. (1980). *A difference in the family.* New York: Basic Books.

Hahlweg, K., Revenstorf, D., & Schindler, L. (1984). Effects of behavioral marital therapy on couples' communication and problem-solving skills. *Journal of Consulting and Clinical Psychology, 52,* 553–566.

Jacobson, N.S. (1977). Problem solving and contingency contracting in the treatment of marital discord. *Journal of Consulting and Clinical Psychology, 45,* 92–100.

Jacobson, N.S., & Gurman, A.S. (1986). *Clinical handbook of marital therapy.* New York: The Guilford Press.

Jacobson, N.S., & Margolin, G. (1979). *Marital therapy: Strategies based on social learning and behavior exchange principals.* New York: Brunner/Mazel.

Kazak, A.E., & Marvin, R.S. (1984). Differences, difficulties, and adaptation: Stress and social networks in families with a handicapped child. *Family Relations, 33,* 67–77.

Lichtenstein, J. (1990). *Behavioral marital therapy for parents of children with developmental disabilities.* Unpublished doctoral dissertation, University of Oregon, Eugene.

Margolin, G. (1982). A social learning approach to intimacy. In M. Fisher & G. Stricker (Eds.), *Intimacy* (pp. 175–201) New York: Plenum.

McCollum, A.T. (1984). Grieving over the lost dream. *Exceptional Parent, 14,* 9–12.

Spanier, G. (1976). Measuring dyadic adjustment: New scales for assessing the quality of marriage and other dyads. *Journal of Marriage and the Family, 38,* 15–28.

Weiss, R.L., & Perry, B.A. (1979). *Assessment and treatment of marital dysfunction.* Eugene: Oregon Marital Studies Program.

"I Don't Know Where We're Going."

Marital Problems and the Young Family

"I don't know what happened," Frank Jones, a short and slender man in his mid-twenties, said quietly. "I just don't know where to begin.

"I guess it all starts with our son, Frank Jr., who just turned three. He was born with serious problems. Last Sunday we celebrated his third birthday and we had Jean's family and mine over. It seems that whenever we have the families together, it's very tense. When everyone went home, we cleaned up and we sat down just by ourselves, I started to cry. I don't think I have cried since I've been three years old. I just don't know what we have for a life. I don't know where we're going and I don't know what we should do. Sometimes, I wish we could start over.

"I find myself resenting attention that anyone gives Jean or my son. I also have begun to envy my friends whether they're married or single. These thoughts make me feel terrible, but I can't stop them. And, last Sunday I felt I'd reached the end of my rope. Jeanie told me she also felt discouraged but couldn't talk to anyone about how her life is going. She suggested that we come to you to see whether you can help us make sense out of what's happened to us and what our life can be.

"I can still remember when we got married. I met Jean when I was 20 and she was 19. I had just finished at community college and I didn't know what I wanted to do. Jeanie was starting a nurse's training program. We went together a couple of years. We had a great time together. We talked a lot about what we were going to do and what kind of family we were going to have. When Jeanie had one more year

to go at nursing school, we decided to get married. She finished
school, and a week later little Frank was born—two months early.

"We were looking forward to a child and thought we'd have a big
family. I still remember the look on the obstetrician's face when he
came to see me. He told me that Dr. Ellison was going to see Frank Jr.
and would tell us what the score was. Dr. Ellison told us there was a lot
of brain damage. He wasn't sure first whether Frank would live and, if
he were to live, how well he would do. He was going to get a specialist
in babies to look at Frankie. And it seemed that life, a part of my life,
ended right then and there.

"We were both upset. I guess I showed it more than Jean. I tend to
get very agitated when I can't settle something. No matter how hard
we try, neither of us can remember that first week. Jean really took
care of Frankie and I guess, me, for a while.

"From that time on, we've been surrounded by Jean's family. She
has two older sisters who live not too far from us. It seems they're
around all the time. It's unfair to look at it that way, I guess, because
they have been very helpful and try to do what they can to help Jean.
At this time Frankie can do so little for himself. He requires constant
attention. But I haven't had any privacy—we haven't had any
privacy—since then. I began to wonder whether I really will ever have
a wife again, or what kind of a wife and husband we're going to be.

"For about a year after the baby was born, our sex life was almost
nothing. And I guess that was both of us. Jeanie certainly is, as I am,
concerned about what would happen if we had another child—would
the same thing happen? Since then, that part of our life has not been
very satisfactory. Sometimes it's because Jean is tired, sometimes it's
because I'm tense. At Frankie's birthday party there were no little kids
his age except his cousins. I really began to wonder, 'Who do I belong
to? Who belongs to me?'

"My family has tried to help some, but they always criticize Jean.
They worry a lot about me. They want to know why I'm not being
taken care of and why I don't look happier. And it's almost as if it's a
constant criticism of Jeanie. I think I feel the same from her parents,
although they don't say it: 'Why aren't I a better husband?' And I
began to say to myself, 'I'm still young. We never go anywhere.' I can't
remember the last time we took a trip together. I get confused about
how I even feel about Jean from time to time. And then I feel terrible.
There's got to be some better way and I just don't know what we
should do."

"I feel some of the same things that Frank talks about." Jean
Jones, a short, dark-haired woman in her mid-twenties, had flecks of

gray in her hair, making her look older than her age. "The thing I miss most is that before Frank Jr. was born, we would talk a lot. We looked forward to seeing each other—I certainly did—at night. And we would talk about our plans for the future.

"We don't do much anymore. We had a lot of friends. I had a lot of friends at nursing school. And slowly but surely, we see fewer and fewer of them. I still see some during the day. Sometimes, when my friends have odd shifts, they'll come over in the afternoon. Most of them are getting married now. Many of them are having children. I feel terrible because, like Frank, I feel jealous. I feel happy that they're having such a wonderful time. They seem so enthusiastic. And then I feel jealous that the ones that have had children are so happy afterwards. I feel terrible about that, and I think the way I feel has meant that I've lost those people as friends also.

"When we first got married, we certainly spent some time each weekend with our families. But we were independent of them. We could go away on a weekend occasionally. Ever since Frankie was born, I feel more like a daughter than a wife. Every day either my mother or one of my sisters comes to help. There is so much to do—special feeding, physical therapy, seizure meds and doctors visits—it seems neverending. I've tried doing it alone but then I'm so tired. I don't know what needs to be done about the marriage or how hard the work is. But when Frank started to cry the other night, I thought it was time to find out what kind of a marriage we have, what kind of a marriage should we have, and what's possible under these circumstances. I don't want to wind up blaming anyone for what's happened. I certainly don't want to wind up blaming Frankie. Because I think what happens is, when we turn to that, then we both feel terrible. I know there's something that can be done. What is it? I'm willing to try anything; I think Frank is, too. I wish I could say clearly that we love each other right now, but I don't know. But I do know that we once loved each other."

SUMMARY AND CONCLUSIONS

The Jones came to discuss their concerns about their marriage. They traced their marital problems to the birth of their son, Frank Jr., who was born with severe disabilities.

Mr. and Mrs. Jones had just celebrated Frank Jr.'s third birthday. When the party was over and their families had gone home, Mr. Jones began to cry. He told his wife that he did not know where their marriage was and what he could do.

Mrs. Jones agreed that their marriage had drifted over the past three years. She felt that the problems stemmed from their involvement with their own families. After Frank Jr. had been born, needing a great deal of help, they turned to their own parents and siblings. Although both of them were uncomfortable about the daily contact, neither had an idea about how to make any change.

The birth of a child is a time of special stress for all parents. When the first child of young parents is born with severe disabilities, the stress on the family is multiplied. They are faced with many questions about the short-term and long-term future of their child, questions they had not been prepared to ask and for which there are few certain answers. Dreams and expectations parents had imagined for their unborn child are suddenly lost, and parents must mourn these losses. At the same time, the daily care of the child requires a great deal of time and energy. The challenges may exceed the financial and emotional resources of the parents.

The impact of stress is shaped, in part, by the stage of family life of the parents. In the Jones family, Frank Jr.'s birth came early in their life together. When young adults marry, they need time to develop patterns of interdependence. They must move beyond their old network of relationships with family and friends, so they can devote themselves to finding ways of sharing their lives. They have to find comfortable ways of doing things together as well as areas in which they may continue to do things by themselves.

One aspect of this change is that young adults have to learn to turn to each other for solving the problems of living rather than turn to the more familiar patterns of turning to parents, siblings and friends. In stressful times, people often turn back to old familiar ways of handling crises.

The continuous stress associated with caring for Frank Jr. seemed to have prevented the Jones from developing new ways of working together on behalf of the child. Married for only a short time, they were still developing their own style of living together as a couple when they had to turn to their families for support. Soon, they found themselves sharing more with their own families than with each other. Although both felt comforted by these experiences, each one also felt uncomfortable about a sense of isolation from the other. Neither felt he or she had a clear sense of direction as to how to meet the needs of their child or how to meet their personal needs together.

Because Mrs. Jones received a great deal of support via her continuous contact with her own family, Mr. Jones had felt her family had taken control of Frank Jr.'s life. The continuous presence of family made the Jones feel more like children than adults.

They were encouraged to find time to visit each of the specialists without their families, in order to define the questions they wished to ask about the child's current program and the expectations of the future. The Jones then discussed what they heard together before they shared any information with their families. They were surprised and delighted when their own parents praised them for these new efforts at independence. As they began to do this they felt emotionally closer to one another and more like husband and wife.

After a year they began to discuss a topic they had been avoiding—having another child. Like many people who have had a child with a disability, the Jones had found it difficult to go back and review with the obstetrician their concerns about having another child.

They also began to define with their parents and families the kinds of support they wanted and how they might use the free time this produced.

For the first time in three years, they were able to take a week's vacation, as they arranged support and respite with their parents. Meeting once a month, they were able to begin to discuss issues that needed to be settled for them to plan ahead for an expanded family.

This case has been selected from private practice and consultation files. The names and circumstances have been changed to preserve confidentiality.

11

Improving Collaborative Communication Between Professionals and Parents

Barbara Walker
and
George H.S. Singer

The purpose of this chapter is to present a set of attitudes, beliefs, and strategies designed to improve working relationships between parents and professionals. The philosophy of professional helping outlined in this chapter is consistent with the family-centered approach to service design (see Singer, chap. 1, this volume) and places particular emphasis on a collaboration orientation to parent–professional relationships. The authors believe that initial expectations for instant formation of collaborative parent–professional partnerships have been presumptuous. Professionals who have been trained primarily to work with children are being asked to take on added orientations toward families and collaborative roles in relationships with parents without the requisite training on how to accomplish family-centered helping or partnership development within the demanding context of special education. In the wake of decades of inattention in professional training programs to family-driven and collaboration goals in parent–professional relationships,

This chapter was supported in part by grants from the U.S. Department of Education, grant no. G008730149 and grant no. H024P10022 to the Oregon Research Institute. The opinions stated in this chapter do not necessarily reflect those of the funder.

considerable adaptations in philosophies of helping, perspectives on families, professional role definitions, and communication strategies are needed to craft and maintain effective parent–professional partnerships.

The authors have been aware for some time that parents and professionals often have difficulty establishing a comfortable way to orient their focus toward family priorities. A study by Dunst and colleagues (Dunst, Trivette, Starnes, Hamby, & Gordon, 1993) found that the ways in which family support workers interact with family members are often not in keeping with family-centered values (see Singer, chap. 1, this volume, for a discussion of these values). Walker (1989a) discovered some specific communication patterns in informal communication between parents and special education teachers that strongly suggested discomfort in the relationship and difficulty in addressing sensitive topics. On the whole, both parents and teachers had difficulty engaging in some of the key communication behaviors considered important as indicators of problem-solving functions and constructive communication. For example, both parents and teachers had difficulty asking one another questions, using assertive statements, and offering one another support. The profile that emerged from Walker's study indicated that, by and large, parents and teachers engaged in conversations where each appeared to be self-directed, as opposed to interactive, in choosing what to say. Furthermore, the communicants appeared to cooperate with one another in remaining on fairly safe ground in their conversations, rather than testing the ability of their relationship to handle more difficult matters.

This profile is consistent with other reports from parents and professionals who indicate confusion and frustration with the absence of effective collaboration and problem-solving in their relationships (Fine, 1991; Rainforth, York, & Macdonald, 1992; Turnbull & Turnbull, 1986). Studies of interactions between physicians and patients have also found that serious miscommunications are commonplace in medical settings. Mischler (1984) analyzed transcripts of discussions between doctors and patients at office visits. His findings were similar to those of Walker (1989a); many of the kinds of relationship skills that typically allow people to communicate and trust one another were lacking.

Much more can be done to assist professionals to more comfortably incorporate a family focus into their work and build collaborative partnerships with parents. In recent years several studies have yielded positive results from efforts to help educators develop more positive attitudes toward parental input and to increase parent–

educator collaboration. Brinckerhoff and Vincent (1986) were able to increase exchanges of information between parents and teachers as well as positive expectations for productive interactions.

Collaboration implies mutual helping. In addition to incorporating more parental input into their thinking about how to plan services, professionals can increase their helpfulness to families by increasing the amount of information and discussion they provide families regarding their own perspective of the child. Walker (1989b) found that systematic efforts to exchange information increased the frequency of communication about the child's progress at home and at school and resulted in positive evaluations of the parent–teacher relationships by both parent and teacher. Lewis, Pantell, and Sharp (1991) showed that providing brief communications and relationship skills training to professionals and family members could increase the way parents and children participated in interactions with family physicians.

Effectiveness as a professional helper in the context of increased emphasis on collaborative parent–professional relationships requires a reevaluation and adaptation of some basic beliefs about what constitutes "professional" help. The development of orientations and strategies that actively promote collaborative relationships between parents and professionals is also needed. The profile of a collaborative professional helper in the context of specialized services for children and families includes competence in several key dimensions. In this chapter, the congruency among professional values, perspectives, roles, and communication strategies and how it affects professionals' ability to achieve collaborative relationships with parents is discussed.

VALUING COLLABORATION

In order to make use of specific collaboration strategies in day-to-day interactions, professionals must embrace some prerequisite, basic relationship values and attitudes. This essential set of values emphasizes equality, cooperation, partnership, and the incorporation of a family-centered focus in parent–professional relationships. Without this set of values and attitudes, the attempt to develop helping roles and to learn specific interpersonal strategies for promoting collaborative partnerships with parents will be unsuccessful. The discussion of relationship strategies in this chapter will be of little value if professionals are not already convinced that flexible sharing of responsibility between coequals should be the hallmark of a professional–familial relationship. It is assumed that the reader of this chapter is already familiar with the values listed in Table 1 and expressed in more detail by a number of authors (Dunst et al., 1993; Singer & Irvin, 1989; Turnbull & Turnbull, 1986). Beliefs held by professionals who value family-centered services ought to include those listed in Table 1.

Many diverse values and beliefs affect the course of any one parent–professional relationship. Sometimes a parent and a particular teacher discover that they are very compatible. Similar cultural backgrounds, social class, values, or personalities may contribute to the ease with which two persons can arrive at mutually accepted definitions of needs or problems and then agree on means for resolving issues. In other parent–professional relationships, however, parents and teachers find that they have a difficult time understanding or agreeing with one another, possibly because of differences in culture, class, and/or personality.

THE DEVELOPMENTAL NATURE OF PARENT–PROFESSIONAL RELATIONSHIPS

In addition to embracing values and beliefs that support collaboration, an understanding of the developmental nature of parent–professional relationships can assist professionals in finding constructive ways to manage relationships with parents. Parent–professional

Table 1. Beliefs contributing to parent–professional collaboration

1. Parents and professionals achieve more constructive outcomes when they work as allies in helping families to achieve their goals and developmental potential. Cooperation increases the likelihood of mutually satisfying outcomes.
2. Professionals can offer a variety of constructive roles to family members. Being flexible in accommodating family preferences enhances the helpfulness of professional roles.
3. Professionals can repeatedly seek informed consent for the actions they take to show respect for a family member's autonomy and judgment.
4. Both parents and professionals have unique knowledge and expertise to bring to collaborative relationships. It is a loss if either is expected to ignore or abandon his or her particular expertise.
5. Both parents and professionals are constrained by the systems in which they live and work, whether it be the family system, the school system, or the health care system. It is important to identify and clarify these constraints as part of their partnership and to either accept or overcome them.
6. Professionals increase their helpfulness to families when they value pluralism; that is, when they respect differences in culture, beliefs, class, family structure, and personal styles.

relationships can be viewed as dynamic and evolving, rather than as static and fixed by individual personalities or temperaments. It is human nature to resort to personal attributions to explain the success or failure of interpersonal interactions. Attribution thinking provides a limiting perspective for understanding parent–professional interactions, however, and leads to stereotyping and blaming behaviors. A developmental perspective on relationships provides a framework for viewing the ups and downs of interpersonal interactions as natural progressions in relationships. It also directs attention toward the creation and growth of a relationship between people, given individual styles and personalities. Trusting, working relationships rarely sprout fully grown out of an initial encounter. They unfold over time. As a relationship grows, the individuals within it can influence its development. Some relationships evolve in a more or less typical fashion and respond to the normal amount of attention and care. Others evolve in less typical ways and need more careful attention, a more carefully controlled environment, and more skilled tending to mature into full working relationships.

Assessing a Parent–Professional Relationship

A developmental perspective on parent–professional relationships provides a set of dynamic, growth-based criteria, rather than static, event-based criteria for evaluating these relationships. The manner in which teachers have typically rated the success or failure of what transpired as they interact over time with parents is considered. Some additional ways to conceptualize parent–professional relationships along developmental and collaboration lines are then suggested to enable professionals to assess whether or not relationships are developing in ways that are conducive to the type of parent–professional collaboration needed in intervention settings.

The way that teachers typically describe a positive parent–professional relationship has also been considered. Oversimplification of the complex nature of parent–professional relationships may result from an attempt to describe a "typical" course of development for a positive parent–teacher relationship. However, studies of parent–teacher interactions have yielded some useful examples of what teachers typically do to establish and maintain positive relationships with parents.

Teachers report considerable variety in their experiences with parents. They do not seem to be particularly mindful of any developmental sequences in their ongoing contacts with parents. Teachers appear more apt to focus mainly on the day-to-day events that characterize contacts with parents. They tend to judge the success of their parent–professional relationships on factors such as: 1) friendly responses to initiations, 2) degree of cooperation with requests, 3) amount of agreement or conflict regarding day-to-day program activities and long-term intervention programming, 4) apparent support or challenge of their efforts to work on the child's behalf, and 5) perceived success or failure of their efforts to influence parents and to be helpful. Teachers also seem to be very mindful of whether or not parents' priorities are compatible with their own and of the relative satisfaction or difficulty they experience fielding parental requests. This approach to conceptualizing parent–teacher relationships, in which satisfaction or success is based on professionals' assessment of their ability to stimulate parental cooperation and accommodation to program-driven goals, is consistent with the child-focused teacher training models used in many professional preparation programs.

Throughout this chapter it is suggested that teachers and other professionals will benefit by conceptualizing their relationships with parents within a developmental model in which collaboration builds over time. Such a model would orient professionals more toward competence in emphasizing give-and-take in their interactions with parents and would allow them the benefits of seeing their own behaviors shaped by parental input. A collaboration model for parent–professional relationships would describe parent–professional contacts in terms of developmental stages with all the various positive, neutral, and negative interpersonal stresses and strains that are natural manifestations of a developing relationship.

Bales (1976) suggests that in group interactions or partnerships that have problem-solving goals, there should be evidence of give-and-take between partners. Both sides will ask questions, state disagreements, express support, and at times criticize. In more superficial relationships, communicative partners are likely to skirt difficult issues. They are unlikely to question one another, unlikely to state criticisms, and unlikely to make statements of support. Walker (1989a) studied telephone conversations between parents and teachers of children with severe disabilities. She found that these conversations fit the pattern common in more superficial relationships. In order to develop a relationship that can bear more risk-taking and mutual involvement, parents and professionals must get to know one another, build a mutual sense of trust, and determine ground rules for how to get along.

A Developmental Framework

The developmental framework for understanding parent–professional relationships, as outlined in this chapter, includes the following stages: 1) getting acquainted and identifying a purpose, 2) setting ground rules, 3) testing the relationship, and 4) modifying ground rules. In the course of any relationship, progression and recycling through these typical developmental stages are expected. Some relationship partners proceed rapidly through the stages while others proceed very gradually. Both the frequency of contact and the individual investment in the relationship affect the rate at which partners advance through the stages and the intensity of their interactions. These stages of professional–family relationships are illustrated below by focusing on the case of parent–teacher relationships.

Getting Acquainted and Identifying a Purpose   It is common for teachers to have some advance knowledge about parents' history with services providers. This information is commonly gleaned from referral documents or meetings or, in school settings, from a previous individualized education program (IEP) meeting where a placement decision was made. Similarly, teachers are aware that their professional reputations frequently precede their initial contacts with parents and can both positively and negatively influence initial and ongoing interactions. With all this in mind, teachers and parents enter into initial contacts as they progress through the getting-acquainted stage of their relationship. These contacts occur in a variety of ways: via letters, phone calls, or face-to-face visits. Some contacts are informal and some are more planned. They may be initiated by a teacher or by parents. In any case, the ways in which professionals orient themselves toward family concerns and toward parents as partners play an important part in determining how encouraged parents are in pursuing working relationships with teachers.

The initiatives described above reflect early getting-acquainted-activities. In this stage, both teacher and parent will eventually attempt to propose their own purposes and identify the other's purposes within the relationship. Teachers' initial reactions to parents' concerns provide information that parents use to assess the likelihood of developing mutual support for a working relationship. Likewise, teachers' communication practices in regard to defining relationship purposes influence the degree to which parents are likely to develop an interest in school activities and ongoing contact with teachers.

Establishing Ground Rules for the Relationship   In the course of getting acquainted teachers and parents also provide one another with information about how they want to interact. Very early on, relationship efforts begin to establish the implicit, if not explicit, ground rules for each parent–teacher relationship and partners adopt a fairly predictable interaction pattern with one another. This pattern becomes a set of relationship norms, or ground rules. Unless challenged by circumstances or by relationship partners, these ground rules dictate the interaction behaviors that characterize the relationship.

Testing the Relationship   Eventually, a demand is placed on the relationship that tests its established ground rules. Urgent contacts, whether initiated by a teacher, a parent, or some external circumstance, place demands on partners in a relationship. These demands test the relationship's ability to serve the individual needs of each partner and tolerate as well the limits of each partner's ability to be responsive. These tests often generate considerable tension. Stressful circumstances often trigger aggressive or submissive behaviors, and communication behaviors are often affected by intense emotions and defensive statements. During intense interactions, people often feel pressure not only to obtain compliance or gratification from their partners, but to defend themselves against demands placed on them. These interactions test the relationship's ability to sustain stresses and crises and to call into play sufficient resources to enable constructive resolutions.

Modifying Ground Rules   Teachers and parents alike react to demands that challenge existing relationship ground rules. Reactions will vary depending on a number of situational, cultural, class, and personality factors. In some cases, relationships return to existing ground rules. In others, patterns of interacting are refined or altered to meet newly identified needs of each partner and to help them avoid unwanted interactive behaviors in the future. As the life of a successful relationship advances, the partnership tends to cycle through nonstressful and stressful times and to weather them, growing stronger or weaker and becoming more explicitly defined after successive cycles of testing and ground-rule modification. Over time, modified interpersonal behaviors become a predictable set of ground rules for the relationship.

When professionals make collaboration a priority in their relationships with parents, they take care to act in ways to demonstrate to parents their commitment to a strong partnership that not only accommodates a high degree of parental demands, but can grow sufficiently strong, efficient, and reliable over the course of its development as a forum within which to address service-related concerns.

ENHANCING EFFECTIVENESS IN PROFESSIONAL ROLES

There are many ways to enhance role effectiveness as a family-focused helper. One way in which professionals can help parents is to be clear in presenting the role they expect to play in providing help. Role clarification includes information about professional mission, the extent and limits of training and experience, individual work style, and procedural preferences in carrying out one's role.

Clarifying the Helping Role

In interviews with parents of children with disabilities (Singer & Walker, 1991), parents reported that they preferred physicians who gave them a clear understanding of their professional mission. For example, some physicians made it clear to parents early in their relationship that they viewed the whole family as being of concern and that they were interested in the parents' emotional adjustment. Other physicians made it clear that they saw their role as focused primarily on the current medical condition of the child. In either event, parents preferred clarity about these roles. Similarly, teachers must be able to clearly define for parents the aims of their classroom and the nature of the relationship they desire with family members. For example, a teacher of children with severe disabilities might define his or her role as working with parents to teach skills and create opportunities for a child to experience a valued life-style in school, at home, and in the community. This view of the teaching role is different from that of a teacher who, for example, believes his or her purpose is primarily to provide a safe, caring environment for the child.

Professional mission, training, experience, and work style are not simply individual matters. They are defined by organizations and by the consumers of human services. Thus, in building cooperative relationships with parents, it is important to gain clarity about the role expected by the larger organization (e.g., clinic, school, hospital, early intervention program) and to be prepared to become active in ensuring that there is a regular process for clarifying service missions.

When a professional has a clear concept of his or her role, it is then possible to give a kind of conceptual road map to family members. A cooperative professional is likely to communicate this conceptual map, or vision of his or her role, on several occasions—in orienting the parent to the classroom or service, in explaining why he or she is concerned about a specific problem or issue, and, when needed, in clarifying his or her role when disagreements arise.

Knowing When To Refer

Professionals who have a clear understanding of their roles are able also to identify instances when a problem is best solved in another forum. In many cases, there are external restrictions placed upon professionals by the limits of their training and experience or by the systems in which they work. For example, physicians are limited by their training in their ability to inform or advise parents on the need or benefits of related services such as speech or hearing therapy, counseling, or physical therapy. They are bounded in other ways by the payment regulations of entitlement programs and insurance companies. Teachers are obligated to administer certain kinds of tests, to construct formal treatment plans in a certain way, and to work with a designated number of students. Each of these conditions places some limits on a professional's ability to deal with problems that families may present. When professionals clearly explain their ability to be helpful within the parameters defining their professional roles, they are better able to assist families in seeking the desired help from appropriately trained professionals or other helpers.

Expanding Helping Roles

As service providers are asked to include family-centered collaboration functions in their work with parents, role definitions must be broadened to include a repertoire of complementary roles. There are many roles that professionals can play to support family-centered and collaborative approaches to services and to increase primary role effectiveness.

Collaboration implies a potential for negotiation of roles within partnerships. Within the parent–professional partnership, this could mean that traditional roles are modified according to mutual agreements among participants. It may also mean that professionals actively assume roles that they have not traditionally filled. For instance, to maintain power equality in the relationship, a professional might assume the role of learner rather than teacher, listener rather than presenter, novice rather than expert, follower rather than director, problem poser rather than problem solver. In shifting to roles that typically have been more ascribed to parents, professionals can demonstrate a desire to share roles in a collaborative fashion. Moreover, by modifying or reversing traditional roles, professionals can enhance their understanding of parents' perspectives and experiences with their children and with the human services system.

In addition to modifying traditional role functions, there are a variety of roles that professionals often assume to complement their primary professional roles in the context of collaboration with families. For example, a language therapist who prefers to provide services in a controlled clinical setting could decide to expand her collaborative activities by planning to meet more regularly with the parents in order to more actively solicit their input and participation in treatment planning and evaluation. Sometimes professionals provide valuable help to families by assuming an advocacy role on behalf of the child or family. For example, a teacher can serve as an advocate for students in regard to bus routes or a physician can argue on behalf of a patient in regard to an insurance ruling.

ENHANCING EFFECTIVENESS
IN PARENT–PROFESSIONAL COMMUNICATION

Since the early 1970s, a variety of communication training programs have been available to help professionals acquire interpersonal skills (Carkhuff & Anthony, 1979; Egan, 1975; Evans, Hearn, Uhlemann, & Ivey, 1984; Ivey, 1988; Krehbiel & Kroth, 1991). These have recently been made available in workshops and training programs for parents of children with disabilities as well (Mendoza, 1983; Walker, 1989b). In addition, researchers and practitioners in the fields of relationship negotiation (Fisher & Brown, 1988) and interpersonal effectiveness (Bolton, 1979) provide readily available and practical suggestions for improving situations where problems must be addressed and where conflict of interest is likely to occur. More recently, strategies for collaboration and partnership-building in parent–professional relationships have become important components of development for professionals working with parents of children with special needs (Fine, 1991; Rainforth et al., 1992).

It is time to give additional attention to specific communication strategies to help professionals in the field of specialized services who are striving to adopt a family-centered collaboration approach in their work. Earlier discussions of professional values and roles and perspectives on relationships are meant to present a framework within which to understand some key communication strategies that affect the development of parent–professional relationships. In this discussion, examples from parent–teacher relationships are used to examine and demonstrate relationship-building strategies.

However, the strategies suggested can be used by anyone interested in fostering collaboration between parents and professionals, including early interventionists, family support workers, health care providers, parents themselves, and young people with disabilities.

In developing a context within which to understand the complexity of communication in parent–professional relationships, it is useful to think about communication occurring on several levels. This discussion will refer to meta-level, intermediate-level, and micro-level kinds of communication. It is important to acquire and implement constructive relationship-building and communication skills on all three levels in order to develop a family-centered, collaborative approach in parent–professional partnerships.

Meta-communication in Interpersonal Interactions

Meta-communication consists of what we say or imply by body language about our values, perspectives, and roles. Professionals convey a great deal about their interests, beliefs, attitudes, and intentions via a variety of meta-messages. Meta-messages affect both the immediate and more long-range development of parent–professional relationships. Meta-messages also provide information—either spoken or nonverbal—about how professionals are involving themselves in particular relationships with parents. Information is conveyed and received via meta-messages and is used to monitor and influence the relationship. Meta-communication skills are used in carrying out many personal and interpersonal executive functions that include awareness, monitoring, and management of oneself and of others during interactions. To master key meta-communication skills, professionals must conduct a thorough examination of their attitudes, beliefs, feelings, and behaviors that influence their interactions with parents. Among other things, meta-messages often reveal a professional's: 1) understanding of the influence of cultural, class, and personality differences and willingness to address these issues openly; 2) ideas about the purpose or goal of a particular parent–professional relationship; 3) understanding of the developmental history of the relationship; 4) understanding and accepting the different ways of thinking and communicating that occur in parent–professional discourse; and 5) understanding and accepting the value of flexible partnerships.

Discussing Cultural, Class, and Personality Differences Earlier the influences of values in parent–professional relationships were discussed. When parents and professionals have different cultural, class, or personality backgrounds, even in small ways, finding a common point of reference or purpose for the relationship can be critical to the relationship that develops between them. Parents in particular may be sensitive or confused by such differences and may rely heavily on professionals' meta-communication to detect whether or not professionals seem open to their perspective. In these instances, professionals can be helpful by acknowledging the differences and working to provide a climate within which parents can feel safe and comfortable in entering into a relationship. Useful meta-communication in such circumstances involves a receptive, relaxed manner and a posture of respectful curiosity. Specific verbal messages might include statements such as:

> I imagine that we have many differences in how we understand your child's needs and what to do to help. I'm interested in finding out what you think is important and what you hope I can do to be helpful to you and your child. I hope we can find ways to combine our interests so that we each feel satisfied with our efforts.

A professional who is skilled in meta-communication will talk openly and sensitively with parents about apparent cultural and other value differences in the relationship.

Talking About the Purposes of the Relationship The purposes of parent–professional relationships within service settings derive from basic values and societal goals. These values and goals are expressed formally in legal mandates; they are then transmitted and interpreted through the policy documents generated by government officials and the teachings of professional leaders in the various human services disciplines. Intentionally or not, professionals then translate these values and goals to parents at a meta-communication level. Parents' first impressions of professional intentions and attitudes toward parent–professional relationships are based on these meta-messages. A teacher working to communicate in this way might say:

> From my point of view the purpose of our relationship is two-fold. I want to be able to provide the kind of classroom experience that will most benefit your child. At the same time I want to be sure I understand what is important to you and that I am working with you to figure out how my services can best help your child learn the things we identify as important to his education.

Thus, being able to provide guidance about the purpose of the relationship is one important meta-communication skill.

A professional who has an understanding of the limits of his or her role can clearly communicate this with parents. For example, a teacher who understands that a transportation issue cannot be solved within the parameters of his or her primary role and who is willing to act collaboratively in an advocacy role might say:

> I understand that you are unhappy with your child's scheduling in the mornings. A lot of the reason he cannot do the things that are important to you has to do with how late the school bus is in getting him here. I am a teacher and not a transportation administrator. But I care about your child and it is very important for me to try to provide a program that meets your child's needs. So I will call and write a letter to the transportation administrator. I'm also going to need your help in getting the system changed. Maybe if we work together we can change the way things are done. Also, I hope you will understand that I have only limited power in this situation and we may not be able to get the changes we want. We may need to get help from an advocacy organization.

This communication conveys the teacher's understanding of her roles in working on the child's and parent's behalf.

Talking About the Relationship's Developmental History   Earlier in this chapter, three stages of developing parent–professional relationships were described in some detail. Professionals must be aware that relationships usually progress through stages. An important meta-communication skill for professionals consists of being able to step back from the relationship and reflect on its developmental sequences, and then talking about them with parents. For instance, a teacher who knows how to reflect upon the history of a relationship would be able to make the following kinds of statements at the beginning of the relationship:

> I think that you and I are just getting to know one another. It would probably help us understand each other better if I told you a little bit about how I like to run my classroom and if you told me about your child's life at home.

Or, at a later date, a teacher might say:

> We have been through some rocky times together in the past. Remember when we disagreed about your son's vocational goals? But we were able to work it out. I bet we can sort this one out too.

Talking About the Difference Between Professional and Family Discourse   Parents and professionals often speak from very different vantage points, have different reasons for interacting the way they do, and use very different language. Darling (1983) and Walker and Erickson (1991) have described the differences between the world view of a professional and that of a parent. Mischler (1984) studied transcripts of hundreds of doctor–patient interactions and came to the conclusion that the two parties were speaking with a different "voice" or world view; the voice of medicine for doctors and the voice of the world for patients. The voice of medicine was problem-focused, efficient, technical, and unemotional. The most typical pattern of speech for the doctors was to ask closed-ended questions and to ignore most of the content of what patients said. The typical pattern of speech for patients was to tell a story, set the context, tell the sequence, and explain how they felt and feel. In a similar fashion, Walker (1989a) studied the transcripts of parent–teacher telephone calls and found that teachers tended to be highly focused, business-like, oriented to a goal, and to speak of students in terms of their goals, progress, or problems. In contrast, parents tended to speak about their children in terms of home life and in more personal terms.

Both modes of discourse have their place and provide important information. However, the problem is that the ways that profession-als speak and interact too often dominate and drive out the "voice of the family." Professionals who are skilled at building partnerships with parents can alternate between these two systems of communi-cation. They can use a meta-message in the form of a bridging or overview statement that orients parents to their professional way of talking about a child. They can acknowledge that their professional view is different and may miss a lot even while it serves an impor-tant technical purpose. For example, a teacher who is skilled in crossing between the two modes of discourse might say:

> I want to tell you a story of something that Jamie did. He had Frank, his peer tutor, push his wheelchair over to the jungle gym. Jamie kept waving and gesturing at Frank until he pushed him right under the bars. Then Jamie pulled himself up out of his chair and hung there grinning. You should have heard him laugh!
>
> Now I need to switch gears a little bit and put on my more formal teacher's hat. I wanted to talk to you about how Jamie is doing with his language board so that I can make sure I keep you up to date. It's important to me that you know what he is learning because I hope he will practice these skills at home.

In this example, the teacher shows an awareness of the two different modes of discourse and has the meta-skill of labeling a transition from one form of discourse to another.

Talking About Flexible Partnerships

An important key to the development of collaborative parent–professional relationships involves professionals' ability and will-ingness to adapt their roles according to parental role preferences and abilities. From the outset, professionals who value parental input and empowerment tend to convey, via meta-messages, a posi-tive orientation toward flexibility in their relationships with par-ents. These professionals cultivate and communicate openly their interest in understanding the other's perspective on the child. In addition, each partner must be sincere in understanding and supporting the parents' efforts to contribute to the child's development and happiness.

In a meta-communication about the value of flexibility, a teacher might say:

> As we get to know one another and how we work best together, we'll probably discover a variety of ways to share responsibilities. I'm comfortable in a number of roles and I'm very willing also to consider a number of ways to let you have as big a role as you want in our work together. Let's try to figure out what each of us can do to make this plan work and see how that works for each of us. We can look at how well we're doing and make some changes down the road if we need to.

As they hear messages of encouragement and support from professionals, parents often develop a greater interest in the assessment, planning, and decision-making process, and may eventually desire a change in their role vis-à-vis professionals. Some parents may want to have more control of all aspects of professional activities related to their child. Others may want less. Professionals who are flexible and comfortable with a variety of roles both for themselves and parents seem better able to maintain cooperative, noncompetitive relationships with parents. Moreover, these professionals are more effective in maintaining a family-centered approach in their work and in empowering parents via their interactions with them.

Intermediate-Level Communication

Meta-level communication addresses the perspectives and attitudes that affect the climate within which parent–professional relationships are developed. Intermediate-level communication addresses the more concrete issue of engineering the environment in which the relationship will play out.

Setting the Stage   In setting the stage for collaborative partnerships, it is important to think about the effects of environmental factors. Setting, time of day, and the particular people in attendance can have a positive or negative effect on participants by the atmosphere they create. It is often possible to schedule conferences at a convenient location for parents as well as for teachers. This effort communicates sensitivity to transportation and setting factors. Some parents do not have convenient or affordable means of transportation for travel to school conferences, and institutional settings may be intimidating for other reasons. These negative environmental factors may be alleviated by offering to meet at a location that is more neutral for parents. Scheduling meetings and phone conversations at times of day that are equally convenient to both parent and teacher help promote the recognition of equality in terms of each partner's time and commitments to activities other than those associated with the student. Arranging meetings so that the parent is familiar with or prepared for the array of professionals who often attend formal IEP meetings and conferences can make a critical difference to the parent's feelings of equality with teachers. Meeting individually ahead of time to discuss the meeting agenda, to identify professionals who will be attending and their respective roles, and to otherwise assist parents in formulating any questions or agenda items in advance can help prepare parents to participate more equally in formal meetings. Giving parents the opportunity to have separate information-sharing or problem-solving meetings with one representative from the IEP professional team might ease the tension often experienced by parents at meetings when they feel significantly outnumbered. Ample opportunity should be offered to parents to bring support people, advocates, or recorders to formal meetings as a way of encouraging them to participate on an equal footing with professionals, whose participation is already assisted by their own record-keeping procedures and collegial support.

Playing the Part of a Collaborative Professional   Professionals can use a variety of intermediate-level messages to demonstrate an early interest in a collaborative parent–teacher relationship. They can be sure to contact parents early in their relationships and to respond positively to early contacts from parents. When these initial contacts occur early in the school year, even before classes begin, and precede or coincide with the early stages of a teacher's contacts with the child, there is a greater likelihood of positive beginnings between parent and teacher. This may occur because for both parents and teachers, anxiety and expectations vis-à-vis one another are higher in the beginning of the relationship. The actual experience of meeting these interpersonal needs and demonstrating intention to build a collaborative relationship is reinforcing to each partner. Early contacts that serve to ease one another's anxieties appear to be important in establishing positive expectations for future parent–teacher interactions.

In addition, ongoing, regular communication seems to play an important role in reassuring parents of legitimate access to professionals and in diminishing the likelihood of breakdowns in communication. Regular communication also helps to prevent misperceptions about one another's thoughts, feelings, and behaviors concerning the student and each other. And finally, explicit messages that convey continued commitment to collaboration better enable the relationship to develop along collaborative lines. Initial "get-acquainted" invitations, the establishment of regular communication systems, arranging meetings in convenient settings and at convenient times, indications of accessibility, and requests for information or input are all examples of intermediate-level messages that show a willingness to give a collaborative parent–professional relationship the best possible chance to flourish.

Micro-level Communication

At the micro-level of communication, professionals are effective to the extent that they have mastered the basic micro-skills of effective interpersonal communication. These skills allow professionals to take advantage of specific moment-to-moment communication opportunities to increase their own understanding of parents' interests and intentions as well as to increase the likelihood that parents will benefit from professional input. The skillful use of micro-level messages addresses immediate needs of the parent–professional relationship and enhances the development of parent–professional rapport.

The first step toward mastery of micro-level communication skills in professional practices is to assess the interpersonal styles that are typically employed in parent–professional interactions. Based on this self-assessment, professionals can then set goals to increase the micro-level communication behaviors that they have already mastered, to identify areas where improvement is needed, and to commit oneself to learn new or modified skills. To master micro-level skills, it is usually necessary to engage in ongoing practice and feedback activities, to implement communication strategies in everyday situations via homework, and to utilize feedback from instructors, observers, or intended beneficiaries to refine developing skills. Achieving mastery in communication skills is easier for professionals who are willing to continually observe their own behaviors and adapt them to serve purposes that support collaboration rather than personal control or comfort in their interactions with parents. Improvement usually requires ongoing situational assessment, coaching, practice, application, and evaluation of effects in contexts where professionals can engage in experiential activities such as role plays and skill enactment. A complete repertoire of micro-level skills includes both receptive or listening skills and sending or influencing skills.

Listening Skills Professionals can use listening skills to enhance collaboration and increase parental input during interactions with parents. Used effectively, listening provides a supportive context in which: 1) parents can clarify and express their thoughts and feelings, 2) professionals can gain an accurate and in-depth understanding of parents' thoughts and feelings, and 3) both parent and professional can safely engage in trust- and rapport-building interactions. Listening behaviors are grouped into three categories: *signaling openness, reflecting,* and *intentional inquiry.* To illustrate their use, examples from parent–teacher interactions are discussed below.

In *signaling openness,* professionals give their full attention to parents and thus convey a willingness to hear parental input. Key behaviors include: friendly, attentive, yet relaxed *facial expressions;* open and relaxed *physical posture,* with the body oriented toward the speaker and avoiding clenched fists, crossed arms, or crossed legs; comfortable *eye contact;* occasional *visual and vocal encouragement* via nods of the head and minimal statements such as "um hmmm" and "I see"; and a consistently *friendly demeanor and tone of voice.* The goal in signaling openness is to indicate receptivity and interest and to allow the focus of the conversation to be controlled by the parent. Any behaviors by professionals that change the topic or take the focus of interest away from parents will interfere with efforts to signal openness to parental input.

Occasionally, professionals wish to provide more tangible evidence that they are following the particulars of what is being said. To do this, they can use a more active form of listening behavior that is referred to as *reflecting messages.* When listening reflectively, professionals use statements that mirror, paraphrase, or summarize what they are hearing, using words that closely match those used by parents. Professionals may reflect the parents' accounts of particular events, thoughts, or feelings. *Mirroring* is the simplest kind of reflecting statement and consists of a simple repetition of words just spoken. Mirroring is especially useful when the parent seems rushed, vague, or confused and the professional is having difficulty understanding actual words or sequences of events presented by the parent. Here is how a teacher might mirror a parent's words:

> Parent: I'm sorry I'm late, but it's my mother's illness, you know. And the car. I'm so disorganized lately. (Pause. . . .)
>
> Teacher: Your mother's ill, and there's something about your car. You're feeling disorganized lately.

The goal in mirroring statements is to allow the parent to hear what he or she has said so that he or she can elaborate if she desires to be more clear. Particular care must be taken to avoid sounding mechanical or trite in the use of simple mirroring statements.

Empathic statements reflect the feelings that are often at the core of a parent's account. It is important for professionals to reserve empathic statements for times when they sense that a parent would benefit from such reflections. For example, when a teacher is sure that he or she has an accurate understanding of a parent's subjective experience, he or she can make an empathic statement reflecting the feelings observed. Often core feelings are more evident in parents' nonverbal behaviors than in their words. For example, in the case of the parent in the above dialogue, the teacher might have sensed some building frustration in the parent from an agitated expression on his or her face, the intensity of the emotional tone in his or her voice, and his or her comment about not knowing what to do. Accordingly, and after using more basic reflecting messages or inquiries to be certain that his or her perceptions were accurate, a teacher might offer an empathic statement such as, "This is a really frustrating dilemma for you, isn't it?" or "It must be frustrating to have to go through so much to arrange a manageable day for yourself." Empathic listening is a powerful agent for building rapport. It should be used sparingly and only when the teacher is confident that it would be constructive for the parent; that is, that it would reassure the parent that thoughts and feelings are understandable and the professional wants to validate them. Used inappropriately, empathic statements can feel intrusive and elicit self-protective responses in parents.

Paraphrasing consists of reflecting key points of a longer account—that is, restating the parent's account in a briefer, more succinct form. Care must be taken to use language similar to that of the parent so that he or she does not have difficulty understanding a paraphrase that is stated in professional terms. The goal of paraphrasing is to convey understanding of the main points of a parent's account and to allow the parent to correct any inaccuracies in the professional's understanding of the main substance of that account. A parent might give a teacher the following description of his or her experience:

> I'm not sure what to do about getting respite care for Todd. I really want to accept my friend's invitation to drive to the coast on Saturday, but I'm very uncomfortable with the thought of asking anyone to watch Todd. His behaviors can really get out of hand and scare a person who's not used to them. I have always been able to get someone in the family to watch him, but no one is available this weekend. And besides, I get the feeling that they're getting burned out with watching him for me.

In paraphrasing this description, the teacher might say:

> You'd really like to go to the coast with your friend, but you're not sure you can find respite care you can trust.

Paraphrasing is a particularly useful listening behavior to use when a parent appears to have completed an account and before the conversation moves to another topic or agenda area. Like other listening strategies, paraphrasing increases accurate understanding and helps safeguard against jumping too quickly to conclusions.

Summarizing consists of reviewing major topics mentioned over an extended conversation, such as an hour-long meeting. Summaries allow a professional to reflect back to a parent his or her understanding of the highlights of a conversation, especially the important points of the parent's presentation of concerns, requests, and any decisions that have been made.

Questions are the most active form of listening behaviors. *Intentional inquiry* is used to gather additional information when professionals are confused about what parents are trying to tell them. A teacher might ask direct, closed-ended questions seeking very specific bits of information, such as, "Which relatives have you asked to provide respite?" or "When are you hoping to go to the coast?" *Closed-ended questions* provide an efficient way to help a professional obtain information quickly, but they can be perceived as attempts to control the conversation and place more focus on the questioner than is often desirable during listening activities. To avoid this, a professional can wait to ask closed-ended questions until there is a natural pause in the conversation and then ask them only to obtain information about important details of the picture being drawn by the parent. For example, closed-ended questions help clarify details such as whom the parent is talking about, which behaviors are of particular importance, and when the parent wants to be contacted.

Direct, open-ended questions typically begin with words like "what" or "how," and are intended to elicit greater detail and to encourage the parent to take more talk-time. For the previous example, they might include questions such as, "What makes you believe finding respite care will be so difficult?" or "How have you dealt with respite problems most effectively in the past?" or "How do you figure out when someone is willing or unwilling to provide respite for Todd?" Open-ended questions such as the last two examples can sometimes orient the speaker toward a solution.

Indirect questions are somewhat gentler and are useful when parents seem to react defensively to direct questions. Statements such as, "I wonder what can be done to find respite for Todd" or "Tell me more about this respite care problem you're having" indirectly invite parents to develop their descriptions further.

Perception-checking questions are more or less rhetorical questions that allow professionals to quickly check the accuracy of their understanding of a situation that a parent is describing. Perception checks are particularly useful when the account is complicated or the professional is confused. For example, in the above situation, the teacher might use the following perception checks before attempting an empathic reflecting statement: "Am I understanding you to say that no one will watch Todd while you go to the coast?" or "You've already asked some people if they're available, then?" These checks would allow the parent to confirm or correct the teacher's perceptions.

When a professional can skillfully and selectively employ a broad repertoire of listening skills to signal openness, to reflect messages accurately, and to make statements and inquiries that assist the parents in clearly defining their experiences and perspectives, opportunities are enhanced for productive work and rapport in the relationship.

Influencing Skills   Listening skills enable professionals to gain accurate insights into parents' perspectives and to demonstrate interest and involvement. However, they are not in themselves sufficient to negotiate a two-way conversation between parents and professionals. There comes a critical time in each conversation when professionals must present their own perspectives and will want to be effective in influencing the course and outcomes of the interaction. Professionals have an obligation to present their perspectives, and parents expect them to do so. The manner in which professionals try to influence parents can greatly affect parents' perceptions of professionals' ability to be helpful.

Influencing messages (Ivey, 1988) include a variety of overt and more subtle messages that guide the course of a conversation. Depending on professionals' roles and desired goals for a particular interaction, they will select different influencing skills. From the outset, a professional enters a parent–professional relationship hoping to offer specialized, often technical, expertise. The professional's identity as a teacher, case worker, speech therapist, physical therapist, or doctor creates the expectation that, at some point, he or she will present his or her view of a child's and family's needs, realistic learning or developmental goals, interventions and service placements, and key players—whether professionals or parents—who can best support the child's intervention program. When used constructively, influencing messages allow the professional to introduce his or her perspective and, at the same time, to empower parents and strengthen the parent–professional relationship. The influencing skills that best promote collaborative partnerships and flexibility in parent and professional interactions are discussed next. These skills have been sorted into four categories: *providing information, providing support, focusing attention,* and *offering help.*

Much of the valuable expertise that professionals bring to parent–professional relationships derives from the *specialized information* that they can provide. The way in which professionals present information about diagnoses of children's developmental difficulties and treatments, for example, greatly influences the understanding that parents develop about their child's condition and the availability of services and resources. Professionals can maximize parents' opportunities to benefit from professional knowledge by presenting information in an objective fashion and adapting the use of technical language to fit the parents' level of familiarity with specialized terminologies. Technical information presented in a simplified, clear, and unbiased manner helps parents understand what professionals envision for their children. It is especially important not to rush through the presentation of technical information. Parents benefit from ample time to digest new information, as do professionals, before evaluating options or making decisions. Language that presents specialized information and recommendations clearly, and specifies a professional intent to inform and empower rather than persuade or control, can be a key tool for empowering parents. In presenting technical information from test results, a teacher might begin by saying:

> As you know, I've been giving some tests to your child to help me understand his situation from a teacher's view of things. I'd like to share the results of the tests with you, because they have an effect on how I think about your child's educational needs. Of course, tests don't tell the whole story, but I'm hoping they will be helpful to you and to me as we think about what we want your child to get out of being in my classroom. (*Pause to allow the parent to ask questions. Proceed if there is encouragement to continue.*) Would it be helpful to you if I described the tests I've used and what they tell me? (*Provide as much information as the parent wants. Be sure to define terms and to include information about the particular information yielded and the limits of each test.*) So, from my point of view as a teacher, these test results help me understand how much your child can do with school-type tasks. They also help me figure out what I should plan to work on with him. When I state my concerns and goals for your child, I rely on information from these tests and on what I see him do in the classroom. I'm hoping that

when we add your information to the information gathered from all the professionals involved, we can come up with a good picture of your child's needs and abilities.

Notice that this teacher sets up the presentation of technical information by describing the value and limits of test results information in objective and easily understood terms. It is clear that the teacher's intent is to inform and collaborate, and that this approach gives the parent ample opportunity to learn comfortably.

Micro-level communication that works to *provide support* consists of the reinforcing statements that professionals use to acknowledge parents' efforts and contributions. Comments that acknowledge evidence of parental involvement, not only as a caregiver to the child but as an important member of the parent–professional team, can add substantially to parents' willingness to become involved in parent–professional relationships. The teacher might say to the parent frustrated by respite concerns, "You've really worked hard to make respite possible, haven't you?" or "You spend so much time caring for Todd. What a good idea for you to get some time for yourself!" Positive statements that are not specific or personalized run the risk of being construed as conventional statements or as credit for someone else, and their supportive intent may be lost. For example, it is common for parents to perceive positive statements about a child's gains as efforts by professionals to obtain credit for their own efforts. To avoid this effect, a teacher might say, "I get the impression that (something the parent is doing) is having a positive effect on your child's language development. She is much more talkative lately, especially during snack time." These statements make clear reference to the parent's contribution.

Micro-level communication that acts to *focus attention* on topics of interest to professionals includes a variety of statements and questions that highlight selected topics. For example, a teacher can refer to something a parent has said regarding a topic of special interest to the teacher and thereby guide the conversation in a desired direction. If this teacher is particularly interested in focusing the conversation on the topic of available respite care (rather than on the parent's desire to go to the coast), he or she could focus the parent's attention on that topic by saying, "So it's the respite problem that's got you stuck." If the teacher wanted to direct the parent's thinking toward working through the dilemma, he or she could guide the parent in that direction by asking, "What would you like to see happen with regard to respite for a trip like that?", "What would have to happen to solve your respite problem?" or "Who's the most likely candidate at this point to provide respite?"

Professionals can also use intentional statements to redirect attention to their own previously mentioned interests or intentions. In focusing on their own perspective, professionals can take care not to usurp talk-time from parents. They can time their focusing statements within appropriate pauses or after requesting and obtaining consent to redirect the conversation. In constructing focusing statements, it is important to include clear personal references to thoughts and feelings and to indicate how points of view and purposes have been derived. This strategy shows an intention to stress a particular point rather than dominate a conversation. For example, in presenting an assessment of a learning need, statements such as, "As a teacher, I feel it is important that we give some special attention to language development. . . " or "My recommendations are influenced by the results of recent language assessments" can be very useful and influential while providing clear references to a particular professional recommendation. These kinds of statements better acknowledge the desire for a balance of power in a parent–professional relationship than do statements such as, "We must do something about the language problems" or "The first priority should be language development."

Much of the influence that professionals exert in their relationships with parents depends on how they *offer help*. Too often, parents resist professional expertise because professionals express a desire to control, persuade, rescue, or prove professional capabilities. Persuasive statements like "you should" and "you need to," and statements inferring that professional knowledge or judgment is more valid than parental experience, can leave parents feeling ignored or discounted. Professionals can state their desire and ability to help in ways that communicate intent to collaborate with family-identified needs and goals. Statements that offer parents choices rather than directions or prearranged plans are more likely to be heard as genuine offers for empowering help. Questions such as, "What can I do that would be most helpful at this time?" can orient professionals to a helping mode when they are tempted to offer advice or directions in a persuasive, domineering, or condescending manner. A teacher who wants to address changing demands in the relationship in a way that stresses his or her intention to be helpful might say, "I'm noticing that you seem to want a more/less active role in (the particular process underway). I'd like to help us figure out how to best coordinate our efforts. Would that be helpful to you as well as to me?" The helping message is preceded by a focusing statement on the relationship and makes the offer in a noncontrolling way. In the context of collaborative parent–professional relationships, the goal of making statements offering professional help is to inform parents of professional insights and abilities to assist with family-identified needs and to provide room for parents to choose among helping options.

In presenting communication strategies for parent–professional relationships, the authors have drawn from their experiences with parents and special education teachers to present some meta-, intermediate-, and micro-communication strategies for increasing opportunities for collaboration in parent–professional relationships. Skillful use of these strategies holds considerable promise for enhancing professionals' effectiveness in using a collaborative partnership approach in their work with families.

HANDLING DIFFICULT INTERACTIONS

In some parent–professional relationships, particularly where there has been difficulty in establishing a satisfactory give-and-take, parents and professionals encounter difficulties in their interactions. It is likely that they will not always agree, especially if their world views are substantially at odds. Factors such as fatigue, discouragement, competitive feelings, frustration with lack of services or progress for the child, misunderstandings about one another's intentions, or disappointments in one another's behaviors can influence their interactions with discouraging regularity, or quite unpredictably and with varying duration and frequency. These and other factors challenge parent–professional relationships and contribute significantly to interpersonal difficulties.

Difficult interactions can be triggered in several ways. Professionals as well as parents sometimes experience some level of discomfort in discussing sensitive topics such as hygiene, test results, or problem behaviors. In other situations, particular parental behaviors such as criticism, anger, or disagreement elicit personal discomfort for professionals, thus making communication difficult. In still others, professionals themselves behave in ways that create impasses in their conversations with parents. For example, teachers may urge parents to adopt a view of the child's functioning or offer unsolicited advice or sympathy in ways that are difficult for parents to accept. Still, there is much that can be done to manage difficult interactions without weakening the parent–professional relationship.

Managing Difficult Behaviors, Thoughts, and Feelings

When a behavior by one partner is perceived as inconsiderate, withdrawn, aggressive, or disparaging by the other, each is prone to defensive reactions that cast either oneself or one's partner in an exaggeratedly negative light. During negative interpersonal interactions, we tend to feel personally attacked and defend ourselves by developing generalized statements at a meta-level in attempts to understand the situation and protect ourselves from aversive experiences. In these situations we often develop negative self-talk about personal traits in ourselves or others, rather than to call on meta-level self-talk that enables us to view upsetting behaviors as logical human responses to conditions of stress and/or frustration. When parents or professionals personalize the intentions of one another's upsetting behaviors and overgeneralize the causes for negative interactions, they can develop negative stereotypes of one another that form obstacles to collaboration in their relationships.

Professionals who face upsetting parental behaviors can utilize some of the communication strategies suggested in this chapter to approach the situation in a manner that preserves the parent–professional friendship. If necessary, professionals can take control of difficult interactions in ways that are respectful of parents' feelings and that rely on assertive strategies rather than aggressive or submissive ones. This often means that professionals must bring intense feelings and/or negative thoughts under control. They can wait to approach the parent until they can formulate some self-regulating meta-level introductory statements that orient them toward a constructive outcome. An example of a constructive outcome might be to understand and validate a parent's intense feelings while continuing to work together on substantive tasks. Professionals can later expect to witness additional upsetting behaviors or emotional statements that are difficult to handle. Still, they can prepare themselves to maintain a neutral stance in response to a parent's upsetting behaviors by concentrating on tracking the substantive content of the parent's words and noting evidence of the parent's emotional state. Remaining neutral and gathering this kind of information are meta-level strategies that often help professionals to avoid judgmental or defensive behaviors when responding to upsetting interpersonal experiences with parents. At the intermediate-level of communication, professionals can ensure that difficult interactions occur in settings where adequate privacy and time are provided.

Assertive communication involves skillful use of both listening and influencing strategies. When used skillfully, assertive communication can help professionals to promote less aversive exchanges with parents during difficult interactions. In using assertive messages, professionals can engage first in active listening to ensure clear understanding of the parent's perspective. If given sufficient opportunity to vent negative thoughts and feelings, people often will modify their behaviors on their own. Likewise, professionals are more likely to gain an accurate understanding of the parent's distress by listening to them before reacting. In addition, they will have a better chance of being on target when focusing or attempting supportive responses. A sensitive, empathic statement is often sufficient to ease tension in the relationship and to move the conversation into a more mutually supportive exchange. Sometimes it is also helpful to precede an assertive message with an overt meta-level message about how the relationship can benefit from paying some attention to the way the interaction is feeling. A professional might say, for example, that he or she is very concerned about the parent's issue and wants to resolve any problems, and at the same time feels that it would be helpful to their relationship if some attention were paid to how each of them is feeling about the present interaction.

To address the tension building between parents and professionals, professionals can make assertive statements following a specific formula:

When X happens, I feel Y because Z.

In this case, X is a reference to a concrete, parent-related behavior or event, Y is the subjective feeling experienced by the professional, and Z provides an explanation of how the professional subjectively interprets and/or reacts to the behaviors or events described as X. Here is an example of an assertive statement by a teacher:

> When you did not come to the scheduled appointment, I became very discouraged and even a little angry, because I began to think that you weren't interested in what we are working on at school.

As noted earlier, assertive statements can be made more effective if the professional precedes an assertive statement with empathic and/or supportive statements. For example, to avoid sounding critical, the following empathic statement can precede the assertive statement above:

> I can imagine that it is difficult for you to come to meetings with me. I can remember how helpful it was to me last spring when you provided input about Pam's activities at home and I miss getting that information. So, when you did not come. . . .

The distinctive characteristics of assertive statements are that they are respectful of the tendency of both parents and professionals to react subjectively. Assertive messages provide concrete references to specific behaviors; they avoid generalizations; they do not make critical, blaming, or negative statements about the other person; and they contain clear references to one's own subjective experience through use of "I" statements. Assertive statements also allow adequate room for the listener to respond nondefensively. The effective professional use of assertive statements often elicits, as opposed to demands, an explanatory or supportive statement from parents who are upset.

In instances where professionals realize that their behaviors are upsetting to parents, they can ease the tension by acknowledging the negative impact created and address and repair any threat to the parent–professional relationship. The quickest way to do this is to begin with an assertive statement in the manner described above as a means of explaining the behavior that was upsetting. Additional statements in which professionals accept responsibility for their own mistakes or lapses and then acknowledge the negative impact are particularly constructive to the parent–professional relationship. And finally, a meta-level statement that reassures parents about professional commitment to a collaborative relationship reestablishes professional intention to keep working within the relationship.

Occasionally, then, it is necessary to work actively to manage negative thoughts and feelings that arise during parent–professional interactions. The professional's use of collaborative frameworks and orientation in relating to parents on a meta-communication level and of constructive communication during difficult interactions on the intermediate- and micro-levels of communication are critical in ensuring the development of a strong parent–professional partnership.

SUMMARY

Family-centered approaches to providing services for children with disabilities require professionals to invest greater effort in the development of collaboration partnerships with parents and other family members. The implementation of family-centered approaches requires a professional orientation that values family and parental perspectives as well as collaboration in parent–professional relationships.

This chapter is aimed at assisting professionals in acquiring the orientation and skills needed to achieve positive outcomes in efforts to interact collaboratively with parents. The importance of valuing a professional orientation that prioritizes collaboration has been discussed and the use of a developmental, growth-oriented framework within which to understand and engineer collaborative parent–professional partnerships has been suggested. In addition, a variety of attitudinal and skill-based communication strategies that professionals can use to enhance collaborative interactions with parents were presented. When professionals genuinely embrace family-oriented and collaboration values in their helping roles with families and achieve congruency in the messages they send from the three levels of thinking and communicating described in this chapter, they will greatly enhance the collaborative nature of their interactions with parents. In addition, they will develop the ability to handle difficult interactions while supporting collaboration goals in parent–professional relationships.

The acquisition of family-centered approaches and collaboration skills is an important goal for professionals who strive to enhance their effectiveness in providing appropriate services to families of children with disabilities. These goals embrace values and behaviors that send clear messages to parents and families about a professional commitment to helping families along their way to empowerment and growth.

REFERENCES

Bales, R.F. (1976). *Interaction process analysis: A method for the study of small groups*. Chicago: University of Chicago Press.

Bolton, R. (1979). *People skills: How to assert yourself, listen to others, and resolve conflicts*. New York: Simon & Schuster.

Brinckerhoff, J.L., & Vincent, L.J. (1986). Increasing parental decision-making at their child's individualized educational program meeting. *Journal of the Division for Early Childhood, 11*, 46–58.

Carkhuff, R.R., & Anthony, W.A. (1979). *The skills of helping*. Amherst, MA: Human Resource Development Press.

Darling, R.B. (1983). Parent–professional interaction: The roots of misunderstanding. In M. Seligman (Ed.), *The family with a handicapped child: Understanding and treatment* (pp. 95–121). New York: Grune & Stratton.

Dunst, C.J., Trivette, C.M., Starnes, A.L., Hamby, D.W., & Gordon, N.J. (1993). *Building and evaluating family support initiatives: A national study of programs for persons with developmental disabilities*. Baltimore: Paul H. Brookes Publishing Co.

Egan, G. (1975). *The skilled helper*. Pacific Grove, CA: Brooks/Cole Publishing Co.

Evans, D.R., Hearn, M.T., Uhlemann, M.R., & Ivey, A.E. (1984). *Essential interviewing: A programmed approach to effective communication*. Pacific Grove, CA: Brooks/Cole Publishing Co.

Fine, M.J. (1991). *Collaboration with parents of exceptional children.* Brandon, VT: Clinical Psychology Publishing Co.

Fisher, R., & Brown, S. (1988). *Getting together: Building a relationship that gets to yes.* Boston: Houghton Mifflin.

Ivey, A.E. (1988). *Intentional interviewing and counseling: Facilitating client development.* Pacific Grove, CA: Brooks/Cole Publishing Co.

Krehbiel, R., & Kroth, R.L. (1991). Communicating with families of children with disabilities or chronic illness. In M.J. Fine (Ed.), *Collaboration with parents of exceptional children* (pp. 103–107). Brandon, VT: Clinical Psychology Publishing Co.

Lewis, C.C., Pantell, R.H., & Sharp, L. (1991). Increasing patient knowledge, satisfaction, and involvement: Randomized trial of a communication intervention. *Pediatrics, 88*(2), 351–358.

Mendoza, J. (1983). *Connections: Developing skills for the family of the young special child, 0–5.* Manual produced by San Diego City Schools, San Diego, CA.

Mischler, E.G. (1984). *The discourse of medicine: Dialectics of medical interviews.* Norwood, NJ: Ablex Publishing Co.

Rainforth, B., York, J., & Macdonald, C. (1992). *Collaborative teams for students with severe disabilities: Integrating therapy and educational services.* Baltimore: Paul H. Brookes Publishing Co.

Singer, G.H.S., & Irvin, L.K. (Eds.). (1989). *Support for caregiving families: Enabling positive adaptation to disability.* Baltimore: Paul H. Brookes Publishing Co.

Singer, G.H.S., & Walker, B. (1991). *Pediatricians and parents of children with disabilities* [Videotape]. Eugene: Oregon Research Institute.

Turnbull, A.P., & Turnbull, H.R. (1986). *Families, professionals, and exceptionality: A special partnership.* Columbus, OH: Charles E. Merrill.

Walker, B. (1989a). *Improving communication between teachers and parents of students with disabilities.* Unpublished doctoral dissertation, University of Oregon, Eugene.

Walker, B. (1989b). Strategies for improving parent–professional cooperation. In G.H.S. Singer & L.K. Irvin (Eds), *Support for caregiving families: Enabling positive adaptation to disability* (pp. 103–119). Baltimore: Paul H. Brookes Publishing Co.

Walker, B., & Erickson, A.M. (1991). *Family focus in school/home collaboration* (Monograph). Eugene: University of Oregon, College of Education.

12

Short-Term Behavioral Counseling for Families of Persons with Disabilities

Nancy E. Hawkins,
George H. S. Singer,
and Charles D. Nixon

The purpose of this chapter is to describe a method for working with families of children and adolescents with severe disabilities. This method can help human services professionals to assess families, to help them to set goals, to teach them skills, to attend to their feelings, and to serve as allies in assisting people to change. This approach does not fall neatly into any of the current schools of family therapy, although it most closely resembles behavior therapy as an umbrella term. The focus and the range of methods that are used in working with families has been enlarged, as has been done by many behaviorists since the early 1980s. This chapter presents an introductory guide to the approach.

POSITIVE ADJUSTMENT TO DISABILITY

Until recently, the presence of a child with a disability or chronic illness was presented as a tragedy in the professional literature. In

Work on this chapter was funded by grant no. G008730149 between the Oregon Research Institute and the U.S. Department of Education, Office of Special Education and Rehabilitative Services. The views expressed herein do not necessarily represent those of the funder.

such instances, the parents were characterized as experiencing chronic sorrow and existential aloneness, siblings as suffering from lowered self-esteem and depression, marriages as being unusually fragile, and families as permanently stuck in earlier stages of the life cycle. The literature seemed to characterize all families of persons with disabilities in this negative manner while rarely mentioning positive adjustment as a possible outcome.

In recent years, however, a number of parents and siblings of children with disabilities have been publishing research that challenges this bleak picture considerably. Turnbull and Turnbull (1986) have been leaders in this intellectual movement by pointing out that in many studies there are insignificant differences between families of children with disabilities and families of children without disabilities and that many parents and siblings report long-term benefits of having a relative with a disability (Turnbull, Guess, & Turnbull, 1988). By studying other literatures concerned with adaptation to difficult life events, Summers, Behr, and Turnbull (1989) presented a coherent theory of positive adaptation through a process of cognitive coping. They went on to develop measures of positive adjustment and benefit in families and have recently collected data demonstrating that a majority of parents, in the long run, come to see their children with disabilities as positive contributors to their quality of life (see also Behr, 1991).

Singer and Irvin (1990) have argued that adaptation is best understood with a model of stress and coping, leading either to maladaption or to resilience and positive benefit. They present evidence for both outcomes. For example, Singer and Yovanoff (1992) conducted meta-analyses of the earlier literature on psychosocial distress in these families and concluded that a majority of parents are not distressed. At the same time, they found consistent evidence for elevated levels of demoralization in parents. In a series of studies examining measures of depression, Singer and Yovanoff's review found that roughly 40% of the mothers of children with disabilities reported symptoms of depression compared to roughly 20% of mothers of children without disabilities. Thus, three things appear to be true: 1) a majority of families of children with disabilities are not distressed; 2) many families benefit in the long run from the experience of living with a member with a disability; and 3) at the same time, there is an unusually high number of mothers (and possibly other family members) who could benefit from extra forms of support in order to resolve obstacles to positive adjustment. From this perspective, the goals of assisting family members are to help them to gain a full appreciation of the lessons and strengths acquired from living with a family member with a disability and to reduce some of the psychological, social, and economic costs that families must bear.

AN ECOBEHAVIORAL PERSPECTIVE

Ecobehavioral perspectives view behavior as embedded in a social and historical context. Ecobehavioral analysis strives to identify the specific impact of contextual variables on human behavior. The ecological approach directs attention to the context that surrounds any problem that families experience. Ecological models are often presented visually as a series of concentric circles. Each circle represents one level of the family social system. The boundaries between any one of these levels of the social system may be troubled. Conversely, there may be untapped resources in these surrounding social networks that could be activated to help.

The ecological perspective leads to a comprehensive assessment of troubled families and a flexible agenda. Help is given to family members to set and work toward goals with respect to any or all of the important social groups that have an impact on them. As a result, flexibility is needed in the kinds of skills that are developed and the tactics that are used. For example, for a troubled mother–child relationship, focusing on behavioral parent training interventions is a priority. For marital conflict, utilizing behavioral marital therapy is likely. With regard to discord with extended family members, assertiveness training and conflict resolution methods may be used. For dealing with the ways families connect with community institutions, the focus may be to link them to advocates and counsel political action.

Although the skills and resources necessary to achieve goals are the constant focus of this approach, at every step of this process family members' thoughts and feelings are important as well. In this aspect, the skills that are commonly taught as essential components of a therapeutic relationship are employed. These include active listening skills such as questioning, paraphrasing, reflecting feelings, sharing personal experiences, and assisting in the process of understanding, articulating, and challenging assumptions. On rare occasions experiential exercises will be used when emotional avoidance appears to be a barrier to making progress. The assumption is made that thoughts and feelings are inextricably interwoven with behavior and need to be clarified and acknowledged in order for people to set goals, learn skills, or activate social support.

INTERVENTION FORMAT

Referral

Parents usually learn about counseling services from other community agencies, such as the public school special education programs and the local developmental disabilities case management system. In many cases the problems for which the families are referred turn out to be the proverbial "tip of the iceberg." Although the initial referral often concerns the behavior of the child with a disability, as the parents continue working in counseling they often request help with relationship issues as well.

Prior to the first session, the counselor talks to the parent over the telephone. Some brief information is given about the counseling in order to clarify what a parent or sibling may expect. Counseling is described as short-term with a focus on first helping the family member to identify his or her goals and then helping him or her to set up steps to accomplish them. The importance of homework as an essential part of the counseling relationship is stressed. It is aimed at prompting people to think about their goals together with their family and, once goals are identified, to practice skills in the real world settings where they are needed.

This initial information is the beginning of the process of obtaining informed consent. People can start to consider whether or not they want to engage in this kind of counseling. People are also informed of the kinds of help that are not offered. For example, problems of addiction or acute mental illness are not directly addressed. If people ask for help with these issues during the initial telephone contact, they are referred to other local services providers who specialize in these problems. Sometimes this referral process takes more than one telephone contact and, occasionally, a counselor may meet with parents solely for the purpose of assisting them in gaining other assistance.

Initial Assessment and Informed Consent

The first appointment with the parents is usually held without the children present. When parents arrive for the first session they are given a written consent form to read and sign. This document spells out in greater detail the information that is given over the telephone. It describes the average number of sessions, their length, the assessments that will be conducted, an explanation of laws concerning the reporting of child abuse, and the general problem-solving approach to treatment. It explains that counseling will involve homework assignments. It also explains methods of protecting confidentiality.

Informed consent is more than a legal formality in working with families. It is a basic stance toward the relationship between the counselor and the family. Both parties enter into a contract. The counselor agrees to provide skilled help. The family members agree to participate actively in the work of solving problems. They are acknowledged as the ultimate holders of power in the counseling relationship. That is, they decide what goals they wish to work on, whether or not they will accede to the suggestions of the counselor, and whether or not they will practice skills and implement plans. They are told that homework assignments will be negotiable each week and that only the ones that they agree upon will be written down and given to them. At the same time, family members are expected to practice homework assignments. While written informed consent is gathered only at the first meeting, verbal consent is requested as part of each session as a way of continuing to develop the client–counselor partnership in treatment.

After obtaining informed consent and completing other procedures, the clinician presents an overview of the treatment approach. With two-parent families the clinician asks *each* parent to tell what he or she is concerned about and what help he or she hopes to get. Often disagreements will immediately arise about the nature of the problem. The explanation is given that family members often have different perceptions of a problem and that these perceptions are valued more than is the "objective truth" of the situation. Family members are asked to take turns speaking and to not interrupt one another with disagreements or comments during this initial presentation.

Identifying Strengths and Resources

During the initial assessment of the problem the counselor tries to obtain as much information as possible and, at the same time, to begin building a relationship with the family. During this process the message that their thoughts and feelings are understandable and valid given their stressful situation is conveyed. The beginning of the assessment process also involves trying to identify the coping skills and social resources available to family members. For example, in one initial interview with a couple whose child had sustained a brain injury, the counselor began to ask about coping and social support:

Counselor:	So far what you've told me is that you are often feeling very sad and frightened about your son. Sometimes you feel so badly that you just don't have the energy to do much. And as a couple, you are feeling isolated from one another. You are talking to each other less than usual and you don't have many enjoyable times together lately. Is that right so far?
Father:	Yes, that's what I'm concerned about.
Mother:	Yes, that's it.
Counselor:	I wonder if you have found anything that has helped you with these problems in the last few months.
Father:	No, not really. Well, come to think of it, we got a baby-sitter last weekend and went off to the coast for the day. But then it all started over again as soon as we got home.
Counselor:	So, getting a break from the house and some time together as a couple seemed to help for awhile.
Mother:	I have a friend; she has been a best friend ever since high school. She has a little boy who was hit by a car and has a brain injury. I feel better when I talk to her on the telephone because she's been through something similar. You know, she never says things to me like, "Maybe there'll be a miracle" or "There's a silver lining in every cloud." I get so sick of hearing that kind of stuff from people at church. My mother is the worst one for that. She just acts like Carl has a flu that's going to go away next week!
Counselor:	So some of the things that people are saying to you about your son are making you feel worse instead of helping. But your friend really understands.
Mother:	(Nods).
Counselor:	You know, I hear other parents say similar things. It's as if people just don't know how to help unless they have been there themselves. Your friend sounds like a real resource for you.
Mother:	Yes. The other thing that helps me feel better is if I get something accomplished during the day. Even if it is something little like getting all of the record albums put away or the bills paid, if I can look at something in the house and feel like I got it finished, I feel better.
Counselor:	So getting some visible task completed during the day helps you to feel better too.
Mother:	Yes.

Counselor: One of the things that I've noticed in working with parents who have children who need extra care is that often parents will stop doing the things that are helpful to them and life gets harder. I want to encourage you to do the things that work for you. In fact, I want to suggest for a homework assignment for next week that you agree to do some of these things that are helpful to you. Are you willing to try? You mentioned three things that work for you: time off together, talking to your friend on the telephone, and getting a task done. What would you like to get done during the week?

Father: I'm going to be on the road this weekend. But we could go out for the evening sometime this week.

Mother: Yes. And I'll call Cherline (friend). I'll call her twice!

Counselor: I'm going to write these down as reminders for you. I also would like you to think about what other problems, if any, you want to work on. Remember, where we are headed is to come up with a list of goals for our work together.

Thus, from the beginning of the counseling, utilizing existing resources and coping strategies is emphasized. A prime goal of this work is to support parents and siblings in their abilities to solve and resolve their problems.

During the first session questions are also asked about each adult and his or her medical history, prior mental health contacts, health practices, mood, and social support. At the end of the first session the clinician explains to clients that one or two more information-gathering sessions will be needed in order to assist them in setting clear goals for treatment. They are asked to help with this process by collecting information during the week. Usually this data collection involves keeping track of stressors and successful coping efforts. If the initial problem presented by a couple concerns marital discord, the couple is given specific instruments to complete. If the problem concerns a child's behavior they are given forms to use to keep track of antecedents, problematic behaviors, and consequences of problems. (For a description of the process of developing a functional analysis, see Lucyshyn & Albin, chap. 14, this volume; for a description of the process of assessment for marital problems see Lichtenstein, chap. 10, this volume.) When parents want to work on a problem with an adolescent, permission is sought to meet separately with the teenager as part of the assessment and goal-setting process. Both parents and adolescents may also be asked to complete questionnaires that identify issues of common concerns.

Identification of Goals

During the first three sessions, the clinician notes possible goals as the parents discuss their concerns and hopes. By the end of the third session both the therapist and the family members usually have several goals in mind. Family members are asked for their suggestions for goals and are also given suggestions that may have become apparent from the assessment.

The therapist writes down the tentative goals and asks the parents to take them home and review them together. They are asked to make any changes in wording or to add or delete goals. Again the process of developing a working partnership and continuing to build the framework of informed consent continues through these sessions.

Setting Criteria and Rating Current Status

At the next session the parents are asked to think about how they would know if they had achieved a goal. They are asked to imagine, on a scale of 1 to 10 in which a "10" is a complete success, what a "10" looks like. For example, the father in the dialogue presented earlier explained that a 10 for the goal of spending more time as a couple would be talking with each other at least three nights a week and going out on a date at least once a week. The mother explained that for her, a 10 with regard to dealing with the other people's comments would be to let people know what she really thought and felt when they said things that were not helpful. The therapist suggested that she might also include as a "10" being able to ask people for the kind of support that is helpful. After the meaning of a success for a goal is defined, clients are then asked to rate how they are doing in achieving the goal at the moment. The same rating system can be used to check progress throughout treatment.

Session Format

Time is taken to set an agenda prior to each session. The plan is based upon notes from the previous week's session and the homework assignment for the week. Table 1 presents the outline of a typical session. Starting each meeting with a statement of the agenda provides a helpful structure. Family members can alter the plan if they have other issues that they wish to include. Gaining initial agreement on a structure for the session and using the agreement to organize the discussion helps to keep a focus especially in working

Table 1. Outline of typical session

Session length:	1 and 1/2 hours
Review agenda:	5 minutes
Review previous week's homework:	25 minutes
Work on goal attainment through problem solving and skill training: 50 minutes	
Assign homework for next week:	10 minutes

with families with multiple problems and ongoing crises. For example, with some parents counselors find themselves referring to the agenda and saying things such as, "Can we move on and address the goals or agenda we set up?" Of course, a counselor must use his or her best judgment in deciding when to pursue an issue that is not on the agenda. Rigid adherence to a plan or a program of skill instruction can also impede spontaneity in discussing feelings about current problems.

During one session with a couple, for example, both parents seemed unusually fatigued and unresponsive. In response to questions about their problem-solving homework, they indicated that they had been somewhat preoccupied that week with a school meeting for their son and had not completed their assignments. They had not yet debriefed one another about their reactions to the meeting and each had strong emotions that distracted them from proceeding with interest in problem solving more minor issues. The focus of the session was changed to their thoughts and feelings about the meeting. The result was some valuable sharing of feelings about a topic that was ordinarily difficult for them to discuss together. They left looking more animated and responsive to one another.

Typically, after reviewing the agenda, family members are asked to discuss the homework from the previous session. The therapist keeps a copy of each week's assignment and refers to it in asking parents how it went. Often the client's experience in trying to meet a goal will bring up issues that become a focus for discussion. Some of these issues imply that more problem-solving and skill training is necessary. Others suggest that the focus should be on thoughts and feelings. The initial emphasis is often placed on changing outward behaviors whenever possible, since thoughts, feelings, and attitudes often change in a positive direction as a result of taking action. When a client is unable to take action or the behavior change does not result in different thoughts and feelings, the emphasis temporarily shifts to cognitive and affective issues.

Skill Training

After the homework from the previous week's assignment has been reviewed the next goal that has been identified by family members is addressed. Table 2 presents examples of goals selected by families. It shows that parents, and sometimes older siblings, often identify a range of concerns and targets for change. There are recurrent themes and these imply sets of interventions that are commonly helpful.

Table 3 lists the major themes along with the skill training focus that fits with these goals. Other chapters in this volume describe in further detail elements of behavioral marital training (Lichtenstein, chap. 10, this volume), communication skill training (Walker & Singer, chap. 11, this volume), and reattribution training (Nixon, chap. 7, this volume). This chapter focuses on the skill training involved in teaching problem solving and interpersonal communication skills based on Robin's work with parent–adolescent conflict (Robin, 1980).

Problem-Solving Training

For many couples and family groups, training in problem-solving and communication is an important focus of joint sessions. The therapist begins by asking each family member to identify a relatively minor issue (a "2" or "3" on a scale of 1–10) for practicing problem-solving skills. By starting with a minor issue, family members are better able to pay attention to learning the process of problem-solving, rather than getting bogged down in controversy. They are asked to follow a highly structured way of talking to one another. Their permission is sought to step in and interrupt their normal

Table 2.   Examples of family goals

1.   Siblings will fight less and play cooperatively before dinner.
2.   The couple will share feelings about their child's disability/illness and care, and withdraw from each other less when they are feeling upset.
3.   The husband will help with laundry and putting away groceries.
4.   The mother will ask for a special meeting to revise the IEP. She will first meet with an advocate. The father will support her by talking with her regularly about the meeting.
5.   The spouses will take turns going out for special activities with the siblings without disabilities.
6.   The mother will practice progressive muscle relaxation three times a week and go for a walk daily.
7.   The father will talk with his two best friends when he feels badly about his child.
8.   Parents will talk with other parents whose child has had behavior problems.

Table 3. Skill training associated with specific problem areas

Unresolved practical problems	• Problem-solving skills • Linkage to social support • Interpersonal problem solving
Marital discord	• Communication training • Increasing positive experiences through planning and problem-solving
Troubled relationships with teenage children	• Interpersonal problem solving
Behavioral and skill deficit problems from child with disability	• Behavioral parent training
Stress problems: insomnia, anxiety, fatigue, low morale due to situational stress	• Relaxation training • Increasing pleasant activities • Skills for recruiting social support • Self-monitoring • Covert rehearsal • Self-coaching and reattribution • Behavioral parent training skills
Conflict with extended family	• Interpersonal problem solving • Assertiveness skills
Conflict with agencies	• Assertiveness and advocacy skills • Linkage to advocacy groups

ways of communicating during the skill training session. Family members are told that this method of talking will feel a little stilted and slow-moving at first and they are asked to be patient.

The therapist needs to be very careful about helping to select a problem that is relatively easy for all family members present. Some issues may appear to be minor at first but may bring up larger and more painful issues. For example, a discussion about putting away the groceries may rapidly open up a general disagreement and long-term resentment over the division of household responsibilities. One of the reasons for starting with an easy, relatively uncontroversial problem is to allow couples to attain initial success. If they have withdrawn from each other or are actively fighting, a constructive conversation over even a fairly minor problem can be encouraging.

Communication training is usually started with modeling and demonstration. Family members are shown ways to talk to each other about the problem. When couples are fighting or extremely conflicted, counselors often work in pairs. Working as a team in this way provides opportunities to model dialogues and listening skills.

Once an easy issue is identified, each partner is asked to state the problem to the other. Throughout communication and problem-solving training counselors are very active; they frequently interrupt with words or gestures in order to try to shape the interaction. Their initial aim is to assist each partner to state the problem in clear, noninflammatory, nonblaming language. They are asked to use a format such as "When you do . . . , this is the consequence for me . . . and this is how I feel." Partners are asked to make eye contact, and they are given descriptive feedback about their facial expressions and body language.

Often several sessions of detailed coaching are needed before parents will begin to talk with one another without falling back into old habits of blaming, referencing the past, generalizing, or verbal sparring.

Cognitive Coaching

With practice, family members become more skilled at turn-taking, making noninflammatory statements of problems, paraphrasing, and communicating with nonaggression. The counselor, in turn, begins commenting on patterns in the way family members appear to interpret each other's communications or beliefs that may be influencing their communication. For example, partners often appear to believe that if they listen to the other person's problem they have an obligation to solve it. If the counselor's observations of the couple suggest that one or both partners hold this idea, it is pointed out and alternative ways of thinking about dealing with problems are suggested. For example, the idea that sometimes simply being listened to is sufficient might be suggested. At other times, particularly when problems are not easily solved, simply sharing feelings about them can be of help. Partners are told that they can say to one another things such as, "I feel so helpless when you tell me what's troubling you. I feel sad when I hear you are having this trouble and I want to be able to fix it but I can't." Beliefs regarding gender roles are also commonly encountered. A frequent one is the belief that men should not talk about their feelings. In families where cultural patterns do not include male expressiveness, male–female teams are set up in which the male counselor talks about the difficulties that men have with this kind of communication. Having the male counselor share some of his own experiences in learning to talk about difficult topics and telling about other men's experiences can be helpful. Some of the problems that can arise when men or women have no way of expressing their private thoughts and feelings when they are in difficult situations are pointed out.

Cognitive Interpretations of a Childhood Disability

During the process of communication skill training, a topic that frequently arises concerns the variety of perceptions that family members hold regarding the child with a disability. One common example has been disagreements over attributions about the cause of behavior problems in children with disabilities. In several cases couples (or siblings and parents) have disagreed over the child's intentions in misbehaving. For example, one family member may attribute the misbehavior to the child's disability whereas another family member may interpret it as an intentional act that reflects badly on the child's character. The members of one family disagreed about how to interact with a young man who had experienced a brain injury in a car accident. Since his injury, he had been involved in repeated problems in the community that were embarrassing to the family. The mother and one sibling attributed the misbehavior to the brain injury and believed that the young man needed help. The father and another brother believed that moral behavior was still under the young man's control and that he had become a bad person; they were much less patient and willing to help.

These kinds of beliefs and attitudinal differences usually emerge in the course of trying to solve practical problems and to reach goals that the family has set. Assisting family members to state their views clearly and to paraphrase one another is the first step in this process. Furthermore, they are encouraged to communicate the way that hearing the others' beliefs makes them feel. At times the counselor intervenes in order to try to change people's beliefs or to encourage them to question their views. Sometimes this process involves giving them information or talking about situations involving other families and persons with disabilities. This open challenging of beliefs can usually only take place later in therapy after considerable trust has been developed. It has to be done with great respect and with a strong sense of empathy. Thus, skill training in areas such as behavior management and communication is frequently interwoven with work on beliefs. In this sense, the approach is cognitive and behavioral.

PROBLEM SOLVING AND COMMUNICATION

Generating and Evaluating Solutions to Problems

Couples or teenagers and parents first work on stating problems clearly, paraphrasing, and reflecting feelings. They then focus on generating solutions to problems. During this stage, the therapist encourages the partners to take turns listing as many possible solutions as they can generate. The therapist writes them down and then asks participants to make suggestions without any evaluative comments in order to avoid stifling the process with judgments. The therapist also suggests solutions. In order to make the process more playful, the therapist often makes patently ridiculous suggestions and also encourages them to make up fanciful ideas. When family members have run out of ideas, the next phase of problem-solving—the process of evaluating the possible solutions—is implemented. The therapist reads the ideas aloud and asks each family member to decide whether or not the solution is one that he or she supports. The counselor records a plus sign (signifying approval) or a minus sign (signifying disapproval) after each option. If one solution emerges as the most preferred, it is chosen. If more than one receive equal ratings, the discussion moves to choosing the preferable solution.

Implementing the Solution

The counselor asks family members to choose one or more of the solutions to implement. At this point the counselor makes a kind of behavioral contract with the couple. It may be formal with written terms, or it may be a verbal agreement. The counselor then asks the couple to try the selected solutions for a certain period of time. He or she asks them to designate who will perform the activities needed to carry out the solution and to specify when they will be accomplished; these steps are usually written down and are assigned as homework. The counselor explains that they will be asked at the next session how well they have succeeded in implementing the solutions. If relevant, he or she works with the family to set up a recording system to determine whether or not the solution is working. For example, one couple wanted to work on a problem that had arisen as a result of remodeling their kitchen. The husband was upset because their daughter, who was deaf, would get into his tools and scatter them through the house while he was away at work. His wife was distressed because she did not have any surfaces available in the kitchen for cooking. They agreed that they would work together to clean up after each remodeling effort and that he would begin to store his tools in a locked tool box. They also planned when they would allow their daughter to play with the tools safely and to help her father with the work. A simple monitoring form was constructed, which they agreed to put on the refrigerator door. It listed the days of the week, provided spaces to write one check mark if they cleaned the counters and another if he locked up his tools. They were asked to bring the written form to the next session for review.

Reinforcement

Reinforcement is a key part of a skill training approach to family change that requires family members to learn and carry out many new ways of acting. Learning research suggests that new learning is best accomplished through the use of much functional reinforcement. Once the counselor has developed rapport with the family, the counselor's praise and encouragement often function as a motivator. Ideally, the process of solving problems and improving the family's situation will in time become an intrinsic reward for the process. In the meantime, genuine respect and enthusiasm are expressed when family members try new solutions, practice new skills, and implement agreements.

Promoting Generalization

The ultimate goal of therapy is that the family will be able to implement these new skills in response to new problems and circumstances without help from the therapist. Several features of the instruction that takes place during therapy are designed to promote generalization and maintenance of skills. The first of these is a gradual fading of the therapist's prompts and assists. The skill training moves from easier tasks to harder ones and from more therapist support to less. The second involves home practice of each skill so that family members gradually initiate the use of skills in their own setting without the therapist present but with weekly guidance from the therapist. The couple might begin to practice the first steps of problem solving for an easy issue during the session and then complete one or two steps, such as the brainstorming or the evaluation of the possible solutions, between sessions. In some cases, the couple is asked to make an audiotape of their home efforts at problem solving. Recording the session ensures that family members actually try the exercise. It also provides the therapist with a sample of their efforts to review. The tapes are listened to, the parts of the interaction that are well done are pointed out, and suggestions for further improvements are made. In addition, recording the exercise provides an opportunity for self-evaluation on the part of family members. They are asked to listen to themselves on the tape and write comments about what they did that enhanced the problem solving as well as what they believe could be improved.

Another element of the treatment design that aims to promote generalization is the timing of sessions. As a family begins making progress, the once-weekly sessions are scheduled 2 weeks apart and eventually 1 month apart. Increasing the time between sessions allows families to have more time to practice skills between sessions as well as more time to test their use of coping skills for the diverse issues that might arise. As the therapist recommends longer spans between sessions, he or she acknowledges confidence in the family's abilities to use the learned skills. Families are always told that they can call if needed for a session sooner than the one scheduled.

HOMEWORK

Assigning homework is an essential element of this skills-based approach to change in families. Assignments cover a range of skills and issues. The assignments are keyed to the stage of therapy. During the assessment phase, the assignments are concerned with gathering data and helping the family members to develop self-monitoring skills. During the intervention stage, the assignments are aimed at practicing skills in the natural environment in order to promote generalization. Later in the course of treatment, the assignments are aimed at promoting generalization to new and more challenging topics.

An important issue with regard to homework is compliance. This skills-based approach to treatment requires family members to carry out efforts at home or in the community between sessions (see Shelton & Levy, 1981, for a comprehensive discussion on compliance with assignments). There are several ways that completing homework assignments is encouraged. The first, as described above, involves explaining from the beginning (and repeating during subsequent sessions) that families must set their own goals and practice skills at home with one another as part of the program. Analogies are often used to explain the importance of practicing these skills. For example, clients are often advised that learning to communicate or manage child misbehavior or to be assertive is like learning a new sport. Merely attending counseling sessions and not practicing the actual skills will not result in making changes, just as one could not learn to play basketball well by sitting in a coach's office once a week and hearing a lecture.

Each session begins with a review of the previous week's homework so that family members know that the first topic for discussion at every meeting will be these assignments. When clients report that they have not completed their homework, they are questioned further to find out what stood in the way of doing the assignments and whether they had even partially completed them. The reasons for incomplete homework may include such things as not understanding the assignment and being too unassertive to ask for clarification; forgetting that they had agreed to do something until the time of the appointment; waiting for the other family member to initiate the assignment when it required both to work on it together; being embarrassed to show their work because of poor reading, writing, or spelling skills; and being reluctant to try for fear of failure of course, sometimes incomplete homework results from an especially stressful week with extra caregiving demands on the family. Before assigning the next homework, the problems that blocked the families from doing the assignments the previous week are addressed. For example, the counselor may do any or all of the following: making certain that the assignment is understood by everyone through modeling in the session, linking the assignments to events that already occur in the family's day (e.g., after the dishes are done and before turning on the television), setting up a specific agreed-upon time to work on the joint assignments, giving permission for written assignments to be in brief note form and not be turned in to the counselor. If the incomplete homework appears to be due to increased stress, family members are praised for taking the time to at least come to the appointment. If possible, a portion of the session may be devoted to working on the assignment before proceeding with the session agenda.

Sometimes the family members may have actually done some but not all of the homework. If they have completed even a portion of the homework, the first focus is on what they did accomplish and how successful it was, and they are reinforced for their efforts. They are encouraged to be more realistic in selecting the number of assignments they agree to do before the next session, so that it is more likely that they will be successful next time. Once any compliance has been reinforced, the counselor returns to a discussion of the family's goals and his or her method of working with people. The importance of doing homework is stressed again, and the suggestion is made that not completing the homework will impede the family's progress through the counseling sessions.

COMMON ISSUES AND METHODS FOR ADDRESSING THEM

Parenting Issues

Many families initially ask for help with problems related to parenting. These include troubles with children with and without disabilities. Behavioral parent training (BPT) is an effective approach to take in addressing these problems. Regular group classes on BPT are offered for parents of children with disabilities. Videotapes and manuals are also available as resources for families.

Parents often disagree over their interpretations of problem behaviors and are often divided in their approaches to handling them. The counselor therefore strives to create a common approach to the problem. These disagreements are important to resolve as a part of creating the necessary conditions that improve the child's misbehavior. For example, in one family a teenager with autism had a fascination with sharp objects. He would carve and cut household objects and the walls of the house. The mother and father dealt with this destructive behavior differently. The father tried to keep all sharp items locked up away from the boy and yelled at his son if he found something sharp. The mother, on the other hand, would occasionally let him use something sharp under her supervision. If he misused it, she would remove the privilege and take away the knife. Whenever the boy did damage an object, his mother and father would begin to fight and blame each other. The nature of this situation suggested that two goals be pursued: 1) that the parents develop ways to agree on parenting issues, particularly with this problem; and 2) that the property destruction stop and the boy learn more constructive behavior. The skills for the first goal are part of communication training. Those for the latter goal are part of behavioral parent training. In this case, first a functional analysis of the problem behavior was conducted in the home. Several recommendations were made about keeping knives and tools locked up and making alternative leisure activities available to the boy along with leisure skill training. Next, marital communication training and other components of behavioral marital therapy were worked on in order to help the couple come to agreements on parenting issues.

Depression

Another common problem encountered by families is depression. (See Powers, chap. 5, this volume, for a more detailed description of grief and depression.) Families who are dealing with the common stresses of contemporary family life, not to mention the difficulties raised by extra caregiving, sometimes face circumstances that can produce depression. In turn, living with a person who is experiencing depression can add further strains to family functioning, thereby compounding the original causal conditions. Consequently, counselors and therapists who work with caregiving families should be prepared to recognize the symptoms of depression and to treat them.

Current treatment methods include many of the cognitive and behavioral skill interventions that have been described previously.

DIFFICULTIES ENCOUNTERED IN
TEACHING SKILLS TO TROUBLED FAMILIES

Differential Parental Involvement

Often one parent, usually the mother, makes the initial request for help. In cases involving two-parent families, both parents are asked to come to the initial interview. The mother sometimes needs to check back with her husband to see if he is willing to come to a meeting. Even though both come in for the first session, sometimes the father indicates that his continued involvement would be difficult at best.

Efforts are made to accommodate work schedules and to work in teams of a male and female counselor when the fathers appear reluctant. In the initial interview, the importance of both partners' participation is emphasized. If the reluctant partner refuses to participate, the therapist clarifies the risks of working with only one parent. Behavioral parent training for only one parent, for example, may give rise to conflict over parenting practices. If relationship issues come to light and the counselor can only hear one partner's viewpoint, stress in the relationship could increase. Attempts to gain informed consent from both partners are made due to the risks involved in only one taking an active role.

A second approach to differential levels of commitment from family members is to create multiple options for involvement. This approach is clearest with regard to behavioral parent training. One partner, usually the mother, will often be the primary caregiver. The father is strongly encouraged to participate as much as possible in a way that is consistent with the family's norms for parenting roles. One option is egalitarian; parents learn the skills equally and implement them equally. Although this approach is becoming more common and is the most democratic one, there are many households where parents do not divide parenting equally. Another option is that the father will learn the skills for the purposes of using them on occasion or for being a backup support to his wife by encouraging her and praising her for using the skills. A less involved role that may be negotiated with the father is that he agrees to talk to his wife frequently about the children and to support her use of behavioral parenting skills. A final and most remote option is that the father simply agrees to let the mother make parenting decisions and will not resist her efforts to use new parenting skills.

Differential Participation in Counseling

As mentioned above, sometimes couples have differential invest- ment in counseling. Even if both are present, both do not necessarily participate in the sessions with equal involvement. Sometimes one member will dominate the discussion while the other will sit back and look bored.

As the therapist becomes aware of differential involvement, he or she can structure activities that require active listening (e.g., paraphrasing). The therapist will also clearly and gently point out the pattern, speculate about its effect, and model and shape appro- priate involvement in order to help the couple develop more success- ful communication patterns.

Changing Issues

Sometimes the family issues most warranting discussion seem to change from one session to the next. While disorganization is toler- ated in the beginning stages of treatment when gathering informa- tion about the family, therapists often have to structure the sessions more in order to keep moving on the selected goals once the assess- ment phase is complete.

In order to keep the sessions focused when new issues arise, the therapist encourages the couple to define new goals around these issues before changing the focus. In addition, the therapist writes an agenda prior to the session and reviews the agenda with the couple at the beginning of the session. On occasion, with couples who are particularly prone to jumping around to different topics, the thera- pist can even provide copies of the agenda so that all of the partici- pants can follow it. The between-session homework (of which the therapist keeps a copy) is reviewed first, in order to tie together issues over time. The goals that the couple have identified are at- tached on a post-it note to the top of the agenda so that the therapist is able to keep them in mind and refer to them at appropriate times. New issues can be discussed within the format of problem solving as well, once it has been introduced.

Unscheduled Breaks in Treatment

At times termination occurs by choice when family members agree that they have reached their goals. However, it also occurs because of situations such as summer vacations, loss of a baby-sitter, or a change in work schedule for one of the parents. Even though maintenance of skills has been built in throughout treatment with the assignment of homework practice, planned reinforcement of each other's efforts, and so on, change is hard work and old habits sometimes reemerge. Couples are encouraged to call for further assistance if the need arises; they are told that asking for help is healthy. Nonetheless, families sometimes report a sense of failure from having to ask for help again.

When family members return to treatment, the notion that progress is not in a straight line but has its ups and downs is reinforced. The previous goals and the progress they made before, as well as what they have managed to maintain, are reviewed. Their attempts at coping before they called, as well as their willingness to call, are respectfully acknowledged. Then their current issues and efforts are identified.

TERMINATING COUNSELING

After 12–15 sessions counseling is normally brought to a close. The primary focus in working with families is to enable them to solve their own problems in the future and to fade the counselor's intervention out of the picture as rapidly as possible. However, a balance between fostering independence and encouraging healthy interdependence must be struck.

One important coping skill involves asking for help from others when needed. Some of the families of children with disabilities must cope with chronic stress as a result of high medical costs, extra caregiving tasks, or negative reactions from others. In these cases families need to know that the counselor will be available in the future. Families are sometimes advised to check in with the counselor every 6–12 months in much the same way they would follow up with a dentist or car mechanic.

For other families whose situation is not marked by chronic stress, a choice of options is offered upon termination. These include making an appointment for 2–3 months in the future, arranging for the counselor to telephone after 2–3 months to see if another appointment is warranted, or leaving it up to the family to contact the counselor if they decide it would be helpful.

Family members often contact counselors for short-term assistance when a new problem has arisen in the family. For example, one couple contacted their counselor several months after termination when the husband was injured in a work accident and confined to the home. After they requested help with adjusting to the situation, the counselor met with them for four sessions. Another couple whose child has a degenerative illness contacted their counselor when there was a major functional change in his health. The best format for counseling for many families is to offer 12–15 sessions with the opportunity to check in with the counselor annually or when the need for extra support arises.

EVALUATION DATA

One way that the efficacy of the short-term problem focused counseling described in this chapter is evaluated is by administering measures such as the Beck Depression Inventory (BDI) (Beck, Ward, Mendelson, Moch, & Erbaugh, 1961) before and after counseling. The same data on waiting list comparison groups for people who have applied for group stress management training and behavioral parent training classes has also been maintained. The repeated testing of waiting list control groups of parents of children and youth with disabilities indicates that, in the absence of intervention, these parents do not normally show significant reductions in depressive symptoms over a 3- to 6-month period. Thus, the changes that are measured can probably be attributed to treatment rather than to the passage of time. However, so far the evaluation of this counseling method has not included random assignment of control groups; thus, these results must be qualified as they derive from a quasi-experimental design.

In order to determine whether or not the amount of change that parents have shown on the BDI is clinically significant, the change scores have been plotted on a graph (see Jacobson & Revenstorf, 1988) that indicates clinically significant score changes. Figure 1 shows this data. The ordinate and abcissa represent pretest and posttest scores on the BDI. The diagonal line is the point on the graph where there is no change from pretest to posttest. A dot that is above the line means that depressive symptoms got worse after treatment. A dot below the line shows that the score improved. The BDI has a "band of error" of approximately ±5 points. This region of error is indicated by the grey area around the diagonal line. A dot located within the band indicates that the change could be due to either measurement error or to actual change. If the data point is outside the band, the change is very likely not due to measurement error. The dotted line on the graph represents the clinical cutoff score for mild depression as determined by extensive research with the BDI. Thus the points that appear in the lower right hand quadrant of the figure represent change from BDI scores that were over

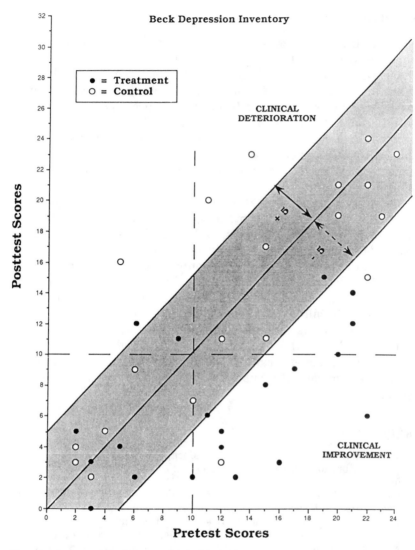

Figure 1. Pretest and posttest scores on the BDI. Triangles represent parents who received treatment. Circles represent parents on a waiting list for 4–6 months. Points located in the lower right-hand quadrant represent clinically significant change. The diagonal represents no change pretest or posttest. Grey band represents measurement error.

the clinical cutoff to those that are below. These data on 16 parents of children with severe disabilities suggest that most parents benefitted from the counseling and that many benefitted at a level that is clinically significant. While clinical trials with random assignment are called for, this data is highly encouraging.

SUMMARY

The literature has shown that although the majority of families of children with disabilites are not distressed but rather benefit from living with a member with a disability, some families need assistance in resolving obstacles to positive adjustment. Because family members may experience problems with respect to any or all of the social groups that have an impact on them, the approach described in this chapter encompasses a variety of skills, each focusing on different groupings of individuals within the family or between nuclear and extended family members, or between family members and the community.

The intervention format is described in detail from the point of referral and the process of obtaining informed consent, through the assessment and setting of goals, to the teaching of skills and termination. Particular attention is given to problem-solving and interpersonal communication skills, not only methods for teaching these skills, but also methods for enhancing their generalization. A number of difficulties encountered in working with families with children with disabilities are discussed. Finally, the efficacy of short-term problem focused counseling is addressed with data on 16 parents of children with severe disabilities. Although the data are derived form a quasi-experimental design that did not include random assignment of control groups, the data suggest that most parents benefited from counseling.

REFERENCES

Beck, A.T., Ward, C.H., Mendelson, M., Moch, T.E., & Erbaugh, J.H. (1961). An inventory for measuring depression. *Archives of General Psychiatry, 4,* 561–571.

Behr, S. (1991). *Final report to the National Institute on Disability and Rehabilitation Research: The Kansas Inventory of Parental Perceptions.* Lawrence: University of Kansas, Beach Center on Families and Disability.

Jacobson, N.S., & Revenstorf, D. (1988). Statistics for assessing the clinical significance of psychotherapy techniques: Issues, problems, and new developments. *Behavioral Assessment, 10,* 133–145.

Robin, A. (1980). Parent–adolescent conflict: A skill-training approach. In D.P. Rathjen & J.P. Foreyt (Eds.), *Social competence: Interventions for children and adults* (pp. 185–210). New York: Pergamon.

Shelton, J.L., & Levy, R.L. (Eds.). (1981). *Behavioral assignments and treatment compliance: A handbook of clinical strategies.* Champaign, IL: Research Press.

Singer, G.H.S., & Irvin, L.K. (1990). Supporting families of persons with severe disabilities: Emerging findings, practices, and questions. In L.H. Meyer, C.A. Peck, & L. Brown (Eds.), *Critical issues in the lives of persons with severe disabilities* (pp. 271–312). Baltimore: Paul H. Brookes Publishing Co.

Singer, G.H.S., & Yovanoff, P. (1992). *Demoralization in parents of children with developmental disabilities: A meta-analysis and review.* Manuscript submitted for publication.

Summers, J.A., Behr, S.K., & Turnbull, A.P. (1989). Positive adaptation and coping strengths of families who have children with disabilities. In G.H.S. Singer & L.K. Irvin (Eds.), *Support for caregiving families: Enabling positive adaptation to disability* (pp. 27–40). Baltimore: Paul H. Brookes Publishing Co.

Turnbull, A.P., & Turnbull, H.R. (1986). *Families, professionals, and exceptionality: A special partnership.* Columbus, OH: Charles E. Merrill.

Turnbull, H.R., Guess, D., & Turnbull, A.P. (1988). Vox populi and Baby Doe. *Mental Retardation, 26,* 127–132.

13

Providing Support to Sisters and Brothers of Children with Disabilities

Betsy Gibbs

There is growing recognition that families function as a system, with different family subsystems affecting one another (Belsky, 1981). The quality of the relationship between husband and wife influences the parent–child relationship. For example, tension and conflict within the marital relationship has been found to diminish the mother's competence in feeding her infant (Peterson, Anderson, & Cain, 1977, as cited in Belsky, 1981). Furthermore, the relationship between a parent and one child will influence the relationship between two siblings as well as the relationship of the parent with the second child. For example, older siblings are more hostile to their newborn siblings when their relationship with their mother prior to the birth of the sibling was intense and playful (Dunn & Kendrick, 1981). If this interrelatedness between individuals and relationships within the family is acknowledged, there is no difficulty recognizing that the birth or adoption of a child into a family system will have effects that ripple throughout the family system, affecting not only the parents but the siblings, grandparents, other family members, and friends as well. This is true for all families, including those with a child with a disability.

When a child within a family has a disability, the lives of the child's parents and siblings will be changed. Some of these changes will be stressful, other changes will bring benefits. Regardless, siblings of children with disabilities share some common experiences and have concerns that must be recognized. This chapter reviews the research describing how children adjust to having a sibling with a disability, the ways in which their lives may be changed and concerns that can arise, and the ways in which parents and professionals can support children who have siblings with disabilities.

Given the prevalence of the nuclear family in society, children's relationships with their siblings often assume an importance second only to their relationships with their parents. In fact, some argue that sibling relationships have significance that is equal to or greater than relationships with parents. In early childhood, siblings often spend as much time with each other as with their mothers and more time with each other than with their fathers (Lawson & Ingleby, 1974). In addition, the sibling relationship typically lasts longer in the overall number of years spent together than the parent–child relationship, with siblings often playing a mutually supportive role for each other as they become elderly (Bank & Kahn, 1982).

Regardless of the importance of sibling relationships above parental relationships, it is clear that siblings play an important role in each other's development (see Dunn, 1983). Their interactions are characterized by a range of emotions from affection to aggression. Some say that siblings "share a world beyond adult reach" (Crnic & Leconte, 1986, p. 76), a world where interactions can occur between relative equals, where the distribution of control is more equalized and variable than between parent and child, where children can take on the role of boss, teacher, learner, friend, enemy, and partner alternately. Within the context of sibling relationships, children master skills such as self-control, sharing, listening, fair play, and negotiation. Given the importance of sibling relationships, it is important to consider the potential impact on brothers and sisters of having a sibling with a disability.

STUDIES EXAMINING THE ADJUSTMENT OF SIBLINGS

Numerous reviews document the research that has examined how children adjust to having a sibling with a disability (see Atkins, 1989; Lobato, 1990; Lobato, Faust, & Spirito, 1988; Powell & Gallagher, 1992; and Simeonsson & McHale, 1981, for extensive reviews).

Until recently, much of the research concerning sibling adjustment has emphasized the negative impact of growing up with a sibling with a disability. The majority of early research documents the adjustment difficulties among siblings of children with disabilities. For example, in her review of the literature, Lobato (1983) cites studies that found that siblings of children with spina bifida were four times more likely to exhibit school-related problems than siblings of children without disabilities. In addition, siblings of children with Down syndrome were found to be twice as likely to be rated by their mother or teacher as displaying some type of deviant behavior.

Some of the earlier studies as well as more recent studies are revealing the positive outcomes for children who have a sibling with a disability. Researchers are only just discovering that growing up with a "difference in the family" (e.g., a sibling who has a disability, a parent who is gay, or parents in an interracial marriage) can offer the child a unique opportunity to confront society's discriminations and gain perspective on the deeper meaning of life (Featherstone, 1980; Riddle, 1978; Skrtic, Summers, Brotherson, & Turnbull, 1984). Atkins (1989) describes a study of adult siblings, 59% of whom report that having a sibling with a disability had an overall negative impact on the family, 18% of whom reported an overall positive impact, and 9% of whom reported no particular effect. Other studies have found a greater proportion of siblings reporting benefits. For example, Grossman (1972) found that almost half (45%) of the siblings of children with disabilities reported that they had benefited from the experience in some way, such as having a "greater understanding of people and handicaps in particular, more compassion, more sensitivity of prejudice, and more appreciation of their own good health and intelligence than peers" (p. 92). Dunn (1988) described siblings of children with disabilities as more considerate and kind. Simeonsson and McHale (1981) cite a study in which three fourths of siblings of children with Down syndrome were reported to be happy and well-adjusted and makes note of the finding that older sisters of children with disabilities are the most likely to pursue careers in the helping professions. Wilson, Blacher, and Baker (1989) asked children how well they got along with their siblings and found that 29% indicated "excellent," 50% indicated "very well," 21% indicated "pretty well," and none indicated "not very well" or "poorly." These school-age siblings endorsed a generally positive attitude toward life with a sibling with a disability, while also acknowledging the caregiving and responsibilities involved. Dyson (1989) discovered that although siblings of children with disabilities were less active in extracurricular activities, overall they did not differ from other siblings in their levels of self-concept, social competence, or the intensity of behavioral issues. In fact, brothers of children with disabilities were found to exhibit less deviant or aggressive behaviors than brothers of children without disabilities. Of particular note is that there was considerable variability in siblings in *both*

groups—with some siblings being well-adjusted and others demonstrating considerable difficulty.

UNDERSTANDING VARIABILITY IN REACTIONS
TO A CHILD WITH A DISABILITY IN THE FAMILY

Why is there such variability in the reaction of families and siblings
to the presence of a child with a disability in the family? The first
step in understanding this variability requires an understanding of
how all families differ in their reactions to the birth of any child,
even a child without an identified disability. Belsky (1981) describes
how the birth of a child may affect the developing relationship between husband and wife. In some cases, the arrival of a first child
can create such stress that it disrupts the marital relationship. In
other instances, the marital relationship remains intact or even improves.

To understand these different outcomes, Belsky argues that the
mutual influences that exist within the family system must be considered. For example, the characteristics of the newborn may affect
the parent–child relationship and the marital relationship. Studies
have documented that when babies display more demanding behavior, parents experience more crisis in their relationship (Russell,
1974, as cited in Belsky, 1981). However, the effect of the child's
characteristics seem to interact with the initial quality of the relationship between husband and wife. Couples with a strong positive
relationship before the birth of a child are better able to cope with
stressful situations that may arise, whereas couples with a tenuous
relationship may break apart under even minor stresses.

Gath (1978, as cited in Belsky, 1981) examined family functioning in families of children with Down syndrome and those of children without disabilities. Equal numbers of marriages in the two
groups were considered to be "good," although more marriages were
disrupted among the families of the children with Down syndrome.
These results suggest that couples who had relationship problems
before the birth of a child with a disability were more vulnerable to
marital crisis, while couples with strong relationships before the
child's birth were able to sustain the quality of their relationship.

Given the interrelatedness within the family system, it is not
surprising that children's adjustment to having a sibling with a
disability is related to their parents' attitude and adjustment. Children observe their parents' emotional reactions and often assume
and voice similar attitudes. In addition, the extent and openness of

parental communication with the siblings is an important factor that contributes to positive adjustment (see Simeonsson & McHale, 1981).

Differences in family reaction also seem to vary as a result of their financial situation or socioeconomic status (SES). For families of limited financial resources, there is major concern about the "burden of care" that the child will impose on the family. Given the financial constraints, more pressure may be placed on siblings to assist either with caregiving or with generating family income. Families of more substantial financial means are often more concerned with the "stigma" of the disability and the child's inability to live up to the family's achievement expectations (Simeonsson & McHale, 1981). Siblings may therefore feel more pressure to overachieve to compensate for their sibling's disability.

Siblings' adjustment may be influenced by other factors, such as birth order, gender, and family size. Research suggests that children born after the child with the disability are more likely to have adjustment problems, given the decreased parental attention and family resources available to them. However, oldest daughters, especially those in low SES families, have consistently been found to have the greatest likelihood of adjustment difficulties (see Lobato, 1983). Older sisters of children with disabilities are also more likely to seek professional help for adjustment difficulties, but as mentioned earlier, they are also most likely to pursue a career in the helping professions (Simeonsson & McHale, 1981). It has been suggested that the adjustment of siblings is better in large families, where the achievement expectations and caregiving responsibility can be spread out across siblings (Skrtic et al., 1984).

One might assume that the greater the severity of the child's disability, the greater the negative impact on the siblings. However, studies have generally not found a clear-cut relationship between sibling adjustment and severity of the disability. Skrtic et al. (1984) suggest that siblings of children with mild disabilities may be more likely to identify with the sibling and perhaps fear that they too may have or acquire a disability. In addition, children with mild disabilities are more likely to be in the same social circles as their siblings, thereby increasing instances of embarrassment about the child's behavior or appearance and the need to protect the child from teasing and ridiculing by the sibling's peers. Furthermore, children whose disabilities are less visible may show less reason for their atypical behaviors. It is clear that the type and severity of the child's disability can affect the family system but it is not a simple linear relationship.

COMMON ISSUES SHARED
BY SIBLINGS OF CHILDREN WITH DISABILITIES

Alteration of Family Patterns and Reallocation of Resources

Whenever a child is born or adopted into a family, the family patterns are altered and there is increased competition for family resources and parental attention. Parents must spend time caring for the new child, thereby reallocating time and energy that was previously available to the other children in the family. This has long been thought to be a source of early sibling rivalry (Dunn, 1983). The addition of a new child, however, also offers an additional resource— a potential new playmate, confidant, and friend to the other siblings. When a child is discovered to have a disability, the time and effort that parents need to care for the child and to adjust emotionally may well be more extensive than usual and may exacerbate the siblings' feelings of invisibility and resentment, as illustrated in this statement: "Because Douglas's presence dominated everything, there was not real time for myself" (Zatlow, 1982, p. 2). As Shulman (1988) suggests, "preoccupation with the handicapped child may prevent the parent from maintaining a normal relationship with the nonhandicapped child" (p. 126). Given the natural tendency for parents to channel extreme amounts of attention and concern to the child with a disability, it is not surprising that children would feel resentful of a sibling with a disability.

As the family adjusts over time, there may be an ongoing need to alter the family patterns, schedule, or vacation times to accommodate the child with a disability. Families, particularly those with limited financial resources, may struggle to pay the additional bills for medical care, adaptive equipment, and therapy for their children with disabilities. It is not uncommon for mothers to give up their paid employment to care for the child or to have to pay increased rates for specialized child care. These financial burdens can place restrictions on the play materials and opportunities open to other children in the family (e.g., bicycles, books, summer camp, ballet lessons).

Increased Caregiving and Household Responsibilities

When a new child enters the family and places increased demands on the family resources, the parents often delegate new responsibilities to the older children to care for themselves more independently and to help with caregiving or household chores. It is not uncommon for older siblings in large families to take on major caregiving responsibility for younger siblings. When a child has a disability, this typical pattern may be exacerbated. Siblings, especially older sisters, may be expected to take on significant caregiving responsibilities for the child with a disability (Lobato, 1983). Siblings may also be expected to take on more responsibility for chores and to curtail some of their own naturally childish behavior.

> The high standards my mother set for my behavior, though, had not only to do with my setting an example; her reasons were also practical. Mindy's impetuous behavior left her with little patience, energy, or time to put up with shenanigans from me. (Hayden, 1974, p. 27)

These demands may contribute to feelings of resentment over the unequal treatment of siblings and the inability to socialize with peers, given their increased household responsibilities. Simultaneously, the opportunity to help out may give the siblings a sense of usefulness.

As siblings enter adulthood and as parents age, there may be an increased likelihood that siblings will take on financial support or guardianship of their brothers and sisters with disabilities. Questions about the extent of responsibility for their siblings may arise as children become adolescents and young adults. These questions may be difficult ones for families to discuss.

Ways of Playing Together

In studies where researchers have actually watched how children interact with their siblings with disabilities, it is clear that the way the siblings play together differs to some extent from the interaction between siblings without disabilities. Crnic and Leconte (1986) cite a study by Miller (1974), who found that children displayed more positive and less negative interactions with their siblings with disabilities than with their siblings without disabilities. They engaged in more instrumental/teaching types of behavior and were more helpful. There was less arguing, teasing, and horseplay. Stoneman and Brody (1984) note that while siblings of children with disabilities assume teacher and manager roles more frequently, siblings without disabilities interact as playmates more often. Similarly, Lobato, Miller, Barbour, Hall and Pezzullo (1991) report that interaction of children with their siblings with disabilities reveals more prosocial behavior, more caregiving, and less agonistic behavior.

Thus, siblings of children with disabilities assume a more complementary, parent-like role and engage less in the reciprocal role typical of siblings. This more affectively positive and adult-like treatment may arise as a result of parents' intolerance of even the normal negative behaviors that occur between siblings. It may also be a natural reaction to the differences in developmental status and ability between siblings. Among siblings without disabilities there is also a greater degree of complementary behavior and less reciprocal behavior in siblings who are more widely spaced in age and developmental ability (Dunn, 1983).

Questions and Misconceptions:
Sharing Information and Feelings

The birth of a child with a disability comes as a complete surprise to most families. Their general knowledge and understanding of disabilities may very well be extremely limited. Unless a family has had a personal experience with an individual with a disability, it is likely that they will have had little exposure to information about disabilities or people with disabilities. Hopefully, this situation will change as children with disabilities are raised at home, educated in regular schools, and live in community settings. However, the current lack of information about disabilities means that parents must gather a great deal of information themselves before they become comfortable explaining to their children why they are so concerned about their siblings. This discomfort can disrupt the parents' ability to communicate openly with their children. Powell and Gallagher (1992) report that in a study of siblings of children with cystic fibrosis, only 47% indicated that their parents had discussed the disability with them.

With little direct information, siblings do their best to understand the situation and in doing so may come up with questions or misconceptions about the situation. They may feel responsible for causing the disability. Children have a remarkable tendency to blame themselves for negative or unpleasant things that they do not understand. They may feel guilty for not having a disability themselves. They may overidentify with the child with a disability and wonder if they also have a disability or whether their sibling's disability is contagious. Some siblings may even feign the symptoms of the child with a disability in order to gain attention (Milstead, 1988).

Coping—Acting Out and Overachieving

If sustained stress pervades the family and the child with a disability usurps a disproportionate amount of parental energy, siblings may become behaviorally difficult themselves in order to express their needs and gain parental attention. Alternatively, they may cope by doing everything they can to make life easier for parents and "assume responsibility for inferred psychological needs of parents" (Simeonsson & McHale, 1981, p. 157). They may take on caregiving responsibilities, bury their negative feelings about the sibling, and try to make up for the sibling's disability by overachieving. Segal (1988) suggests that children who display the latter pattern may appear to be coping beautifully, but may in fact be equally, if not more, in need of support.

Surpassing the Child with a Disability in Skill Level

Typically, older siblings have and maintain a headstart in ability over younger siblings, especially in cognitive ability. Although it is not uncommon for siblings to differ from each other in temperament and specific abilities (i.e., a younger sibling excelling relative to an older sibling in some domain such as sports, music, or mathematics), it is less common for siblings to completely surpass older siblings in ability. For some younger siblings, this progression may be uncomfortable and cause them to feel guilty for developing skills that their older siblings with disabilities have not yet mastered.

Dealing with Teasing and Ridiculing by Peers

Children tease and ridicule children who are different, whether the difference is being of a different race, being overweight, being short, or having a disability. The word *retard* is thrown out as one of childhood's most degrading insults. If a child's brother or sister actually has mental retardation or another disability, he or she must deal with these insults being directed at himself or herself or their sibling. As the following quotation exemplifies, siblings often react to these incidents with a mix of embarrassment and protectiveness:

> One day in particular, they all started laughing and teasing and calling him retarded. I remember how upset that made me. I tried to defend him, but there was something in me that prevented me from doing so. I was afraid that they wouldn't like me either. This made me very confused and angry. (Atkins, 1989, p. 271)

METHODS AND RESOURCES FOR SUPPORTING SIBLINGS

Involving Siblings in a Family-Centered Program

As program staff begin to examine how family-focused they are, they must examine the methods by which they address the needs of siblings. Do they ask parents how the child's brothers or sisters are doing? Do they discuss siblings' needs and help parents identify means to meet sibling needs? Do they create specific programs or activities to meet sibling needs? Siblings serve as lifelong supports for children with disabilities. By recognizing siblings' needs, assisting the family in coping with sibling issues, and promoting positive sibling interactions, professionals are developing a strong foundation of support for children with disabilities. Below are some of the specific approaches that can be helpful in supporting siblings.

Information and Open Communication

Professionals can assist families in recognizing the needs of siblings and encouraging open communication. All too often, professionals reinforce the unitary focus on the child with a disability. As is so clearly stated by Smith (1988) in the following quote, the neglect of siblings without disabilities is generally quite unintentional.

> Marianne was three years old when her sister Jane was born. The next two years in Marianne's life are a blur in my memory. Yet, I can recall vividly what happened to Jane during that time. You see, Jane was born with a disability. We did not confirm her disability until she was 14 months old. Those first 14 months were filled with apprehension, concern and crying, and the fussing and fretting of a demanding little baby. The next 12 to 14 months, the months after the diagnosis, were filled with more concerns, confusion, distress, dismay, and heartbreak . . . I wonder where Marianne was during those two and a half years. What was she thinking during that time and what was happening to her? (p. 9)

Professionals can make information and resources about siblings of children with disabilities available to families. A particularly good, easy-to-read introduction to sibling issues is presented in an issue of *Special Parent* Special Child* by Murphy and Corte (1989). This article describes the common sibling reactions and suggests ways of addressing sibling needs, including (in a nutshell) being honest, finding time, reading children's books about disabilities, planning family meetings, helping the child deal with friends, and joining a sibling network. For families interested in additional reading, Powell and Gallagher's (1992) book *Brothers & Sisters—A Special Part of Exceptional Families* (2nd edition) is a good, comprehensive starting point, a must-read for professionals who work with children with disabilities and their families.

Children's books about kids with disabilities can be particularly helpful to families as they try to discuss disability and sibling feelings. When selecting books, it is important to keep in mind the child's age and ability to understand. In addition, some books are designed to share information or address specific issues about disabilities or sibling reactions. Others simply show children with disabilities as characters in a story, without focusing on disability issues. The latter can provide a very positive introduction to the abilities and normality of individuals with disabilities and can provide a very open-ended context for eliciting children's questions. The more didactic books are useful for addressing the child's needs for information about the sibling's particular disability or to discuss certain feelings. The Sibling Information Network (1991) has produced a useful annotated bibliography, *Children's Literature for Sisters and Brothers of Children with Special Needs,* that not only describes each book but also indicates the age/developmental level to which the book is geared. Professionals and families are encouraged to share this bibliography with their local libraries. The Sibling Information Network has also produced an annotated bibliography of audiovisual materials, publishes a newsletter for siblings, and is a good source of ongoing information about sibling issues, needs, and programs. In addition, local or regional parent support groups may have information about programs or resources for siblings.

TRAINING OR INVOLVING SIBLINGS AS TEACHERS, TRAINERS, AND PLAYMATES

Parents and siblings may benefit from information and instruction on ways to interact successfully with the child with a disability. Early intervention and preschool professionals often help parents learn to read their children's cues and follow their children's leads in an effort to promote responsive parent–child interaction (Mahoney, Robinson, & Powell, 1992). In addition, parents may also be taught to use specific behavioral approaches or disciplinary methods to cope with inappropriate behavior. Being a tutor or behavioral therapist to one's sibling with a disability can help brothers and sisters develop skills for interacting more effectively with their siblings and for coping with the siblings' inappropriate behavior (Simeonsson, & McHale 1981).

One of the earliest training methods involved siblings as behavior therapists (see Lobato, 1983; Powell & Gallagher, 1992). For example, Weinrott (1974) trained siblings as behavior therapists during a 6-week summer camp program. Following training, parents reported that the children engaged in less custodial care and more instruction with their siblings with disabilities. Schreibman, O'Neill, and Koegel (1983) trained siblings of children with autism to use general behavior modification procedures such as prompting, shaping, consequences, and discrete trials. They found that siblings could learn to use a behavioral approach with a high degree of proficiency, that their use of this approach generalized to less structured types of settings than the training setting, and that this approach resulted in improvement in the responses of their siblings with autism. The training also resulted in the children making fewer negative statements such as,

"He never does anything fun with me, because he doesn't know how" (p. 136), and more positive statements about their siblings with disabilities such as, "We get along better when I make him pay attention" (p. 136). While most behavioral training has involved older school-age children, Lobato (1983) describes some successful interventions that have involved preschool-age siblings.

Given the limited amount and quality of research on training siblings in behavioral methods, it is important to consider the potential benefits and drawbacks of involving siblings in this way. The formal training of siblings in behavioral intervention may inhibit the more natural, playful forms of interaction that normally occur between siblings. However, if introduced appropriately, the use of behavioral methods could serve to help children manage the inappropriate behavior of their siblings with disabilities more effectively and elicit positive behaviors, thereby improving the quality and likelihood of sibling play.

Given the desire to involve siblings and encourage sibling play, it is important to include the siblings of children with disabilities in early intervention and preschool programs. When the program is home-based, the home visitor should include the siblings in his or her intervention efforts. All too often, when the home visitor arrives, the siblings are relegated to another room to play by themselves and are scolded if they "interfere" with the "therapy." Just as there is a movement to integrate therapies into the context of classroom activities rather than using "pull out" methods (Hampton University Mainstreaming Outreach Services, n.d.), home-based programs must integrate therapies into the ongoing routine of the family. This can include working with siblings, watching them interact and play together, and modeling behaviors that can help children understand the behavioral cues and elicit appropriate responses from their siblings with disabilities. When siblings of children with disabilities are involved in in-home therapy sessions, they seem to readily pick up (often without direct instruction) ways of interacting successfully with their siblings.

There is an increasing emphasis in the early childhood literature on promoting social interaction among peers. The social skills of children with disabilities not only lag well behind their age peers but are also more delayed than their cognitive level would warrant (Guralnick, 1990). Strain and Odom (1986) have developed programs for teachers and peers to facilitate successful social behavior in peers. For example, children are taught ways of prompting social interaction from a child with a disability (i.e., use the child's name, touch the child to get attention, try something else if the child does not respond). Although there is little information on using these approaches with siblings, it would not appear difficult to adapt them. Powell and Gallagher (1992) do report that a social skills training package has been developed by Powell for use in promoting interaction between siblings.

SIBLING SUPPORT GROUPS

A number of individuals have developed and implemented sibling support groups. Most of these groups have been offered to school-age siblings (Chinitz, 1981; Grossman, 1983; McLinden, Miller, & Deprey, 1991; Meyer, Vadasy, & Fewell, 1986; Summers, Bridge, & Summers, 1991). Lobato (1985, 1990) has also developed and evaluated a program specifically for young siblings.

The sibling support groups developed to date are fairly similar in form and content. Generally, siblings within a 5-year age span (3–8 or 7–12) are brought together for weekly meetings lasting $1\frac{1}{2}$ hours each. Most last for 6 weeks, although Chinitz's group runs for 8 weeks and Grossman's group runs for 10 weeks. In addition to a number of playful activities to help the children get to know each other, the programs generally cover the following issues:

- Similarities and differences among all people
- Sharing information about each other's families
- Sharing information about their siblings' disabilities and learning about different disabilities
- Recognizing and identifying feelings in general and their positive and negative feelings regarding their siblings with disabilities
- Problem-solving reactions to sibling behaviors or peer reactions

Grossman's group has an additional component where the children observe their siblings' intervention or education program. Lobato's group offers hands-on contact and information about adaptive equipment.

Sibling support groups provide a valued learning and emotional support opportunity for many siblings. Wilson et al. (1989) found that 55% of siblings (mean age 11 years) of children with disabilities expressed interest, and an additional 32% expressed tentative interest, in participating in a sibling group. They expressed interest in learning about different disabilities, in learning how to teach their siblings, and in the opportunity to share experiences with other siblings.

Very few people have systematically evaluated the benefits of participating in sibling support groups. Lobato (1985) found that following her sibling workshop program, the young children were able to describe disabilities more accurately and used more positive verbalizations when describing both their families and themselves. Summers et al. (1991) report that children became less controlling with their siblings with disabilities. McLinden et al. (1991) found that compared to a group of siblings who did not participate in a support group, siblings who did participate reported higher levels of social support. In addition, their mothers reported decreased negative interactions and increased positive interactions between siblings. However, they did not find any differences in behavior problems, self-concept, or attitudes. Given the limited amount of information on effectiveness, there is a need for individuals who conduct sibling support groups to recruit siblings who express an interest in attending the group and to carefully monitor the children's reactions to the program.

FAMILY THERAPY OR INDIVIDUAL COUNSELING

Families sometimes experience so much stress or siblings have so much difficulty adjusting that they should be encouraged to seek out family or individual therapy. In addition, interested families should be encouraged to use therapy and counseling to help promote family coping rather than wait until extremely problematic situations arise. Shulman (1988), recognizing the tendency for families to become overly involved with their children with disabilities, suggests that "therapeutic intervention should emphasize the balance of attachment and separateness" (p. 132). Gaining a degree of separateness can help the family recognize the needs of siblings without disabilities. Powell and Gallagher (1992) also encourage siblings to seek out counseling in order to gain a deeper understanding of their feelings, to develop skills and attitudes that assist them in handling problems, to assist siblings in identifying and pursuing their own life goals, and to strengthen their relationships with their siblings with disabilities.

SUPPORTING SIBLINGS OF CHILDREN
WITH DISABILITIES: A DEVELOPMENTAL PERSPECTIVE

Of all children receiving special education, 80% have siblings (Summers et al., 1991). Yet until recently, little attention has been given to meeting the needs of siblings of children with disabilities. Given the recent emphasis placed on providing family-focused services to children with disabilities and their families (Education of the Handicapped Act Amendments of 1986; Americans with Disabilities Act of 1990), it is a good time for services providers to rethink how they could better meet the needs of siblings.

When considering how to support siblings, one must assume a developmental perspective. Different issues will assume different importance depending on the developmental status of the sibling without a disability, the age of the sibling with a disability, and the family reaction, among other factors discussed earlier. It is also important to recognize that the feelings children have about their siblings with disabilities are not static; they fluctuate over time. Certain issues take on more importance at different points in the life span and, on a more short-term basis, feelings may vary from day to day depending on the specific issues that confront the child. The issues most common at different ages are reviewed below.

Preschoolers

For infants and preschool-age siblings, the amount of time and attention that they receive will have an influence on their adjustment. Older siblings of newborn children with disabilities are particularly at risk of losing their parents' attention, given the parents' emotional state. For the younger sibling of an older child with a disability, the parents are likely to have passed the most emotionally stressful period following the diagnosis of the older child's disability, but may be anxious about whether this younger child will also exhibit a disability. The parents may also need to provide a great deal of care to the older sibling, reducing their physical and emotional availability to the younger sibling without a disability. At this age, it is important to find ways to give the young child attention and emotional care. This can be achieved by seeking out support from extended family, friends, and professionals in order to find time to spend with the younger sibling of a child with a disability. Parents can be encouraged to spend some time alone with siblings without disabilities and to make sure some of the siblings' priority activities get into the family schedule. Encouraging the children to be the "parent's helper" can make them feel involved, but should be used as a way for the parent to interact with and provide attention to the siblings without disabilities, not to burden them with caregiving responsibility. Given the intensity of the time following diagnosis, professionals can play an important role in encouraging parents to attend to the needs of siblings and to keep the family patterns as similar as possible to those they would choose if the child did not have a disability. For example, early interventionists can encourage families to maintain contact with their communities through programs such as religious groups, story hours, or play groups in ways that they would if their children did not have disabilities.

During the early years, it is important to allow children to express the normal range of emotions that siblings typically express, including anger and aggression, and to help them resolve sibling conflict in the same way as would siblings without disabilities. Rather than curtail negative interactions altogether and thereby make children feel guilty for these natural feelings, parents can acknowledge the appropriateness of these feelings: "I know you're mad at Jeremy for knocking over your tower." Parents can also offer the child an alternate way of coping: "Tell Jeremy that you're playing with the blocks now. Tell him to play with something else, like his cars." Efforts can also be made to promote positive play between siblings through modeling or direct teaching of behavioral or interaction skills to siblings without disabilities.

It is also important during the early to later childhood years to assure children that they are not the cause of their sibling's disability. This subject can be addressed using children's books on disability to open the subject and to facilitate discussion about the child's own sibling. Books can also be a useful tool to share information with children about what a disability is. Sibling groups have also been run successfully with preschool-age siblings (see Lobato, 1990).

School-Age Children

As children enter school, their circle of friends widens and their need for peer contact and acceptance becomes more salient. School-age children want to spend more time with friends and may feel the restrictions imposed by caregiving responsibility and financial constraints. Parents must make sure that children who cope by becoming model helpers are also encouraged and allowed to pursue their own interests and activities without guilt for leaving their parents "stranded."

As with younger siblings, school-age siblings should be encouraged to engage in typical sibling play and interactions with the child with a disability—and this may include getting angry with the child. In addition, siblings can also be taught to use the same therapeutic interventions that parents are using; this creates consistency across the family and improves children's ability to interact successfully with their siblings who have disabilities. This can include learning to use sign language with their siblings or learning behavior management techniques. Again, care should be taken not to restrict the child to the role of teacher, but to provide the child with different ways of interacting successfully with his or her siblings.

Siblings of children with disabilities may become self-conscious or embarrassed by their sisters or brothers because their peers may not easily understand or accept their siblings' atypical behavior or appearance. At the same time, they may often be fiercely protective of their siblings and try to shield their siblings from teasing and degrading remarks. They may also be afraid to bring friends home to play. If the children themselves have little information about their siblings' disabilities, they will have a more difficult time dealing with peers' reactions. It is important to offer children opportunities to learn about their siblings' disabilities and to think through how they can respond to different comments and reactions from peers.

Questions about whether they caused the disability or whether they have or will acquire a disability in some way remain salient for school-age children, as shown in the following statement by one parent:

> One day Tony had a fever and we decided to take him to the doctor. He put up such a fuss you wouldn't believe it. Finally, he asked us in this really scared voice, 'Is the doctor going to say I catched cerebral palsy?' (Segal, 1988, p. 24)

With school-age children, parents can more easily provide information about the disability and should provide opportunities for their children to bring up questions. Again, books about children with disabilities can help create opportunities for discussion. As always, it is important to keep the information at a simple level that children can understand. Asking questions can help adults clarify how the child has understood what he or she has been told. Keeping family communication open through family meetings can also be helpful for all families, but can be an especially effective way to provide siblings of children with disabilities with a medium through which their questions and concerns can be heard (Murphy & Corte, 1989). In addition, groups for school-age siblings have been developed and many, though not all, siblings are interested in attending such groups (Wilson et al., 1989).

Late Adolescence and Adulthood

As siblings of persons with disabilities begin to contemplate having families of their own, the question of whether they are at risk of having a child with a disability often arises. They also wonder what role they will be expected to play as their parents become less able to care for the sibling with a disability. Parents can anticipate these questions and approach them directly. Genetic counseling can be sought if uncertainty exists regarding the possible inheritability of a disability. Finally, parents can involve the siblings in making plans for future guardianship and financial care of the sibling with a disability upon their deaths. *Disability and the Family: A Guide to Decisions for Adulthood,* by Turnbull, Turnbull, Bronicki, Summers, and Roeder-Gordon (1989), is a useful resource for families of adults with disabilities.

SUMMARY

Siblings of children with disabilities are integral parts of their families. As family-focused support and intervention begin to be offered to families, the various needs of siblings must be recognized and met. In this chapter, the common issues and reactions that emerge for siblings of children with disabilities have been reviewed. The various resources that can be useful both to professionals and parent and the various types of programs that can be offered to siblings have also been described. Professionals must recognize that each child has a different perspective on what it means to have a sibling with a disability. As always, professionals must listen to the needs and beliefs of each individual and tailor their support to meet these unique needs.

REFERENCES

Americans with Disabilities Act of 1990 (ADA), PL 101-336. (July 26, 1990). Title 42, U.S.C. 12101 et seq: *U.S. Statutes at Large, 104,* 327–378.
Atkins, S.P. (1989). Siblings of handicapped children. *Child and Adolescent Social Work, 6*(4), 271–282.
Bank, S., & Kahn, M.D. (1982). *The sibling bond.* New York: Basic Books.
Belsky, J. (1981). Early human experience: A family perspective. *Development Psychology, 17*(1), 3–23.
Chinitz, S.P. (1981). A sibling group for brothers and sisters of handicapped children. *Children Today, November-December,* 21–24.
Crnic, K.A., & Leconte, J.M. (1986). Understanding sibling needs and influences. In R.R. Fewell & P.F. Vadasy (Eds.), *Families of handicapped children: Needs and support across the lifespan* (pp. 75–98). Austin, TX: PRO-ED.
Dunn, J. (1983). Siblings relationships in early childhood. *Child Development, 54,* 787–811.
Dunn, J. (1988). Sibling influences on child development. *Journal of Child Psychology and Psychiatry, 29*(2), 110–127.
Dunn, J., & Kendrick, C. (1981). Interaction between young siblings: Association with the interaction between mother and first-born. *Developmental Psychology, 17,* 110–132.
Dyson, L. (1989). Adjustment of siblings of handicapped children: A comparison. *Journal of Pediatric Psychology, 14*(2), 215–219.

Education of the Handicapped Act Amendments of 1986, PL 99-457. (October 8, 1986). Title 20, U.S.C. 1400 et seq: *U.S. Statutes at Large, 100,* 1145–1177.

Featherstone, H. (1980). *A difference in the family: Life with a disabled child.* New York: Basic Books.

Gath, A. (1978). *Down's syndrome and the family: The early years.* New York: Academic Press.

Grossman, B. (1983). *A manual for conducting a support group for siblings of physically handicapped and developmentally delayed children.* (Available from The Arc–Fresno, The Children's Center, 5755 E. Fountain Way, Fresno, CA 93727.)

Grossman, F.K. (1972). *Brothers and sisters of retarded children.* Syracuse, NY: Syracuse University Press.

Guralnick, M.J. (1990. Peer interactions and the development of handicapped children's social and communicative competence. In H.C. Foot, M.J. Morgan, & R.H. Shute (Eds.), *Children helping children* (pp. 275–305). New York: John Wiley & Sons.

Hampton University Mainstreaming Outreach Services. (n.d.). *Resource services . . . in the classroom? Yes! In the classroom!* Washington, DC: U.S. Department of Education (Grant no. G008530165).

Hayden, V. (1974). The other children. *Exceptional Parent, 4,* 26–29.

Lawson, A., & Ingleby, J.D. (1974). Daily routines of preschool children: Effects of age, birth order, sex, social class, and developmental correlates. *Psychological Medicine, 4,* 300–315.

Lobato, D.J. (1983). Siblings of handicapped children: A review. *Journal of Autism and Developmental Disorders, 13*(4), 347–364.

Lobato, D.J. (1985). Preschool siblings of handicapped children—Impact of peer support and training. *Journal of Autism and Developmental Disorders, 15*(3), 345–350.

Lobato, D.J. (1990). *Brothers, sisters, and special needs: Information and activities for helping young siblings of children with chronic illness and developmental disabilities.* Baltimore: Paul H. Brookes Publishing Co.

Lobato, D., Faust, D., & Spirito, A. (1988). Examining the effects of chronic disease and disability on children's sibling relationships. *Journal of Pediatric Psychology, 13*(3), 389–407.

Lobato, D.J., Miller, C.T., Barbour, L., Hall, L.J., & Pezzullo, J. (1991). Preschool siblings of handicapped children: Interactions with mother, brothers and sisters. *Research in Developmental Disabilities, 12,* 387–399.

Mahoney, G., Robinson, C., & Powell, A. (1992). Focusing on parent–child interaction: The bridge to developmentally appropriate practices. *Topics in Early Childhood Special Education, 12*(1), 105–120.

McLinden, S.E., Miller, L.M., & Deprey, J.M. (1991). Effects of a support group for siblings of children with special needs. *Psychology in the Schools, 28,* 230–237.

Meyer, D.J., Vadasy, P.F., & Fewell, R.R. (1986). *Sibshops: A handbook for siblings of children with special needs.* Seattle: University of Washington Press.

Miller, S.G. (1974). An exploratory study of sibling relationships in families with retarded children. *Dissertation Abstracts International, 35,* 2994–2995.

Milstead, S. (1988). Siblings are people, too! *Academic Therapy, 23*(5), 537–541.

Murphy, L., & Corte, S.D. (1989). Sibling. *Special Parent* Special Child, 5*(1), 1–6. (ERIC Document Reproduction Service No. ED 309 605)

Peterson, F., Anderson, B., & Cain, R. (1977, March). *An approach to understanding linkages between the parent–infant and spouse relationships.* Paper presented at the biennial meeting of the Society for Research in Child Development, New Orleans, LA.

Powell, T.H., & Gallagher, P.A. (1992). *Brothers and sisters; A special part of exceptional families* (2nd ed.). Baltimore: Paul H. Brookes Publishing Co.

Riddle, D.I. (1978). Relating to children: Gays as role models. *Journal of Social Issues, 34,* 38–58.

Russell, C. (1974). Transition to parenthood: Problems and gratifications. *Journal of Marriage and Family, 36,* 294–301.

Schreibman, I., O'Neill, R.E., & Koegel, R.L. (1983). Behavioral training for siblings of autistic children. *Journal of Applied Behavioral Analysis, 16*(2), 129–138.

Segal, M. (1988). *In time and with love: Caring for the special needs baby.* New York: Newmarket Press.

Shulman, S. (1988). The family of the severely handicapped child. *Journal of Family Therapy, 10,* 125–134.

Sibling Information Network. (1986). *Audiovisual materials: Siblings of children with special needs.* (Available from Sibling Information Network, A.J. Pappanikou Center on Special Education and Rehabilitation, 991 Main Street, East Hartford, CT 06108.)

Sibling Information Network. (1991). *Children's literature for sisters and brothers of children with special needs.* (Available from Sibling Information Network, A.J. Pappanikou Center on Special Education and Rehabilitation, 991 Main Street, East Hartford, CT 06108.)

Simeonsson, R.J., & McHale, S.M. (1981). Research on handicapped children: Sibling relationships. *Child: Care, Health and Development, 7,* 153–171.

Skrtic, T.M., Summers, J.A., Brotherson, M.J.M., & Turnbull, A. (1984). Severely handicapped young children and their brothers and sister. In J. Blacher (Ed.), *Severely handicapped young children and their families* (pp. 215–246). New York: Academic Press.

Smith, P.M. (1988). Where is Marianne? *NICHCY New Digest, 11,* 9–10.

Stoneman, Z., & Brody, G.H. (1984). Research with families of severely handicapped children: Theoretical and methodological considerations. In J. Blacher (Ed.), *Severely handicapped young children and their families.* New York: Academic Press.

Strain, P.S., & Odom, S.L. (1986). Peer social interactions: Effective intervention for social skills development in exceptional children. *Exceptional Children, 52*(6), 543–551.

Summers, M., Bridge, J., & Summers, C.R. (1991). Sibling support groups. *Teaching Exceptional Children, 23*(4), 20–25.

Turnbull, H.R., Turnbull, A.P., Bronicki, G.J., Summers, J.A., & Roeder-Gordon, C. (1989). *Disability and the family: A guide to decisions for adulthood.* Baltimore: Paul H. Brookes Publishing Co.

Weinrott, M.R. (1974). A training program in behavior modification for siblings of the retarded. *American Journal of Orthopsychiatry, 44,* 362–375.

Wilson, J., Blacher, J., & Baker, J. (1989). Siblings of children with severe handicaps. *Mental Retardation, 27*(3), 167–173.

Zatlow, G. (1982). A sister's lament. *Sibling Information Network Newsletter, 1*(5), 2.

14

Comprehensive Support to Families of Children with Disabilities and Behavior Problems

Keeping It "Friendly"

Joseph M. Lucyshyn and Richard W. Albin

This chapter describes a consultation approach to providing behavioral support for families of school-age children with severe disabilities and severe behavior problems. This comprehensive approach strives to be "friendly" to the family. Its foundation rests on current best-practice themes in three areas: 1) positive behavioral support to individuals with severe behavior problems, 2) professional support to families of children with disabilities, and 3) behavioral consultation. This chapter briefly reviews the need for behavioral support to families, outlines the basic themes of the approach, and then provides a detailed description of the consultation process and procedures. Examples drawn from clinical experiences are presented to illustrate the approach.

THE NEED FOR COMPREHENSIVE SUPPORT

The current experience of families of children with disabilities suggests that many of these families may benefit from behavioral consultation and support. As a result of legislation that mandates community-based developmental and educational services, increasing numbers of children with disabilities are remaining at home with their families and attending neighborhood schools (Turnbull & Turnbull, 1991a). Advocacy efforts by parents and professionals have contributed to a positive perspective toward family life. Families are regarded as "their child's most powerful, valuable, and durable resource" (Dunlap & Robbins, 1991, p. 188). The home and the local school are viewed as the best contexts for the child's development and the creation of lifelong social support (Goetz, Anderson, & Laten, 1989; Singer & Irvin, 1989).

At the same time, many of these children and their families are not functioning well in the home and community (Hawkins & Singer, 1989; Snell & Beckman-Brindley, 1984). Families of children with disabilities face serious challenges in terms of their caregiving capacities. The presence of severe behavior problems such as aggression, self-injury, and property destruction provides one of the biggest challenges. These behavior problems are a significant source of stress for family members (Quine & Pahl, 1985) and strongly influence out-of-home placement decisions by parents (Bromley & Blacher, 1991). Unless these behavior problems are ameliorated, these children are at risk of separation from their families and face institutional placement. At the same time, their families are at risk of demoralization, social isolation, and marital distress (Singer, Irvine, & Irvin, 1989).

The consultation approach described here is designed to address these issues. Its goals are to improve the child's behavior in the home and community, to enhance the family's capacity to support the child, and to strengthen the family as a whole. In order to achieve these goals, a family support process has been developed with features that are based on best practice themes drawn from the positive behavioral support and family support literatures. Process recommendations from the behavioral consultation literature have also been incorporated. These themes are briefly outlined below.

BEST PRACTICE THEMES

The present approach is based on 10 best practice themes, five derived from the current literature on positive behavioral support and five from the theoretical and applied literature on family support. Brief outlines of the themes that have influenced and shaped the approach are presented in Tables 1 and 2. The reader is referred to other sources for more detailed descriptions of positive behavioral support approaches (e.g., Horner et al., 1990; Horner, O'Neill, &

Flannery, 1993; LaVigna, Willis, & Donnellan, 1989; Meyer & Evans, 1989) and family support approaches (e.g., Bernheimer, Gallimore, & Weisner, 1990; Dunst, Trivette, & Deal, 1988; Patterson, 1980; Turnbull & Turnbull, 1991a).

OVERVIEW OF THE CONSULTATION PROCESS

Seven steps in the process of consulting with family members and school personnel are followed: 1) referral, 2) comprehensive assessment, 3) preliminary support plan and implementation plan design, 4) support team planning meeting and plan finalization, 5) plan implementation support, 6) evaluation, and 7) follow-up. These steps have been adopted from the work of Bergan and Kratochwill (1990) and Sprague, Flannery, and O'Neill (1992) on behavioral consultation to school and group home personnel. An overview of the steps and features of the family support process is presented in Figure 1.

Although this chapter is about consultation support to families, the importance of the child's school in the support effort cannot be ignored. In order to promote behavioral and life-style change, parents and school personnel should collaborate in the development and implementation of a behavioral support plan. The classroom teacher and other school personnel (e.g., the child's language therapist) play leadership roles in teaching the child new behaviors or skills. For many parents, their child's teacher is a source of emotional support as well. This chapter, however, does not detail the school's involvement in the consultation process. The involvement of school personnel is described only at those times in the support process where the family and the school work together. For the most part, this chapter focuses on the family.

REFERRAL

Referrals for behavioral consultation with families may come from the family directly, from school personnel, or from a psychologist or social worker working with a family in private practice. When a referral is received, general information about the child and the nature of the problem is first requested, typically by completing a brief telephone interview with the individual making the referral. Information of interest includes the child's disability, the behaviors of concern, the situations in which the child engages in these behaviors, and the support strategies currently being used. Next, the persons, or stakeholders, who will need to participate in the develop-

Table 1.   Best practice themes in positive behavioral support

Theme	Major features	Sources
1. A focus on life-style change	a. Behavioral support must ensure health and safety, and result in durable improvements in the quality of life of persons with severe behavior problems. b. Outcomes of successful support plans include: 1) reductions in problem behaviors to near-zero levels across home and community settings for a durable period of time, 2) increases in adaptive behavior that meet individual needs and are referenced to the local community, and 3) opportunities for participation in community life and for development of social relationships.	Horner, Dunlap, Koegel, Carr, Sailor, Anderson, Albin, and O'Neill (1990); Meyer and Evans (1989)
2. Attention to child-focused ecological variables	a. Effects of ecological and setting event variables on the occurrence of problem behaviors need to be addressed in both the assessment and design of behavioral support plans. b. These variables may include activity patterns (e.g., prevalence of preferred activities); physical and social setting conditions (e.g., crowded conditions, rapport with others in a setting); predictability of schedules and other occurrences; physical and medical status (e.g., sleep patterns, illness); and social interaction opportunities.	Horner, Albin, and O'Neill (1991)
3. Completion of a comprehensive functional assessment	a. Interviews, direct observations, and experimental manipulations are used to develop hypotheses about	O'Neill, Horner, Albin, Storey, and Sprague (1990)

Table 1. (*continued*)

Theme		Major features	Sources
		the functions of problem behaviors, setting events, antecedent stimuli, and consequences relevant to the maintenance of problem behaviors and the promotion of adaptive behavior.	
	b.	This information provides the foundation for designing interventions that are logically linked to hypotheses about the functions of problem and the promotion of adaptive behavior.	
4. Design of a comprehensive behavioral support plan	a.	The broadened, ecological, and behavioral perspectives have resulted in the design of behavioral support plans with multiple components.	Dunlap, Kern-Dunlap, Clarke, and Robbins (1991); Horner, O'Neill and Flannery (in press)
	b.	There are five categories of potential intervention strategies: 1) ecological or setting event interventions, 2) immediate antecedent event interventions, 3) response and skill training interventions, 4) consequence interventions, and 5) emergency procedures.	
5. Social validation of support plans	a.	Family members, teachers, and other persons who implement behavioral support plans should evaluate the social validity of these plans.	Wolery and Gast, 1990
	b.	They should evaluate the acceptability of: 1) plan goals, 2) intervention procedures, and 3) behavioral and life-style outcomes.	

Table 2.   Best practice themes in family support

Theme	Major features	Sources
1. The importance of understanding the ecology of the family	a. Several ecological theories of the family contribute to the assessment of family needs and the provision of support to the child and family. These theories include family system theory, family life cycle theory, and ecocultural theory. b. Family assessment should highlight the family's perspective and be conducted in a manner that contributes to family empowerment. c. Support plans need to be individualized to the family and fit well into the family's social and material ecology.	Gallimore, Weisner, Kaufman, and Bernheimer (1989), Turnbull and Turnbull (1991a, 1991b)
2. Development of collaborative partnerships	a. Collaborative goal-setting is an essential feature of a family–professional partnership. b. A value-based process for collaboratively deciding goals and interventions involves: 1) families selecting goals that represent their priorities; 2) listing intervention options and negotiating preferences; and 3) ensuring that goals and interventions are consistent with family values, resources, and life-style.	Bailey (1987); Kaiser and Hemmeter (1989)
3. Standards and practices that strengthen the family	a. The aim of family support should be the strengthening of the family system and the empowerment of individual family members. b. Standards for strengthening families include: 1) improving the capacity of	Dunst, Trivette, and Deal (1988); Kaiser and Hemmeter (1989); Turnbull (1988)

Table 2. (*continued*)

Theme		Major features	Sources
		family members to solve problems related to child development in the home, 2) enhancing family use of informal and formal supports, 3) encouraging family members to attribute success to their own effort, and 4) providing families with emotional support as well as instrumental support.	
4. Identification of family strengths and child's positive contributions	a.	Recent research has recognized the strengths of families who raise children with disabilities and the positive contributions these children make to the family.	Summers, Behr, and Turnbull (1989)
	b.	Interventions and support activities should build on family strengths and child's positive contributions to the family.	
5. Identification of sources of stress	a.	In addition to the stress associated with a child's behavior problems, there may be other sources of stress in the family.	Robbins, Dunlap, and Plenis (1991), Singer and Irvin (1989)
	b.	These other stressors (e.g., disruption of sleep patterns, money worries, marital distress) may contribute to difficulties that family members have in implementing support procedures and effectively caring for their child.	
	c.	Family-focused support goals that may reduce these stressors include respite care, stress management training, or marriage counseling.	

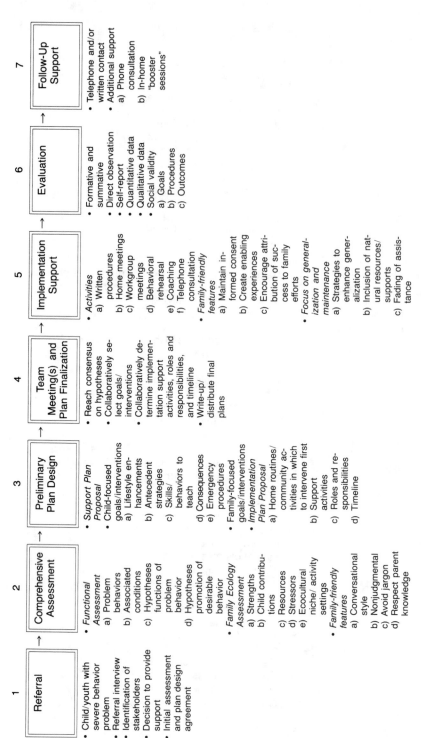

1

Referral

- Child/youth with severe behavior problem
- Referral interview
- Identification of stakeholders
- Decision to provide support
- Initial assessment and plan design agreement

2

Comprehensive Assessment

- *Functional Assessment*
  a) Problem behaviors
  b) Associated conditions
  c) Hypotheses functions of problem behavior
  d) Hypotheses promotion of desirable behavior
- *Family Ecology Assessment*
  a) Strengths
  b) Child contributions
  c) Resources
  d) Stressors
  e) Ecocultural niche/ activity settings
- *Family-friendly features*
  a) Conversational style
  b) Nonjudgmental
  c) Avoid jargon
  d) Respect parent knowledge

3

Preliminary Plan Design

- *Support Plan Proposal*
- Child-focused goals/interventions
  a) Lifestyle enhancements
  b) Antecedent strategies
  c) Skills/ behaviors to teach
  d) Consequences
  e) Emergency procedures
- Family-focused goals/interventions
- *Implementation Plan Proposal*
  a) Home routines/ community activities in which to intervene first
  b) Support activities
  c) Roles and responsibilities
  d) Timeline

4

Team Meeting(s) and Plan Finalization

- Reach consensus on hypotheses
- Collaboratively select goals/ interventions
- Collaboratively determine implementation support activities, roles and responsibilities, and timeline
- Write-up/ distribute final plans

5

Implementation Support

- *Activities*
  a) Written procedures
  b) Home meetings
  c) Workgroup meetings
  d) Behavioral rehearsal
  e) Coaching
  f) Telephone consultation
- *Family-friendly features*
  a) Maintain informed consent
  b) Create enabling experiences
  c) Encourage attribution of success to family efforts
- *Focus on generalization and maintenance*
  a) Strategies to enhance generalization
  b) Inclusion of natural resources/ supports
  c) Fading of assistance

6

Evaluation

- Formative and summative
- Direct observation
- Self-report
- Quantitative data
- Qualitative data
- Social validity
  a) Goals
  b) Procedures
  c) Outcomes

7

Follow-Up Support

- Telephone and/or written contact
- Additional support
  a) Phone consultation
  b) In-home "booster sessions"

Figure 1. Steps in the comprehensive family support process.

ment of a support plan that promotes durable, life-style changes are identified. Potential stakeholders include family members, the child's teacher, classroom teaching assistants, related service professionals, or a counseling psychologist. Because the support process is designed to build collaborative partnerships between family members and school personnel, both are requested to make a formal commitment to participate in a cooperative effort to provide the child with comprehensive positive behavioral support. This is typically done by asking the family and the school to write a letter expressing their willingness to participate in such an effort.

At this point in the referral a decision is made, based on available time and resources, whether to provide consultation services or to refer the family or professional to another behavioral consultant and/or formal resource. If a decision to provide consultation is made, the family and school are contacted. The consultation process is described, and an agreement for assessment and preliminary plan development is negotiated.

By way of illustration, a parent named Beth sought help regarding Luke, her 8-year-old son. Luke was deaf and was diagnosed as having autism. During the day he attended a special education class in a residential school for students who are deaf. He lived at home with Beth and his stepfather, David. Beth referred her son for consultation because of severe tantrum behaviors at home and in the community, and numerous incidences of hitting others and running away. Beth was asked to contact the school and solicit a letter of support for a comprehensive assessment and the preliminary development of a support plan. After receiving the school's support, Beth and the supervisor of the school program were contacted. The assessment and preliminary plan development process was described, the necessary consents were obtained, and a time for the first assessment activity was arranged.

COMPREHENSIVE ASSESSMENT

Two kinds of assessment are completed to gather information about the child, the family, and the broader ecology in which both interact. The first is a functional assessment of the child's behavior problems. During this assessment the assessment protocol and guidelines described by O'Neill, Horner, Albin, Storey, and Sprague (1990) are followed. Assessment activities include a functional analysis interview; observations in home, school, and other relevant settings; and interactions with the child to test hypotheses about the functions of his or her behavior problems. Information from this assessment

contributes to the development of interventions that are individualized for the child (e.g., ways to minimize the effect of child-specific
setting events, strategies for reinforcing desirable behavior, positive
procedures for de-escalating the behavior problems).

   The second assessment activity involves a focused look at family characteristics and ecology. This is accomplished through an in-
depth interview with the family. The first half of the interview is
based on the work of Turnbull and her associates (Turnbull & Turnbull, 1991a; see also Summers, Behr, & Turnbull, 1989). Open-ended
questions are asked about family strengths, positive contributions of
the child to the family, resources and social supports, and sources of
stress in the family. The second half of the interview uses features of
ecocultural theory, developed by Gallimore and his colleagues (Gallimore, Weisner, Kaufman, & Bernheimer, 1989; see also Bernheimer et al., 1990), to understand the family's ecology and culture. Open-
ended and semi-structured questions are asked to understand how
the family has include their child with a disability in daily routines
in the home and community. Information from this assessment contributes to the selection of interventions that are individualized to
the family (e.g., the need for respite care services, child-focused
interventions that capitalize on family strengths, accommodations
that decrease stress in the home).

Guidelines During Assessment

Several guidelines that contribute to a process that is "friendly" to
the family are followed during assessment activities. Interviews are
conducted in an unhurried manner, and a conversational style of
asking questions is used. That is, although many specific questions
are asked, attention is given to questions that parents ask, and time
is taken to listen to family members' interpretations of the problems
that they are experiencing with their child.

   Making judgments about what parents discuss is avoided.
When parents share information that is potentially embarrassing,
efforts are made to be empathetic. If parents, for example, say that
their childen sometimes make them feel angry or discouraged, they
are often told about a situation in which others have experienced
similar feelings.

   Care is taken to diminish the potentially stifling effect of professional knowledge by avoiding the use of special education or psychological jargon. Parents also are encouraged to share their knowledge
about promoting adaptive behavior with their children. Their insights are acknowledged and are recommended for inclusion in their
child's support plan. For example, one parent informed the consul-

tant that her daughter was more cooperative when she offered her daughter choices. In this child's plan, offering choices became a prominent component.

Functional Assessment

At least seven relevant characteristics are learned about the child and his or her behavior problems during the functional assessment: 1) the behavior problems, including their topography, frequency, and intensity; 2) escalating sequences of interaction between the child and the parent or teacher; 3) the environmental features (e.g., persons, places, activities) relevant to the occurrence of behavior problems; 4) the medical/physiological factors associated with behavior problems; 5) educational or skill factors (e.g., communication skill deficits) relevant to behavior problems; 6) potential functions of behavior problems and maintaining reinforcers; and 7) personal reinforcers (e.g., events, activities, objects).

The functional assessment is begun by interviewing the parent(s) and stakeholders from the child's school. Stakeholders who are interviewed may include the classroom teacher, a language specialist, and/or a behavioral consultant from the school district. Parents and school personnel are either interviewed individually or together in a small group. During a group interview, efforts are made to ensure that the parent is equally valued as an informant.

Observations also are conducted of the child in the home, the school, and other community settings where behavior problems are manifested (e.g., a day-care center). A functional analysis observation form is used to directly observe behavior problems, associated setting events and discriminative stimuli, possible functions, and consequences. Other observations may include frequency counts of positive and negative interactions between the child and persons in his or her environment, and a checklist that assesses environmental features of the classroom (e.g., functional curricular activities, sufficient staffing, opportunities to make choices). The consultant also may ask a parent or teacher to use a functional analysis observation form for 1 week in the home or school. The consultant shows the parent or teacher how to use the form, calls a few days later to learn how data collection is progressing, and answers any questions about recording data. Figure 2 presents the functional analysis interview summary for Luke.

After completing the interview and collecting observation data, the consultant summarizes the behaviors of concern as well as the personal and environmental features that are associated with problem behavior and adaptive behavior. This information is usually

Person: Luke
Date(s) of interview(s) 11-2-90
Person(s) interviewed Beth (parent), Mary (teacher), Rachel (autism specialist),
Theresa (school program supervisor)

Behavior Description
1. Behaviors of concern
    Hits people, kicks people, pounds on something, throws something,
    knocks things over, screams, runs away, falls to the ground

2. Behaviors occurring together as a group
    a. Pulls, grabs, points, signs repeatedly (appears agitated)
    b. Hits, kicks, screams, pounds (runs and/or falls to ground)
    c. Sometimes knocks things over, throws things
    d. Sometimes sobs

Potentially Relevant Personal and Environmental Features
1. Environmental features
    a. Transitions: ending a high interest activity; getting on school bus
        in A.M.; getting off school bus in A.M. or city bus in P.M.; leaving a
        preferred person; leaving day-care
    b. Unexpected changes in a routine or event
    c. Expressions of choice or preference that are not honored; these
        include reasonable and unreasonable requests
    d. Requests to do nonpreferred tasks or activities
    e. Waiting for a preferred activity or person

2. Medical/physiological and educational or skill factors
    a. Receptive and expressive communication skills at a concrete level;
        doesn't understand concepts such as time; doesn't use language to
        express negative feelings; doesn't understand social rules
    b. Self-management skills: Poorly developed

Potential Functions/Maintaining Reinforcers
1. What were the potential functions that the behaviors were described as
    serving? What were the maintaining reinforcers or consequences that were
    described?
1) *Tantrums.* Functions: a) get object, activity, or person, b) avoid or
    delay the ending of preferred activity or the start of a nonpreferred
    activity. Maintaining contingencies: exert control over his
    environment; people's reactions.
2) *Hits others.* Functions: a) same as above; b) testing behavior that
    attracts negative attention. Maintaining contingencies: Vigorous
    hand movement, facial expressions, and physical contact that
    accompanies negative attention.
3) *Runs away.* Functions: a) same as 2b. above. Maintaining
    contingencies: Exerts control over his environment; people's
    reactions.

Figure 2.   Functional analysis interview summary form.

sufficient for generating hypotheses about the functions of problem behavior and hypotheses about the promotion of adaptive behavior. If it is not, the consultant then conducts one or more sessions of hypothesis testing with the child in the home or school in order to confirm these hypotheses.

A description of the functional assessment for Luke will serve to illustrate this process. Interviews with Luke's parents and teachers, and observations of Luke at his school, home, and day-care center, revealed that he engaged in intense tantrum behavior; he hit and kicked others, pounded his open palm or closed fist on flat surfaces, knocked things over, screamed, and/or ran away. In addition, Luke engaged in less intense hitting and running away behavior at other times and in other places. Information from the functional analysis interview and observations suggested the following hypotheses about the functions of Luke's behavior problems: 1) Luke engaged in tantrums and/or hit others to avoid a transition from a preferred activity, place, or person; 2) Luke engaged in tantrums and/or hit others to obtain a desired object, activity, or person; and 3) Luke hit others and/or ran away to obtain negative attention.

Additional personal and environmental features associated with the occurrence of problem behavior or adaptive behavior contributed to the development of hypotheses about the promotion of adaptive behavior. First, Luke had serious deficits in receptive and expressive language skills, which made it difficult for him to make predictions about his day and negotiate preferences. Second, Luke received few opportunities at home to make choices about things to get, activities to do, and people to see. Third, Luke used a daily picture schedule at school and did not engage in tantrum behavior during transitions pictured on his schedule. Finally, when Luke ran away from an instructor at school, and the instructor nonchalantly turned his or her back and attended to the other children, Luke consistently returned to the instructor. Hypotheses about the promotion of adaptive behavior that emerged from these features included: 1) Luke may calmly transition from a preferred activity, place, or person if he uses a picture schedule to help him predict the steps in the transition; 2) Luke may behave more cooperatively if he is offered a wider variety of meaningful choices throughout his day; 3) Luke may accept natural limitations on choice if he is taught receptive and expressive sign language about transitions, unexpected changes, and making choices (e.g., What's next? Sorry, no one's home. Sorry, no money.); and 4) Luke may return to the adult from whom he runs away if the adult remains calm and actively ignores Luke (e.g., nonchalantly walks to the car without looking back). Together, hypotheses about behavior problems and the promotion of adaptive behavior provided a direct link to the subsequent design of a preliminary positive behavioral support plan.

Before concluding functional assessment activities, the consultant talks with the family and school personnel about potential child-focused goals. He or she first asks family members and teachers to describe child-focused goals that are important to them. The consultant then suggests additional goals that are based on the hypotheses generated during the functional assessment. He or she explains the reasoning behind the suggestions and solicits parent and teacher reactions. For example, after completing observations, the consultant met with Luke's parents at their home and discussed potential goals for Luke. In addition to eliminating behavior problems, Beth felt strongly about improving Luke's sign language skills. Both parents wanted Luke to develop friendships with typical peers in his neighborhood. The consultant expressed his agreement with these goals and offered two additional suggestions. He recommended that Luke learn to use picture schedules to make predictions and self-manage his activities. He also suggested that family members and school personnel offer Luke a variety of meaningful choices throughout his day. After the consultant offered his rationale for these suggestions, Beth and David expressed their agreement with these goals.

Recommendations During Crisis Situations

Parents or school personnel sometimes express an interest in implementing interventions before a formal support plan is negotiated during the team meeting. The severity of the child's or youth's behavior problems may require action before the assessment and plan design process is completed. In these cases, teachers or family members may be encouraged to make an "emergency" change in the pattern of activities and interactions that the child experiences. These changes serve to minimize the presence of tasks, activities, interactions, or persons highly associated with behavior problems until a comprehensive support plan can be put into place. For example, it may be recommended that the child receive a break from vocational activities at school that are consistently associated with problem behaviors. It may be suggested that the parents refrain from using the word "no" at home if it is highly associated with self-injurious behavior.

Teachers or family members may also be encouraged to immediately use interventions discussed during the functional assessment when there is sufficient information, based on clinical judgment, to support the efficacy of the intervention. In Luke's case, severe tantrums at school were reported to occur only during weekly outings in the community. After the first observation of Luke in the classroom, his teacher, Mary, was encouraged to: 1) make a picture schedule of the community outing, 2) include a picture of a reinforcer at the end of the sequence, and 3) deliver the reinforcer contingent upon calm completion of the outing. The following week Mary reported that she developed and implemented these interventions and Luke did not have tantrums. To be sure, "emergency interventions" rarely are sufficient for promoting durable, life-style enhancement for the child and his or her family. Other functional assessment information and information about the family's ecology usually suggest the need for a more comprehensive set of interventions.

Assessment of Family Characteristics and Ecology

Two additional meetings with the parent(s) following the functional assessment interview are scheduled in order to learn about important characteristics of the family and features of the family's ecology. The consultant conducts the assessment in the family's home with one or both parents. With the family's permission, he or she may invite a stakeholder from the school (e.g., the family consultant) to participate.

During the first half of this interview, family members are asked about their strengths, the positive contributions that their son or daughter makes to their family, the resources and social supports that the family uses, and the sources of stress that exist. This dialogue appears to contribute to the development of rapport and trust with the family. As these topics are discussed with the family, respect for the family's experience and perspective is communicated. In addition, each topic may contribute to the design of a support plan that is individualized to the family.

Understanding family strengths helps to develop support strategies that build on these strengths. A discussion of family strengths may also contribute to a parent's sense of self-efficacy. Luke's mother Beth, for example, was fluent in American Sign Language (ASL). During the support effort, Beth played a central role in the development of a language program for Luke that taught him about the language of change and choice. Luke's stepfather David was good at helping Luke participate in leisure activities with other children. During the support effort, David played a leadership role in fostering a friendship between Luke and an 11-year-old boy who lived nearby.

Discussing a child's positive contributions may serve to revital-
ize a family's appreciation for their child despite his or her behavior
problems. During the consultant's discussion with Beth, for example, Beth commented that she never realized how many positive
contributions her son had made to her knowledge, experience, or
career. Thanks to her son and his need for ASL, she would soon be
graduating from a professional sign language interpreter program
at a local college.

Understanding the resources and social supports available to
the family allows them to be included in the support plan that is
designed. Beth and David, for example, shared a circle of friends
who provided emotional support and occasional respite care. In addition, the family had recently begun to receive funds from the state
to hire respite care providers. Through this discussion it was
learned that respite care services were available. A subsequent conversation about sources of stress suggested the need to enhance this
resource.

The first half of the interview is concluded with a discussion
about sources of stress. This information allows the family's need for
other forms of family support to be considered, including respite
care, financial assistance, or marital counseling. Knowledge of specific stressors also contributes to the selection of child- or family-
focused interventions that may diminish stress. Beth and David, for
example, reported that they were usually exhausted by the end of
the week after caring for Luke and seeing to their other responsibilities. They also told the consultant that, although they had respite care funds, finding and training skilled respite care providers
was difficult. Thus, the development of a network of skilled respite
care providers became an important component of the support plan
for Luke and his family.

During the second half of the interview, parents are asked to
describe the activity settings of daily routines in which their child
participates in the home and community. These routines include, for
example, getting ready for school in the morning, having supper,
and going shopping with a parent. The purpose of asking parents to
describe child activity settings is to understand how the family has
included their child in the ecology and culture of the family. This
understanding helps in developing interventions that fit well into
the ecological and cultural features of each routine. It also facilitates
a dialogue with family members about features of routines that are
not working well and that they may wish to change or enhance.

For each routine it is important to learn about: 1) the persons
present; 2) the tasks that must be performed; 3) the goals, values, or
beliefs that are expressed; 4) the themes or scripts that are present

(e.g., conversations about the day, prompts to complete tasks); 5) the child's positive contributions; and 6) the sources of stress. The interview is usually begun by asking parents to describe each routine in general terms. Often this initial open-ended question is sufficient for gaining much of the information listed above. When additional information is needed, more specific questions are asked (e.g., "What are some goals or values that are part of the morning routine?").

A discussion of child routines provides a window into the larger ecology of the family. Routines give access to information about: 1) child care tasks, 2) the role of the father and mother in child care, 3) the child's peer and play groups, 4) the safety and convenience of the home and neighborhood, and 5) the accessibility of educational and other services. Also, some understanding of the family's goals, values, and beliefs related to child care, disability, and family life are gained. Finally, the family's proactive efforts to accommodate the needs of their child within specific routines are brought to light. The success of these accommodations can then be assessed in terms of their: 1) congruence with the child's characteristics; 2) consistency with the family's goals, values, and beliefs; and 3) sustainability over time.

By way of illustration, the consultant discussed Luke's morning routine with Beth and David. He learned that David woke Luke up at 6:30 A.M., prompted him to get dressed, and then began to prepare breakfast for the family. Beth woke up 15 minutes later and the family ate breakfast together in the kitchen. At about 6:50 A.M., David left for work. At that time Beth continued with the child care task of getting her son ready for the school bus. This included helping him get his shoes and coat on, getting his backpack, and sitting on the living room couch together while waiting for the bus. Goals and values expressed during the routine included: 1) egalitarian sharing of child care and domestic tasks; 2) telling Luke, through sign language, that he was loved and that the family would gather together again in the late afternoon; 3) ensuring Luke's safety as he left the house to board the school bus; and 4) effecting a smooth transition for her son to school.

A belief of David's that influenced his interactions with his stepson was that children should not be praised for doing things that they "should do anyway." Common scripts (i.e., patterns of interaction) included: 1) parent directions to get ready, 2) David signing "no" to Luke's requests, 3) Beth talking to Luke about his day, and 4) Beth requesting and demanding that Luke get on the bus. Luke's positive contributions to the routine included his ability to dress himself, his ASL skills, and occasionally helping to prepare breakfast. Sources of stress included Luke demanding more or different breakfast items, running away when the bus arrived, and having a tantrum when his mother chased him. A description of this routine revealed accommodations that were successful, such as the sharing of child care tasks and using sign language to give Luke directions to get ready. Less successful accommodations also were revealed, such as Beth running after Luke when he ran out of the house and away from the school bus. This well-intentioned action, done out of Beth's concern for Luke's safety, inadvertently reinforced Luke's running away and tantrum behavior.

Following a discussion of child activity settings, the consultant and the parent(s) collaboratively choose one or two routines in which to first introduce interventions. They choose activity settings that reflect family priorities and that are most likely to lead to success. Beth, David, and the consultant agreed first to introduce a multi-component intervention for Luke during the morning routine. They made this decision because Beth expressed a strong preference for initiating the intervention during this routine, and because Beth could ensure Luke's success in walking to the bus by providing physical assistance for a brief period of time across a short distance.

After selecting one or two activity settings in which to first intervene, parents are asked to describe what these routines would look like if they were sucessful. This discussion is guided by the components of routines described above (e.g., persons present, tasks that must be performed), and the characteristics of successful routines (e.g., congruent with child characteristics, consistent with family values and goals). Beth and David described the features of a successful morning routine in the following way: Beth and David would continue to share child care tasks. Luke would complete each step in the morning routine with little to no assistance. During the routine, he would receive choices of clothes to wear and food to eat. While waiting for the bus, Beth and Luke would have a friendly conversation in ASL. Finally, when the bus arrived he would walk to the bus calmly and cooperatively. Luke's parents agreed that with the addition of positive behavioral support interventions (e.g., a picture schedule, a visually mediated reward for getting on the bus), the organization of the routine would be more congruent with Luke's strengths and needs, family goals and values would be supported, and the sustainability of the routine would be enhanced.

The interview is concluded with a brief discussion about additional family-focused goals for the support plan. During this discussion, the consultant and the family discuss goals that may further strengthen the family and reduce sources of stress. For example, Beth and David stated that they would like to develop a network of skilled respite care providers for their son so that they could get away on Friday evenings and at least one weekend day each week. David said that he would like to increase his ASL skills so that he could communicate with Luke more effectively.

PRELIMINARY SUPPORT PLAN
AND IMPLEMENTATION PLAN DESIGN

Behavioral Support Plan Design

After the completion of the comprehensive assessment, the information is used to design a multicomponent positive behavioral support plan. The plan that is designed will subsequently be presented to parent(s) and other stakeholders at a planning meeting. At this meeting, the stakeholders, or support team, will collaboratively decide the goals and interventions to be implemented. Thus, the plan that is designed is a proposal, one that will be subject to change based on input from other members of the support team.

The components of the proposed plan may include: 1) ecological or life-style interventions, 2) antecedent interventions, 3) new behaviors or skills to teach, 4) reinforcement strategies, 5) procedures to de-escalate behavior problems, and 6) emergency procedures to prevent injury. Interventions are proposed that are: 1) logically related to the hypotheses generated from the functional assessment, 2) informed by family strengths, 3) likely to reduce stress in the family as a whole, and 4) consonant with features of the family's ecology.

The task of generating a multicomponent support plan is simplified by outlining potential interventions in the form of a table, as shown in Table 3. At the head of each column the consultant writes the category of the plan components (e.g., ecological/lifestyle, antecedent, teaching new behaviors/skills). At the beginning of each row he or she briefly notes the hypotheses for problem behavior and adaptive behavior. The consultant begins with the column for ecological/lifestyle interventions and briefly writes down child-focused interventions that are directly linked to each hypothesis. As the consultant goes through the hypotheses, he or she also considers relevant information from the assessment of the family's ecology. This information may contribute to the selection of either a child-focused intervention that builds on family strengths or a family-focused intervention that uses available resources. After noting potential ecological/life-style interventions, the consultant continues the same process for each subsequent intervention category. The

Table 3. Proposed family support plan interventions

Hypothesis	Ecological/life-style	Antecedent/proactive	Teach new behaviors/skills	Reinforcement procedure	De-escalation strategy	Emergency procedure
Tantrums/hits to avoid transition from a preferred activity Calmly transition with picture schedule; contingent reward When agitated, will calm down if given clear, firm redirection	Increase predictability by using picture schedules	Red-flag critical transitions and prepare Luke beforehand: a) review schedule b) select and review reward	Self-management skills: using picture schedules with less help Language skills related to transition, change, and choice	Choice of reward for calmly completing transition Contingent delivery of praise and reward for cooperative transition behavior	When he is agitated: firmly say "Come here"; no eye contact; relaxation routine; redirect to next activity; praise cooperation	When tantrum begins, use nonaversive restraint procedure until calm
Tantrums/hits to obtain desired object, activity, or person Cooperative if offered meaningful choices Accept limits if taught language skills about transition, change, and choice	Increase opportunity to make choices Develop friendships with peers of similar age	Offer free choices (e.g., "Yes, you can") and limited choices (e.g., "You can brush your teeth now or in 5 minutes") If preference cannot be honored, then calmly, concisely redirect	Language skills related to transition, change, and choice (e.g., "Check your schedule," "Sorry, it's closed," "Yes, but later")	Social reinforcement for accepting limits on choice Social reinforcement includes expressive signing, positive facial expression, and positive physical contact	Same as above	Same as above
Runs away or hits to obtain negative attention Return if you remain calm and actively ignore			Language skills for asking for attention or activity (e.g., "Let's talk" "Let's go to the park")	Social reinforcement for asking for attention or activity Signed praise specific; social attention vigorous	If he hits you, then block and redirect; remain calm If he runs, actively ignore him; when he returns, redirect	

Additional family-focused interventions: skilled respite care two times per week; David enhances skills in ASL.

completed table defines interventions that the consultant believes are necessary and sufficient for promoting durable life-style change. Table 3 illustrates a list of proposed interventions for Luke and his family. For a thorough description of how to design effective behavior support plans, the reader is referred to Horner, Flannery, and O'Neill (1993).

Implementation Plan Design

The activities that will constitute implementation support, the person or persons who will provide support, and the time when support will be initiated and concluded are briefly outlined in this plan. Again, this plan is viewed as a proposal that will require input from other members of the support team during the team meeting. At a minimum, the proposed plan specifies the support activities in which the consultant is willing to engage, a timeline for the length of his or her participation in the above support process, and a set of suggestions and/or questions about the roles and support activities of other members of the team.

Recommended implementation support strategies are drawn from the literature on behavioral consultation and behavioral parent training (see Bergan & Kratochwill, 1990; Dunlap, in press; O'Dell, 1985). Table 4 lists potential support strategies and factors that guide their selection.

Based on the information in Table 4, the consultant selects support activities that seem to best fit the skills, resources, and concerns of the family and the classroom teacher. For example, Beth possessed many parenting skills going into the support effort. Luke's teacher possessed a number of important skills in teaching students who have hearing impairments and intellectual disabilities. The teacher's supervisor valued and supported the teacher's efforts to provide Luke with a quality educational program (e.g., functional activities, a focus on language training). At the same time, the family lived in a small community that was far from Luke's school and isolated from formal support services. David was not a skilled signer and did not often socially reinforce Luke for desirable behavior. Finally, the level of trust between home and school was not very high. Neither the teacher nor Luke's family members expressed much confidence in the other's ability to raise or educate Luke. Based on this information, the consultant proposed a plan that emphasized both direct support in the home by a member of the consultation group and the enhancement of trust and cooperation between the home and the school. The proposed implementation support activities included: 1) written procedures to guide the acquisition of sup-

Table 4. Support strategies for implementation in the selection of strategies

Support strategies for implementation

1. Written descriptions of intervention procedures
2. Meetings with family members to develop home-based interventions
3. User-friendly implementation checklists
4. Behavioral rehearsal of specific interventions with family members and/or school personnel
5. Work group meetings with team members to develop materials for home- and/or school-based interventions
6. Direct coaching of parents in the home or community
7. Follow-up telephone consultation

Factors in the selection of strategies

1. The amount of time available to commit to implementation support
2. Family member and/or teacher preferences for implementation support (e.g., role-play sessions, coaching at the school or in the home)
3. The skills possessed by family members (e.g., using praise effectively, accurately implementing written instructions)
4. The skills possessed by the classroom teacher (e.g., using errorless teaching procedures, developing functional curricular activities)
5. Additional implementation support resources available to the family and the school (e.g., home visits by the family consultant, support to the classroom teacher by the school district's behavioral consultant)
6. The quality of the relationship between the parent(s) and the classroom teacher (e.g., the presence of trust and good communication, the absence of same)

port procedures; 2) meetings with family members in the home to develop materials (e.g., a home picture schedule) and to practice intervention strategies (e.g., effective use of praise); 3) workgroup meetings by family members and school personnel to develop materials (e.g., language programs, strategies for choice giving) and practice strategies; and 4) implementation checklists to facilitate the acquisition, generalization, and maintenance of support procedures.

SUPPORT TEAM PLANNING MEETING AND PLAN FINALIZATION

Following the development of a proposal for a behavioral support plan and an implementation support plan, the family and the school are contacted to schedule a time for a 2-hour planning meeting. If 2 hours are not adequate to complete the meeting's agenda, then a second meeting is scheduled. The meeting is usually held at the school at a time that is convenient for the parent(s) and school personnel. Attendance is encouraged for persons who work directly with the child as well as for persons in consultant or supervisory roles. At a minimum, participants include the parent(s), the classroom teacher, and the family and/or behavioral consultant to the classroom. Additional participants may include the teacher's supervisor, the child's language therapist, or a psychologist who is counseling the family.

The main goals of the team meeting are to strengthen collaborative relationships among team members and to foster a commitment to improving the behavior and life-style of the child. Progress toward these goals is achieved through the specific objectives of the meeting. These objectives include reaching a consensus on hypotheses about behavior problems and the promotion of adaptive behavior, collaboratively selecting goals and intervention strategies, and finalizing implementation support activities.

The consultant prepares for the meeting by summarizing the assessment and intervention information on large pads of paper (27" × 34") that attach to an easel. On the first sheet he or she writes out the meeting agenda. Subsequent sheets contain the following information: 1) functional assessment information (e.g., behaviors of concern, associated conditions, related skill deficits); 2) hypotheses about problem behavior and adaptive behavior; 3) potential goals; 4) potential interventions organized by category of intervention (e.g., ecological/life-style); and 5) recommended implementation support activities.

Negotiating the Behavioral Support Plan

The consultant first reviews the agenda and briefly explains the purpose of the meeting. He or she begins the negotiation process with a brief review of the behaviors of concern and personal and environmental features associated with behavior problems. If team members describe additional associated conditions, the consultant then adds these to the written list. Next, he or she reviews the hypotheses for both problem and adaptive behavior. The consultant answers any questions that team members may have about particular hypotheses and writes down testable hypotheses that are suggested by team members.

After the team has reached a consensus of understanding about the assessment information and the hypotheses for both problem and adaptive behavior, the consultant guides a review of the proposed goals and interventions. During the review of goals, team members negotiate changes or additions to the goals listed and prioritize a final set of goals. During the review of each intervention category, team members negotiate changes or additions to the interventions listed and finalize the interventions that will be implemented in the home, the school, and/or other relevant settings.

The consultant then leads a brief discussion of measurement strategies for evaluating progress toward plan goals. He or she recommends measures of problem behavior (e.g., frequency of tantrums), implementation fidelity (e.g., how well a picture schedule strategy is being used), and social validity (e.g., the acceptability of a de-escalation procedure). Team members agree on the kinds of data that will be collected, the persons who will collect the data, and the general frequency of data collection (e.g., daily for tantrum behavior, weekly for fidelity of implementation). The outcome of this negotiation process is a collaboratively determined behavioral support plan. The negotiated support plan for Luke and his family is outlined in Table 5.

Negotiating the Implementation Plan

The last task of the planning meeting is the collaborative finalization of an implementation plan. The consultant first reviews the list of proposed support activities and asks team members for their opinions and recommendations. He or she notes any changes or additions that team members suggest and negotiates their inclusion in the implementation plan. Next, the consultant leads a discussion about potential implementation support activities of other team members. During this discussion, for example, the family consultant may agree to conduct a monthly home visit and to help family members solve problems in implementation. The classroom supervisor may agree to conduct an observation of the teacher and the student twice each month and give the teacher feedback on implementation fidelity. After the group agrees on specific support activities, the consultant writes down the initials of the person(s) responsible for each activity and the date when the activity will begin. Finally, the consultant negotiates a date to conclude his or her involvement in the support process. The duration of involvement will vary depending on the comprehensiveness of the plan, the skills and resources of team members, and the nature of the child's behavior problems. The typical length of direct involvement in the implementation phase of the process is between 2–6 months. For Luke and his family, it was agreed that participation in support activities would be for a 4-month period.

Following the planning meeting, the consultant writes a positive behavioral support plan and an implementation support plan that summarize the decisions made during the meeting. He or she sends a copy of each plan to the members of the support team. An excerpt from the implementation support plan for Luke is presented in Table 6.

Table 5.   Summary of family support plan goals and interventions

GOALS
Child-Focused Goals
1. Increase Luke's opportunities to make meaningful choices.
2. Increase predictability for Luke by using a flexible picture schedule at home and school.
3. Support Luke in the development of a friendship with a peer without a disability.
4. Increase Luke's self-management skills.
5. Increase Luke's sign language skills.
6. Decrease Luke's tantrum, aggression, and running away behaviors.

Family-Focused Goals
1. Family receives respite care 2 days a week (Friday evening and 1 weekend day).
2. Recruit and train respite care providers.
3. Father increases his sign language skills.

BEHAVIORAL SUPPORT PLAN INTERVENTIONS
Life-Style/Ecological Interventions
1. Provide Luke with choice-making opportunities throughout his day.
2. Use flexible picture schedules with Luke at home and during transitions between activities, weekend outings, and family vacations.
3. Luke's father facilitates leisure activity outings with a peer without a disability who lives near the family.

Antecedent Interventions
1. Red-flag transition situations and prepare Luke beforehand: a) review his schedule with him, and b) offer him a choice of a reward for calmly completing the transition.
2. When Luke's preference cannot be honored, be clear, concise, and calm as you redirect him.

Teaching Interventions
1. Use "whole task" teaching methods to teach Luke to use his picture schedule to initiate tasks and activities with less assistance.
2. Use incidental language teaching methods to teach Luke sign language about transition, change, and choice.

Reinforcement Interventions
1. Contingent delivery of a tangible reinforcer for cooperative transition behavior
2. Social praise and attention for accepting a limitation on choice
3. Social praise that is specific, enthusiastic, and includes warm physical attention

De-escalating Strategies
1. When Luke is agitated, but before he tantrums, firmly say, "Come here" and don't give eye contact; prompt him through relaxation routine; praise cooperation.
2. If Luke runs from you, actively ignore him; when he returns, redirect him.

Table 6. Implementation support plan outline

Activity	Goals		Tasks		Who	By when
Home meetings and family support	1.	Family members will skillfully use positive behavioral support interventions.	a. b. c. d.	Schedule weekly home meetings. Develop materials (e.g., picture schedules, reinforcer menu). Role play intervention procedures. Review self-evaluation data, discuss progress, and solve problems.	Beth, David, Joe	Jan. 24 thru May 23
	2.	David will help Luke develop a friendship with a nondisabled peer.	a. b. c.	Consult with David on friendship development strategy. Schedule supervised leisure activities with new friend. Provide problem solving support to a new friend.	Joe David David	Feb. 7 Ongoing from February 14
	3.	Beth and Joe will recruit and train respite care providers	a. b. c.	Recruit respite care providers. Review intervention procedures with respite care providers. Develop user friendly behavioral support manual.	Beth Beth, Joe Joe	Ongoing from Feb. 14 May 23
Evaluation	1.	Family members and school personnel self-evaluate use of interventions once per week.	a. b.	Design self-evaluation forms. Self-evaluate implementation once per week	Joe Beth, David, Mary, Tom, Joy	Feb. 21, March 21 March 1 thru May 24
	2.	Monthly and final evaluation of Luke's support plan.	a. b. c. d.	Review and evaluate progress monthly. Implement changes; provide additional support as needed. Interview school personnel and family members. Write final evaluation report; distribute copies to team members.	Theresa, Joe Team Joe Joe, Theresa	March 14 April 11, May 23 May 23 June 1

PLAN IMPLEMENTATION SUPPORT

Two interdependent goals are addressed during implementation support. The first goal is to improve the quality of life of the child. This goal requires that problem behavior be reduced to a near-zero level across all home, school, and community settings for a durable period of time. It also requires broad life-style improvements such as the development of adaptive behavior and the expansion of opportunities to do preferred activities and to interact with peers without disabilities. This first goal is achieved through implementation of the comprehensive positive behavioral support plan. The second goal is to strengthen the capacity of the family and school personnel to effectively support and educate the child. This second goal is achieved through the activities of the implementation support plan.

During implementation support, parents and school personnel learn to implement interventions with sufficient fidelity to improve the behavior and life-style of the child. As described above, several different strategies are used to help parents and school personnel implement behavioral support interventions with fidelity. General guidelines that are followed when supporting families, four implementation support activities typically used with family members, and strategies used to promote generalization and maintenance are described in the following section.

General Guidelines

Several guidelines are adhered to during implementation support that contribute to a "family-friendly" process. At the beginning of a home visit, parents are asked for their informed consent before initiating support activities. The consultant reviews the prepared agenda, negotiates additions to or changes in the agenda, and begins activities after receiving verbal consent to do so. If the consultant wishes to introduce a new implementation activity (e.g., coaching), the rationale for the new activity is explained, its features are described, and consent is requested.

The expression of emotions by family members are valued and supported. Expressions of feelings are never considered to be off task. On the contrary, clinical experience suggests that if a parent's feelings are not recognized and validated, problems may arise in the consultation relationship or during opportunities to use specific interventions. Support is provided by actively listening to a parent's feelings about his or her child's progress and the use of specific interventions. When a parent's feelings interfere with constructive action, an effort to resolve the impasse is made in a way that promotes child growth and family empowerment. For example, Beth was initially reluctant to use the active ignoring procedure when Luke ran away from her. She was afraid for him because he could not hear traffic going by in the street. Her strategy of running after him was also based on feelings of love for her son and a desire to protect him from harm. The consultant expressed his understanding and acceptance of these legitimate feelings. The consultant and Beth discussed different circumstances where these feelings had long-term benefits for her son. They also discussed the short-term gains and long-term problems created by running after Luke. They reviewed the assessment information, which indicated that when he was actively ignored at school, he reliably came back. They also discussed the school's observation that Luke did not run into a street when he attempted to run away. Through this dialogue Beth and the consultant developed an acceptable compromise. Where streets and traffic were not a cause of concern, Beth would try to actively ignore Luke when he ran away. When physical safety was a concern, Beth would use physical assistance to help Luke stay with her (e.g., hold his hand, walk with her arm around his shoulder).

Family members are encouraged to attribute improvement in their son's or daughter's behavior to their own effort. Many families tend to be hesitant to accept credit for enhancing the behavior and life-style of their child. Rather, they may attribute their child's improvement to the effort of the consultant or to some nonspecific factor such as maturation. Since these attributions do not contribute to the empowerment of family members, the influence of the parents' efforts and skillfulness with their child is emphasized.

Parents also are encouraged to talk about their successes in enhancing their child's behavior and quality of life. When parents report successes, admiration for their expertise and effectiveness is expressed. When family members have mastered the use of intervention strategies, they are encouraged to play a leadership role in solving problems in their child's behavior or in interacting with other professionals and service providers. Leadership activities might include telling their child's teacher about the use of a particularly effective support strategy (e.g., picture schedules, star charts), showing respite care providers how to work with their son or daughter, or solving a new problem with their child's behavior without professional assistance.

Written Procedures

The behavioral support plan that was written and distributed to team members serves as the primary document to guide the imple-

mentation support effort. This plan is written as clearly and suc-
cinctly as possible so that it can be easily understood and used by
parents and school personnel. When specific behavioral interventions such as antecedent or reinforcement strategies are described,
the hypothesis that prompts the use of the intervention is stated, a
brief title for the procedure is written, and the rules or steps of the
procedure are briefly listed. The procedure may also be illustrated
by providing a brief example of the intervention in practice. Figure 3
describes an antecedent strategy from Luke's support plan.

Meetings with Family Members

Holding regular meetings with family members in their home is
another important implementation support activity. Typically, the
meetings are held weekly at a time that is convenient for the mother
and/or father and are from 1 to 2 hours in length. During these
meetings several implementation support tasks are performed.
These include: 1) the development and/or purchase of materials for
use in the home (e.g., picture schedules, reinforcer menus, new toys
or games); 2) the behavioral rehearsal of specific interventions (e.g.,
using praise effectively, using natural contingency statements to
increase the likelihood of child compliance); and 3) the review of
progress data on behavioral and implementation objectives (e.g.,
frequency of tantrums during the past week, parent self-evaluation
of implementation fidelity).

As the child's parents begin to use interventions in the home or
local community, problems may arise. Family members and the con-

---

Hypothesis 1. Luke has tantrums or hits to avoid a change in activity, event, or person.

Proactive Strategy

A. "Red-flag" critical situations *before* they occur. These include leaving a preferred activity, event, or person.
   1. At the start of a preferred situation, sign through Luke's picture schedule with him; make an impromptu schedule using line drawings if needed.
   2. Negotiate a reward he can receive for calmly transitioning to the next situation. Place or draw a picture of the reward on his schedule.
   3. Right before the change, remind Luke of what will happen next and review his schedule.
   4. If Luke calmly completes the transition, praise him and give him his reward.

Figure 3. Antecedent strategy from Luke's support plan.

sultant typically discuss problems in implementation during the review of progress data. When a problem develops, an attempt is first made to assess its source. A behavioral intervention may need to be modified because it is poorly designed and thus ineffective. Parents may find it difficult to implement an intervention with their child at times when other home tasks, such as meal preparation, compete for their attention. Family members may have difficulty implementing a life-style intervention because they realize, soon after they begin the intervention, that it conflicts with their values and beliefs about parenting.

After the reason for the implementation problem has been assessed, a solution is sought that is acceptable to the parents and effective in improving the behavior and quality of life of the child. If, for example, an intervention conflicts with the parents' values or beliefs about parenting, then permission may be requested to discuss this values conflict and an attempt to find an acceptable solution made. For instance, a life-style intervention for Luke included increasing his opportunities to make choices throughout his day at home and school. After this intervention was initiated, the classroom teacher and Luke's mother reported that they were offering Luke many more choices. They also reported that Luke had become more cooperative with them. Luke's stepfather, however, reported that he continued to have difficulty offering Luke choices. He also reported that Luke continued to hit him and did not comply with his requests or instructions. When the consultant learned of this problem, he asked David if he would be willing to participate in a dialogue about this issue. The consultant explained that the dialogue would involve a sharing of perspectives and information. The outcome of the dialogue would involve some additional support to David if he so wished. Following this explanation, David consented to participate.

During this dialogue the consultant learned that David was raised in an authoritarian household where his parents did not offer their children choices. In David's mind, a father should control his children by telling them what to do and what not to do. The consultant responded to David's comments with both empathy and information. He assured David that he was not alone in this regard—that it is not uncommon for parents to raise their children in this way. He then presented evidence that gave weight to an alternative style of parenting. The consultant described how recent research has shown that children with severe disabilities are more cooperative when they are given choices. He suggested that by giving Luke more choices in his life, he is given an opportunity to learn about responsibility—how to make his own choices and control his own actions, rather than be controlled by others most of the time. David expressed his appreciation for this new way of thinking, and reaffirmed his interest in adopting this new style of parenting. However, he expressed his concern that old habits are difficult to break. David and the consultant agreed to incorporate into their weekly meetings a brief review of how well David was doing with this intervention. Beth agreed to support her husband by expressing appreciation for his effort.

Implementation Checklists

A self-evaluation form, called an implementation checklist, is another strategy used to support family members and school personnel. The form is composed of a list of intervention steps or procedures and a 5-point Likert scale. The checklist may focus on a particular home or community routine that the family is attempting to enhance (e.g., the morning routine, coming home from day-care) or sample a range of intervention strategies the family is using throughout the day (e.g., picture schedules, praising calm acceptance of changes). The parent reads each step or procedure on the list and self-evaluates how well he or she implemented it. An abridged sample of an implementation checklist for Luke is presented in Figure 4. The checklist was used by Luke's parents during their implementation of the interventions for the transition from the day-care routine.

Family members derive several benefits from using this kind of self-evaluation tool. It helps a parent remember the steps or procedures that he or she is learning to implement. For example, Luke's mother reported that she would quickly read the form before leaving for the daycare center, in order to remind herself of what to do. It

		Completely unable to do this			Did this very well	
1.	Prepared choice of reinforcers.	1	2	3	4	5
2.	Day-care teacher reviewed schedule before I arrived.	1	2	3	4	5
3.	Kept Luke's attention focused on steps in leaving.	1	2	3	4	5
4.	Gave brief praise for completing steps.	1	2	3	4	5
5.	Actively ignored running away.	1	2	3	4	5

Figure 4.   Abridged implementation checklist for the day-care to home transition routine.

also serves as a problem-solving tool. During meetings with the family, the consultant may review the recently completed checklists with the child's parent(s) and help the parent(s) solve problems with implementation. For example, a review of Luke's day-care transition checklist indicated that his stepfather sometimes forgot to praise Luke when he gave him the reinforcer for cooperatively leaving the day-care center and getting into the family's car. This information prompted the consultant to give David additional assistance. David and the consultant discussed the importance of this procedure for strengthening the value of social praise for Luke. David also agreed to participate in a behavioral rehearsal of this procedure. Following these support activities, David reported that he consistently remembered to praise Luke before he gave him his reward.

The checklist also helps family members solve implementation problems on their own. For example, Beth reported that one day when she arrived at the day-care center to pick Luke up, he ran out of the building and entered another family's car. In trying to identify the reason for this problem, she asked the day-care aide if she remembered to review Luke's transition schedule with him. The day-care aide reported that she had forgotten to do this. Beth noted this on her checklist later that evening. The next day she called the day-care center and asked the director to remind the staff to review Luke's schedule with him just before she arrived. When Beth arrived, Luke was cooperative and got into his family's car. The aide working with Luke reported that she had reviewed his schedule with him.

Behavioral Rehearsal

For some families, behavioral rehearsal is a useful supplemental activity for promoting implementation fidelity. During behavioral rehearsal, family members and the consultant role-play situations in which interventions are to be used. The consultant develops a script of vignettes in preparation for a role-play session. The vignettes sample the range of situations where the intervention should be implemented, and the range of skills the parent is supposed to use. For instance, the consultant for Luke's family designed a role-play script for teaching Luke's parents to use reinforcement skills. The script contained 12 vignettes. Situations sampled included tasks or activities in which Luke engaged, settings, times of day, and persons providing reinforcement. Skills sampled included gaining the child's attention, ensuring the congruence between language content and nonverbal behavior, using descriptive praise, and using primary reinforcers. An example of one role-play vignette is presented below:

3. *Situation:*   Home in the early morning. Luke has finished break-
    fast and is getting his coat and backpack. Today he does this with
    greater independence compared with yesterday.
    Player: Beth
    What to do: You want to praise Luke for completing the morning
    routine with greater independence. After Luke gets his pack and
    jacket, gently get his attention. When he looks at you, sign "Jacket.
    Pack. By yourself. Great!" When you do this, make sure that your
    signs' meanings are congruent with your nonverbal behavior. That
    is, make sure your facial expression is relaxed and positive, and
    your gestures are graceful in movement.

During role play sessions, the consultant emphasizes the rules that guide the effective use of interventions. For example, in the vignette described above, the consultant emphasized the importance of getting the child's attention, and making one's affect congruent with signed praise. Behavioral rehearsal is a particularly effective strategy for teaching these rules or discriminations. After a parent has role-played the use of an intervention, the consultant can point out the rules that the parent effectively followed. When the consultant takes the role of the parent, he or she can purposely make common errors in implementation and then ask parents to describe the errors that the consultant made. In this way family members learn to discriminate skillful implementation from errorful implementation of specific interventions.

Promoting Generalization and Maintenance

The ultimate goal of the support process is the empowerment of the family and the promotion of durable, life-style improvement for the child with a disability. In order to achieve this aim, issues of generalization and maintenance are addressed throughout the assessment and intervention process. Successful generalization occurs when family members use new skills across all of the relevant situations (e.g., time of day, place, activity) where problem behavior has occurred, and when child behavioral improvement occurs across all of the relevant situations that have been associated with problem behavior (e.g., persons, activities, settings).

Generalization is promoted in several ways throughout the consultation process. During the comprehensive assessment, the consultant identifies the full range of relevant situations in which problem behaviors occur. He or she identifies all of the settings where interventions will be necessary, and all of the persons who will need to implement interventions. During plan design, the consultant identifies a comprehensive set of interventions that may promote life-style improvement for the child and the family. During implementation support, the consultant introduces a variety of strategies to promote generalization. The consultant and parent(s) may agree to sequentially introduce interventions into new activity settings (e.g., the evening routine) after the child's behavior has improved in one or two settings (e.g., the morning routine and the transition from the day-care routine). The consultant may design an implementation checklist that family members use to mediate generalization to nontrained settings. During behavioral rehearsal, the consultant may design role-play vignettes that sample the range of situations associated with problem behavior and the response requirements of intervention skills. When parents report a lack of success in using interventions in nontrained settings, the consultant and family members participate in problem-solving activities together and try to find a solution that is both acceptable to the parent(s) and effective for the child. When the strategies described above are not sufficient to promote generalization, the consultant may coach the parent(s) in the natural setting where behavior problems continue to occur.

During plan implementation for Luke, for example, Beth and David had to generalize the use of picture schedules, visually mediated reinforcers, and social reinforcement across several nontrained situations. These situations included trips to the local grocery store, evening visits to the homes of family friends, weekend hiking trips, and a week-long vacation to Idaho. All of these conditions were associated with tantrums in the past. Over the course of implementation support, Beth and David reported that they had begun to use the intervention procedures during these conditions. They also reported that Luke had begun to calmly complete the transitions associated with each situation. Beth, for instance, enthusiastically reported that they had used picture schedules during their visit to Idaho. At the start of each day, Beth would think through the events of the day, have Luke participate in a few events, and then organize the pictures in his schedule book. Throughout the day, she would review the schedule with Luke. When he completed difficult transitions calmly, Beth and David would vigorously praise Luke and give him his reinforcer. With a clear sense of accomplishment, Beth reported that Luke did not have a tantrum during the trip.

Successful maintenance of parenting skills and of life-style improvement for the child occurs when parents receive sufficient social support for the changes they have initiated, and when the child receives both adequate opportunity to use new adaptive behaviors and reinforcement for their use. Several strategies are used to promote maintenance. During assessment, the consultant identifies members of the parents' support network who may encourage the mother and/or father to use positive behavioral support interventions. During intervention design, he or she recommends interventions that fit well with the family's ecology and that diminish stress. During implementation support, he or she encourages the development of collaborative relationships between the family and school personnel.

When the child shows sustained improvement in his or her behavior across all relevant settings, assistance is gradually faded. The consultant may design an abbreviated implementation checklist that includes only those intervention procedures that have proven most effective. He or she begins to meet with the family less often. Instead of meeting once a week, for example, the consultant and the family may meet once every 2 weeks or once a month. The consultant also starts to rely on telephone calls more often to provide support. The consultant offers less instruction during meetings or telephone contacts. He or she encourages family members to share their successes, lead problem-solving discussions, and attribute child progress to their own effort. The consultant and the family also discuss strategies that the family can use to maintain child improvement after the consultant has stopped providing implementation support (e.g., use of formal and informal support networks, use of abbreviated implementation checklists).

One month before implementation support for Luke and his family was concluded, Beth and David decided to return to their original home in Idaho. This presented the family with a unique challenge in terms of maintaining Luke's improvement and the family's social support. In preparation for this move, the consultant and the family participated in several maintenance-enhancing activities. They met only once during the last month of the support effort and relied on telephone contacts more often to discuss progress and solve problems. During these contacts, the consultant encouraged family members to lead problem-solving discussions and to provide each other with social support for their continued successes with Luke. The consultant also organized a notebook of intervention programs and implementation checklists. Beth and David agreed to use the materials in the notebook as a reference for behavioral support interventions and a manual to train new respite care providers. Finally, the consultant encouraged Beth and David to contact him if they felt that further telephone consultation was necessary.

EVALUATION

Progress toward support plan goals is evaluated throughout the implementation of the support plan. At the conclusion of the consultant's involvement, a final evaluation of progress is completed. During ongoing and final evaluations, four basic questions are addressed: 1) Has the child's behavior, skills, and/or life-style improved in a meaningful way? 2) Have family members and school personnel implemented the interventions with sufficient fidelity? 3) Do family members and school personnel find the goals, interventions, and outcomes of the support effort acceptable? 4) Has the support effort strengthened the family as a whole?

During implementation support these questions are answered both formally and informally during meetings with family members and/or school personnel, during telephone conversations, and during observations in the home, the school, or other relevant settings. During these activities, the consultant reviews parent or teacher self-report measures, listens to verbal reports about progress or problems, and observes the child interacting with his or her parents and/or teacher. Other members of the support team also participate in evaluation activities. For example, the classroom supervisor may observe the teaching staff and provide feedback on implementation fidelity. The family consultant for the school district may visit the family's home and discuss progress toward home goals. By sharing formative evaluation tasks with other team members, these forms of local support will hopefully remain after the consultant's involvement has ended.

Family members and direct teaching staff participate in evaluation activities by completing self-report measures of child behavior, implementation fidelity, and social validity. Excerpts from self-report measures used by Luke's parents and/or school staff are presented in Figures 5 and 6.

Evaluation data are used to make ongoing decisions about intervention procedures and implementation support activities. Behavioral data may indicate a need to change an intervention because it is not having the desired effect on the child's behavior problems. Implementation fidelity data may suggest a need for additional assistance to a parent. Social validity data may require a change in an intervention because it is difficult to implement in the home or local community. These data may also necessitate a change in procedure because the outcome of the intervention, although positive for the child, has a negative effect on another member of the family.

		Disagree				Agree	
1.	The goals of the behavioral support plan are appropriate for my child.	1	2	3	4	5	6
2.	The interventions are difficult to carry out in the home and in the community.	1	2	3	4	5	6
3.	The interventions are effective in improving my child's behavior and quality of life.	1	2	3	4	5	6
4.	The outcomes of the support effort have been beneficial to my family as a whole.	1	2	3	4	5	6

Figure 5.   Self-report items of social validity.

At the conclusion of the consultant's involvement in the behavioral support effort, final evaluation of progress toward support plan goals is completed. The consultant summarizes self-report data collected by family members and school personnel during plan implementation, interviews parents and school personnel about child progress on specific goals, and asks team members to complete a social validity evaluation form. He or she organizes this information into a final evaluation report and distributes copies to team members.

A final evaluation of the behavioral support plan goals for Luke and his family occurred in May 1991, 4 months after implementation support began. Overall, interviews and self-report data indicated that Luke, his parents, and school personnel made progress

5.	During critical situations (e.g., leaving a preferred activity or person), I prepared Luke *beforehand* by reviewing his schedule. I did this during the preferred situation and right before the change occurred.				
	Unable to do this			Did this very well	
	1	2	3	4	5
6.	During critical situations in which I was with Luke, he became very agitated:				
	Once	Twice	Three times	Four times	Five or more times
7.	When Luke became very agitated, and before he entered a full tantrum, I used the deceleration procedure with him.				
	Unable to do this			Did this very well	
	1	2	3	4	5

Figure 6.   Self-report items of child behavior and implementation fidelity.

toward attaining several of the goals of the support plan. Informal observation of Luke's behavior at home and school supported the information gained from the interviews and self-report forms. Fidelity data on the use of specific support strategies indicated that family members and school personnel became increasingly more proficient in the use of interventions. There was also evidence that a mutually supportive relationship had developed between the parents and the classroom teacher. Daily notes exchanged between home and school no longer expressed contention and doubt. Rather, the messages were mostly exchanges of information and occasionally comments of appreciation.

In terms of the quality of Luke's life, several areas evidenced improvement. Luke performed several tasks and routines at school and home with less assistance. He used picture schedules to make predictions and calmly transition between activities or events. He understood and used more sign language associated with scheduled activities, changes, and choices (e.g., Later. We'll go tomorrow. What want?). Luke was provided with opportunities to make meaningful choices, and he experienced the development of one friendship with a typical peer in his neighborhood. Finally, Luke engaged in tantrums, hitting, and running away behavior significantly less often. Beth and David subjectively evaluated the improvement in Luke's quality of life as being substantial. Beth candidly stated, "I'm not scared anymore. He's much calmer, much more respectful to me. He's made a great improvement."

Self-reported behavioral data and verbal reports by Luke's parents and teacher indicated a reduction in the frequency, intensity, and duration of tantrums. Data indicated that Luke engaged in one tantrum at school since interventions were begun in January. Beth and David reported that since February, when the family began using support strategies, Luke had four tantrums. This compared favorably with a report of four to five tantrums per week before the support effort began. They also noted that the duration of tantrums was much shorter than in the past, and fewer problem behaviors were associated with each tantrum.

Behavioral data and verbal report also indicated improvement in the frequency of Luke's running away and hitting behaviors. Teacher and parent self-reported frequency data indicated that Luke ran away or hit others on an average of 4.3 times per week at school and 5.6 times per week at home. Before interventions were initiated his parents reported eight to ten episodes of hitting per day and two episodes of running away per day.

In order to further improve the quality of Luke's life and to further strengthen the family, several recommendations were made in his final evaluation. These included: 1) providing Luke with a comprehensive program of positive behavioral support at his new school and community in Idaho, 2) providing this support within the context of a life skills curriculum that emphasized the mastery of age-appropriate activities and functional academic skills, 3) continuing to offer Luke meaningful choices at home and school, and 4) developing a network of skilled respite care providers in order to provide Beth and David with a rest from child care responsibilities.

FOLLOW-UP

After the consultant's involvement in the support effort is concluded, additional consultative support may be provided in order to help families maintain their children's behavioral and life-style improvements. During the final evaluation interview family members are encouraged to request further assistance if needed. At a minimum, the family is contacted by letter or telephone 1–3 months after the conclusion of support activities. During this contact the maintenance of behavioral and life-style improvement is assessed. When family members report continued success, admiration and respect for their skillfulness is expressed. If families report that behavioral and life-style difficulties have increased, consultative assistance via telephone is provided. If telephone consultation proves ineffective, a visit to the family's home and a "booster session" in the use of support plan interventions may be conducted.

During follow-up assistance there is also concern for the maintenance of social support to the family. For example, if parents inform the consultant that they are having difficulty maintaining positive behavioral interventions, they are asked if they are receiving the social support needed to maintain these interventions (e.g., respite care during the weekend, the father providing the mother with a break from child care duties after supper). If this social support has diminished, the family is counseled to rebuild this support back into their lives.

Two months and 5 months after Luke's family moved to Idaho, the consultant contacted the family and inquired about Luke's behavioral and lifestyle gains. On both occasions, Beth informed the consultant that Luke continued to do well. The family did not request further consultative assistance. During the second follow-up contact, Beth and David provided a detailed description of Luke's behavior and the family's lifestyle since returning to Idaho. Beth stated that Luke and the family were doing "surprisingly well." She expressed her satisfaction with Luke's new school and said that he had a very individualized educational program. Her major concern was that Luke was not having opportunities to interact with peers without disabilities.

Beth and David stated that Luke rarely had tantrums, reporting only two incidents since their return. Beth and David reported that they continued to use picture schedules and contingent reinforcement for calm transition behavior. They added that Luke continued to hit others and run away, but the frequency and intensity of the behaviors were acceptably low. During the month of October, they reported that Luke ran away from them once or twice a week. He hit them with his open palm 7–12 times per week. In terms of family support, Beth informed the consultant that the family was receiving respite care funds from the state. With this financial assistance, they recruited and trained a small group of respite care providers and received 20–25 hours of respite care relief each week. Beth concluded her description by stating:

> I think that while we still have some problems . . . we now have the tools to go back and figure out what we could do differently and can see what we need to work on. We have the skills now that we didn't have before. It's been a world of difference between this November and last November. I doubt that the family would have held together if we hadn't . . . been involved in the support program. It's really amazing how things are working out.

SUMMARY AND CONCLUSION

In this chapter, a comprehensive approach to behavioral consultation that is "friendly" to families has been described. Luke's family's participation in the support process serves as one example of how the process works in actual practice. The family-friendly features of the process, such as honoring the family's perspective and collaboratively agreeing on goals, interventions, and support strategies, make it easier for families to adopt positive behavioral support in the home and local community. This ease of adoption in turn increases the likelihood that families will successfully promote durable life-style enhancement for their children and for the family as a whole.

One of the major elements of the process is the partnership that develops between the family and the consultant, a partnership characterized by trust, mutual respect, and collaborative problem-solving. Essential to the development of this partnership is the dialogue between the consultant and the family, as illustrated with Luke's parents. In the context of this dialogue, Beth and David developed an understanding of their child's behavior problems that enabled them to ameliorate these problems. By listening closely to Luke's parents, the consultant was able to design interventions that fit well with the family's values and life-style. When family beliefs or values interfered with implementation fidelity, the dialogue between the family and the consultant enabled them to find acceptable and effective solutions. Finally, the dialogue contributed to Beth's and David's confidence that the successes they experienced with Luke were due to their own efforts. Given this growing conviction, Luke's family became increasingly capable of applying solutions in novel settings and solving new problems on their own.

A final element that bears emphasis is the bidirectionality of influence between the consultant and the family. Although the consultant plays a leading role in the recommendation of interventions and implementation support activities, family members play a significant role in the selection of support goals, the adaptation of specific interventions for use in the home or community, and the types of implementation support activities that are used. Through this reciprocal influence, issues of treatment adherence become less problematic. Rather, in an atmosphere of mutual trust and respect, the difficulties of raising a child with a severe disability at home and in the local community are brought to light. The challenges families face in adopting and adapting new technology to meet the needs of their child are shared with professionals. Finally, improvement in the behavior of the child and the life-style of the family is more likely to endure because family members and members of the family's support network have actively participated in creating these positive outcomes.

REFERENCES

Bailey, D.J. (1987). Collaborative goal-setting with families: Resolving differences in values and priorities for services. *Topics in Early Childhood Special Education, 7*, 59–71.

Bergan, J.H., & Kratochwill, T.R. (1990). *Behavioral consultation and therapy.* New York: Plenum.

Bernheimer, L.P., Gallimore, R., & Weisner, T.S. (1990). Ecocultural theory as a context for the individual family service plan. *Journal of Early Intervention, 14*(3), 219–233.

Bromley, B.E., & Blacher, J. (1991). Parental reasons for out-of-home placement of children with severe handicaps, *Mental Retardation, 29*, 275–280.

Dunlap, G. (in press). Promoting generalization: Current status and functional considerations. In R. Van Houton & S. Axelrod (Eds.), *Effective behavioral treatment.* New York: Plenum.

Dunlap, G., Kern-Dunlap, L., Clarke, S., & Robbins, F.R. (1991). Functional assessment, curricular revision, and severe behavior problems. *Journal of Applied Behavior Analysis, 24,* 387–392.

Dunlap, G., & Robbins, F.R. (1991). Current perspectives in service delivery for young children with autism. *Comprehensive Mental Health Care, 1,* 177–194.

Durst, C.J., Trivette, C.M., & Deal, A.G. (1988). *Enabling and empowering familier: Principles and guidelines for practice.* Cambridge, MA: Brookline Books.

Gallimore, R., Weisner, T.S., Kaufman, S.Z., & Bernheimer, L.P. (1989). The social construction of ecocultural niches: Family accommodation of developmentally delayed children. *American Journal on Mental Retardation, 94,* 216–230.

Goetz, L., Anderson, J., & Laten, S. (1989). Facilitation of family support through public school programs. In G.S.H. Singer & L.K. Irvin (Eds.), *Support for caregiving families: Enabling positive adaptation to disability* (pp. 239–252). Baltimore: Paul H. Brookes Publishing Co.

Hawkins, N.E., & Singer, G.H.S. (1989). A skills training approach for assisting parents to cope with stress. In G.H.S. Singer & L.K. Irvin (Eds.), *Support for caregiving families: Enabling positive adaptation to disability* (pp. 71–84). Baltimore: Paul H. Brookes Publishing Co.

Horner, R.H., Albin, R.W., & O'Neill, R.E. (1991). Supporting students with severe intellectual disabilities and severe challenging behaviors. In G. Stoner, M.R. Shinn, & H.M. Walker (Ed.), *Interventions for achievement and behavior problems* (pp. 269–287). Washington, DC: National Association of School Psychologists.

Horner, R.H., Dunlap, G., Koegel, R.L., Carr, E.G., Sailor, W., Anderson, J., Albin, R.W., & O'Neill, R.E. (1990). Toward a technology of "non-aversive" behavioral support. *Journal of The Association for Persons with Severe Handicaps, 15,* 125–132.

Horner, R.H., O'Neill, R.E., & Flannery, K.B. (1993). Effective behavior support plans from functional assessment information. In M. Snell (Ed.), *Instruction of persons with severe handicaps* (4th ed.) (pp. 184–214). Columbus, OH: Charles E. Merrill.

Kaiser, A.P., & Hemmeter, M.L. (1989). Value-based approaches to family intervention. *Topics in Early Childhood Special Education, 8,* 72–86.

LaVigna, G.W., Willis, T.J., & Donnellan, A.M. (1989). The role of positive programming in behavioral treatment. In E. Cipani (Ed.), *The treatment of severe behavior disorders: Behavior analysis approaches* (pp. 59–83). Washington, DC: American Association on Mental Retardation.

Meyer, L.H., & Evans, I.M. (1989). *Nonaversive interventions for behavior problems: A manual for home and community.* Baltimore: Paul H. Brookes Publishing Co.

O'Dell, S. (1985). Progress in parent training. In M. Hersen, R.M. Eisler, & P.M. Miller (Eds.), *Progress in behavior modification* (Vol. 9, pp. 57–108). New York: Academic Press.

O'Neill, R.E., Horner, R.H., Albin, R.W., Storey, K., & Sprague, J.R. (1990).

Functional analysis of problem behavior: A practical assessment guide. Sycamore, IL: Sycamore Publishing Co.

Patterson, G.R. (1982). *Coercive family process.* Eugene OR: Castalia Publishing Co.

Quine, L., & Pahl, J. (1985). Examining the causes of stress in families with severely mentally retarded children. *British Journal of Social Work, 15,* 501–517.

Robbins, F.R., Dunlap, G., & Plienis, A.J. (1991). Family characteristics, family training, and the progress of young children with autism. *Journal of Early Intervention, 15,* 172–184.

Singer, G.H.S., & Irvin, L.K. (1989). Family caregiving, stress, and support. In G.H.S. Singer & L.K. Irvin (Eds.), *Support for caregiving families: Enabling positive adaptation to disability* (pp. 3–25). Baltimore: Paul H. Brookes Publishing Co.

Singer, G.H.S., Irvine, A.B., & Irvin, L.K. (1989). Expanding the focus of behavioral parent training: A contextual approach. In G.H.S. Singer & L.K. Irvin (Eds.), *Support for caregiving families: Enabling positive adaptation to disability* (pp. 85–102). Baltimore: Paul H. Brookes Publishing Co.

Snell, M.E., & Beckman-Brindley, S. (1984). Family involvement in intervention with children having severe handicaps. *Journal of The Association for Persons with Severe Handicaps, 9,* 213–230.

Sprague, J., Flannery, K.B., & O'Neill, R.E. (1992). *Effective consultation: Supporting the implementation of positive behavior support plans.* Eugene, OR: University of Oregon, Specialized Training Program, Division of Special Education and Rehabilitation.

Summers, J.A., Behr, S.K., & Turnbull, A.P. (1989). Positive adaptation and coping strengths of families who have children with disabilities. In G.H.S. Singer & L.K. Irvin (Eds.), *Support for caregiving families: Enabling positive adaptation to disability* (pp. 27–40). Baltimore: Paul H. Brookes Publishing Co.

Turnbull, A.P. (1988). The challenge of providing comprehensive support to families. *Education and Training in Mental Retardation, 23,* 261–272.

Turnbull, A.P., & Turnbull, H.R., III. (1991a). *Families, professionals and exceptionality: A special partnership.* Columbus, OH: Charles E. Merrill.

Turnbull, A.P., & Turnbull, H.R., III. (1991b). Family assessment and family empowerment: An ethical analysis. In L.H. Meyer, C.A. Peck, & L. Brown (Eds.), *Critical issues in the lives of people with severe disabilities* (pp. 485–488). Baltimore: Paul H. Brookes Publishing Co.

Wolery, M., & Gast, D.L. (1990). Reframing the debate: Finding middle ground and defining the role of social validity. In A.C. Repp & N.N. Singh (Eds.), *Perspectives on the use of non-aversive and aversive interventions for persons with developmental disabilities* (pp. 129–144). Sycamore, IL: Sycamore Publishing Co.

Index

Page numbers followed by t *and* f *denote tables and figures, respectively.*